Peter in Early Christianity

Peter in Early Christianity

Edited by

Helen K. Bond and Larry W. Hurtado

WILLIAM B. EERDMANS PUBLISHING COMPANY
GRAND RAPIDS, MICHIGAN / CAMBRIDGE, U.K.

Published 2015 by
Wm. B. Eerdmans Publishing Co.
2140 Oak Industrial Drive N.E., Grand Rapids, Michigan 49505 /
P.O. Box 163, Cambridge CB3 9PU U.K.

Printed in the United States of America

21 20 19 18 17 16 15   7 6 5 4 3 2 1

Library of Congress Cataloging-in-Publication Data

Peter in early Christianity / edited by Helen K. Bond and Larry W. Hurtado.
        pages   cm
    Includes index.
    ISBN 978-0-8028-7171-8 (pbk.: alk. paper)
    1. Peter, the Apostle, Saint.
    2. Church history — Primitive and early church, ca. 30-600.
    I. Bond, Helen K. (Helen Katharine), editor.

    BS2515.P474   2015
    225.9′2 — dc23

                                                        2015028072

www.eerdmans.com

Contents

CONTRIBUTORS   viii

ABBREVIATIONS   x

Introduction   xvi

Helen K. Bond and Larry W. Hurtado

1. The Apostle Peter in Protestant Scholarship:
   Cullmann, Hengel, and Bockmuehl   1

   Larry W. Hurtado

THE "HISTORICAL PETER"

2. The Fisherman from Bethsaida   19

   Sean Freyne

3. From Shimon to Petros — Petrine Nomenclature
   in the Light of Contemporary Onomastic Practices   30

   Margaret H. Williams

4. Was Peter behind Mark's Gospel?   46

   Helen K. Bond

5. Did Peter Really Say That? Revisiting the Petrine Speeches
   in Acts   62

   Jonathan W. Lo

6. "Another Shall Gird Thee": Probative Evidence
for the Death of Peter   76
Timothy D. Barnes

PETER IN THE NEW TESTAMENT

7. Reassessing Peter's Imperception in Synoptic Tradition   99
John R. Markley

8. The Centrality of Discipleship in the Johannine
Portrayal of Peter   109
Jason S. Sturdevant

9. Moving the People to Repentance: Peter in Luke-Acts   121
Finn Damgaard

10. The Tradition of Peter's Literacy: Acts, 1 Peter,
and Petrine Literature   130
Sean A. Adams

11. Why Are There Some Petrine Epistles Rather Than None?   146
Matthew V. Novenson

PETER IN LATER CHRISTIAN TRADITIONS

12. Images of Peter in the Apostolic Fathers   161
Todd D. Still

13. Peter in Paul's Churches: The Early Reception of Peter in
1 Clement and in Polycarp's *Philippians*   168
Paul A. Hartog

14. On the Trail of the Scribal Peter: Petrine Memory, Hellenist
Mission, and the Parting of the Ways in *Peter's Preaching*   181
William Rutherford

15. "Gnostic" Perspectives on Peter   196
Tobias Nicklas

16. Peter in Noncanonical Traditions   222
Paul Foster

17. When Did Peter Become Bishop of Antioch?   263
    Paul Parvis

18. Traces of Peter Veneration in Roman Archaeology   273
    Peter Lampe

CONCLUDING REFLECTION

19. Scripture's Pope Meets von Balthasar's Peter   321
    Markus Bockmuehl

INDEX OF MODERN AUTHORS   341

INDEX OF SCRIPTURE AND OTHER ANCIENT WRITINGS   349

Contributors

SEAN A. ADAMS
University of Glasgow

TIMOTHY D. BARNES
University of Edinburgh

MARKUS BOCKMUEHL
University of Oxford

HELEN K. BOND
University of Edinburgh

FINN DAMGAARD
University of Copenhagen

PAUL FOSTER
University of Edinburgh

SEAN FREYNE
Trinity College Dublin, d. 2013

PAUL A. HARTOG
Faith Baptist Seminary

LARRY W. HURTADO
University of Edinburgh

PETER LAMPE
University of Heidelberg and University of the Free State

JONATHAN W. LO
Hong Kong Baptist Theological Seminary

JOHN R. MARKLEY
Liberty University

TOBIAS NICKLAS
University of Regensburg

MATTHEW V. NOVENSON
University of Glasgow

PAUL PARVIS
University of Edinburgh

WILLIAM RUTHERFORD
University of Texas at Austin

TODD D. STILL
Baylor University, Truett Seminary

JASON S. STURDEVANT
North Carolina State University

MARGARET H. WILLIAMS
University of Edinburgh

Abbreviations

Journals, Series, Reference Works, Modern Editions of Ancient Works

AB	Anchor Bible
ABD	*Anchor Bible Dictionary.* Edited by David Noel Freedman. 6 vols. New York: Doubleday, 1992
AGJU	Arbeiten zur Geschichte des antiken Judentums und des Urchristentums
AnBib	Analecta Biblica
BA	*Biblical Archaeologist*
BASOR	*Bulletin of the American Schools of Oriental Research*
BBR	*Bulletin for Biblical Research*
BCNH	Bibliothèque copte de Nag Hammadi
BECNT	Baker Exegetical Commentary on the New Testament
BETL	Bibliotheca Ephemeridum Theologicarum Lovaniensium
BG	Berlin Gnostic Papyrus
BGU	*Aegyptische Urkunden aus den Königlichen Staatlichen Museen zu Berlin, Griechische Urkunden.* 15 vols. Berlin: Weidmann, 1895–1937
BHG	*Bibliotheca Hagiographica Graeca.* Edited by François Halkin. 3rd ed. 3 vols. Brussels: Société des Bollandistes, 1986
BHLAMA	*Bibliotheca Hagiographica Latina Antiquae et Mediae Aetatis.* 2 vols. Brussels: Société des Bollandistes, 1898-1901
BHT	Beiträge zur historischen Theologie
BNTC	Black's New Testament Commentary
BRS	Biblical Resource Series
BTB	*Biblical Theology Bulletin*
BZ	*Biblische Zeitschrift*

BZNW	Beihefte zur *Zeitschrift für die neutestamentliche Wissenschaft*
CBQ	*Catholic Biblical Quarterly*
CCSA	Corpus Christianorum: Series Apocryphorum. Turnhout: Brepols, 1983-
CCSL	Corpus Christianorum: Series Latina. Turnhout: Brepols, 1953-
CIG	*Corpus Inscriptionum Graecarum.* Edited by August Boeckh. 4 vols. Berlin, 1828–1877
CIL	*Corpus Inscriptionum Latinarum.* Berlin, 1862–
CJCZ	Gert Lüderitz. *Corpus jüdischer Zeugnisse aus der Cyrenaika.* Wiesbaden: Reichert, 1983
CPG	*Clavis Patrum Graecorum.* Edited by Maurice Geerard. 5 vols. Turnhout: Brepols, 1974-1987
CPJ	*Corpus Papyrorum Judaicarum.* Edited by Victor A. Tcherikover. 3 vols. Cambridge: Harvard University Press, 1957-1964
CPL	*Clavis Patrum Latinorum.* Edited by Eligius Dekkers. 2nd ed. Steenbrugis: Abbatia Sancti Petri, 1961
CSCO	Corpus Scriptorum Christianorum Orientalium. Edited by Jean Baptiste Chabot et al. Paris, 1903
CTQ	*Concordia Theological Quarterly*
DOP	*Dumbarton Oaks Papers*
DRev	*Downside Review*
EHPR	Etudes d'histoire et de philosophie religieuses
EKK	Evangelisch-katholischer Kommentar
ETR	*Etudes théologiques et religieuses*
EvQ	*Evangelical Quarterly*
EvT	*Evangelische Theologie*
ExpTim	*Expository Times*
GCS	Die griechischen christlichen Schriftsteller der ersten [drei] Jahrhunderte
GNS	Good News Studies
HTR	*Harvard Theological Review*
HTS	Harvard Theological Studies
ICC	International Critical Commentary
ICUR	*Inscriptiones christianae urbis Romae.* Edited by Giovanni B. de Rossi. Rome: Officina Libraria Pontificia, 1857–1888
ILCV	*Inscriptiones Latinae Christianae Veteres.* Edited by Ernst Diehl. 2nd ed. Berlin: Druckerei Hildebrand, 1961
JBL	*Journal of Biblical Literature*
JECS	*Journal of Early Christian Studies*
JRS	*Journal of Roman Studies*
JSJ	*Journal for the Study of Judaism in the Persian, Hellenistic, and Roman Periods*

JSNT	*Journal for the Study of the New Testament*
JSNTSup	*Journal for the Study of the New Testament* Supplement series
JTS	*Journal of Theological Studies*
L&N	Johannes P. Louw and Eugene A. Nida, eds. *Greek-English Lexicon of the New Testament: Based on Semantic Domains.* 2nd ed. New York: United Bible Societies, 1989
LCL	Loeb Classical Library
LNTS	Library of New Testament Studies
NA^{27}	*Novum Testamentum Graece,* Nestle-Aland, 27th ed.
NHC	Nag Hammadi Codices
NHL	*Nag Hammadi Library in English.* Edited by James M. Robinson. 4th rev. ed. Leiden: Brill, 1996
NHMS	Nag Hammadi and Manichaean Studies
NIGTC	New International Greek Text Commentary
NovT	*Novum Testamentum*
NovTSup	Supplements to *Novum Testamentum*
NTL	New Testament Library
NTS	*New Testament Studies*
NTTSD	New Testament Tools, Studies, and Documents
OECGT	Oxford Early Christian Gospel Texts
OLA	Orientalia Lovaniensia Analecta
PG	Patrologia Graeca [= *Patrologiae Cursus Completus:* Series Graeca]. Edited by Jacques-Paul Migne. 162 vols. Paris, 1857-1886
PL	Patrologia Latina [= *Patrologiae Cursus Completus:* Series Latina]. Edited by Jacques-Paul Migne. 217 vols. Paris, 1844-1864
PNTC	Pillar New Testament Commentary
PRSt	*Perspectives in Religious Studies*
RevScRel	*Revue des sciences religieuses*
RFCC	Religion in the First Christian Centuries
RSLR	Rivista di storia e letteratura religiosa
SBLDS	Society of Biblical Literature Dissertation Series
SBT	Studies in Biblical Theology
SHR	Studies in the History of Religions (supplements to *Numen*)
SJT	*Scottish Journal of Theology*
SNTSMS	Society for New Testament Studies Monograph Series
SNTU	*Studien zum Neuen Testament und seiner Umwelt*
SSAC	Sussidi allo studio delle antichità cristiane
ST	*Studia Theologica*
TENTS	Texts and Editions for New Testament Study
TLZ	*Theologische Literaturzeitung*
TS	*Theological Studies*
TSAJ	Texte und Studien zum antiken Judentum

TU	Texte und Untersuchungen
TUGAL	Texte und Untersuchungen zur Geschichte der altchristlichen Literatur
TynBul	*Tyndale Bulletin*
VC	*Vigiliae Christianae*
WA	*D. Martin Luthers Werke* [Weimarer Ausgabe]. Weimar: Böhlau, 1883–1993
WBC	Word Biblical Commentary
WMANT	Wissenschaftliche Monographien zum Alten und Neuen Testament
WUNT	Wissenschaftliche Untersuchungen zum Neuen Testament
ZAC	*Zeitschrift für Antikes Christentum*
ZKG	*Zeitschrift für Kirchengeschichte*
ZNW	*Zeitschrift für die neutestamentliche Wissenschaft und die Kunde der älteren Kirche*
ZTK	*Zeitschrift für Theologie und Kirche*

Ancient Works

1 Clem.	*1 Clement*
2 Clem.	*2 Clement*
Acts Pet.	*Acts of Peter*
Ap. Con.	*Apostolic Constitutions*
Apoc. Pet.	*Apocalypse of Peter*
Augustine	
Conf.	*Confessiones*
Serm.	*Sermones*
Aulus Gellius	
Noct. Att.	*Noctes atticae*
Bede	
Com. Acts	*Commentary on the Acts of the Apostles*
Clement of Alexandria	
Adumbr.	*Adumbrationes in Epistulas canonicas*
Paed.	*Paedagogus*
Protr.	*Protrepticus*
Strom.	*Stromata*
Cyprian	
Ep.	*Epistula*
Ep. Apos.	*Epistula Apostolorum*
Ep. Pet. Phil.	*Letter of Peter to Philip*
Epiphanius	
Pan.	*Panarion*

Eusebius of Caesarea
    H.E.   *Historia ecclesiastica*
Gos. Mary   *Gospel of Mary*
Gos. Pet.   *Gospel of Peter*
Gos. Thom.   *Gospel of Thomas*
Gregory the Great
    Epp.   *Epistulae*
Herm.   *Shepherd of Hermas*
Hippolytus
    Haer.   *Refutatio omnium haeresium*
Ignatius
    Magn.   *To the Magnesians*
    Rom.   *To the Romans*
    Smyrn.   *To the Smyrnaeans*
    Trall.   *To the Trallians*
Irenaeus
    Adv. haer.   *Adversus haereses*
Jerome
    Vir. ill.   *De viris illustribus*
John Chrysostom
    Hom. Act.   *Homiliae in Acta apostolorum*
Josephus
    Ant.   *Antiquities of the Jews*
    J.W.   *Jewish War*
Jub.   *Jubilees*
Justin Martyr
    1 Apol.   *First Apology*
    Dial.   *Dialogue with Trypho*
Minucius Felix
    Oct.   *Octavius*
Optatus
    De schism. Donat. *De schismate Donatistarum*
Origen
    C. Cels.   *Contra Celsum*
    Comm. Jo.   *Commentarii in evangelium Joannis*
    Comm. Matt.   *Commentarium in evangelium Matthaei*
Philip of Side
    H.E.   *Historia Ecclesiastica*
Philo
    Migr.   *De migratione Abrahami*
Philostratus
    Vit. Apoll.   *Vita Apollonii*

Plutarch
    Reg. imp. apophth.   *Regum et imperatorum apophthegmata*
Polycarp
    Phil.   *Epistle to the Philippians*
Pseudo-Clement/Pseudo-Clementines
    Hom.   *Homilies*
    Rec.   *Recognitions*
Quintilian
    Inst.   *Institutio oratoria*
Sozomen
    H.E.   *Historia ecclesiastica*
Strabo
    Geogr.   *Geographica*
T. Ab.   *Testament of Abraham*
Tacitus
    Ann.   *Annals*
Tars.   pseudo-Ignatius, *To the Tarsians*
Tertullian
    Apol.   *Apologeticum*
    Praescr.   *De praescriptione haereticorum*
    Pud.   *De pudicitia*
Xenophon
    Mem.   *Memorabilia*

Codices and Papyri

Codex Berol.   Codex Berolinensis
CT   Codex Tchacos
P.Cair.   Papyrus Cairensis
P.Heid.   Papyrus Heidelbergensis
P.Oxy.   Oxyrhynchus papyri
P.Ryl.   Rylands papyri
P.Vindob. G.   Papyrus Vindobonensis Greek

Introduction

Helen K. Bond and Larry W. Hurtado

The essays gathered together in this volume are some of the highlights of a conference organized by Edinburgh University's Centre for the Study of Christian Origins in July 2013. After years of playing second fiddle to Paul, Peter has been the focus of a number of scholarly works over the last decade, and so it seemed like an opportune time to gather together an international team of experts to reconsider the apostle and his legacy within the early church. The conference was a great success, attracting over seventy delegates and twenty-two papers. The constraints of space meant that we could not publish all the proceedings — the essays reproduced here are those the editors consider to be the most significant, with an eye also to even coverage of the first three centuries in particular.

Two authors in the collection deserve special mention: one for his presence, the other for his absence. Although the conference was not specifically designed around the work of Professor Markus Bockmuehl, he quickly emerged as the undisputed guest of honor. As the author of two major recent works on Peter,[1] virtually all of our contributors interacted with his scholarship in one way or another. We are extremely grateful to Professor Bockmuehl for his good-humored discussions throughout the conference and are pleased to be able to include his reflections on Hans Urs von Balthasar as the concluding essay in the volume. The second author is Sean Freyne. Professor Freyne

---

1. Markus Bockmuehl, *The Remembered Peter in Ancient Reception and Modern Debate*, WUNT 1/262 (Tübingen: Mohr Siebeck, 2010); *Simon Peter in Scripture and Memory: The New Testament Apostle in the Early Church* (Grand Rapids: Baker Academic, 2012).

agreed with great enthusiasm to offer a paper at the conference, and we had looked forward to learning from his extensive knowledge of Galilean archaeology. Sadly, he became ill shortly before the conference and died not long after. He did manage to send us a copy of what he intended to say, however, and after editing it lightly we have included it in the collection.

We have arranged the papers (as at the conference) in roughly chronological order, starting with the "historical Peter" and then moving on to the apostle's literary afterlives, both within the New Testament and in later, noncanonical literature. A chapter is also devoted to early traditions concerning Peter as evinced by Roman archaeology.

Larry Hurtado sets the scene for our discussion of Peter in the opening paper. He considers the portraits of Peter from three generations of Protestant scholars spanning the mid-twentieth to the early twenty-first centuries — Oscar Cullmann, Martin Hengel, and Markus Bockmuehl. He asks what prompted their interest in Peter, discusses what aims and context are being addressed, and shows how their reconstructions illustrated contemporary Protestant scholarship just as much as the historical Peter they purported to describe.

Our next five essays are devoted to the "historical Peter." Hurtado's paper warned us that the historical Peter might prove as elusive as his historical master, and rather than present overarching portraits of the apostle (three of which have already been given by Hurtado), the papers in this section all seek to contribute to a particular aspect of the historical Peter. Sean Freyne draws on his prodigious knowledge of both the writings of Flavius Josephus and archaeology of first-century Galilee to provide a portrait of the fishing industry on Lake Tiberias. Recent work at Bethsaida, Tarichea, and the many harbors along the shore — including the famous "Galilee boat" — have contributed to our knowledge not only of fishing and associated industries but also of their contribution to the local economy. All of this may not help us to understand Peter directly, but it paints a picture of a world with which he was familiar.

Margaret Williams analyzes Jewish onomastic practices to chart the various names by which Peter was known. In a beautifully argued piece, she suggests that Peter grew up as "Simon bar Yonah," and that his name was changed to "Kephas" by Jesus at the start of his ministry. Strangely perhaps, only Peter and the sons of Zebedee seem to have received nicknames, but we should not be particularly surprised if we find it hard now to work out what they meant — as Williams observes, it is in the nature of nicknames that they are only really meaningful to insiders. Later on, as he established himself within the Jerusalem church, our apostle began to be known as "Peter" (the Greek translation of Kephas), and was known in this way both in Rome and also the West, where a Greek, non-Jewish name was an advantage.

The next two essays deal, in rather different ways, with the question of Peter's theology. Helen Bond tackles the vexed problem of Papias's claim that Peter had some connection with Mark's Gospel. Scholars are rightly wary of Papias's testimony, noting its apologetic aim to give the Gospel more status by linking it with the leading apostle. But the bishop's clear apologetic agenda does not necessarily mean that his testimony is of no value whatsoever. Beneath the rhetoric, Bond suggests, there might be a genuine recollection that Peter did in fact have a connection to the author of Mark. Taking the work of Joel Marcus as a test case, she analyzes the reasons why the Petrine connection is often rejected, suggesting that some are rather dated nowadays, and attempts to carve out a more moderate position by drawing on social memory, Mark's links with the biographical tradition, and the evangelist's use of Peter as a literary character. She concludes that there might well have been a link between Peter and Mark's Gospel, though any attempts to reconstruct Peter's theology would be perilous in the extreme.

Jonathan Lo asks if Peter really said the things attributed to him in the speeches of Acts. This, of course, is a long-standing debate within scholarship, with a spectrum of opinion ranging from those who argue that the speeches are solely products of Lukan invention through to those who assert that Luke drew on existing sources and traditions. Lo explores the topic through three lenses: Greco-Roman conventions, Luke's literary style, and the Christology of Acts. He concludes that the issue of historicity may well have been more important to the author of Acts than is generally supposed, though he is suitably wary of taking the speeches as verbatim reports. What the narrative of Acts does confirm, however, is the historical Peter's prominence in the early church, and his role as primary witness to his resurrected Lord.

In the final essay in this section, Timothy Barnes considers Peter's death in Rome, robustly arguing that Peter was not crucified (as tradition asserts) but burned alive. The primary evidence here is John 21:18-19, which makes it clear that Peter was to be *clothed* prior to his death, not stripped naked as was the case with crucifixion. This fits perfectly with Tacitus's description of Nero's execution of Christians in Rome in 64, where large numbers were executed on the charge of arson. Nero included additional and innovative mockeries to the spectacle, including dressing some in animal skins and setting others alight with their arms extended as if on crosses. This, however, was not a modified form of crucifixion (as is generally supposed), but a modified form of burning alive. The association of Peter's death with Nero's atrocities finds corroboration in *1 Clement,* the *Ascension of Isaiah,* and the *Apocalypse of Peter.*

The next group of essays focuses on Peter in the New Testament, either as a literary character or a putative author of letters. John Markley considers Peter's apparent lack of understanding in the Synoptic tradition. He rightly highlights the problems with the use of terms such as "positive" and "negative," used widely by redaction critics and more recently within literary analyses. Instead, he identifies "human imperception" as a theme in apocalyptic literature, employed particularly when a human being is faced with divinely revealed mysteries beyond his or her comprehension. If this is indeed the background to the Synoptic presentation of Peter's slowness to comprehend, then the portrayal of Peter in these Gospels is not "negative," but rather serves to cast him as a recipient of revelation.

Jason Sturdevant looks at the character of Peter in the Fourth Gospel. Noting that Peter has tended to be contrasted with the Beloved Disciple, he charts the change in scholarship from seeing Peter as a negative symbol of the mainstream church to the more popular view today in which Peter and the Beloved Disciple are both perceived in a positive, yet different, manner (with the Beloved Disciple as the ideal witness and Peter as Jesus' successor as the protector of the flock). Even this more nuanced reading, he suggests, misses a key component in Peter's characterization: the presentation of Jesus as Peter's guide throughout the Gospel, correcting and teaching Peter in his journey to discipleship. Through close attention to a number of key texts, Sturdevant charts Peter's development from initial self-reliance to a mature and full submission to God's will.

Finn Damgaard looks at Peter in Luke-Acts, noting that these two works offer what is probably the most positive portrait of the apostle in the New Testament Gospels. Given Luke's favorable portrait of Peter, however, he asks why this evangelist decided to include a heavily edited version of the denial scene rather than simply omitting it. The answer, he suggests, lies in Luke 22:32, with its instruction to Peter to "strengthen your brothers," a command that refers not simply to the disciples (as is often thought) but to the people more generally. The denial scene allows Luke to show that Peter, like Paul, experienced a change or reversal prior to his new ministry as a preacher of repentance. Peter's denial and subsequent turning reflect the people's involvement in the crucifixion and their subsequent repentance. It also parallels Paul's "conversion," as Peter's own paradigmatic experience of repentance/conversion. Although Peter does not himself refer to his denial and repentance in his missionary speeches in Acts, the implication of Luke's narrative seems to be that it is precisely his own denials that enable him to strengthen the people and take up a leading position in the church.

Sean Adams examines the representation of Peter as literate, a "text broker," across several early Christian writings, beginning with references in the Acts of the Apostles, and then turning to texts ascribed to Peter. His survey includes the New Testament writings, 1 Peter and 2 Peter, and the other texts in the "Petrine corpus": *Gospel of Peter, Apocalypse of Peter, Acts of Peter, Preaching of Peter, Epistle of Peter to James, Epistle of Peter to Philip,* and *The Homilies and Recognitions* of the pseudo-Clementine literature. Adams argues that the ascription of literacy to Peter expressed in 1 Peter and the early acceptance of Peter's authorship of the writing likely provided the foundation for the subsequent treatment of Peter as literate and a writer of texts.

The key question pursued by Matthew Novenson is why there are *epistles* in particular ascribed to Peter. He contends that the canonical 1 Peter seems to have been the earliest text written in Peter's name, and was likely influential on the author of 2 Peter. Thereafter, we have the two apocryphal writings, *The Epistle of Peter to James* and *The Epistle of Peter to Philip,* neither of which seems to show much dependence or direct inspiration from either of the two New Testament writings. Novenson's general conclusion is that "there was nothing inevitable about the production of this small corpus of Petrine letters," that other apostles were ascribed apocryphal gospels and acts, but not epistles. So he judges that the Petrine epistles are "an anomaly in early Christian literature, a happy accident."

Todd Still surveys references to Peter in the collection of early Christian writings known today as "the Apostolic Fathers." Judging that in these texts Peter is not a "flat" character, but instead has a certain complexity, it is difficult to reduce it to some simple picture. In general, however, Peter serves variously as "a paragon of, and a paradigm for the faith" shared by the various authors of these texts.

Paul Hartog probes the reception of Peter in two early texts more often linked with Pauline Christianity: *1 Clement* and Polycarp's *Epistle to the Philippians.* Despite the paucity of overt references to Peter, Hartog argues that there is subtle evidence of a reception of Peter in the Pauline circles reflected in these two texts, Peter "framed within a more fundamental imaging of Paul." Offering the analogy of the Russian *matryoshka* doll, Hartog proposes "the reception of Peter *nested within* the overt reception of Paul."

Addressing a topic related to the focus of Sean Adams's essay, Will Rutherford contributes a detailed analysis of the representation of Peter as having a "scribal" competence, with special reference to the text known as *The Preaching of Peter* (preserved as a set of excerpts in Clement of Alexandria's *Stromata*). But Rutherford also seeks the social provenance of *The Preaching of Peter*, proposing that it lies in some circle of Alexandrian Jewry.

Tobias Nicklas gives an extended study of perspectives on Peter in so-called gnostic texts, and finds several. In some, there is an explicit and/or implicit polemic against Peter. In some others, Peter is compared (somewhat unfavorably) to other figures ascribed superior revelations. In still others, Peter holds a certain authority, and is claimed by the particular "in-group" behind each of these texts. Nicklas also notes with some puzzlement that texts reflecting very different views of Peter were sometimes put together in the same codex, as if those who read the texts in question did not perceive or care deeply about the differences.

In a wide-ranging study of Peter in noncanonical gospels, epistles, apocalypses, and acts, Paul Foster provides a further survey that complements several of the other contributions to this volume. He notes a striking diversity, Peter peripheral in some cases, a central and heroic figure in others, a more negative figure in still other texts. Foster argues that this radical diversity works against Bockmuehl's contention that the representation of Peter in early Christianity continued to be shaped in some measure by "living memories."

In light of the more well-known tradition connecting Peter with Rome, Paul Parvis asks the somewhat puckish question: When did Peter become bishop of Antioch? The serious point of Parvis's essay is to trace when and why Peter came to be referred to (by some early Christians, but not all) as the first/founding bishop of Antioch. Parvis shows that the Antioch connection comes clearly into view sometime in the late fourth century, and he proposes that it reflects various factors, including the desire of individuals (e.g., Jerome) and also churches of the East to assert their importance.

With Peter Lampe's paper we turn our attention to archaeology, specifically views of Peter in third- and fourth-century Rome, as they can be reconstructed from epigraphy and (particularly funeral) iconography. Lampe looks both at the traditional location of Peter's burial (held to be at the site of the Vatican since the mid-second century) and also the memorial to Saints Peter and Paul at St. Sebastian on the Via Appia, which Lampe suggests came to prominence during the persecution of Valerian when Christians were prevented from visiting their cemeteries. Also surveyed here are catacomb frescoes and sarcophagi, many of which (particularly the latter) contain images of Peter, variously depicted as denier, teacher, new Moses, or intercessor. Lampe suggests that the upper-class owners of the sarcophagi liked to associate themselves with Peter, thereby linking themselves to church authority and leadership.

Markus Bockmuehl concludes the volume by taking us into present-day questions about the role of Peter, popes, and church leadership, focusing on references to Peter in the celebrated Catholic theologian Hans Urs von Balthasar. Bockmuehl concludes that von Balthasar's treatment of Peter is too abstract to serve these continuing questions in much of a practical way.

Finally, the editors would like to thank the Centre for the Study of Christian Origins committee for organizing the conference: Sean Adams, Frank Dicken, Paul Foster, Ray Lozano, Matthew Novenson, Paul Parvis, Sara Parvis, and Margaret Williams. Invaluable IT help was provided by Mark Batluck and Andrew Kelley, and abundant administrative support from Jean Reynolds in the School of Divinity office. Special thanks go to Ray Lozano and his team of helpers at the conference itself, who ensured the smooth running of the whole event. Particular mention should be made of Joshua Coutts and Joshua Mann, who, with Ray's careful guidance, kept the bar going, and ensured that Edinburgh is now the home of the legendary G&T.

CHAPTER 1

The Apostle Peter in Protestant Scholarship: Cullmann, Hengel, and Bockmuehl

Larry W. Hurtado

When it comes to apostles, Protestant scholars write about Paul, overwhelmingly. Ever since Martin Luther's discovery in Paul's letters of what was for him a revolutionary understanding of God's righteousness as a gift received through faith, Protestant scholars have found in Paul the unrivaled focus of their scholarly attention. To be sure, Paul, uniquely among the apostles, left us with several letters, all of which are invaluable snapshots of earliest Christianity (perhaps especially the Corinthian letters), some of them (especially Romans and also Galatians) remarkable discourses on Christian faith that justifiably have occupied scholars down the centuries.

Peter, on the other hand, has not fared so well, at least among Protestant scholars. He has been hailed sometimes subsequently as "Prince of the Apostles," and the first bishop of Rome, from whom (in Roman Catholic tradition) the papal office is posited as deriving. He is presented in all four Gospels as the spokesman for the Twelve, and is cited by Paul as the first one in the list of those chosen witnesses to whom the risen Jesus appeared (1 Cor. 15:3-8). Nevertheless, at least in Protestant scholarship, Peter has not received anything like the attention given to Paul.[1] Indeed, at the risk of some exaggeration, one could say that Paul is the de facto chief apostle for Protestants, and Peter is for

---

1. I take the "Cephas" (κηφᾶς) in 1 Cor. 15:5 (as in Paul's other uses of this name) to be Paul's way of referring to the figure more known subsequently as "Peter." On the issue, see, e.g., Bart D. Ehrman, "Cephas and Peter," *JBL* 109 (1990): 463-74; Dale C. Allison, "Peter and Cephas: One and the Same," *JBL* 111 (1992): 489-95; earlier, J. K. Elliott, "Κηφᾶς: Σίμων Πέτρος: ὁ Πέτρος: An Examination of New Testament Usage," *NovT* 14 (1972): 241-56; and now Margaret H. Williams in this volume, pp. 30-45.

Roman Catholics. Protestants revere and study Paul particularly for his theology, whereas Roman Catholic tradition has revered and emphasized Peter as the figure who represents the notion of Jesus' authority being conferred, that authority claimed in the Roman Catholic Church itself.[2] Indeed, it may be that one reason for the comparative neglect of Peter among Protestant scholars has been precisely that Roman Catholic tradition has ascribed to him such significance, particularly in asserting the claims for the Roman Catholic Church, and especially for the papacy.

So, when Protestant New Testament scholars give Peter their serious attention, it is worth noticing, and worth asking why they do so. In this presentation, I consider three important instances of Protestant New Testament scholars of the twentieth and early twenty-first centuries who have produced significant studies of Peter.[3] In each case, I consider what seems to have prompted the work and/or what aim and context are addressed, and so what each work tells us about Protestant scholarship at the time, as well as what these scholars tell us about Peter. My aim here, obviously, is not a complete survey of Protestant writings on Peter, but rather to consider these three particularly significant efforts, each of them from an important New Testament scholar in his own generation.

Oscar Cullmann

Among New Testament scholars of the mid-twentieth century, Oscar Cullmann (1902-1999) was certainly a prominent figure.[4] Cullmann's book on

2. The scholarly studies of Paul's theology form an ocean that cannot be charted here. Illustrative is the huge study by James D. G. Dunn, *The Theology of Paul the Apostle* (Grand Rapids: Eerdmans, 1998).

3. So, I do not consider here valuable studies by Roman Catholic scholars, e.g., Rudolf Pesch, *Simon Petrus. Geschichte und geschichtliche Bedeutung des ersten Jüngers* (Stuttgart: Anton Hiersemann, 1980); Pheme Perkins, *Peter: Apostle for the Whole Church* (Columbia: University of South Carolina Press, 1994; republished Minneapolis: Fortress, 2000); Christian Grappe, *Images de Pierre aux deux premiers siècles,* Études d'histoire et de philosophie religieuses 75 (Paris: Presses Universitaires de France, 1995).

4. Although Rudolf Bultmann might be cited by many as the most salient and influential NT scholar of that time, I think Cullmann has to be seen as the NT scholar who in some ways offered the major Continental alternative to Bultmann, and who was the most significant competitor. From 1948 onward, Cullmann simultaneously held chairs in Basel, the Sorbonne, and the Protestant theological faculty in Paris. In the English-speaking world in the 1950s-1960s, Cullmann's works were translated earlier and were more widely read than Bultmann's. For a

Peter is commonly cited as a landmark study, and it remains important to this day. The first edition appeared in 1952 in German and in French, with an English translation (of the German) in 1953.[5] The multilingual publication of the book shows that he clearly intended it to be noticed, and also that he had a wide readership interested in what he wrote. A second edition, "a complete and thorough revision of almost the entire volume," in which Cullmann engaged "the historical and exegetical problems" raised by his discussion, appeared in 1960 (German), and an English translation of this edition followed in 1962.[6] In his preface to the second edition of the English translation, Floyd Filson hailed Cullmann's book as, to that date, "the most thorough and informative study of Peter by any Protestant scholar."[7] The work is noteworthy for several reasons.

We may begin by noting the impressive scope of the study. Though not a large book (242 pages in the English translation), it covers considerable ground. As indicated more clearly in the title of the English-language editions, Cullmann addressed both the major historical and the major theological questions. Moreover, in his discussion of historical questions (which occupies the greater part of the book) Cullmann engaged in considerable depth both the varied textual data in the New Testament and other early Christian writings, including "liturgical sources" that refer to festivals observing the martyrdom

---

brief description of Cullmann's work together with a bibliography, see "Cullmann, Oscar," in *Dictionary of Biblical Interpretation,* ed. John H. Hayes (Nashville: Abingdon, 1999), 1:234-35. In commemoration of Cullmann's role in the establishment of the Ecumenical Institute of Tantur (Jerusalem), a fuller account of Cullmann, focusing on his ecumenical activities and especially his role in, and response to, Vatican II, is given by André Birmelé, "Oscar Cullmann: In the Service of Biblical Theology and Ecumenism," Institute for Ecumenical Research, October 2012, http://www.ecumenical-institute.org/wp-content/uploads/2012/11/ActuelCullmann Jerusalem2012English.pdf. There is a brief autobiographical account in Karl Barth and Oscar Cullmann, "Karl Barth and Oscar Cullmann on Their Theological Vocation," *SJT* 14 (1961): 229-33 (225-33).

5. Oscar Cullmann, *Petrus. Jünger, Apostel, Märtyrer: Das historische und das theologische Problem* (Zürich: Zwingli-Verlag, 1952); Cullmann, *Saint Pierre: Disciple, apôtre, martyr. Histoire et théologie* (Paris: Delachaux & Niestlé, 1952); Cullmann, *Peter: Disciple, Apostle, Martyr. A Historical and Theological Study,* trans. Floyd V. Filson (London: SCM, 1953).

6. In my discussion I refer to this English translation of the second edition: London: SCM, 1962, reprint edition, Waco: Baylor University Press, 2011. I cite here Cullmann's foreword to the second edition, p. 15. The third German edition (Zürich: Theologischer Verlag, 1985) seems essentially a reprint of the second edition. At a couple of points Cullmann (*Peter,* preface and p. 184 n. 80) referred to another book that he planned to produce, *Peter and the Pope,* but it never appeared.

7. Floyd V. Filson, preface to Cullmann, *Peter,* p. 8.

of Peter, and also the archaeological evidence purporting to concern Peter in Rome, some of which had come to light only shortly before Cullmann's book appeared.[8] One has to admire the breadth of Cullmann's scholarship and the sure-footed manner in which he threaded his way through this wide-ranging and diverse material.

So, a brief review of some of his conclusions is appropriate here. Surveying the various names that Peter bears in the New Testament, Cullmann proposed that "Symeon" and/or the "native Greek" "Simon" could have been Peter's given name(s), noting the presence of Greek language in Galilee from the fourth century BCE, and citing a probable analogy in "Paul/Saul."[9] As for "Kēpha(s)" (כיפא), a common noun in Aramaic and not evidenced as a given name among ancient Jews, Cullmann judged that it originated as a title given to Peter/Simon by Jesus, citing as analogy the report that Jesus gave the epithet "Boanerges" to the two sons of Zebedee (Mark 3:17).[10]

But, for Cullmann, the *occasion* when Jesus likely first called Peter "Kēpha" was an important matter too. Noting the various settings given in the Gospels in which Peter is given the title "rock" (see Mark 3:16; John 1:42; Matt. 16:18), Cullmann devoted a lengthy chapter (pp. 164-217) to making a case that Je-

---

8. Cullmann's discussion of excavations: *Peter,* pp. 131-56. He concluded (p. 156), "The archaeological investigations do not permit us to answer in either a negative or an affirmative way the question as to the stay of Peter in Rome. The grave of Peter cannot be identified." But he also judged that the evidence speaks "in favour of the report that *the execution of Peter took place in the Vatican district.*" In 1968, Pope Paul VI declared that the bones of Peter had been identified, but this has by no means settled the question. See esp. Graydon F. Snyder, "Survey and a 'New' Thesis on the Bones of Peter," *BA* 32(1969): 2-24; and for an analysis by a Roman Catholic scholar, Daniel W. O'Connor, *Peter in Rome: The Literary, Liturgical, and Archaeological Evidence* (New York: Columbia University Press, 1969); O'Connor, "Peter in Rome: A Review and Position," in *Christianity, Judaism and Other Greco-Roman Cults,* ed. Jacob Neusner (Leiden: Brill, 1975), 2:146-60. For a still more recent review of the Vatican excavations, see Peter Lampe, *From Paul to Valentinus: Christians at Rome in the First Two Centuries,* trans. Michael Steinhauser (Minneapolis: Fortress, 2003), pp. 104-16, who judges that the tropaion found is that mentioned by Gaius (ca. 200 CE, quoted in Eusebius, *H.E.* 2.25.7), and that "around the middle of the second century . . . Christians stood on the Vatican at a place they identified as a grave," which they likely identified as Peter's grave (pp. 104-5).

9. Cullmann, *Peter,* p. 19.

10. Cullmann, *Peter,* pp. 21-23. Mark (3:17) renders "Boanerges" (Βοανηργές) as "sons of thunder" (υἱοὶ βροντῆς), which seems a somewhat free translation of the likely Hebrew or Aramaic expression in question, e.g., Hebrew בני רגז (= "sons of agitation/tumult"). See, e.g., the discussion in Adela Yarbro Collins, *Mark,* Hermeneia (Minneapolis: Fortress, 2007), pp. 219-20.

sus' saying in Matthew 16:17-18, specifically Jesus' positing Peter as "this rock" upon which Jesus will build his church, preserves something of an incident in Jesus' ministry in which the title "Kēpha" was first given to Peter. Cullmann also urged as "a very strong exegetical probability" that the actual/original historical occasion for this was in "the framework of the Last Supper," in the hours before Jesus' looming arrest and death, and that Matthew relocated the bestowal of the title (somewhat awkwardly) into the Caesarea Philippi exchange.[11] Matthew's reason for doing so, says Cullmann, was to balance and soften the reference a few verses later (16:22-23) to Peter as "the instrument of the devil."[12] Nevertheless, although Cullmann devoted a sizeable space in the book to making this argument, he concluded it by urging that the authenticity of the tradition that Jesus gave the title "Kēpha" to Peter and the reason for his doing so were what mattered, and that these did not "stand or fall with the acceptance of this theory concerning the original setting."[13]

As to how to take the saying, judging that "all Protestant interpretations that seek in one way or another to explain away the reference to Peter [as the rock upon which Jesus says he will build his *ekklēsia*] seem to me unsatisfactory," Cullmann insisted that this saying in Matthew 16:18, "upon this rock I will build my church," really does designate "the person of Simon" as the foundation-rock in question.

> Upon this disciple, who in the lifetime of Jesus possessed the specific advantages and the specific weaknesses of which the Gospels speak, upon him who was then their spokesman, their representative in good as well as in bad, and in this sense was the rock of the group of disciples — upon him is to be founded the Church, which after the death of Jesus will continue his work upon the earth.[14]

Traditional Roman Catholic exegesis, thus, was correct in rejecting other referents for the "rock" in the saying; but Catholic tradition in turn errs, insisted Cullmann, "in an even more arbitrary way when it tries to find in this

---

11. Cullmann, *Peter*, pp. 164-91, citing p. 191.

12. Cullmann, pp. 184-86.

13. Cullmann, *Peter*, p. 191. As indicated in the interconfessional study, *Peter in the New Testament*, ed. Raymond E. Brown, Karl P. Donfried, and John Reumann (Minneapolis: Augsburg; New York: Paulist Press, 1973), p. 85, "Cullmann has not had much following in this hypothesis; and there is greater support for the thesis that the pre-Matthean setting, in whole or in part, was post-resurrectional."

14. Cullmann, *Peter*, p. 213.

text a reference to 'successors.'" There is "not a single word" in the passage that justifies positing successors of Peter.[15] Likewise, the reference to Peter (John 21:16-17) as summoned by the risen Jesus to feed the "sheep/lambs" "*is certainly limited by his martyrdom!*"[16] In the Matthew 16:18 saying, it is only the building of the *ekklēsia* that proceeds into the future, "*not the laying of the foundation of the rock* on which [it] is built."[17] To quote Cullmann, "In Matthew 16:18 Peter is addressed in his unrepeatable apostolic capacity."[18] Cullmann granted that *functions* of Peter rightly continue, specifically mentioning the reference to "the keys of the kingdom of heaven" (Matt. 16:19) as referring to "church leadership," but this should not be restricted to one form of leadership or one office, such as that of the bishop of Rome. Cullmann insisted that, just as Jesus' death and resurrection are one-time events with continuing force/significance, so Peter as "rock" and the "loosing and binding" promised to him pertain to Peter alone, who "represents once for all the earthly foundation, the beginning who supports the whole structure of the *ekklēsia* that is to be built in the future."[19]

Time does not permit a further survey of the various matters Cullmann addressed. Instead, I want to consider the situation and purposes behind his book, a work in which he obviously invested a great deal of effort. As noted already, the original edition appeared in 1952, when Europe was still recovering from World War II, the "Cold War" was developing, and, most relevantly, there were fervent efforts to promote ecumenical relations among the various Christian denominations. Cullmann was himself profoundly concerned to promote ecumenicity and to help shape it, with a particular emphasis that church unity could only be a unity in diversity, the various Christian communions complementing and correcting imbalances in one another, not aiming for some uniformity in beliefs, structures, or practices.[20]

---

15. Cullmann, *Peter,* p. 213.

16. Cullmann, *Peter,* p. 214 (emphasis original).

17. Cullmann, *Peter,* p. 214 (emphasis original). In support, Cullmann cited other NT passages that refer to the foundation of the church, e.g., Eph. 2:20; Rom. 15:20; 1 Cor. 3:10; Gal. 2:9; Rev. 21:14, 19.

18. Cullmann, *Peter,* p. 215.

19. Cullmann, *Peter,* p. 217. It is interesting, not to say a bit curious, but probably deliberate, that the collective study project, *Peter in the New Testament* (n. 13 above), did not engage this question about whether Matt. 16:18-19 provides a basis for Roman Catholic teaching about succession as embodied in the pope.

20. I draw here on Birmelé, "Oscar Cullmann," cited earlier. In later years Cullmann continued promoting his vision, publishing a more thorough expression of it in a book: *L'unité par la diversité* (Paris: Cerf, 1986); German edition, *Einheit durch Vielfalt* (Tübingen: Mohr, 1986).

It seems obvious that Cullmann's work on Peter was intended to focus on him as a figure particularly iconic for bridging different versions of Christianity.[21] It is significant that nearly 40 percent of the book is devoted to the exegetical and theological issues surrounding Jesus' saying addressed to Peter in Matthew 16:17-19, with a special concern to determine whether and how this saying to Peter might validly apply to later church leadership.[22] As we have noted, Cullmann's own position was that both traditional Roman Catholic and Protestant claims were wrong, and he sought to promote a corrective to them, in which the figure of Peter was both unrepeatable in his role as "rock," and yet also indicative of the continuing validity and importance of church leadership and the shepherding of the church.

The date of the second edition of Cullmann's *Peter* book (German 1960, English 1962) reflects his continued concern and involvement in interconfessional matters. Cullmann was deeply interested in the developments reflected in Vatican II (1962-1965), and was invited as a personal guest of both John XXIII and Paul VI, the only guest invited to four of the council's sessions, and "often invited to private engagements to offer his theological and personal advice."[23] He remained firm in his rejection of the Roman Catholic papal claim of exclusive succession to Peter: "Neither from Scripture nor from the history of the ancient Church can a divine right for the primacy of Rome be derived."[24] Nevertheless, he clearly sought to reach out in friendly dialogue and debate with Roman Catholic scholars in those heady days when there seemed such a readiness to reexamine traditional dogmas and practices.[25]

---

21. As noted by Perkins, *Peter,* p. 5, "Cullmann clearly framed his discussion so that historical and exegetical analysis might provide the foundation for a theological convergence between Protestant and Roman Catholic viewpoints."

22. Pp. 159-242 of the English edition of 1962 deal with "the exegetical and theological question" about this saying. Not counting the prefatory material, there are 226 pp. of text.

23. Birmelé, "Oscar Cullmann," section 2.1. Noting that "many conversations were held with Cullmann, and he probably offered his advice on many texts of the Council," Birmelé suggested three areas "where Cullmann's influence is recognizable": the council's "biblical hermeneutic," the relationship of Scripture and tradition, and the understanding of the church (sections 2.2-2.4).

24. Cullmann, *Peter,* p. 241.

25. Cf. Perkins, *Peter,* p. 6, who notes, "The second Vatican council shifted attention away from using the Petrine texts as evidence for papal jurisdiction and infallibility to understanding Peter as the head of the apostolic college. In his relationship to the larger group of apostles, Peter is the foundation for the unity of the church." But then (pp. 6-7) she continues, "Though Peter may not have exercised the juridical or teaching functions characteristic of later popes, his role in guiding the group of disciples provides the basis for legitimating later developments."

Martin Hengel

I turn now to a small book by Martin Hengel that he described as "ancillary" to a projected four-volume history of Jesus and the early church, in which he sought to correct what he saw as the underestimation of Peter's historical and theological importance within Protestant and Catholic exegesis.[26] Noting that the earliest references to Peter accord him a special status, for example, as the first-named witness to the risen Jesus in 1 Corinthians 15:1-11, Hengel particularly emphasized a need "to examine critically how Protestantism has underestimated Peter theologically."[27] Hengel argued that Peter must have conveyed "a powerful, Spirit-filled proclamation" from the earliest days, or he would not have been leader in the Jerusalem church and "the Man of Rock" figure in early sources. Peter, Hengel urged, must have "participated in giving decisive shape to *the development of the pre-Pauline beginnings of Christology and soteriology.*"[28] One should not deny Peter's "particular theological competence" for "the Man of Rock was certainly not merely an average 'theologian who passed on the theology of others.'"[29]

In a section on Peter's theology, Hengel declared Peter to have been "the leading figure for the *auctor ad Theophilum,*" paradigmatic among the "eyewitnesses and ministers of the word."[30] Although Hengel alleged "significant tensions" between Peter and Paul, with Cullmann, he also posited "a basic consensus" between them on key theological matters, for example, on not requiring circumcision or full observance of Torah for gentile believers, Peter's position something of a middle ground between more extreme views of Judaizing believers and Paul's gentile-oriented message.[31] Granted, as reflected in Galatians 2:11-21, so Hengel proposed, to avoid making problems for Jewish believers "who lived under pressure of the Zealots," Peter withdrew from "Eucharistic table fellowship" with gentile believers in Antioch.[32] But,

---

26. Martin Hengel, *Der unterschätzte Petrus. Zwei Studien* (Tübingen: Mohr Siebeck, 2006); English: *Saint Peter: The Underestimated Apostle* (Grand Rapids: Eerdmans, 2010), which I cite here (preface). It is unfortunate that the translator rendered the German *evangelisch* as "evangelical," whereas "Protestant" is what is meant. To my knowledge, only the first of the planned four-volume work appeared before Hengel's death in 2009: Martin Hengel and Anna Maria Schwener, *Jesus und das Judentum* (Tübingen: Mohr Siebeck, 2007).

27. Hengel, *Saint Peter,* p. 36.

28. Hengel, *Saint Peter,* p. 34 (emphasis original).

29. Hengel, *Saint Peter,* p. 35.

30. Hengel, *Saint Peter,* p. 80.

31. Hengel, *Saint Peter,* p. 83. Cullmann, *Peter,* p. 24.

32. Hengel, *Saint Peter,* p. 84, and p. 65 (and n. 212) for slightly fuller discussion of Hengel's view of the pressure from Zealots on Judean Christianity.

notwithstanding this wobble, Peter was not himself a Judaizer. Indeed, the Petrine speeches in Acts may not be "quite as completely worthless as is generally suggested," and their "antiquated" and "unpretentious" Christology and soteriology may well reflect Peter's teaching.[33]

Acknowledging that any attempt to lay out a "Petrine theology" would be possible "only in a purely hypothetical sense," and that the "ancient Christological confessional statements" should not be ascribed to Peter alone, Hengel nevertheless contended that Peter "would have played a decisive, if not *the* decisive role in the development of the earliest kerygma."[34] Hengel also posited that Paul's decision in his first postconversion trip to Jerusalem to make an extended visit with Peter alone (Gal. 1:18) surely reflects Peter's importance, and in that visit "Paul would have certainly learned more from Peter than vice versa," particularly, but not exclusively, traditions about Jesus.[35] In sum, positing Peter's likely influence on the authors of the Synoptics, and even on Paul and John, Hengel urged (in a characteristic rhetorical flourish), "one could even say, *concerning the apostolic witness,* that [Peter] is — without having left us with a single sentence that he himself wrote — the teacher of us all."[36]

In addition, Hengel contended that Peter was also "a *successful organizer and 'mission strategist,'*" which in turn "played an important role in the conflict between the two opponents."[37] Peter, Hengel submitted, certainly played a role, "actually *the* most significant role," in consolidating the young Jesus movement in the Jewish motherland in the early years after the first Easter.[38] Furthermore, Peter's influence spread thereafter translocally, and there developed "a network of communities that would have been aligned with Peter," including, crucially, Antioch, where Paul was displaced in influence by Peter, and "for a time" something similar seemed likely in Corinth as well. In Rome, "there would have been Pauline and Petrine house communities" next to one another, with occasions for conflict always "close to the surface."[39] In Hengel's view, we can account for the high regard for Peter reflected in various texts, including the Gospels, Acts, 1 Peter, Clement of Rome, and Ignatius only by positing that "the Western communities

---

33. Hengel, *Saint Peter,* p. 85.
34. Hengel, *Saint Peter,* phrases cited from pp. 86, 88.
35. Hengel, *Saint Peter,* p. 88.
36. Hengel, *Saint Peter,* p. 89 (emphasis original).
37. Hengel, *Saint Peter,* p. 89 (emphasis original).
38. Hengel, *Saint Peter,* p. 90.
39. Hengel, *Saint Peter,* p. 90.

knew the apostle himself or learned about him from messengers" sent out by him.[40]

A tension between Peter and Paul is one of the striking emphases that runs through Hengel's study, and receives a sustained discussion in pages 48-79. This strong assertion of a tension between Peter and Paul distinguishes Hengel from Cullmann and, as we shall see, from Bockmuehl. Hengel gives extended description of a *"protracted split"* between Paul and Peter arising from the incident in Antioch mentioned in Galatians 2:11-21, the effects of "the Petrine (rival-)mission" in Corinth that caused "significant problems" there for Paul, and the "tension-filled years" after the "clash in Antioch" during which "Peter was the direct missionary opponent of Paul."[41] Irritatingly for us, however, although the author of Acts knew otherwise, he avoided mentioning the disagreement in Antioch and subsequent tensions between the Pauline and Petrine missions, tensions resulting from "the way the Man of Rock forced his way into the Gentile Christian mission territory of Paul."[42] In light of Hengel's portrait of Peter's rival mission and specifically his interference in Paul's churches, one wonders how Peter could be seen as a symbol of ecumenicity and Christian collegiality. For all Hengel's concern to raise the estimate of Peter's importance in early Christianity, Peter also comes across as a bit of a nuisance in some ways, or at least not entirely a constructive figure, in his effects if not in his intention.

Although Hengel admits that we must remain agnostic about whether Peter and Paul eventually reconciled with each other, he considers it to have been possible, perhaps particularly in the years immediately preceding Nero's persecution of Roman Christians, during which time they were both in Rome.[43] Hengel offers as "a small indicator" that Paul and/or the Pauline tradition sought to close the gap between them and Peter/Petrine churches in the inclusion of Mark (otherwise linked with Peter) among Paul's fellow workers in Philemon 24, Colossians 4:10, and 2 Timothy 4:11.[44]

---

40. Hengel, *Saint Peter*, pp. 48-49. See also pp. 95-97, where Hengel refers to Peter's "considerable" influence outside of Palestine and in the West, especially in Rome.

41. On the Antioch conflict, Hengel, *Saint Peter*, pp. 57-65; on Corinth, pp. 66-72. Phrases cited (sequentially) from pp. 57, 66, and 74.

42. Hengel, *Saint Peter*, p. 79.

43. Hengel, *Saint Peter*, p. 97.

44. Hengel, *Saint Peter*, p. 97. See Mark's link with Peter in 1 Pet. 5:13. Hengel also notes the mention of "the faithful brother" Silvanus in 1 Pet. 5:12 as another expression of an effort to link Pauline and Petrine circles. Curiously, Hengel mentions the corresponding explicit endorsement of Paul's letters as Scripture in 2 Pet. 3:15-16 only in p. 98 n. 331.

As to the classic question about what significance Peter has for subsequent church tradition and structures, Hengel offered only a few brief, but typically direct, comments. He pointed to Peter, Paul, and also John *together* as *"the weight-bearing pillars"* and "the *apostolic witness* that is the foundation for our common faith and the starting point for all ecumenical reflection." Moreover, Hengel insisted that their witness is unique and "their authority cannot be replaced or expanded." So, there can be no "office of Peter" in particular that can set forth "ever new, developing authoritative claims." Instead, Hengel posited, the key Petrine texts, such as Matthew 16:18-19, Luke 22:31-32, and John 21:15-18, point to *"the special, unique 'apostolic service' that the Man of Rock performed for the growing church."*[45] In short, although Hengel urged a far greater recognition of Peter's significance, even in some ways as equal or rival to Paul, Peter is not the rock on which a continuing papal office rests.

Markus Bockmuehl

The most recent scholarly work we consider here is by Markus Bockmuehl, who has now published two valuable books on Peter arising from over a decade of work on him. The earlier volume, *The Remembered Peter* (2010), is a collection of a number of studies (mostly previously published ones) in which Bockmuehl lays out his approach (which involves close attention to the posthumous representation of a historical figure such as Peter) and then carries out various in-depth explorations of particular matters and bodies of evidence.[46] In the later volume, *Simon Peter in Scripture and Memory* (2012), Bockmuehl draws on the research reflected in the earlier book and offers a more synthesized discussion intended for a wider readership, describing it as "a narrative of exegetical engagement with the NT Peter and his reception in the second century."[47]

In both books, Bockmuehl notes a movement in scholarship on Peter in the later twentieth century, describing its direction in the first volume as "away from its earlier polarized anti-Pauline mode . . . to a much more 'centrist' view of the Apostle, according to which his place in early Christianity is indeed that

---

45. Hengel, *Saint Peter,* p. 99 (emphasis original).

46. Markus Bockmuehl, *The Remembered Peter in Ancient Reception and Modern Debate,* WUNT 1/262 (Tübingen: Mohr Siebeck, 2010).

47. Markus Bockmuehl, *Simon Peter in Scripture and Memory: The New Testament Apostle in the Early Church* (Grand Rapids: Baker Academic, 2012).

of a bridge figure and a symbol of unity."[48] In his later volume Bockmuehl refers to the study of Peter as enjoying "a remarkable literary renaissance" in the preceding two decades, arising from "the impulse set by Oscar Cullmann" several decades earlier and now bearing "impressive fruit" that "helps correct several centuries of neglect and distortion."[49] Indeed, Bockmuehl describes his own original ambition, "a 'new Cullmann'," as overtaken by the pace and volume of this recent scholarly work on Peter.[50] Nevertheless, Bockmuehl's two books on Peter constitute a significant body of work that also presents a distinctive approach to the historical appreciation of him and his impact.[51]

As indicated already, Bockmuehl's approach is to attend carefully to how Peter was "remembered" in the early church, especially in the first two centuries, a time Bockmuehl characterizes as giving access to the "living memory" of Peter. Bockmuehl describes his studies of Peter as constituting "a kind of test case" of an approach that he advocates for New Testament studies more generally, in which the *Wirkungsgeschichte* of the New Testament writings, and the figures and ideas in them, should be included programmatically as integral to the discipline.[52] So, whereas for Cullmann "the historical question" required a kind of archaeological work on earliest extant texts and other data to see what could be regarded as the most secure and earliest evidence and resulting picture, Bockmuehl additionally devotes substantial attention to the ways that Peter is depicted in Christian traditions of the first couple of centuries or so, "attempting to find clues to the range of Petrine memory in the early reception history."[53] On the convictions that "the effects and consequences that people generate are as vital to historical understanding as their causes and original circumstances," and that historical figures are more adequately appraised with a bit of hindsight, albeit by people with some "living memory" of them, Bockmuehl contends that Peter's "enormous profile in the subsequent tradition of early Christian faith and thought can be harnessed as a significant asset for historical study, rather than being discarded as an inconvenient liability."[54]

Thus one key feature of the context for Bockmuehl's work on Peter is his

48. Bockmuehl, *Remembered Peter*, p. 8.
49. Bockmuehl, *Simon Peter*, p. xiii.
50. Bockmuehl, *Simon Peter*, p. xiv.
51. Note also Bockmuehl's website on Peter: http://simonpeter.bodleian.ox.ac.uk.
52. Bockmuehl, *Simon Peter*, pp. xiv-xv. Bockmuehl lays out his approach more fully in *Seeing the Word: Refocusing New Testament Study* (Grand Rapids: Baker Academic, 2006).
53. Bockmuehl, *Simon Peter*, p. 19.
54. Bockmuehl, *Remembered Peter*, p. 11, and also pp. 18-22.

concern about the fragmentation of the discipline of New Testament studies, and what he regards as in some scholarly circles an overly narrowed view of what counts as historical and "critical" knowledge. As to the latter concern, granting that his approach "will not produce clear-cut 'historical results'" that will satisfy either strict empiricists or Christian apologists, nonetheless, Bockmuehl urges that it is valid to examine the ways Peter was depicted, especially in the century or so after his death, as indicative of "the impressions he left on those around him," "Peter's footprint in the memory of the first two centuries."[55]

So, a substantial part of both of his books is devoted to examining the representations of Peter in an impressive list of ancient Christian writings. In his later book, working in each case from comparatively later to earlier sources, Bockmuehl investigates "the Eastern Peter" (considering Serapion of Antioch, Justin Martyr, Ignatius of Antioch, "Syrian Noncanonical Gospels," the Pseudo-Clementines, the Gospel of John, the Gospel of Matthew, 2 Peter, and Galatians), and "the Western Peter" (beginning with various references to Peter in Rome, then Dionysius of Corinth, Marcion, Phlegon of Tralles, Clement of Rome, Luke-Acts, 1 Peter, Gospel of Mark, and Romans, winding up with a brief discussion of "local memory" of Peter in Rome).

I must admit that it is still not entirely clear to me what the results of this are for a historical view of Peter. The sources contemporary with, or close to, the lifetime of Peter are of obvious usefulness. But reports and references from the second century tell us essentially that Christians (of various types) found it useful to refer to, and/or claim, Peter and characterize him in certain ways. These sources *may* also, to some degree, reflect something of an earlier impact of the historical figure, but one needs cogent criteria by which to determine this. To be sure, Bockmuehl acknowledges the problem and offers reasons for his judgments at every point, specifically why he thinks that this or that later source might preserve something authentic of Peter. But it will likely require more time for scholars to test the warrants and results of what Bockmuehl offers.

I should also mention that, as did Cullmann, Bockmuehl includes archaeological data in his investigation. His chapter "Simon Peter and Bethsaida" in his earlier book is a fascinating and valuable assessment of questions about Peter's relationship to Bethsaida (Bockmuehl judges that Peter grew up there), what kind of place Bethsaida was (Bockmuehl thinks it was heavily hellenized and that Peter grew up thoroughly bilingual and acquainted with Hellenistic influences), and archaeological questions about where Bethsaida actually was

---

55. Bockmuehl, *Remembered Peter*, pp. 15-16, 29.

(probably the site known as et-Tell, but perhaps also inclusive of el-Araj as a fishing "outpost" of the town).[56]

In his later book, Bockmuehl also briefly discusses questions about the tomb of Peter under the Vatican, judging that archaeological work there has discovered "the site remembered by second-century Christians as the tomb of Peter," as reflected in the statement by the Roman presbyter Gaius in the early third century.[57] On the other hand, as to "the tricky question" of whether the bones of Peter have been identified, Bockmuehl considers that the story of their claimed discovery "does not inspire confidence," and that "it seems right to join the majority of scholars in being cautious about Pope Paul VI's claim in 1968 that these are indeed the bones of Peter."[58] In an irenic statement, however, that reflects Bockmuehl's forthright combination of scholarship and faith, he urges that "a properly Christian approach to such claims ought to be reluctant in practice but sympathetic in principle."[59]

On the classic question of what Peter's significance is for subsequent church leadership, Bockmuehl judges Cullmann and traditional Protestant views "both profoundly right and profoundly misguided." Although "the remembered Peter" is neither "an authority nor an institution," and so not the basis for traditional Catholic papal claims, the shepherd ministry assigned to Peter (e.g., in John 21) pertains "as long as the church endures," and so "there must be a question of the proper succession to this Petrine ministry." As to whether the papal office validly "embodies this Petrine succession," Bockmuehl thinks that this "remains a perennially useful question."[60] Although consensus on this and related matters can remain only "an eschatological hope," Bockmuehl insists that "it seems patently untrue to assume, as many Protestants continue to do, that Peter's task self-evidently 'expired with his death.'"[61] In

---

56. Bockmuehl, *Remembered Peter*, pp. 158-87. Bockmuehl draws on this discussion also in *Simon Peter*, pp. 166-76.

57. Bockmuehl, *Simon Peter*, pp. 148-49, citing p. 149. Gaius is quoted by Eusebius, *H.E.* 2.25.6-7 as pointing to "the trophies of the Apostles" to be found on the Vatican hill (the site of Peter's burial) and the Ostian Way (the site of Paul's burial).

58. Bockmuehl, *Simon Peter*, p. 149. Bockmuehl refers to Margherita Guarducci's book, *La tomba di San Pietro: Una straordinaria vicenda* (Milano: Saggi Bompiani, 2000), but curiously does not seem to know of some other relevant works critical of Guarducci's claims, e.g., Snyder, "Survey and 'New' Thesis on the Bones of Peter"; O'Connor, *Peter in Rome*; O'Connor, "Peter in Rome."

59. Bockmuehl, *Simon Peter*, p. 149.

60. Phrasing quoted in this paragraph all from Bockmuehl, *Simon Peter*, p. 182.

61. Bockmuehl, *Simon Peter*, p. 183, Bockmuehl citing critically Jürgen Becker, *Simon Petrus im Urchristentum* (Neukirchen-Vluyn: Neukirchener, 2009), p. 139.

response, one might note that the continuation of Peter's "task" or "ministry" is one thing, but the Roman Catholic claim about the *authority* of the papal *office* as *unique successor* to Peter is quite another. With due appreciation for their irenic quality, Bockmuehl's statements here might be seen more as stepping carefully around the latter difficult issue rather than engaging it.

Conclusion

As indicated at the outset, this has been a selective discussion. The quality of the works considered here justify selecting them for attention, and the scholars in question represent three distinguishable generations across the last sixty years. Certainly, however, there are indications of a wider scholarly interest in Peter in recent decades, even confining attention to other Protestant scholars.[62] Though they vary in the evidence considered and the approaches taken, and reflect different circumstances and occasions for their works, Cullmann, Hengel, and Bockmuehl surely show that Peter is now firmly a topic for serious, thoughtful investigation by Protestant scholars rightly concerned more with historical knowledge than with church polemics.

---

62. E.g., the eloquent appreciation of Peter stated by James D. G. Dunn, *Unity and Diversity in the New Testament* (Philadelphia: Westminster, 1977), p. 385, referring to Peter as "probably in fact and effect the bridge-man who did more than any other to hold together the diversity of first-century Christianity," echoed later by him in *The Canon Debate,* ed. Lee Martin McDonald and James A. Sanders (Peabody, MA: Hendrickson, 2002), pp. 576-77.

The "Historical Peter"

CHAPTER 2

The Fisherman from Bethsaida

Sean Freyne

When I was invited to bring some archaeological color to these proceedings, I jokingly suggested showing some slides of Galilean rocks! However, a little reflection caused me to jettison that idea and to decide that a discussion of the Galilean fish industry would seem to be appropriate. Simon son of Jonah and his brother Andrew were fishermen (Mark 1:16), and came from Bethsaida originally (John 1:44), as also did Philip (John 12:21). Mark tells us that another pair of brothers, James and John, on receiving Jesus' call to follow him left their father Zebedee with the hired servants and also followed Jesus (Mark 1:19-20). These call stories are located by both Matthew and Mark in the region of Capernaum, and it is this town rather than Bethsaida that features more prominently in the career of Jesus subsequently.[1]

This fact is quite interesting, since Bethsaida was in the territory of Philip, and later Agrippa II, whereas Capernaum was in Antipas's territory. It would appear that two quite different environments operated even though the two locations are situated very close to each other. As is well known, Herod Philip had no qualms about honoring the Augustan era on his coins whereas Antipas adhered to a noniconic policy in order to avoid offending the vast majority of his Judean subjects.[2] Yet the manner in which Capernaum and Bethsaida were

---

1. For Capernaum, see Mark 1:21; 2:1; 9:33; Matt. 4:13; 8:5; 11:23; 17:24; Luke 4:23, 31; 7:1; 10:15; John 2:12; 4:46; 6:17, 24, and 59. For Bethsaida, see Mark 6:45; 8:22; Matt. 11:21; Luke 9:10; 10:13; and John 1:44 and 12:21.

2. See the discussion in Morten H. Jensen, *Herod Antipas in Galilee: The Literary and Archaeological Sources on the Reign of Herod Antipas and Its Socio-Economic Impact on Galilee*, WUNT 2/215 (Tübingen: Mohr Siebeck, 2006), pp. 203-9.

interconnected through kinship relations suggests that there was a strong Judean presence in both places, something that has been confirmed with regard to Bethsaida also on the basis of recent archaeological finds at et-Tell, the most likely site for ancient Bethsaida.[3] Thus it would seem that two different boundaries were operative, one religious and the other political, and this should be recognized when we hear of Jesus crossing over to the other side. He is not thereby necessarily entering gentile territory.

Mark's account of the call of the first disciples is laconic, lacking social and psychological details; the incident begs to be filled out from what we know about ancient fishing and its economic potential in the Mediterranean world generally. One suspects that evangelical rather than social world concerns have shaped the accounts: the suddenness of the call and the prompt response of the two brothers have all the hallmarks of an early Christian conversion story. Even the mention of the hired servants may indicate that this was a relatively affluent household with all its members engaged in making the business successful. As such it could be an early example of the rich young man syndrome when the lure of wealth could have easily got in the way of responding to the call of the gospel (Mark 10.17-31 and pars.).

Luke fills out the picture somewhat, mentioning two boats and referring to the occupants as partners (*metochoi,* Luke 5:7), suggesting a cooperative arrangement of some sort. Certainly the discovery of more than twenty harbors, breakwaters, and fish ponds around the lake indicates that fishing was an important aspect of the local economy and was more than just a part-time occupation.[4] The fact that Magdala on the western side of the lake had its name changed, probably in the Hellenistic period already, to Tarichea, with reference to the salting of fish, as Strabo informs us (*Geogr.* 16.2.45), is further evidence that the resource of the lake was fully exploited in terms of the preservation and export of the produce. This in turn would have fed into other aspects of the economy — boat building and repair, pottery making, and overland transportation of salt and other ingredients being the most obvious elements in such a network. As we shall see, these aspects can be illustrated from some of the recent archaeological finds in the region. However, it also gives rise to a

---

3. Rami Arav, ed., *Bethsaida, A City by the North Shore of the Sea of Galilee,* 4 vols. (Kirksville, Mo.: Truman State University Press, 1999-2007); Heinz-Wolfgang Kuhn, "Bethsaida und et-Tell in frührömischer Zeit," Part I, *ZNW* 101 (2010): 1-32; Part II, *ZNW* 101 (2010): 174-203.

4. M. Nun, *Sea of Galilee: Newly Discovered Harbours from New Testament Days* (Kibbutz Ein Gev: Kinnereth Sailing Club, 1988); M. Nun, *The Sea of Galilee and Its Fishermen in the New Testament* (Kibbuz Ein Gev: Kinnereth Sailing Club, 1990).

number of issues to do with the Galilean economy more generally, especially the disputed issue of who was likely to benefit from the proceeds, the Herodian elites or the fishing families themselves.[5]

Demand for Fish in the Ancient World

In order to understand better the role that fishing might have played in the Galilean economy, it is worth looking briefly at the demand for fish in the Roman world more generally. In the Greek world cereals and meat were deemed more suitable for a healthy diet than fish, especially when it was imported.[6] Indeed fish and fishermen were often lampooned by the Greek dramatists in Athens of the classical period.[7] However, all that was to change later, and while we are dependent on Galen and his younger contemporary Athenaeus for our information, these second- and third-century-CE writers were heavily dependent on earlier works, only fragments of which have survived.[8]

One aspect of the discussion in both writers that has direct bearing on the Galilean situation is the manner in which different types of fish are classified in terms of the type of water in which they are to be found. Thus, for example, Galen mentions that there are two types of mullet, one that is to be found in the sea and another that is to be found in pools, swamps, and rivers that run through large towns, where they eat human dung and other such foods, and are therefore bad for human consumption unless they are pickled.[9] This information is quite significant as far as the quality of the fish in the Sea of Galilee is concerned. Josephus mentions a special kind of fish found in the lake called the coracin, a type of black eel, only found elsewhere in the lake of Alexandria, he claims (*J. W.* 3.521). Earlier in this same passage — an encomium on the Plain of Gennosar and its fertility — Josephus describes the waters of the lake in the following glowing terms:

5. K. C. Hanson, "The Galilean Fishing Economy and the Jesus Tradition," *BTB* 27 (1997): 99-111.

6. Plato, *Republic* 372; Ovid, *Fasti* 6, 169-86.

7. James N. Davidson, *Courtesans and Fishcakes: The Consuming Passions of Classical Athens* (London: HarperCollins, 1997), pp. 3-35.

8. J. Wilkins, "Fish as a Source of Food in Antiquity," in *Ancient Fishing and Fish Processing in the Black Sea Region,* ed. T. Bekker-Nielsen (Aarhus: Aarhus University Press, 2005), pp. 21-30.

9. Galen, *On the Properties of Foodstuffs* 3.24; Mark Grant, *Galen on Food and Diet* (London: Routledge, 2000).

Notwithstanding its extent, its water is sweet to the taste and excellent to drink. Clearer than the marsh water with its thick sediment, it is perfectly pure, the lake everywhere ending in pebbly and sandy beaches. Moreover when drawn it has an agreeable temperature, more pleasant than that of the river or spring water, yet cooler than the great expanse of the lake would lead one to expect. It becomes cold as snow when one has exposed it to the air, as the people of the country are wont to do during the summer nights. The lake contains species of fish, different both in taste and appearance from those found elsewhere. (*J. W.* 3.506-8)

Elsewhere I have suggested that Josephus's description of the lake and the properties of its water recalls the Hippocratic treatise *On Airs, Waters and Places.*[10] Not only does he speak of the water in the glowing terms just cited, but he also describes the air as *eukrasia,* that is, temperate or moderate (*J. W.* 3.519). Thus it is clear that he also sees the lake as an important food resource, given the quality of the water. Indeed of the many possible reasons for Jesus' seeming transfer to the valley region, one might easily be that as a folk healer he too was conscious of both the air and water quality of the region.

Despite the very different perspectives of Josephus's *Vita* and the Gospels, especially that of Mark, it is interesting to note that both narratives do focus on the lake region in terms of the activity of the main characters. In the case of Josephus, the primary motive for making Tarichea his headquarters was to be close to Tiberias, where one of his main rivals, Justus, was based. Both Tarichea and Tiberias "with their toparchies" technically belonged to the territory of Agrippa II, on the basis of a bequest from Nero, as early as 54 CE (*J. W.* 2.252-53; *Ant.* 20.159). By setting up his quarters in Tarichea and seeking to control Tiberias, he was, therefore, making a political statement that refused to accept existing Roman divisions of the land, while avoiding being sucked into the internal politics of Tiberias.

In Mark's account the lakefront and its busy boating activity are never far from the author's mind in describing Jesus' movements. Unlike Josephus, however, he never visits either Tarichea or Tiberias, with the more northerly Capernaum providing him with something of a home base. The emphasis is more on Jesus' constant movements around the lake and in the villages of the region. Boats are regularly at hand to ferry him across the lake, and crowds

---

10. Sean Freyne, *Jesus, a Jewish Galilean: A New Reading of the Jesus Story* (London: T&T Clark, 2005), pp. 56-57.

seem to gather wherever he disembarks.[11] While these movements may well be part of the Markan description of the opening out of the mission to non-Jews in the immediate post-70 period, they are quite realistic for the period of Jesus' ministry also, in view of the many harbors that are on the eastern side of the lake, some presumably belonging to gentile centers such as Hippos and Gadara, and others, such as Ein Gev, belonging to Jewish communities.[12]

Josephus, too, can avail of the movement of boats on the lake to his advantage on a number of occasions. One instance was when "the Judeans" of Tarichea were insisting that some noblemen from Trachonitis who had sought refuge among them should undergo circumcision if they were to stay in their city. By describing this group as *Ioudaioi*, rather than the more usual *Galilaioi* or *hoi en Tarichaea katoikountes*, Josephus was indicating a rigorist group within the city, possibly the remnant of the older Hasmonean nationalists whose loyalties were more rooted in Judean practices than the more recently arrived Herodians. At all events, Josephus did not want to support this xenophobic demand and gives a speech to that effect (*Vita* 112-13). However, shortly afterward the refugees again came under extreme pressure and Josephus was forced to get them out of the city by having a canal cut from their dwelling to the harbor and accompanying them by boat to Hippos across the lake. A second incident is even more telling in terms of the boat traffic on the lake. Tiberias had revolted against Judean control by declaring its support for King Agrippa, and excluded Josephus from their city.[13] However, he was able to commandeer the whole Tarichean fleet of boats and launch a mock attack on Tiberias. According to the *Jewish War* account there were 230 boats in all, each with four sailors on board, whereas in *Vita* Josephus says that he ordered the heads of households to launch a vessel, but without giving the actual numbers (*J. W.* 2.635; *Vita* 163). By ordering the boats to anchor well offshore the Tiberians believed that they were about to be subjected to a massive sea attack and as a result they threw down their arms and surrendered!

Clearly both incidents are intended to extol Josephus's magnanimity and cleverness, avoiding bloodshed in his successful conduct of affairs in Galilee.[14] Inevitably there is a lively imagination at work in these narratives. Yet one cannot dismiss the accounts completely, especially the presence of boats on the lake, and the fact that many of the population of Tarichea were engaged

11. Mark 1:16; 2:13; 4:1-2, 36; 5:1-2; 6:45, 53; 7:31; 8:10.

12. Nun, *Newly Discovered Harbours*; Nun, *Sea of Galilee and Its Fishermen*.

13. Josephus, *Vita* 155-73; *J. W.* 2.632-46.

14. Steve Mason, *Flavius Josephus: Life of Josephus, Translation and Commentary* (Leiden: Brill, 2003), pp. 88-91.

in the fishing industry. The name of this place is associated with fish (Semitic: *Migdal Nunya,* "fish tower"), and the Greek name Tarichea refers to the salting of fish, as noted by the first-century-CE writer Strabo (*Geogr.* 16.2.45).

However, none of the ancient sources dealing with Galilee broaches the topic of the various types of fish by-products that we know about from other Greco-Roman writings. These include not just salted fish but also various fish-based sauces such as garum and salsamenta. The differences between these various by-products depended largely on the parts of the fish used, the amount and provenience of salt, the variety of other ingredients added as well as the types of containers in which the by-product was stored. On the basis of remarks from Seneca and Pliny, especially about the smells emanating from them, modern scholars tended to overlook the importance of these for the ancient populations. However, the increased emphasis on the archaeological data, especially that emanating from the western Mediterranean, as well as a greater interest in everyday life patterns including diet at different social levels, has begun to change the view with regard to the importance of the various products.[15] Unfortunately, as we shall discuss presently, archaeology has so far not uncovered evidence for these production processes at Tarichea. We must presume that they would have been carried out there also, and contributed to the local and regional economy, even if K. C. Hanson's proposals of a social and economic network that reached as far as the Herodian court may be somewhat overcooked.[16] The absence of fish symbols on all of the coins minted in the region is a notable omission, if the fish industry was as highly developed and managed as is claimed. Certainly the Galilean fishermen were not in a position to emulate their first-century-CE counterparts at Ephesus, who were sufficiently affluent as a guild of fishermen and fishmongers, to erect a public toll building by the harbor and dedicate it suitably, with the amount of contributions from all the members listed.[17]

Archaeology and Fishing in the Region

Thus far the material evidence for Tarichea's engagement with the fish industry is not as significant as one might expect, mainly because excavation at

15. R. I. Curtis, "Sources for Production and Trade of Greek and Roman Processed Fish," in Bekker-Nielsen, *Ancient Fishing and Fish Processing,* pp. 31-46, here pp. 31-39.

16. K. C. Hanson and Douglas E. Oakman, *Palestine in the Time of Jesus: Social Structures and Social Conflicts* (Minneapolis: Fortress, 1998), especially pp. 99-104.

17. G. H. R. Horsley, "A Fishing Cartel in First Century Ephesus," in *New Documents Illustrating Early Christianity* (Sydney: Macquarie University, 1989), 5:95-114.

the site has until lately concentrated on the alleged synagogue and the streets surrounding it. However, one of the archaeological teams at the site, that of the Franciscans, under the direction of Stefan de Luca has now uncovered the harbor, among other aspects of Greco-Roman town planning, following the Hippodamic grid pattern and with an underground drainage system. In addition a large bathhouse has been uncovered, a peristyle surrounding an open courtyard with separate bathrooms with pools, basins, and other installations.

East of this complex the harbor is separated from the city by a plastered wall. Massive foundations of a tower have been uncovered as well as a large L-shaped basin with a breakwater and six mooring stones with iron hooks for tying up the boats. The archaeologists believe that they can decipher two phases in the building of the harbor, one pre-Herodian datable to the first century BCE, when Galilee came under the control of the Hasmoneans, and the other from the first-century-CE Herodian period, virtually contemporaneous with Herod the Great's building project at Caesarea Maritima. The Magdala harbor is the first such in the region to have been fully excavated, and therefore accurately dated on the basis of the stratigraphy of the site. It is also of considerable size and clearly capable of accommodating a large number of boats, as suggested by Josephus's numbers, exaggerated though they may be.[18]

West of the bathhouse, the discovery of a mosaic at the entrance vestibule to a first-century villa, depicting a fishing galley and other objects provides an interesting insight into the life of an upper-class Tarichean in this relatively prosperous town.[19] The prominence of the galley in the mosaic suggests that the owner of the villa has acquired his wealth from the fish industry. The mosaic is simply executed, but it is based on firsthand observation rather than an artisan's "pattern book." Three different colors of tesserae are used: black for the most part, a white line near the top of the hull and light brown for the sail and oars. The depiction of the boat is side on, moving under oar, three on the side facing. As well as the depiction of the galley the mosaic in question has a number of other objects that have been interpreted to reflect the

18. J. Zangenberg, "Archaeological News from the Galilee: Tiberias, Magdala, and Rural Galilee," *Early Christianity* 1 (2010): 471-84, here pp. 475-77; see also the Magdala Project website, www.magdalaproject.org.

19. V. Corbo, "Piazza et Villa urbana a Magdala," *Liber Annuus* 28 (1978): 232-40; J. Zangenberg, *Magdala am See Gennesaret,* Kleine Arbeiten zum Alten und Neuen Testament 2 (Waltrop: Spenner, 2001), pp. 50-56; J. R. Steffy and S. Wachsman, "The Migdal Boat Mosaic," in *The Excavation of an Ancient Boat in the Sea of Galilee (Lake Kinneret),* 'Atiqot, ed. S. Wachsman, English Series 19 (Jerusalem: Israel Antiquities Authority, 1990), pp. 114-18; R. Arav, "A Note on the Roman Mosaic at Magdala on the Sea of Galilee," *Liber Annuus* 41 (1991): 455-58.

aspiration of the villa's owner. They include objects associated with the bath-house and the sports arena (i.e., recreational pursuits), knapsacks for carrying food and liquids, a beautifully crafted *kantharos,* or large drinking cup, and most significant of all, the fishing boat with mast and sail as well as posts for three oarsmen on either side and a helmsman. Clearly this mosaic represents an affluent lifestyle, more Greco-Roman than Jewish, and is indicative of the possibility for generating wealth that the fish industry in this place provided. Separate from the main mosaic but close by is a Greek inscription *(KAI SU),* which has been interpreted as part of an apotropaic formula to avert the "evil eye" from the household and protect its prosperous lifestyle.[20]

The discovery in 1986 of a first-century-CE boat close to Tarichea and its subsequent restoration open a further window on this world of fishing in the region. The "Galilean Boat" has been painstakingly restored and beautifully presented at a small museum attached to Nof Ginosar, a few kilometers north of the site of Magdala. Study of the construction of the boat and the various types of wood that have been used has assisted greatly in our understanding of the ancillary trades that were required in order to service the fishing industry, since the manner in which the timbers were prepared and mortised illustrates the ways in which first-century boatwrights worked. This particular sample would appear to have had a long life and had undergone repairs many times with different timbers being used. Of the forty-two timbers that have been ex-amined, Lebanese cedar and oak constitute the majority, but there are samples of Aleppo pine, hawthorn, willow, and redbud — all locally grown except for the cedar. According to E. Werker this variety of timber types, some of which were unsuitable for seafaring, indicates either a shortage of wood or the fact that the boat's owner could not afford any better, even though the hull was originally crafted by someone familiar with Mediterranean seafaring.[21] It is a large boat, 8.2 meters long and 2.3 meters wide at its maximum. At the stern, where it is best preserved, the depth is 1.2 meters high. The boat would have required four oarsmen and a helmsman captain, similar to the boat depicted in the Magdala mosaic and mentioned also by Josephus in relation to the launching of the boats from Tarichea for the mock attack (*Vita* 163; cf. Mark 1:20; John 21:2-3). Presumably this boat also had a mast and sail, but the mast step had been removed already in antiquity.

20. R. Reich, "A Note on the Roman Mosaic at Magdala on the Sea of Galilee," *Liber Annuus* 41 (1991): 455-58.

21. E. Werker, "Identification of the Wood," in Wachsman, *Excavation of an Ancient Boat,* pp. 65-76.

Fig. 1. The Galilee boat (courtesy Sean Freyne)

It has been suggested that the location of this boat may have been a repair yard as some timbers from other boats were also found in the mud that had covered the boat for centuries. Equally fascinating are some of the other items discovered in the immediate vicinity: household pottery including a lamp, an arrowhead, coins, and anchors. The pottery finds are particularly interesting in that they match similar finds at Capernaum, and Magdala, representing some well-established samples of Kefar Hanania ware, a ceramic production center in the center of Galilee. Israeli archaeologist David Adan-Bayewitz has made a detailed study of this ware in terms of both form and distribution patterns. The samples from the boat site represent Kefar Hanania types 3A and 4A of Bayewitz's analysis of the pottery, and they also match similar finds in stratified digs from nearby Capernaum and Magdala.[22] Thus they can be confidently dated to a period between the mid-first century BCE and the late first century CE, that is, the early Roman period. The fact that none of the later pottery types from Kefar Hanania was found at the site suggests that in the wake of the collapse of the Galilean campaign, the yard may have closed,

22. D. Adan-Bayewitz, *Common Pottery in Roman Galilee: A Study of Local Trade* (Ramat Gan: Bar-Ilan University Press, 1993), pp. 83-154.

probably because of Vespasian's destruction of the Tarichean fleet, as reported by Josephus (*J. W.* 2.522-31).[23]

As mentioned previously, Bethsaida/et-Tell is another site in the region that has come in for special archaeological attention in recent times. The site is of particular interest because at least three of Jesus' first followers were from Bethsaida (Peter, Andrew, and Philip). However, some scholars are unsure of the identification of this site with Bethsaida Julias of the first century. Several objections have been mounted, not least the distance from the lakefront and the relative scarcity of Roman-period buildings and artifacts. The Bethsaida team under the direction of Rami Arav has mounted a vigorous defense of the identification, explaining the distance from the lakeshore, partly on the basis of a misreading of Josephus, and partly on the seismic geological shifts in the region over the centuries. In particular, the German New Testament scholar Heinz-Wolfgang Kuhn has produced a closely argued defense of the site as being that of Bethsaida Julias. On the basis of a coin that describes Philip as *ktistēs,* dated to 31 CE, he points out that in all probability Philip did not have the resources or the time to adorn the place in best Roman style, before his death in 34 CE. Kuhn has collected the evidence for Roman-style artifacts, such as coins, pottery, cooking wares, Rhodian jar handles, glassware, and personal ornaments, all indicating that it was inhabited in the Roman period. He also discusses the possibility of a Roman temple at the site. However, the evidence for identifying the structure in question as a temple is to a large degree circumstantial, with the discovery of an incense shovel and a female figurine in close proximity.[24]

Of more immediate interest in this context is the evidence for Bethsaida/et-Tell as a fishing village. A Hellenistic/Roman-period house in area B, of peristyle layout, had been designated by the first excavators as "the Fisherman's house" due to the number of items to do with fishing discovered there.[25] However, subsequent work at the site has led to the conclusion that there was no specific fisherman's quarter but that implements to do with fishing have been discovered all over the site. These include iron and bronze hooks, lead basalt and limestone weights and anchors, as well as needles for repairing nets.[26]

23. D. Adan-Bayewitz, "The Pottery," in Wachsman, *Excavation of an Ancient Boat,* pp. 89-96.

24. Kuhn, "Bethsaida," I, pp. 25-28; II, pp. 177-87; cf. C. Savage, "Supporting Evidence for a First-Century Bethsaida," in *Religion, Ethnicity and Identity in Ancient Galilee,* ed. Jürgen Zangenberg, Harold W. Attridge, and Dale B. Martin (Tübingen: Mohr Sieback, 2007), pp. 193-206.

25. Arav, *Bethsaida* I, pp. 26-27.

26. S. Fortner, "The Fishing Implements and Maritime Activities of Bethsaida-Julias," in Arav, *Bethsaida* II, pp. 269-80.

While archaeology may not so far have provided the kind of data that could enable us to reconstruct the Galilean fishing industry satisfactorily, it does confirm and in interesting ways supplements the literary evidence. Nor has it assisted directly in giving us a better understanding of Peter's decision to join the Jesus movement. Was he driven by a desire to challenge the Roman presence in the persons of Antipas and Philip? Or was it the putative temple to Julia the wife of Augustus that prompted a reaction, especially Philip's minting of a coin that portrayed her as Ceres, the goddess of plenty? Perhaps it was the fact that the fruits of his labors were being eroded by the taxes imposed by the Herodian elite in order to maintain their luxurious lifestyles. Undoubtedly these and other motives may well have come into play in his decision "to leave all" and "follow Jesus." We cannot rule out personal feelings and motivations also. Nevertheless, it is interesting to note that in one version of the postresurrection traditions, on returning to Galilee after "the failure" in Jerusalem, he and his Galilean companions were assumed to have engaged, if only temporarily, in their original pursuits as fishermen (John 21).

CHAPTER 3

From Shimon to Petros — Petrine Nomenclature in the Light of Contemporary Onomastic Practices

Margaret H. Williams

Changes of name were not uncommon either in the Palestinian Jewish environment into which "Simon Peter" was born or in the wider Greco-Roman world in which he was subsequently to operate as a Christian missionary. The most famous example from the latter is that of Augustus, the ruler of that world when Peter was born. It is also one of the best documented: we know the exact occasion of his transformation from Gaius Octavius to Gaius Iulius Caesar[1] and precisely when and why he made the final, breathtakingly original addition to his nomenclature — the brand-new name Augustus.[2] With Peter, such exactitude is impossible. Although we know that he started out as Shimon and ended up, at least in the West, as Petros, it is far from clear when that particular onomastic change occurred or why. Nor is that the only problem with Petrine nomenclature: his patronymic is variously given — Jonah in one Gospel, John in another; and a further source of difficulty and debate has been his Aramaic nickname, Kepha.[3] Making sense, then, of

1. It was in the aftermath of the murder of his great uncle, the dictator Julius Caesar, on the Ides of March, 44 BCE. For Caesar's bequest to his great nephew of both the bulk of his fortune and, crucially, his name, see Suetonius, *Augustus* 7.2; and Barbara Levick, *Augustus — Image and Substance* (Harlow, U.K.: Pearson, 2010), pp. 25-26.

2. For the date (January 16, 27 BCE), see Victor Ehrenberg and A. H. M. Jones, *Documents Illustrating the Reigns of Augustus and Tiberius* (Oxford: Clarendon, 1955), p. 45; for the reasons, see Suetonius, *Augustus* 7.2; and Cassius Dio, *Roman History* 53.16.6-8.

3. On this topic, the fundamental study remains Joseph A. Fitzmyer's "Aramaic Kepha' and Peter's Name in the New Testament," in *Text and Interpretation: Studies in the New Testament Presented to Matthew Black,* ed. Ernest Best and R. McL. Wilson (Cambridge: Cambridge

the nomenclature of an individual referred to more variously than any other New Testament figure is no small matter.[4] However, by viewing the Petrine evidence against the backdrop of onomastic practice among Jews in both Palestine and the Diaspora, as well as of onomastic practices in the wider non-Jewish world, it becomes possible to construct an entirely coherent, even if not precisely datable, name profile for this apostle. What enables us to do this is the considerable amount of contemporary onomastic data at our disposal, Palestine in the late Second Temple period being one of the most richly documented areas of the early Roman Empire. Besides the voluminous writings of Josephus, there is an extensive body of epigraphic evidence. Mostly this consists of short epitaphs either scrawled or incised in Aramaic, Hebrew, and Greek on ossuaries found primarily in Jerusalem and its environs, but the inscribed potsherds from Masada also provide significant amounts of information. Since in both of these cases (ossuaries and ostraca) essentially we are dealing with identification labels, unsurprisingly the predominant element in them consists of names.[5]

In constructing a name profile for our apostle, the approach here will be chronological. Hence we will start with the name conferred on "Peter" by his parents on the eighth day after his birth — Shimon (שמעון), a popular Hebrew/Aramaic name, the most common transliterated form of which in Greek was Σίμων (Simon). Our sources agree that this was his original name, Petros (or its Graecized Aramaic equivalent Kephas) being an additional name, a *supernomen* or *signum,* acquired much later in life.[6]

University Press, 1979), pp. 121-32, now reprinted in Joseph A. Fitzmyer, *To Advance the Gospel: New Testament Studies* (New York: Crossroad, 1981), pp. 112-24.

4. For full documentation of the eight different ways in which Peter's name is given in the New Testament, see O. Odelain and R. Séguineau, *Dictionary of Proper Names and Places in the Bible,* trans. Matthew J. O'Connell (London: Robert Hale, 1991), s.v. "Peter." For detailed treatment of Petrine nomenclature, the discussions of Oscar Cullmann, *Peter — Disciple, Apostle, Martyr,* trans. Floyd V. Filson, 2nd ed. (London: SCM, 1962), pp. 19-23; and Markus Bockmuehl, *The Remembered Peter in Ancient Reception and Modern Debate,* WUNT 1/262 (Tübingen: Mohr Siebeck, 2010), pp. 135-54, are particularly useful.

5. Access to this documentary material is most easily gained by consulting Tal Ilan, *Lexicon of Jewish Names in Late Antiquity: Part I — Palestine 330 BCE-200 CE* (Tübingen: Mohr Siebeck, 2002). For the most recent edition of the inscriptional material from the Jerusalem area, see Hannah M. Cotton et al., eds., *Corpus Inscriptionum Iudaeae/Palestinae,* vol. 1, part 1, *Jerusalem* (Berlin: de Gruyter, 2010) (hereafter, *CIIP* 1.1).

6. For this common onomastic practice in Greco-Roman antiquity, see G. H. R. Horsley, "Names, Double," in *ABD,* 4:1012-7.

Peter's Original Personal Name

With the name Shimon we find ourselves on comfortingly firm ground. There is a mass of evidence from late Second Temple-period Palestine for this ancient Hebrew patriarchal name.[7] Our sources, literary and epigraphic, are unanimous in making this and its Greek variant, Simon, the commonest male name by far at that time. According to Tal Ilan, it occurs over 250 times and so comes out way ahead of all of its nearest rivals.[8] As to why it was so popular, there can be little doubt that it was because of its nationalist, patriotic associations. Until Simon Maccabee comes to dominate the scene in the third quarter of the second century BCE, the patriarchal name Shimon hardly ever occurs in the Palestinian Jewish onomasticon,[9] a fact that is not surprising given the less-than-glorious part played by that particular son of Jacob in the biblical narrative. After Simon Maccabee's successes in ridding the Palestinian Jews of Seleucid control around 140 BCE and so effectively turning Judea into an independent state,[10] the popularity of the name Shimon rockets, a trajectory shared by virtually all the Hebrew names found in his family. That applies not just to the male names (e.g., Judas and John) but to the female names too, most notably Miriam (Greek form, Mariamme).[11]

Many factors, of course, may be operating when a choice of name is made. It should not automatically be assumed that when our Peter was given his original name, political considerations alone motivated his parents. Familial traditions in naming, for instance, could well have been an influence too:[12] papponymy and patronymy are both well-attested practices at that time.[13]

---

7. For its first occurrence and popular etymology, see Gen. 29:33.

8. See Ilan, *Lexicon,* p. 56 (table 5), and pp. 218-35 (שמעון — Simon).

9. See Odelain and Séguineau, *Dictionary of Proper Names,* s.v. "Simeon."

10. E. Mary Smallwood, *The Jews under Roman Rule from Pompey to Diocletian,* 2nd ed. (Leiden: Brill, 1981), pp. 7-8.

11. Tal Ilan, "The Names of the Hasmoneans in the Second Temple Period," *Eretz-Israel* 19 (1987): 238-41 (Hebrew section); and Ilan, *Lexicon,* pp. 6-8. Margaret H. Williams, "Palestinian Jewish Personal Names in Acts," in *The Book of Acts in Its First Century Setting,* vol. 4, *Palestinian Setting,* ed. Richard Bauckham (Grand Rapids: Eerdmans, 1995), pp. 79-113 (esp. pp. 106-9), now reprinted in Margaret H. Williams, *Jews in a Graeco-Roman Environment* (Tübingen: Mohr Siebeck, 2013), pp. 289-315 (esp. pp. 310-13).

12. As the story of the naming of John the Baptist at Luke 1:59-61 shows.

13. Rachel Hachlili, "Hebrew Names, Personal Names, Family Names and Nicknames of Jews in the Second Temple Period," in *Families and Family Relations as Represented in Early Judaisms and Early Christianities: Texts and Fictions,* ed. Jan Willem van Henten and Athalya Brenner (Leiderdorp: Deo, 2000), p. 88.

However, when the onomastic evidence for late Second Temple Palestine is considered as a whole, the most striking feature of it is the extraordinarily close relationship that existed between personal name and politico-religious stance. Consequently it is not unreasonable to hypothesize that politico-religious considerations may well have played at least some part in determining the choice of the future apostle's first name. When, in addition, we factor in the evident enthusiasm for the preaching of John the Baptist of Simon's brother Andrew and Simon's own eagerness to make the acquaintance of the new "messianic" preacher Jesus (John 1:35-42), the conclusion seems inescapable that theirs was a family for whom the renewal of Israel almost certainly was an issue.

Simon's Patronymic

When formally expressing their identity, male Palestinian Jews did not simply cite their personal name but supplied that of their father too. Hence the formulations *x* ben *y* (Hebrew) and *x* bar *y* (Aramaic). That being the case, we must now consider Simon's patronymic.

In the New Testament, Simon's patronymic is variously given, thus affording New Testament scholars ample opportunities for lengthy and, at times, some extremely subtle exegesis. In the solitary citation of the patronymic in the Synoptic Gospels, at Matthew 16:17, we find Simon at that critical point in the narrative, namely, his public declaration at Caesarea Philippi that Jesus is the Messiah, formally addressed by Jesus as *bariōna* ("son of Yonah"), an appellation set out in some manuscripts as a single word and in others split into two. In the manuscripts of the Fourth Gospel, however, where Jesus is made to give utterance to Simon's patronymic at two key junctures in the narrative — namely, his initial meeting with Jesus (1:42) and his final pastoral commissioning by the risen Lord (21:15-17) — the onomastic differences are more substantial: while some manuscripts, those in the early tradition, offer "son of Jonah," so giving rise to the *filius Ionae* found in early editions of the Vulgate,[14] others read "son of John."

There is no room in a study as short as this to rehearse the long-running debates among *Neutestamentler* to which this conflicting testimony has given rise. All I can do here is offer an ancient historian's take on the matter. Having viewed this problem as I would any other in ancient history arising from a contradiction in the sources, my conclusion is that the weight of the evidence

---

14. Bockmuehl, *Remembered Peter*, p. 141 n. 29.

clearly favors the interpretation that Yonah was Simon's patronymic. Though a very rare name in the Jewish onomasticon throughout antiquity, Yonah does crop up from time to time here and there, especially in Galilee, home of the first-attested bearer of the name, the prophet Jonah. Evidence for this is partly rabbinic and partly epigraphic.[15] Crucially for us, two of those occurrences are in pre-70-CE Jerusalem. The name has been deciphered there on a couple of ossuaries of the late Second Temple period. On one, an ossuary excavated at Isawiya, a village near Jerusalem, it is written in Aramaic;[16] on the other, an artifact that turned up on the antiquities market in Jerusalem and whose exact provenance is therefore unknown, it appears in Greek in an epitaph that runs *Mariamme gyne Iona* = "Miriam, wife of Yonah."[17] Given these attestations, there can be no justification for continuing to claim that the name did not exist in first-century Palestine.[18] Nor is it likely that Matthew's Iona is an abbreviation for John, as some would have it, for the shortened form of the name Yehohanan was Yoḥai.[19]

But if Simon's patronymic was Yonah, how are we to explain the reading "son of John"? Markus Bockmuehl has suggested that it probably arose from "an author with Jerusalem connections attempting to explain the unfamiliar Galilaean patronym in terms of a more recognisable name."[20] That conjecture, in which he was anticipated by Barnabas Lindars,[21] seems entirely reasonable to me. While Yonah was a very rare name, the Hasmonean name John is among those most frequently attested in the late Second Temple period.[22]

So much for the formal nomenclature that the future apostle would have acquired around the time of his birth. Was he given in the pre-Capernaum, pre-Jesus phase of his life, when he was still resident in the largely gentile set-

---

15. Bockmuehl, *Remembered Peter,* p. 142.

16. Joseph A. Fitzmyer and Daniel J. Harrington, *A Manual of Palestinian Aramaic Texts* (Rome: Biblical Institute Press, 1978), pp. 180-81, and p. 244 (134C) = Ilan, *Lexicon,* s.v. "יונה — Yonah," no. 4.

17. Ilan, *Lexicon,* s.v. "יונה — Yonah," no. 3.

18. As does, for example, John F. McHugh, *John 1-4* (London: T&T Clark, 2009), p. 156 n. 11 (commenting on John 1:42).

19. For detailed discussion of this point, see Bockmuehl, *Remembered Peter,* p. 145.

20. Bockmuehl, *Remembered Peter,* pp. 145-6.

21. See Barnabas Lindars, *The Gospel of John* (Grand Rapids: Eerdmans; London: Marshall, Morgan and Scott, 1981), p. 115 — "As Jonah is rare, but John common, the change (*sc.* to John in the MS tradition) is more readily explained if Jonah is original."

22. Ilan, *Lexicon,* p. 56 (table 5). On the textual grounds for slightly preferring Yonah to John, see John Nolland, *The Gospel of Matthew: A Commentary on the Greek Text,* NIGTC (Grand Rapids: Eerdmans, 2005), p. 666.

tlement of Bethsaida, any of the other names by which he is sometimes known? In his recent publications on Peter, Bockmuehl has suggested that it was there, at some unspecified point in time, that Simon may also have acquired the rare Greek name Petros.[23] How plausible is that hypothesis? One can easily understand why this scholar favors the idea of Simon acquiring such a name at an early stage in his life: since for him Simon is the bridging figure par excellence in the early Christian movement,[24] equipping him with nomenclature that can show him at ease in both a Jewish and a Greek milieu virtually *from the word go* is clearly highly desirable. But while it may be desirable to underpin the bridging case in this way, it cannot, in my opinion, be justified — in the first place, because the evidence on which this hypothesis is based is so weak; in the second, because the counterevidence is so strong.

Petros a Bethsaidan Acquisition?

The main grounds for advancing the hypothesis that the name Peter was acquired at Bethsaida is the fact that both Matthew and John use it in reference to the future disciple from the very outset of their respective narratives.[25] That cannot be gainsaid: for in the opening chapter of the Fourth Gospel (1:40), John does indeed refer to the subject of this volume as Simon Peter *(Simon Petros)* and at 4:18 of his Gospel Matthew unquestionably introduces the future apostle as *Simōna ton legomenon Petron* = "Simon called Peter."[26] Bockmuehl's explanation, however, is not the only one that can be advanced for the evangelist's choice of names in those passages. It is not uncommon when referring to an individual whose name has changed over time to use the one with which the listener or reader has come to be most familiar rather than the one that, strictly speaking, is correct. One good example of this can be

23. Bockmuehl, *Remembered Peter,* p. 156; and Bockmuehl, *Simon Peter in Scripture and Memory — The New Testament Apostle in the Early Church* (Grand Rapids: Baker Academic, 2012), p. 22. In this belief, he was preceded by Cullmann (*Peter,* p. 19), who believed that "Peter, like his brother Andrew, had been given a Greek name *from the outset*" (emphasis added).

24. Bockmuehl, *Remembered Peter,* p. 60 — "He is a unique bridge figure who embodies important connections from Jesus to the Jewish and Gentile missions, both historically and theologically."

25. Bockmuehl, *Remembered Peter,* p. 151; and Bockmuehl, *Simon Peter,* pp. 58-59 (John) and p. 71 (Matthew).

26. On the various formulas used in Greco-Roman (including NT) sources for registering the possession of an additional/alternative name, see Horsley, "Names, Double," 4:1012-14.

found in literature relating to the emperor Augustus, whose name, as we saw earlier, changed several times in the course of his long life. Strictly speaking, his final name, Augustus, should be used only for the period *after* January 15, 27 BCE.[27] However, it is not uncommon to find him called Augustus *before* that date, sometimes by people who ought to know better. From this and the many other examples that could be cited (the observant reader will have noted the anachronistic use of the name Palestine in both the foregoing discussion and the titles of several of the works cited in the footnotes[28]), we can see that there is no need to assume that because Peter is named as such by both Matthew and John at the start of their respective narratives that is what he must have been called in his pre-Jesus days. Most likely these writers introduced him by that name because, as we shall see below, that was the name by which he had come to be known in the Christian circles in which they moved at the time when they embarked on their Gospel accounts.

But it is not just the evidence for the hypothesis that is weak. Far more serious are the onomastic and literary considerations that can be brought against it. We shall take the onomastic first, prefacing them with a brief overview of Palestinian Jewry's most distinctive onomastic practice during Peter's lifetime — alternative naming.

In Palestinian Jewish society during the late Second Temple period it was extremely common for male Jews to be assigned or to adopt an alternative name. Primarily (though not exclusively,[29] as we shall see in a moment) this was because such a tiny number of names were favored by such a large proportion of the male population. To give one example out of the many that could be cited: according to Tal Ilan's calculations, over 30 percent of the male population whose names are known (i.e., about eight hundred men) bore one of the six universally acknowledged Hasmonean names — Matthew, Judah, John, Jonathan, Eleazar, and of course Simon. If Joseph were to be counted as a Hasmonean name too, as is sometimes done on the basis of 2 Maccabees 8:22, then that figure rises to around 40 percent (i.e., around one thousand individuals).[30] The result of this general unwillingness to use more than a tiny fraction of the vast number of names available either from the biblical repertoire or from the local gentile name pools, whether Semitic

27. See n. 2 above.

28. See, for instance, nn. 5 and 11.

29. On the various reasons for alternative naming in Jewish society, see Margaret H. Williams, "The Use of Alternative Names by Diaspora Jews in Graeco-Roman Antiquity," *JSJ* 38 (2007): 307-27.

30. Ilan, *Lexicon*, pp. 6-8.

or Greek, was that not only did large numbers of male Jews have the same personal name but many found themselves possessing the same patronymic as well.[31] Distinguishing between homonymous individuals, then, often was no easy matter. Hence the prevalence of second names, the majority of which took the form of nicknames in Aramaic, the everyday language of most of the population.

But if second-naming was such a common practice in Peter's day, why do I consider it unlikely that the young Simon bar Yonah with his common Hasmonean name acquired the second name Petros during his early years in Bethsaida? The main reason is that the social conditions that fostered the practice of alternate naming in much of Palestine, necessitated it even, were probably not present there. Archaeologists have deduced from the total absence of Jewish artifacts discovered at the site most likely to have been ancient Bethsaida that the number of Jewish families living there was probably very small.[32] If that deduction is correct, then the chances of our Simon being confused with any other Simon living there will have been minute. If the rarity of his patronymic is taken into account as well, those chances surely will have been reduced to zero. To all intents and purposes, Bariona functioned as a nickname, as Ilan has pointed out.[33] Nor would the future disciple of Jesus have needed a specifically Greek name, such as his brother Andrew had, to function in the hellenized society of Bethsaida, for in Shimon/Simon he already possessed the perfect bridging name. Such was its chameleon-like character that when used in an Aramaic-speaking context it could be construed as שמעון, but when used among Hellenes it could be taken as Σίμων, the snub-nosed one.[34]

But it is not only onomastic considerations that make the suggestion of a Bethsaida-acquired second name unlikely. The whole weight of the Gospel evidence is against it too. According to most of the Gospel writers, it was Jesus who gave Simon his new name.

---

31. Ilan, *Lexicon,* p. 46.

32. For Bockmuehl's endorsement of this interpretation of the archaeological evidence, see *Remembered Peter,* pp. 184-85.

33. Ilan *Lexicon,* p. 18.

34. See Victor A. Tcherikover, *Corpus Papyrorum Judaicarum* (Cambridge, Mass.: Harvard University Press, 1957), 1:29-30. For hard documentary examples of the chameleon-like character of the name, see Richard Bauckham, "Paul and Other Jews with Latin Names in the New Testament," in *Paul, Luke and the Graeco-Roman World: Essays in Honour of Alexander J. M. Wedderburn,* ed. Alf Christophersen, Carstin Claussen, Jörg Frey, and Bruce Longenecker, JSNTSup 217 (Sheffield: Sheffield Academic, 2002), p. 205, n. 7.

Jesus' Renaming of Simon

If we look at the Gospel evidence for the renaming of Simon, the picture it presents is surprisingly unclear, given the weight that it is often required to bear. Manifestly by the time the Gospel texts came to be written, memory of that event had faded to the extent that *precisely* when and *precisely* where it had occurred were beyond recall.[35] Indeed, none of the evangelists, apart from Matthew, appears to have any interest at all in the meaning of that act. For our purposes, that lack of precision and apparent indifference do not matter. The key thing is that most of the Gospel writers believed (1) that Jesus was responsible for the new name and (2) that the new name had been conferred right at or very near the beginning of Simon's discipleship with Jesus (Mark 3:16; Luke 6:14; John 1:42).[36] Such a scenario is entirely plausible given what we know about contemporary naming practices, both Jewish and non-Jewish. In the society of which Simon bar Yonah was part, embarkation on a new stage in life, whether the context was secular or religious, was, if not invariably, certainly often marked by the bestowal or the adoption of a new name. That was the case whether you were, say, a provincial signing up for military service in one of Rome's auxiliary units[37] or an individual entering a Roman household as a slave.[38] The most famous instance of name change is, of course, the adoption by Rome's first emperor of the name Augustus at the time of his first constitutional settlement, the measure that established the Principate in 27 BCE. That startling innovation (overfamiliarity with the name Augustus has blinded us as to its "fantastic novelty"[39]) was to mark the start of a new phase both for both him personally and for the Roman

---

35. So, correctly, Cullmann at *Peter,* p. 23.

36. The odd man out is Matthew. He is the only evangelist who does not explicitly make Jesus responsible for Simon's additional name. See Nolland, *Gospel of Matthew,* p. 179 (commenting on Matt. 4:18). It is this lack of specificity on Matthew's part that enables Bockmuehl to privilege his testimony over that of the other Gospel writers.

37. A much-discussed text in this regard is BGU 2.243, a second-century CE papyrus letter sent from Italy by a Roman naval recruit to his father back in Egypt. Originally called Apion, this individual had found himself renamed Antonius Maximus on joining the imperial fleet based in the Bay of Naples. For text and discussion, see Adolf Deissmann, *Light from the Ancient East,* trans. Lionel R. M. Strachan (London: Hodder and Stoughton, 1927), pp. 179-83.

38. On the owner's right to decide on his slave's name, see Jane F. Gardner and Thomas Wiedemann, *The Roman Household — A Sourcebook* (London: Routledge, 1991), p. 70 n. 1; and Sandra R. Joshel, *Slavery in the Roman World* (Cambridge: Cambridge University Press, 2010), pp. 94-95, citing Varro, *The Latin Language* 8.21.

39. So described by John A. Crook in *The Cambridge Ancient History,* 2nd ed. (Cambridge: Cambridge University Press, 1996; online ed., 2008), 10:79.

state as a whole. But we do not have to go to Rome and the pinnacle of Roman society to find examples of this practice. Ossuary inscriptions from Palestine broadly contemporaneous with Simon bar Yonah provide several pertinent cases. From two ossuary inscriptions found at Jericho, one Greek and the other Aramaic, relating to a former Jewish slave of the empress Agrippina, it has been deduced that this individual had been named Nathanel at birth but renamed Theodotos on entering gentile captivity.[40] Among the ossuary texts found in the Jerusalem area there are at least three referring to individuals who had marked their conversion to Judaism by assuming that quintessentially Jewish name, Judah.[41] The positioning, then, in the Gospels of Jesus' renaming Simon at the start of his discipleship (this is particularly clear in Mark and Luke) is entirely plausible — it was at points of transition such as that that the conferral of a new name was most likely to occur.[42]

So far so good. But before we leave the renaming episode, there is one puzzling feature of it that also needs to be addressed. If renaming was so important, why was it that out of the twelve disciples selected by Jesus for special operations and so the abandonment of their former way of life only three were given a new name — Simon himself and the two sons of Zebedee? At the time when Simon was renamed Peter or Kephas (see discussion below), that duo, according to Mark's unique testimony (Mark 3:17), were given the joint Aramaic nickname Boanerges, whose meaning allegedly was Sons of Thunder. Why just these three? That the purpose of those nicknames was simply to distinguish Simon, James, and John from their fellow disciples is unlikely: Simon's unusual patronymic, bar Yonah, meant that he will have been easily distinguishable from Simon *ho Kananaios* (Matt. 10:4; Mark 3:18), otherwise known as Simon the Zealot *(Simōna ton kaloumenon zēlōtēn)* (Luke 6:15). There can have been no risk of confusing James son of Zebedee with James son of Alphaeus (Matt. 10:3; Mark 3:18; Luke 6:15). In the lists of the Twelve, there is only one John. However, as I pointed out in passing above, nicknames, though *generally* given to deal with the problem of homonymity, were not given *for that reason alone*. Another motive was (and is) to demonstrate and to foster intimacy. That factor, I suspect, will have been the operative one here. From Mark's narrative subsequent to the choosing of the twelve disciples, it is clear

40. R. Hachlili, "The Goliath Family in Jericho: Funerary Inscriptions from a First Century A.D. Jewish Monumental Tomb," *BASOR* 235 (1979): 33 and 45-47.

41. *CIIP* 1.1, nos. 174, 304, and 551.

42. I am, of course, aware that there are Old Testament precedents too — e.g., God's renaming of Abram and Sarai in Gen. 17. However, I think that it is important to realize that Peter's renaming can be explained equally well in contemporary terms.

that those three were closer to Jesus than the other nine, for we find them again and again at the very heart of his inner circle. Nicknaming, then, will have been Jesus' way of flagging up the privileged position that he envisioned them occupying in the new phase of their life that was about to begin.

As to the meaning of the nicknames he gave them, that is not at all obvious. That should not surprise, for a large part of the attraction of nicknames is that they form part of a private communication system and so, by their very nature, are often difficult for outsiders to construe.[43] Boanerges, the joint nickname given to John and James, has never been satisfactorily explained, despite the tireless and ingenious efforts of many New Testament exegetes.[44] And who knows what Jesus had in mind when he gave Simon bar Yonah his new name? Although in due course huge ecclesiological significance was to be attached to it, or at least to the Greek version of it, as the elaborate wordplay on Petros and *petra* at Matthew 16:18 shows,[45] Jesus' motives at the time of assigning it may have been, indeed they probably were, quite different. They need not have been theological at all.[46] I consider it significant that the only nicknames (just two) for which we are given an explanation in our sources were invented by the Jewish *public* for a *public* figure. One of those nicknames was Dikaios ("the Just"), as the second-century-BCE high priest Simon son of Onias came to be called on account of his exemplary piety toward God and men (so Josephus at *Ant.* 12.43). The other was Thrakidas (Thracian), the Jews' derogatory name for King Alexander Jannaeus. Translated in the Loeb as "Cossack," it was given to Jannaeus, according to Josephus (*Ant.* 13.383), because of his excessive cruelty. Arrived at by common consent, these names were understood by all.[47] Privately conceived nicknames, however, were another matter. Hence the difficulty outsiders past and present have in construing their meaning.

---

43. For comments on the "usually inexplicable" character of ancient Jewish nicknames, see Ilan, *Lexicon,* p. 46.

44. Commentaries on Mark abound in explanations of the nickname, among which the two most widely favored are that (1) it reflects the volatile personalities of James and John and (2) it has an eschatological significance. For a brief assessment of the most common explanations on offer, see Morna Hooker, *The Gospel according to St Mark* (London: Black, 1991), p. 112.

45. For detailed discussion, see Chrys C. Caragounis, *Peter and the Rock* (Berlin: de Gruyter, 1990), pp. 88-112.

46. See W. D. Davies and Dale C. Allison, *A Critical and Exegetical Commentary on the Gospel according to St Matthew* (Edinburgh: T&T Clark, 1991), 2:626, citing Peter Lampe.

47. The nicknames accorded some of the Ptolemies by their "irreverent" Alexandrian subjects (e.g., Physkon/Potbelly; Lathyros/Chickpea) are clear parallels. On this topic, see Peter Green, *Alexander to Actium: The Hellenistic Age* (London: Thames & Hudson, 1993), p. 82 and p. 538.

The New Name

So far I have merely alluded to Simon's new name. We must now examine it more closely. Here, once again, we find considerable inconsistency in the Gospels: while Mark and Luke both state categorically that the additional name that Jesus gave to Simon was Peter (Mark 3:16; Luke 6:14), John (1:42) gives the new name as Kephas. Neither of these names is a *novum*, as used to be thought. Petros, the more frequently attested of the two, not only has been found in a late-first-century-CE pagan context outside Palestine,[48] but has now turned up in a couple of Jewish documentary sources from Palestine as well, one of them also of indisputable first-century date: since Masada fell in 73/74 CE, the Petros son of Istomachos whose name is written in Hebrew characters on a potsherd found there must have flourished before that date.[49] Nor is that the only attestation of the name. It has also been deciphered in a papyrus document of the Bar Kokhba period (P. Yadin 46) found in a cave in the Judean desert (Naḥal Ḥever).[50] Although this comes from a period somewhat later than the one with which we are concerned here, it is worth including in the discussion here since it shows that the name did have a certain currency in first- and second-century Palestine.

That is more than can be said for Kephas, for although the name is attested (just once), the date of that solitary mention is the late fifth century BCE[51] and the place, the Jewish military colony at Elephantine on Egypt's southern frontier.[52] Jesus, we can confidently assume, will not have been aware of the naming practices of Jews living in a different country half a millennium before his time, let alone influenced by them. Consequently, when, if John is to be believed, he hit on Kephas as a fitting alternative name for Simon, the probability must be that he was simply inventing another nickname along the lines of the Boanerges mentioned by Mark.

So here we have two very different-looking names put forward by the Gospel writers as Simon bar Yonah's newly minted *supernomen* — and so a serious conflict in the evidence, it would be justified to think. However,

---

48. In a poll tax receipt from Egypt, dated 100/101 CE. According to Caragounis (*Peter and the Rock*, p. 23), this "leads to the conclusion that the name Πέτρος was given around 60-70."

49. Ilan, *Lexicon*, s.v. "Πέτρος — Petrus," no. 5.

50. Ilan, *Lexicon*, s.v. "Πέτρος — Petrus," no. 4, dated to 134 CE.

51. The name figures as the patronymic of a witness to a legal document clearly dated to 416 BCE. See Bezalel Porten and Ada Yardeni, *Textbook of Aramaic Documents from Ancient Egypt* (Jerusalem: Hebrew University, 1986), 2:84-85 (B3.9, line 10).

52. See Fitzmyer, "Aramaic Kepha' and Peter's Name," pp. 127-28.

this difference is more apparent than real, for both names have roughly the same semantic range, which can be anything from bedrock at one end of the scale to stone at the other.[53] That this broad congruity was recognized in early Christian circles is clear from the words with which the renaming incident is brought to a close at John 1:42 — *sy klēthēsē Kēphas, ho hermēneuetai Petros,* which the AV sonorously translates, "Thou shalt be called Cephas, which is, being interpreted, A stone." More recent translations prefer "rock."[54]

But although the Gospel evidence is not as contradictory as it appears at first sight, questions still remain about the relationship between the different versions of Simon's *supernomen* given in the New Testament. To start with the most basic: which of those two names did Jesus actually give to Simon? It is most unlikely that Simon received both names from him at the same time. Notwithstanding the fact that Matthew, Mark, and Luke never use the name Kephas at all and John does not use it except in the passage just cited, it surely must have been Kephas. For first-century Palestinian nicknames generally were Aramaic, since the circles in which they were invented and used were largely Aramaic-speaking. That will have been the case with the coterie around Jesus, even though a few of its members (e.g., Andrew and Philip) will have spoken Greek as well. However, to answer the question just posed, namely, which was the prior form of the *supernomen,* we do not have to rely on mere inference. For we have the explicit testimony of Paul that in post-Easter Jerusalem the name by which the former leading disciple was known was Kephas: at Galatians 1:18 he writes, "Then after three years I went up to Jerusalem to visit Kephas, and remained with him fifteen days."[55] The almost total avoidance of this name in the Gospels, then, must be a deliberate anachronism. As to the reason for that, it is probably because by the time the writers of the Gospels came to compose their accounts of Jesus' life, the Aramaic version of Simon Peter's second name had fallen into disuse in the predominantly Greek-speaking circles in which they moved.

That development prompts our second and final question: when was it

---

53. See Caragounis, *Peter and the Rock,* pp. 9-16, for the various meanings of *petros,* and pp. 26-30 for discussion of *kepha.*

54. As, for instance, the NEB, which here offers: "You shall be called Cephas (that is, Peter, the Rock)."

55. A minority of scholars argue that the Kephas mentioned here and elsewhere in the Pauline corpus (1 Cor. 1:12; 3:22; 9:5; 15:5; Gal 2:9, 11, 14) was a different person from Peter. I follow the majority opinion in rejecting that view. Given the singularity of the name Kephas, it seems most unlikely that there will have been two figures of authority bearing that name in the early Christian community in Palestine.

that the Greek form of Simon's *supernomen* came into use? Any answer to this question inevitably will involve considerable speculation, as the evidence for Peter's career after the death of Jesus is so poor. On the basis of the few hard facts that we have about him, plus our knowledge of onomastic practices among Jews at that time, a likely scenario can easily be envisaged.

From Kephas to Peter

According to the narrative presented in Acts, after Jesus' death and resurrection Peter was initially based in Jerusalem, where he took the lead in "spreading the word." How long his residence there lasted it is not possible to say, but almost certainly it must have been for several years, if the timescale presented at Galatians 1:18 is accepted. Was it during that time that he began to be called Petros at least by some of the people with whom his work as an evangelist brought him into contact? That seems extremely likely, given the fact that Jerusalem was such a cosmopolitan place and Greek one of the main languages spoken there:[56] besides local Jews, such as Peter, who were fluent in both Greek and Aramaic,[57] there would have been hundreds, if not thousands, of Jewish pilgrims from the eastern provinces of the Roman Empire, some even from Rome itself, for whom Greek was their mother tongue. Peter's original name, Shimon/Simon, would of course have been the ideal communication tool in a society of that cultural makeup. However, so associated with his Jesus-bestowed nickname had Simon bar Yonah become that that obvious onomastic strategy seemingly was not resorted to. (The fact that it was Jesus who had given him his nickname must have made it seem very special.) Instead the Greek name deemed to be equivalent to Kephas seems to have emerged and come into use.

One can see very easily why such a development might have come about: translation names were a long-established feature of the Palestinian Jewish onomasticon, traceable at least as far back as the second quarter of the second century BCE. That can be seen quite clearly by consulting the entries in the first volume of Ilan's *Lexicon* under Dositheos and Theodotos, the Greek

---

56. Lee I. Levine, *Jerusalem — Portrait of the City in the Second Temple Period (538 B.C.E.–70 C.E.)* (Philadelphia: Jewish Publication Society, 2002), pp. 270-76.

57. On the likely extent of bilingualism in the first-century C.E. Palestine, see the careful discussion in Emil Schürer, *The History of the Jewish People in the Age of Jesus Christ*, vol. II, revised by Geza Vermes, Fergus Millar and Matthew Black (Edinburgh: T. & T. Clark, 1979), pp. 74-80.

equivalents of Jonathan and Nathanel. And they were particularly popular in Diaspora communities too, especially those of Egypt and Cyrene, as can be easily documented by consulting Rokeah's prosopographical register in *CPJ* 3 and the name index in *CJCZ*.[58] Now, Jews from both those areas are often attested in first-century Jerusalem. Besides being mentioned in the narrative in Acts of the first, post-Easter Pentecost (Acts 2:10), they are well represented in the epigraphic record: among Diaspora Jews clearly identifiable as such in the ossuary inscriptions from Jerusalem, those from Cyrene, for instance, easily constitute the largest group.[59] It is not inconceivable, then, that it was through their influence or the influence of people like them that over time Peter increasingly came to be addressed by his Greek name at least when operating in a Greek milieu.

With the acquisition by "our hero" of his last and final name, all that remains now is to briefly outline the role played by names in the final stage of the life of Shimon bar Yonah a.k.a. Kephas a.k.a. Petros, when he extended his operations as a Christian missionary to the wider Greco-Roman world.

Peter as a Christian Apostle

Furnished now with a Greek as well as an Aramaic name, the former first disciple was now perfectly equipped for missionary work as an apostle in the Greco-Roman world: while in communities of a more Semitic character he could present himself as a Semite, among Hellenes he could assume more of a Greek persona. That partly explains why, when he eventually came to Rome (as I believe he did at some point[60]), the name he chose to be known by there was Peter: that was the main language spoken by his prime missionary target there, the nonelite, Greek-speaking inhabitants of the capital.[61] But that probably was

---

58. D. Rokeah, "Prosopography of the Jews in Egypt," in *Corpus Papyrorum Judaicarum*, ed. Victor A. Tcherikover, Alexander Fuks and Menahem Stern (Cambridge, Mass.: Harvard University Press, 1964), 3:167-96; Gert Lüderitz, *Corpus jüdischer Zeugnisse aus der Cyrenaika* (Wiesbaden: Reichert, 1983), pp. 217-27 (index 1.1).

59. *CIIP* 1.1, nos. 20, 98, 170, 324-32.

60. That is the clear implication of 1 Pet. 5:13, "whether or not the letter with its salutation from 'the chosen church in Babylon' was in fact written by Peter," as is correctly observed by Timothy D. Barnes, *Early Christian Hagiography and Roman History* (Tübingen: Mohr Siebeck, 2010), p. 23. On the Petrine letters, see Matthew V. Novenson in this volume, pp. 146-57.

61. Ramsay MacMullen, "The Unromanised in Rome," in *Diasporas in Antiquity*, ed. Shaye J. D. Cohen and Ernest S. Frerichs (Atlanta: Scholars Press, 1993), p. 47.

not his only reason for opting to be called Petros. Late Julio-Claudian Rome was not an especially friendly environment for Jews, as Claudius's various measures against them, for instance, show.[62] And Seneca's outright condemnation of them as a *gens sceleratissima* ("most wicked race") gives a clear indication of how Jews were regarded in elite Roman circles at the very least.[63] Such being the climate of opinion, Peter will not have been surprised to find that several of his fellow Christian workers preferred to use their Greek and Latin names rather than their Hebrew and Aramaic ones. With Silas, for instance, calling himself Silvanus, John Mark preferring his Latin *supernomen* (1 Pet. 5:12-13), and, if Richard Bauckham is to be believed, the apostle Junia apparently choosing not to be known by her Hebrew name Joanna,[64] it is not surprising that "our hero" opted to be called by his non-Semitic name too (1 Pet. 1:1). And so it came about that it was as Peter that he was martyred[65] and as Peter that he came to be remembered, at least in the West.[66] For in the East the name Kepha endured.

62. For a brief overview of the difficult and much-disputed evidence on this topic, see John M. G. Barclay, *Jews in the Mediterranean Diaspora* (Edinburgh: T&T Clark, 1996), pp. 303-6.

63. See Menahem Stern, *Greek and Latin Authors on Jews and Judaism* (Jerusalem: Israel Academy of Sciences and Humanities, 1974), vol. 1, no. 186 (citation from Augustine, *De Civitate Dei* 6.11). For the generally hostile tone of contemporary literary references to the Jews, see Margaret H. Williams, "Latin Authors on Jews and Judaism," in *The Dictionary of Early Judaism*, ed. John J. Collins and Daniel C. Harlow (Grand Rapids: Eerdmans, 2010), pp. 870-5 (esp. p. 872).

64. Bauckham, "Paul and Other Jews," p. 220.

65. Burnt alive in the Neronian persecution of 64 CE, according to Barnes. See *Early Christian Hagiography*, p. 9; and chapter 6 below.

66. As shown by, for instance, *1 Clement* 5.4.

CHAPTER 4

Was Peter behind Mark's Gospel?

Helen K. Bond

Peter has been linked with the Gospel of Mark since at least the mid-second century CE. Our earliest, and most extensive, witness is Papias the bishop of Hierapolis in Asia Minor (ca. 60-130 CE). In a famous passage, he claimed that Mark had been Peter's *hermēneutēs* (interpreter? translator?), and that he had written down accurately, though not in order, all that he remembered of Peter's anecdotes (or *chreiai*). Elsewhere he claimed that those who heard Peter begged Mark, a follower of the apostle *(akolouthen onta Petron),* to commit the apostle's teaching to writing — a development that, it appears, delighted Peter.[1]

Most modern critical scholars, however, have questioned Papias's testimony. To some extent they are quite right to do so: the bishop's account is clearly exaggerated, and it is difficult not to agree with Chris Tuckett that the "link alleged between Mark's gospel and Peter is probably part of a second-century attempt to give the gospel more status by linking it with the leading apostle."[2] But does the bishop's clear apologetic agenda necessarily mean that

---

1. The relevant passages are cited by Eusebius, *H.E.* 3.39.15-16 and 2.15.1. For full texts, see the contribution of Todd Still in this volume, pp. 161-67. In addition to Papias, the link with Peter appears in the *Anti-Marcionite Prologue*, Justin Martyr (*Dial.* 106.3), Irenaeus (*Adv. haer.* 3.1.2), and Clement of Alexandria (cited by Eusebius, *H.E.* 2.15.2, 6.14.6-7, *Adumbr. in 1 Pet.* 5.13), though all of these later authors may well be familiar with Papias. For a useful overview of the texts, see Vincent Taylor, *The Gospel according to St Mark: the Greek Text* (London: Macmillan, 1952), pp. 1-8.

2. Christopher M. Tuckett, "Mark" in *The Oxford Bible Commentary,* ed. J. Barton and J. Muddiman (Oxford: Oxford University Press, 2000), pp. 886-922, here p. 886. Similar asser-

his testimony is of no value whatsoever? Beneath Papias's overblown claims, might there be a genuine recollection that Peter did in fact have a connection to the author of our earliest Gospel? In this essay I intend to explore this possibility a little further, first by looking at the reasons why most critical scholars question the link between Peter and Mark, and second to carve out a more moderate position by drawing on social memory, Mark's links with the biographical tradition, and the evangelist's use of Peter as a literary character.

Arguments against a Petrine Connection to Mark

Papias's testimony is clearly quite ancient. Depending on how we interpret the statement, it is possible to push it back into the late first century, that is, within thirty years or so of the writing of the Gospel.[3] Why, then, are many modern critics so reluctant to trust it? In the following study, I have chosen to analyze Joel Marcus's arguments. There are three reasons for this: first, Marcus's commentary on Mark is reasonably recent (the first volume was published in 2000); second, he engages with the question of authorship at some length;[4] and third, Marcus's commentary is simply one of the best, most thoughtful and sensitive readings of Mark's Gospel on the market. On all these grounds, his arguments deserve careful attention.

Marcus rightly notes that *external* evidence — the testimony of Papias — is inconclusive. Some see the bishop's work as entirely tendentious, claiming that he derived the link between Mark and Peter solely on the basis of 1 Peter 5:13, promoting an apostolic link in the face of competing (often Gnostic) gospels.[5] Others, however, with reference to the rather critical element in Papias's

---

tions are made by J. Dewey, "The Survival of Mark's Gospel: A Good Story?" *JBL* 123 (2004): 495-507; and Joel Marcus, *Mark 1–8: A New Translation with Introduction and Commentary*, AB 27 (New York: Doubleday, 2000), p. 30.

3. The crucial section of this testimony seems to be dependent on Papias's memories as a young man of the teaching of "the Elder" (John?); if so, this would push his testimony back into the first century. For a full discussion, see Richard Bauckham, *Jesus and the Eyewitnesses: The Gospels as Eyewitness Testimony* (Grand Rapids: Eerdmans, 2006), pp. 202-39.

4. The relevant discussion can be found at Marcus, *Mark 1–8*, pp. 17-24.

5. This is in fact Marcus's preferred option, *Mark 1–8*, pp. 21-24; see also the classic treatment of Kurt Niederwimmer, "Johannes Markus und die Frage nach dem Verfasser des zweiten Evangeliums," *ZNW* 58 (1967): 172-88, especially pp. 185-86; Austin Farrer, *A Study in St Mark* (London, Dacre, 1951); and Gerd Theissen and Annette Merz, *The Historical Jesus: A Comprehensive Guide* (London: SCM, 1998), pp. 26-27. It is clear from Eusebius, *H.E.* 2.15.2, 3.39.17 that Papias knew 1 Peter.

comments about Mark (specifically its lack of order, or *taxis*), argue that he is in fact defending it in relation to the more popular Gospels of either Matthew or John (or both) — in which case it is only an alleged (and inherited) claim to Petrine inspiration that commends the Markan Gospel to the bishop.[6] In what follows, I shall not discuss Papias in any more depth; instead, I shall concentrate on Marcus's *internal* arguments, derived from the text of the Gospel itself. Broadly, there are seven of these:

1. Marcus notes, in general terms, that "Mark does not give the impression of being any *closer* to the events he describes than are Matthew and Luke, the later evangelists who appropriated his work."

2. He points out that "the supposition that between Jesus and Mark there was a lengthy course of development with many tradents helps to explain how, for example, two versions of the same narrative, the feeding of the multitude (6:30-44 and 8:1-9), had had time to crystallize before their incorporation into the Gospel."

3. Many Markan stories lack the kind of detail we would expect from close association with a participant.

4. The Gospel contains a number of stories that do not contain disciples (such as 1:1-15 or 14:43-52), or where disciples seem to have been added to stories originally told about Jesus alone (e.g., 1:21-28 or 2:15-17 or 3:1-6).

5. Throughout the Gospel, Peter appears not as an individual, but as a "type."

6. If there were a special Petrine connection, we would expect that disciple to be particularly prominent in Mark, but this is not the case. In fact, Matthew contains stories about him that are not in Mark (e.g., Matt. 14:28-31; 16:17-19; 17:24-27).

7. Mark's picture of Peter is "generally a rather negative one."

Overall, Marcus suggests, "The truth is that, were it not for Papias, one would never suspect that the second Gospel was particularly Petrine" and concludes that the Gospel "probably was written by someone called Mark, but this Mark probably had no special connection with Peter."[7]

---

6. See, e.g., Martin Hengel, *Studies in the Gospel of Mark* (London: SCM, 1985), pp. 47-53; Bauckham, *Eyewitnesses*, pp. 203-30. For a detailed (and mediating) assessment, see C. Clifton Black, *Mark: Images of an Apostolic Interpreter* (Edinburgh: T&T Clark, 2001), pp. 82-94, 195-223.

7. Marcus, *Mark 1–8*, p. 24. Matters are often complicated by the identification of the author of the Second Gospel with the John Mark of the New Testament, a Jerusalemite who became a missionary and accompanied his kinsman Barnabas, Paul and later Peter on their

Surveying the list, I am struck by how dated some of the arguments now appear (and I stress once again that Marcus is simply representative of a wide body of critical opinion). Arguments 1-3 are heavily indebted to the work of the form critics, and while their legacy is still of enormous importance for New Testament studies, certain aspects have been nuanced and often superseded by recent studies, particularly of social memory and identity formation. Arguments 4 and 6 sit awkwardly with the fact that the evangelist's literary activity has been repeatedly stressed in recent decades. If Mark presents his material in a particular way, our first question should not be, What does this tell us about his source? but, Why has this author shaped his material in this manner? and, How does it contribute to his overall literary (and theological) aims? And, finally, the figure of Peter has been a favorite topic in many recent literary studies of Mark's Gospel, with the prevailing opinion nowadays suggesting that the evangelist is not really so negative toward Jesus' closest disciple as an earlier generation might have supposed (arguments 5 and 7).

In what follows, I shall discuss each of these observations under the following headings: (1) Peter and the social memory of Mark's Christian audience; (2) Mark as a biographer; and (3) Mark's portrait of Peter. For the purposes of illustration, I shall assume that Mark wrote in Rome, to a Christian assembly that was not founded by Peter, but that had, at some point, benefited from the apostle's company.[8] (Such a setting, however, is not entirely essential to my argument.)

---

travels (Acts 12:12, 25; 13:5, 13; 15:37, 39; Col. 4:10; Philem. 24; 2 Tim. 4:11; 1 Pet. 5:13). In opposing this identification, scholars have noted that the Gospel seems too Pauline to have been written by an associate of Peter, too gentile to have been written by a Jew, and that it has too hazy an idea of Palestinian geography to have been written by a Jerusalemite (see again Niederwimmer, "Johannes Markus"). None of these assertions are decisive, but more importantly for our present purposes it has to be stressed that the traditional identification does not necessarily have a bearing on the Gospel's links with Peter. It is perfectly possible that the Gospel was written by an unknown Mark who was later identified (on the basis of 1 Pet. 5:13) with the only Mark in the New Testament. "Marcus" was, after all, one of the most common Roman names, and we may see here a perfectly understandable early Christian wish to know more about the author of an important text (this position has been held by a number of German commentators, see e.g. Rudolf Pesch, *Markusevangelium* [Freiburg: Herder, 1976], 1:9-11; and Dieter Lührmann, *Das Markusevangelium* [Tübingen: J. C. B. Mohr, 1987], pp. 5-6). In what follows, I wish to remain entirely agnostic on the question of whether the evangelist was the John Mark of tradition.

8. This is, of course, the "traditional" view. For fuller argument, see Hengel, *Studies in the Gospel of Mark*, pp. 1-30; more recently, see Brian J. Incignieri, *The Gospel to the Romans: The Setting and Rhetoric of Mark's Gospel* (Leiden: Brill, 2003), esp. pp. 59-115. Marcus, however, argues for a Syrian province, "The Jewish War and the Sitz im Leben of Mark," *JBL* 111 (1992): 441-62.

1. Peter and the Social Memory of Mark's Christian Audience

The form critics famously regarded Gospel pericopes not so much as windows onto actual events from the time of Jesus, but rather as reflections of the situation (or *Sitz im Leben*) of early Christian communities. The lack of vivid eyewitness detail in the Gospels, they claimed, supported their view that individual pericopes had become detached from the original eyewitnesses at an early period, and that they had been smoothed over and reshaped by repeated use within early Christian preaching. Stories and traditions were retained and repeated, not out of historical or antiquarian interest, but primarily because they spoke to the needs of emerging Christian audiences, specifically their growing sense of identity and debates with opponents.[9]

These insights are still of value for understanding the reception of Jesus tradition within early Christian communities, though today some of the most interesting work is being done less in terms of the study of oral transmission and folklore and more in the context of social (or collective) memory. Memory theorists stress the importance of social memories in forging both a group's distinctive history and its present identity (what we might call a "shared story").[10] The assembled group provides environments, or social frameworks, in which memories can exist and have meaning. A dynamic relationship exists between the group's past and present, such that the shared distant past (perhaps represented by the story of Israel and/or specific interpretations of the Hebrew Scriptures) provides typological frames for representing shared group "memories" in the present. And although "what

---

9. The classic works here are of course those by K. L. Schmidt, Martin Dibelius, and Rudolf Bultmann. Commenting specifically on Mark's Gospel, B. H. Branscomb could confidently assert that "there is no impression of freshness and exactness of detail such as to suggest an immediate personal source" (*The Gospel of Mark* [London: Hodder & Stoughton, 1937]); and D. E. Nineham, in a thorough discussion, noted that even where Mark's Gospel did contain what appeared to be vivid, circumstantial details, it was possible to suggest theological reasons for their inclusion, for example at 3:5; 1:40-45; and 2:3-5 ("Eye-Witness Testimony and the Gospel Tradition I," *JTS* 9 [1958]: 13-25). Even V. Taylor and C. E. B. Cranfield, both of whom were reluctant to jettison the apostolic link altogether, were able to argue only that certain sections of the Gospel were derived from Peter (largely those actually involving the disciple).

10. Influential here is the work of M. Halbwachs, J. Assmann, and B. Schwartz. For an introduction, see A. Kirk, "Social and Cultural Memory," in *Memory, Tradition, and Text: Uses of the Past in Early Christianity,* ed. Alan Kirk and Tom Thatcher (Atlanta: SBL, 2005), pp. 1-24; also Chris Keith, "Social Memory Theory and Gospels Research: The First Decade," *Early Christianity* 6 (2015), forthcoming.

really happened" may still be important, present concerns are primarily what determine the formation and articulation of the past. In the case of Mark's Christian audience, we can assume an ongoing process of "re-membering" the Jesus tradition in the light of crises (including the crucifixion itself), new opportunities (the mission to Gentiles), and ongoing challenges (perhaps hostility from the local synagogue). All of this contributed to the way that the story of Jesus was told, or remembered, within the group, to the way these early Christians presented themselves to outsiders, and to their sense of identity and shared purpose.

What role an individual such as Peter would have had in all of this is difficult to determine.[11] As a prominent member of Jesus' inner circle, Peter's autobiographical recollections would have been eagerly received by the majority of early Christian gatherings, including the church in Rome: these early congregations would have been eager for more anecdotes about Jesus, particularly those that cohered with their own developing story. From Peter's perspective, however, three aspects need to be considered. First, it is clear that there were many differing ways of articulating Christian existence in the early decades. Unless we are to assume that Peter's proximity to the earthly Jesus gave him a strong sense of his own authoritative position (for which the admittedly scanty evidence of Acts and Paul's letters gives no support), there is no reason to assume that Peter *imposed* his views on the Christian assemblies he encountered as he journeyed around the Mediterranean. Second, Peter's own recollections would have been subject to all the usual deteriorations and erosions of memory (forgetfulness of detail, blurring of differing events, false recollection, and so on[12]). Memories of Jesus' ministry would have been radically shaken by the traumatic and barely credible events of the cross and the resurrection, the efforts of other disciples to make sense of this extraordinary event, and continued reflection on the identity of the one at the center of their proclamation. Peter's stories were attempts to extrapolate the significance of what he and fellow disciples had experienced, and would of course have been told differently depending on the demands of the situation. Third and finally, in a society where the group rather than the individual was paramount, there would have been every reason for both

11. An edition of the journal *Memory* was recently devoted to this issue; see the editorial by A. J. Barnier and J. Sutton, "From Individual to Collective Memory: Theoretical and Empirical Perspectives," *Memory* 16 (2008): 177-82, and the ten essays gathered together in the volume.

12. See in particular the studies of J. C. S. Redman, "How Accurate Are Eyewitnesses? Bauckham and the Eyewitnesses in the Light of Psychological Research," *JBL* 129 (2010): 177-97; and Robert Kerry McIver, *Memory, Jesus, and the Synoptic Gospels* (Atlanta: SBL, 2011).

Mark's Roman church and Peter to bring their memories into conformity with one another.[13] Peter would have shared his memories with the gathered Christians, and this group context would have exerted a powerful pull on the way those memories were presented and heard. The assembly's sense of its own past, its shared memories of Jesus tradition, and its view of its present vocation and place in the world would have conditioned the way Peter's stories were heard and interpreted within their assembly, ultimately transcending Peter's individual memory. We might surmise, then, that Peter's presence provided new material for Mark's Christian church, that it supplied new ideas, insights, and emphases, but that it did not radically change their shared memories and communal "story."

How, then, does this help our study of Mark's Gospel? It is striking that the work gives no sense of recording the recollections of an individual for those who are not well informed; in fact, quite the opposite. The Gospel is clearly written for *insiders,* for those who know the story: they do not need to be persuaded to join the movement (otherwise the call stories of 1:16-20 have to be regarded as completely inadequate) or to be told what happens after the empty tomb (once again, it is hard to imagine any hearer not knowing the sequel to 16:8!). The impression we get is of a shared basic story set down in (perhaps an innovative) narrative form.[14] This should certainly cause us to question Papias's stress on Mark's efforts to recollect precisely what Peter had told him (which in any case draws on conventional stereotypes[15]), but it does not necessarily force us to disconnect Peter from Mark altogether. It would still be fair to categorize these as Petrine memories, even testimony, despite the fact that they had been largely absorbed into the group's social memory.

A further point also needs to be taken into consideration. Despite Papias's concern to show that Peter approved of Mark's Gospel (surely an apologetic flourish?), modern scholarship broadly agrees that the bishop got his timing all wrong. If Peter died during the Neronian persecution of 65 and the Gospel was

13. For discussion, see Redman, "How Accurate Are Eyewitnesses," p. 187; C. B. Harris, H. M. Paterson, and R. I. Kemp, "Collaborative Recall and Collective Memory: What Happens When We Remember Together?" *Memory* 16 (2008): 213-30; I. Wessel and M. L. Moulds, "Collective Memory: A Perspective from (Experimental) Clinical Psychology," *Memory* 16 (2008): 288-304.

14. As Ernest Best notes, the Gospel was written to help and encourage like-minded Christians: "The Role of the Disciples in Mark," *NTS* 23 (1976/1977): 377-401, here p. 378.

15. The note that a writer did not omit or misrepresent anything is found in a variety of forms in much ancient literature (Philo, *De Vita Mosis* 2.34; Josephus *Ant.* 1.5, 17; 4.196; 10.218).

written in the late 60s, or perhaps more likely early 70s,[16] Peter must already have perished before the evangelist began to write.[17] Nor were these tranquil years: Mark's Christian community had to come to terms not only with a fierce wave of imperial recrimination, which held them responsible for the fire of Rome, but also the failed Jewish revolt and (quite probably) the destruction of the Jerusalem temple. These were seismic events, which shook them to the core and required group memories to be constantly adapted to incorporate newer insights. It may be, however, that it was these turbulent events, coupled with the passage of time and the deaths of the "originating" Christians (including of course Peter), that spurred our evangelist to pen his own account.

In this regard, Werner Kelber and Chris Keith have both drawn on Jan Assmann's concept of a *Traditionsbruch* (or breakdown in tradition) to explain the emergence of Mark's Gospel. Assmann suggested that the communicative memory of a living group *(kommunikative Gedächtnis)* encounters a crisis at around the forty-year mark as the originating generation dies out. If the memories are to survive, these oral memories must be transformed into cultural memory *(kulturelle Gedächtnis),* which extends beyond the present generation and becomes embedded in the authoritative cultural repertoire of the group. Writing the memories down into some kind of a literary text provides an effective way of transforming them into cultural memories, of stabilizing group identity, and of providing an expanded context *(zerdehnte Situation)* in which the writer of the text can speak to new generations of hearers without actually being present. Both Kelber and Keith suggest, with some plausibility, that this accounts for Mark's decision to write a foundational narrative at this precise time. We do not have to specify a *particular* crisis — as we have seen, a range of events took place at around the forty-year point — but it may have been particularly *Peter's* death that required the production of a text, in effect to take the place of a revered leader. Mark's suitability for the task, we may assume, lay precisely in his connection (whatever it may have been) to Peter.[18]

---

16. On Peter's death, see the essay by Timothy Barnes in this present volume. On the date of Mark, see Tuckett, "Mark," p. 886; and Marcus, *Mark 1-8,* pp. 37-39.

17. As is assumed by the *Anti-Marcionite Prologue* and Irenaeus, *Adv. haer.* 3.1.1-2.

18. Jan Assmann, *Cultural Memory and Early Civilization: Writing, Remembrance, and Political Imagination* (Cambridge: Cambridge University Press, 2011; German original 1992); Assmann applied his work specifically to the book of Deuteronomy. Werner Kelber, "The Works of Memory: Christian Origins as MnemoHistory — A Response" in Kirk and Thatcher, *Memory, Tradition, and Texts,* pp. 221-48, here pp. 243-44; Chris Keith, "Prolegomena on the Textualization of Mark's Gospel: Manuscript Culture, the Extended Situation, and the

But Mark was not simply a compiler and editor of tradition; recent scholarship has repeatedly stressed the evangelist's creative handling of his material. In the next sections, we need to consider the genre of Mark's Gospel, and how this might have affected both his use of Petrine material and his portrayal of Peter as a literary character. I shall consider each of these in turn.

2. Mark as a Biographer

Over the last few decades, an emerging scholarly consensus holds that Mark wrote a *bios,* an ancient biography.[19] The biographical genre was well suited for his story of Jesus — it allowed him to present a portrait of the types of things that Jesus did and said, to reveal his identity, and to offer his life as a model for others to emulate. Our author presumably gathered together well-known and loved material, some of it perhaps originating with Peter, and cast it as a life of Jesus. Although an ancient *bios* could be fluid and adaptable, as a literary genre it would have been thoroughly familiar to his audience. The question that concerns the present discussion is: what effect would this literary genre have had on Mark's material?

Surveying a wide range of biographical literature, and highlighting both the similarities and the acceptable idiosyncrasies within the genre, Thomas Hägg sees Mark as a type of "professional biography" that focuses only on the important section of a person's life, in the case of Jesus, of course, on his ministry and death.[20] Three features of biography are worth noting. Somewhat surprisingly, perhaps, Hägg observes that, except in the case of imperial subjects, ancient biographies typically stressed their hero's public life but often said nothing (or very little) concerning their private or intimate details. Even when the author knew his subject well, such information is often not supplied.[21]

Emergence of the Written Gospel," in *Memory and Identity in Ancient Judaism and Early Christianity: A Conversation with Barry Schwartz,* ed. Tom Thatcher (Atlanta: Society of Biblical Literature, 2014).

19. See, e.g., the studies of Charles H. Talbert, *What Is a Gospel? The Genre of the Canonical Gospels* (Philadelphia: Fortress, 1977); David E. Aune, *The New Testament in Its Literary Environment* (Cambridge: James Clarke, 1988); Vernon K. Robbins, *Jesus the Teacher: A Socio-Rhetorical Study of Mark* (Philadelphia: Fortress, 1984); Richard A. Burridge, *What Are the Gospels: A Comparison with Graeco-Roman Biography,* 2nd ed. (Grand Rapids: Eerdmans, 2004).

20. Thomas Hägg, *The Art of Biography in Antiquity* (Cambridge: Cambridge University Press, 2012).

21. Xenophon, for example, knew Agesilaus well from serving under him on the battlefield and later lived for over twenty years on his estate, yet in his biographical encomium of

Second, like other ancient writers, biographers were often reluctant to give their sources.[22] More surprisingly, however, is the fact that even when the author knew his subject, or was a witness of events, there is often a curious reluctance to mention this fact.[23] And third, it is common for anecdotes in biographies to lack temporal, geographic, or spatial indicators.[24] The reason for this is quite simple: in *bioi* aiming to give a sense of the man and his way of life, the typical took the place of the specific, and details of time and place were simply irrelevant.

While Mark's account may strike modern readers as somewhat odd, then, his lack of intimate details relating to Jesus, his lack of reference to sources, and his lack of specifics relating to time and place would all have been within the acceptable boundaries of the biographical genre, and would not have seemed particularly surprising to his audience (most of whom, presumably, were quite well aware of any Petrine connection to their group and did not need it to be spelled out). All of this was anticipated over thirty years ago by T. F. Glasson, who argued that names, dates, and places had disappeared from the Gospel narratives, not because they had been worn down by transmission within early Christian communities (as the form critics argued), but because they were

---

his patron he tells us nothing of his childhood, his education, or appearance and chooses to focus his account exclusively on the Spartan king's forty-year reign. Much closer to Mark's own time, Tacitus's account of Agricola similarly says almost nothing of his father-in-law's private life (about which Tacitus obviously knew a great deal), and even the governor's physical appearance is only given almost as an afterthought in the epilogue; once again, it is the public life that is important; other details are irrelevant.

22. When they *did* give their sources, it was often to indicate how they differed, and to give a scholarly air to their writing. An example of this is the "learned" style of Diogenes Laertius's *Lives and Opinions of Eminent Philosophers* (see Hägg, *Biography*, pp. 305-18, for discussion).

23. Even in his *Memorabilia*, a largely eyewitness account of his teacher Socrates, Xenophon rarely notes his own presence; when he does, he refers to himself in the third person, and only seldom uses expressions such as "I heard him" or "I was present" (see Hägg, *Biography*, p. 26, for discussion). Despite Tacitus's obviously close relationship to his subject, it is extremely rare for him to mention his sources or his own eyewitness recollections (only at *Agricola* 4.3; 22.4; and 24.3; see Hägg, *Biography*, p. 209).

24. In his *Evagoras*, for example, Isocrates appears to have arranged his material in a broadly chronological manner, though he rarely gives any temporal markers or allows us to see how events connect with one another. On the occasions where specific times or dates do occur, their use is to make a specific point — for example, the reference to "winter" in 2.31 is given not to date the event, but to show how the aging king "defied the elements to do his duty to the state" (Hägg, *Biography*, p. 47). And even when, in *Memorabilia* 3.3, Xenophon says that he remembers an event, there is no indication of the occasion, date, or place. Such information was clearly not regarded as necessary.

immaterial to the main points being made by the evangelists.[25] Hägg's work on biographical literature tends to corroborate this view. If Mark omitted details concerning places and times, or the kind of "vivid eye-witness detail" that the form critics sought in vain, it may not be because he had no access to it, but rather because the expectations of the biographical genre he had chosen for his work did not require them.

We saw earlier that among the reasons Joel Marcus rejects a link with Peter are that Mark does not appear to be any closer to Peter than the other evangelists (argument 1) and that his Petrine passages lack detail (arguments 5 and 6). He writes:

> If, for example, the first Markan narrative that features Peter, the story of his call in 1:16-18, were a genuine personal reminiscence, we should expect more details, such as an explanation of what it was about Jesus that made Peter and Andrew drop everything to follow him.[26]

This, however, is to confuse a "genuine reminiscence" (in the sense of an event told for its own sake) with a story retold as part of an ancient *bios*. Peter may well have had a clear recollection of the first time he set eyes on Jesus, of the tremendous impact it made on him. Perhaps (to allow our imaginations some free rein) he remembered other strange, inconsequential details as we sometimes do in connection with important events: maybe it was the day before his son's *bar mitzvah*, or a week he was trying out some new nets, or even during that long drought when the water levels were low and he was forced to go out far into the lake — but none of these details would have been relevant to Mark's biographical enterprise.[27] The evangelist was not interested in supplying his audience with details of *Peter's* own call experience, but in raising the call to discipleship to a level of abstraction that would include his audience, and emphasizing to them (whatever Peter's own call experience might have been like) that following Jesus required immediate and wholehearted commitment. The Gospel is not a biography of Peter, but of *Jesus,* and all material is turned to the portrayal of the central character and the demands of following him. Thus inconsequential details concerning Peter would simply be out of place. With this in mind, we must turn finally to the role of Peter as a character in the narrative.

---

25. T. F. Glasson, "The Place of the Anecdote: A Note on Form Criticism," *JTS* 32 (1981): 142-50.

26. Marcus, *Mark 1–8,* p. 23.

27. So also Bauckham, *Eyewitnesses,* p. 172.

3. Mark's Portrait of Peter

The character of Peter in Mark's Gospel has been a perennial problem for interpreters. Whereas Eusebius was content to attribute less favorable characteristics to Peter's humility,[28] others (such as the Tübingen school) took a less positive approach. The most extreme modern interpretations of the disciple were published by Tyson, Schreiber, Weeden, and Kelber in the 1960s and early 70s. Together they argued that the Twelve (and Peter in particular) had been deliberately cast in a negative way because they represented a Palestinian Christology to which the evangelist was opposed, creating a divide between Mark's Hellenistic Christianity on one hand and the Palestinian Christianity of Peter, James, and the Jerusalem church on the other.[29] There was clearly no room in this reconstruction for any view of Peter as an eyewitness source for Mark.[30] Although these views have been challenged on a number of grounds by recent scholarship, the idea that Mark portrays the disciples in a "negative" light remains remarkably persistent.

Most recent *literary* studies of Mark's Gospel, however, have seen things rather differently. The disciples tend to be regarded as fallible humans, who struggle to follow Jesus but are often thwarted by their lack of understanding or preoccupied with their own importance and competitive instincts. Frequently they act as little more than a foil to Jesus, as questioners who draw their master out in his teaching, with Peter acting as the spokesman of the group, exemplifying their hopes, fears, and misunderstandings. Rather than regarding Peter and the disciples as ciphers for a heretical faction, most literary critics suggest that readers are to *identify* with them; they embody the situation of most readers, struggling to follow Jesus to the best of their ability. Thus, although Peter can exhibit both positive and negative qualities, the reader remains sympathetic toward him.[31]

---

28. Eusebius, *Demonstratio Evangelica* 3.3.

29. J. B. Tyson, "The Blindness of the Disciples in Mark," *JBL* 80 (1961): 261-68; J. Schreiber, "Die Christologie des Markusevangeliums," *ZTK* 58 (1961): 154-83; T. J. Weeden, "The Heresy That Necessitated Mark's Gospel," *ZNW* 59 (1968): 145-58; and W. H. Kelber, "Mark 14,32-42: Gethsemane, Passion Christology and Discipleship Failure," *ZNW* 63 (1972): 166-87.

30. So Kelber, "Gethsemane," p. 186 n. 59.

31. See, e.g., Robert C. Tannehill, "The Gospel of Mark as Narrative Christology," *Semeia* 16 (1979): 57-95; David Rhoads and Donald Michie, *Mark as Story: An Introduction to the Narrative of a Gospel* (Philadelphia: Fortress, 1982), pp. 122-29; Elizabeth Struthers Malbon, "Fallible Followers: Women and Men in the Gospel of Mark," *Semeia* 28 (1983): 29-48; and Thomas E. Boomershine, "Peter's Denial as Polemic or Confession," *Semeia* 39 (1987): 47-68. Drawing on the work of C. H. Turner, Richard Bauckham argues for a "Petrine perspec-

These studies have proved extremely important as approaches to Mark's narrative. There are, however, two weaknesses: first, narrative studies often assume that it is possible to present a portrait of Mark's Peter that will make coherent sense; second (and related to this) is the common idea that the text is a unified story world.[32] As a *bios*, however, Mark's Gospel is not the same as a fictional story where characterization is entirely at the discretion of the author. Mark's central focus was on Jesus, and even he barely becomes a "rounded" character. All other actors in the drama are there in a supporting role: to illustrate aspects of Jesus' teaching, to embody what it means to be a disciple, or to contrast with the hero's endurance. If the subjects of biographies could easily become "types," or embodiments of virtues, we should hardly wonder if the same is still more true of supporting characters, even those known to their author.[33] The evangelist presumably had no interest in providing us with a consistent view of Peter's motives or character.[34] It comes as no surprise, then, to find "narratorial slumbers," where the author has forgotten to tie in apparently conflicting portraits of the disciples (for example, Peter plays a prominent role in the transfiguration scene, as if the awkward and humiliating exchange of six days earlier had not happened![35]). The focus is so thoroughly on Jesus that other characters are of importance only in how they interact with him at any

---

tive" in the Gospel, in which Peter's original "we" has been changed by the evangelist into "they" (*Eyewitnesses*, pp. 155-82); see also Markus Bockmuehl, who speaks more generally of Mark seeing and hearing through Peter's eyes and ears (*Simon Peter in Scripture and Memory* [Grand Rapids: Baker Academic, 2012] pp. 5, 131-41). This may well be true, though Bauckham's attempt to stress Peter's individuality (*Eyewitnesses*, pp. 168-71, drawing here on T. Wiarda, "Peter as Peter in the Gospel of Mark," *NTS* 45 [1999]: 19-37) is less successful, and in my opinion unnecessary.

32. For similar criticisms, see P. Merenlahti and R. Hakola, "Reconceiving Narrative Criticism," in *Characterization in the Gospel: Reconceiving Narrative Criticism,* ed. David Rhoads and Kari Syreeni (Sheffield: Sheffield Academic, 1999), pp. 13-48; see also in the same volume Kari Syreeni, "Peter as Character and Symbol in the Gospel of Matthew," pp. 106-52.

33. On "typological characterization" in ancient literature more generally, see A. Smith, "Tyranny Exposed: Mark's Typological Characterization of Herod Antipas (Mark 6:14-29)," *Biblical Interpretation* 14 (2006): 259-93. More broadly on characterization in biographical literature, see C. Gill, "The Question of Character Development: Plutarch and Tacitus," *Classical Quarterly* 33 (1983): 469-87; and Burridge, *What Are the Gospels*, pp. 120-21.

34. Augusti Borrell, *The Good News of Peter's Denial: A Narrative and Rhetorical Reading of Mark 14:54, 66-72* (Atlanta: Society of Biblical Literature, 1998), p. 23; also Best, "Role of the Disciples in Mark," pp. 377-401.

35. So Syreeni, "Peter," p. 149 (from whom I also borrowed the term "narratorial slumbers").

given point. Peter is at his most "rounded" in the denial scene: not only is he the central character, but the reader is also exposed to his mounting agitation and later remorse (14:54, 66-72). Yet even here it quickly becomes apparent that the scene is to be read alongside the story of Jesus before the high priest (14:53, 55-65), and the actions of Peter, although significant in themselves, are presented on a wider canvas as a contrast to those of his Lord.

If Mark was writing for a Christian group that knew of most of the actors in the story (as his abrupt introduction of most of them suggests), then we also have to take this into account in his portrait of Peter.[36] Stories of his obtuseness and lack of faith, or his questioning and empty bravado, take on a very different light in the knowledge of his subsequent Christian activity and years of loyal service on the mission field. Even his denial takes on a different hue. Reports of Peter's failings, particularly his denial, could only have come from Peter in the first instance; perhaps, like Paul's persecution of the early church, he made it into an important part of his preaching, drawing on its parenetic value (as Mark still does). As Thomas Boomershine notes, these

> are the stories of men who have experienced the forgiveness and power of God to overcome their weaknesses and failures. How does one tell such a story? One tells such a story as a confession and as an invitation to others who had the same feelings to identify with the story and make it their own.[37]

Just as Paul's persecuting activity acquired a different tone by what his congregations knew of his subsequent Christian activity, so Peter's denial and failings must be seen against his later devotion — quite possibly, too, the knowledge that, in the end, he did follow his master, even to death.[38] Writing at a time of persecution and difficulty, Mark's Peter reassures Christians that following Jesus is hard, that even the greatest of the disciples had his moments of failure, but that, like him, even those who fail can still hope for restoration (14:28; 16:7).

---

36. See Augustine Stock, *Call to Discipleship: A Literary Study of Mark's Gospel* (Wilmington, Del.: Glazier, 1982), pp. 39-43.

37. Boomershine, "Peter's Denial," pp. 60-61; similar points are made by Bauckham, *Eyewitnesses,* pp. 178-80; and Bockmuehl, *Simon Peter,* p. 140. I see little evidence for Marcus's claim that Peter could ill afford to weaken his precarious position in the church by passing on stories that cast himself in a poor light (*Mark 1–8,* p. 24); this seems to me to make too much of the Tübingen school's antithesis between the two men.

38. So Best, "Role of the Disciples," p. 400; and Wiarda, "Peter in the Gospel," p. 558.

Concluding Thoughts

Writing in the 1950s, Vincent Taylor perceptively warned that Papias's testimony only becomes vulnerable when too much is based on it.[39] This seems to me to be an eminently sensible judgment. In this essay I have looked at some of the most common arguments against a connection between Peter and the Markan evangelist and found them to be less than convincing. I am quite aware, however, that rebutting arguments against a proposition is a very different thing from proving that the proposition is true in the first place. In this instance, though, it is difficult to see how one would go about *proving* a Petrine connection. All we have is a memory from the second century (which perhaps goes back to the first), an account that tells the story of Jesus from just before Peter's arrival on the scene, and a Gospel that proved remarkably enduring even when superseded by Matthew and Luke. If it has demonstrated that a Petrine link to Mark's Gospel is not as self-evidently impossible as many critical scholars suppose, this essay will have served its purpose.

It is worth, however, clarifying one final issue. Many of those arguing for a Petrine connection to Mark do so for a particular reason: if Peter stands behind the Gospel, it is assumed, the material contained in it must be historically reliable. My earlier comments should make it clear that I do not hold this view. On a very general level, we have access to the kind of things Jesus said and did, but there is still a great deal of scope for the distortion of memory (both Peter's and Mark's) and perhaps more importantly the present needs of the Christian group to which they belonged as it sought to explain itself following the cataclysmic events of persecution, revolt, and the fall of the temple. Furthermore, the requirements of a biographical narrative imposed their own burden on Mark's material; unlike today, when we expect at least an attempt at historical accuracy (however illusory such a thing might be), the central concern of an ancient *bios* was to give an insight into the hero's character and way of life, a concern that could take precedence over precise historical information. In Hägg's words, "The establishment of any form of higher truth — be it poetic, psychological, philosophical, or religious — overrules demands for the truth of facts."[40] Given the role of creative imagination within the biographical genre,

---

39. Taylor, *Gospel*, p. 8; so also Morna Hooker, *A Commentary on the Gospel according to Saint Mark* (London: Black, 1991), p. 6.

40. Hägg, *Biography*, pp. 3-4.

it would be unwise to ask the Gospel to deliver more historical material than it is able to do.

If there is a connection between Mark and Peter, as I have argued, it is tempting to speculate whether some of Mark's theology also goes back to Peter. Quite possibly it does.[41] Yet it is not clear to me what principle one would use to separate the theology of Peter from a theology shared by others in the early church, or even from that of Mark himself. And that, of course, would be well beyond the scope of this essay.

41. William L. Lane finds the outline of the Gospel in Peter's sermon of Acts 10:36-41, and claims to hear Peter's voice in Mark 1:29, 35-37; *The Gospel According to St Mark* (London: Marshall, Morgan & Scott, 1974), p. 12.

CHAPTER 5

Did Peter Really Say That?
Revisiting the Petrine Speeches in Acts

Jonathan W. Lo

The speeches in the Acts of the Apostles contain the majority of the extended discourses attributed to the apostle Peter within the New Testament canon, but did Peter really say the things Luke attributes to him? A conservative dating of Acts might put its composition around 75 CE, a staggering forty years after the founding of the nascent Christian movement.[1] Given that many historical writers were prone to inventing entire speeches, could the eight Petrine speeches in Acts be fictitious compositions?[2] The speeches exhibit Lukan style, grammar, and vocabulary; they also have programmatic functions within their narrative contexts and within the larger framework of Acts — all of which have led critical readers to question their authenticity.[3]

In Luke-Acts scholarship, there has been an enduring debate about the authenticity of these speeches. Some scholars contend that the speeches in Acts are solely products of Luke's literary invention and have no real relation to Peter.[4] Others are convinced that Luke did not create the speeches ex nihilo,

---

1. Frank Dicken places the terminus a quo of Acts at 75 CE, "The Author and Date of Luke-Acts: Exploring the Options," in *Issues in Luke-Acts,* ed. Sean Adams and Michael Pahl (Piscataway, N.J.: Gorgias, 2012), pp. 7-26.

2. This tabulation follows the treatment of the speeches in Acts by Marion L. Soards, *The Speeches in Acts: Their Content, Context, and Concerns* (Louisville: Westminster John Knox, 1994), pp. 18-22.

3. Martin Dibelius, "The Speeches in Acts and Ancient Historiography," in *The Book of Acts: Form, Style, and Theology,* ed. K. C. Hanson (Minneapolis: Fortress, 2004), pp. 49-86.

4. E.g., Dibelius, *Book of Acts,* pp. 32-33, 67, 141. See also, Ernst Haenchen, *The Acts of the Apostles: A Commentary,* 2nd ed. (Philadelphia: Westminster, 1971), p. 43.

but adapted existing sources, using his own language and modifying traditional material to conform to his literary purpose and theological outlook.[5] The debate is complicated by the fact that the same phenomena can be used to support either position. While it is clear that all of the speeches are written in Luke's hand and woven rather seamlessly into the narrative of Acts,[6] Luke's literary prowess can be an explanation both for his free invention and for his adaptation of existing sources.

The aim of this essay is to revisit the question of the historical value of the Petrine speeches in Acts and to provide an overview of the debate in light of current developments in Luke-Acts research. The debate over the authenticity of the Petrine speeches in Acts centers on three major issues: (1) comparisons with Greco-Roman literary conventions, (2) Luke's literary style, and (3) Lukan theology. Arguments constructed from these categories are used independently, and also combined, to argue for and against the historicity of the speeches.

Comparisons with Greco-Roman Literary Conventions

In accordance with the pioneering observations of Henry J. Cadbury and Martin Dibelius, many have sought to understand Acts through the writings of Greco-Roman historians.[7] The obvious comparison for Acts is with the genre of Greco-Roman history,[8] because their authors also detail historical events and intersperse them with extended discourses by important characters.[9]

5. See Ward Gasque, "The Speeches of Acts: Dibelius Reconsidered," in *New Dimensions in New Testament Study*, ed. Richard N. Longenecker and Merrill C. Tenney (Grand Rapids: Zondervan, 1974), p. 247; Jacques Dupont, *The Sources of Acts: The Present Position* (London: Darton, Longman & Todd, 1964); C. H. Dodd, *The Apostolic Preaching and Its Developments* (New York: Harper, 1936); and F. F. Bruce, *The Speeches in the Acts of the Apostles* (London: Tyndale, 1943).

6. Luke Timothy Johnson, *The Gospel of Luke* (Collegeville, Minn.: Liturgical Press, 1991), pp. 6-7.

7. Henry J. Cadbury, *The Making of Luke-Acts* (London: Macmillan, 1927); and Martin Dibelius, *Book of Acts;* Marion L. Soards also agrees that the strongest parallels to the form of the speeches in Acts are to be found in the speeches of Greco-Roman historiography, but he contends that with respect to content, they are closer to the Septuagint. *Speeches in Acts*, pp. 134-61.

8. Craig S. Keener, *Acts: An Exegetical Commentary*, vol. 1, *Introduction and 1:1–2:47* (Grand Rapids: Baker Academic, 2012), p. 269.

9. The consensus among scholars is that Luke is employing the tools of ancient histo-

Some ancient historians' speeches include embellishments and free inventions that cannot be regarded as authentic. Polybius's critique of Timaeus's careless handling of speech materials, for example, demonstrates that there existed a range of historians with varying concerns for the historicity of the speeches they report.[10] For rhetorical historians such as Isocrates, Dionysius of Halicarnassus, and Josephus, their invented speeches primarily served to entertain, to defend a certain viewpoint, and to demonstrate their literary skill and polished rhetoric.[11] Even classical historians such as Herodotus and Tacitus have been known to invent speeches and to present their own words as those of the characters in their narratives;[12] as Lucian of Samosata points out, the task of the historian is to entertain as well as to be historically appropriate.[13]

Conrad Gempf argues that despite their creative liberties, some Roman historians such as Sallust, Livy, and Tacitus attempted to preserve the general sense of what the speakers said, when those sources were available.[14] Therefore, some have taken the classical historian Thucydides' explanation of the composition of his speeches in his *Peloponnesian War* (1.22.1) as instructive for understanding those of Luke. Thucydides' comments reveal four clues for understanding the use of speeches in ancient historical writing.

First, discourses of important figures at key events are considered to be significant and worthy of remembrance; Thucydides mentions speeches being reported back to him. Second, Thucydides acknowledges the difficulty of remembering the exact wording of a speech with precision. Third, he admits to exercising a degree of freedom in the writing of the speeches by attributing to speakers words fitting their disposition. In other words, Thucydides uses available sources, along with his knowledge of the speakers, to compose the speeches in his account of the war. Finally, it can be seen that while the precise wording of a speech and the exact circumstance in which a speech was

riography to report some kind of history, although other proposals, such as novel, Homeric epic, biography, etc., have been raised. See Sean A. Adams, "The Genre of Luke and Acts," in Adams and Pahl, *Issues in Luke-Acts,* pp. 97-120.

10. Polybius, *Histories* 12.25a.4-5.

11. Keener, *Acts,* p. 265. On the rhetorical liberty of Josephus in his speech writing, see pp. 303-4. Conrad H. Gempf notes that even the rhetoric of Isocrates and Dionysius was employed to adapt a speech or event for a new audience. See "Public Speaking and Published Accounts," in *The Book of Acts in Its First Century Setting,* vol. 1, *Ancient Literary Setting,* ed. Bruce W. Winter and Andrew D. Clarke (Grand Rapids: Eerdmans, 1993), pp. 259-303.

12. Keener, *Acts,* pp. 265, 272.

13. Lucian, *How to Write History,* 58.

14. Gempf, "Public Speaking", pp. 283-85.

originally given cannot be ascertained, Thucydides considered his work to be faithful to the essence of the speech. The import of these statements for the study of the Petrine speeches should be obvious: it is possible for a writer to compose speech material that is both innovative and faithful to the existing sources and traditions.[15] Thucydides' discussion on his use of speeches illustrates the complexities involved in determining the historical value of a speech; consequently, the contention that the speeches in Acts have some grounding in existing sources or traditions cannot be summarily dismissed simply because there is evidence of Lukan redaction or adaptation. Craig Keener notes that "ancient historiographic theory allowed a writer to put a speech in his own words, provided he did not invent the content." When sources were available, it seems reasonable to suppose that most historians retained the essential substance of the speeches they were reproducing.[16]

Be that as it may, this observation must also be tempered with the expectations of the contemporary audience of the ancient historical genre. Verbatim reports of speeches were not possible, expected, or desirable in ancient historiography;[17] rather, the speeches were intended to instruct as well as to entertain.[18] Historians writing for more educated audiences employed speeches to demonstrate their literary skills, with "rhetorical appropriateness" being a particularly sought-after element.[19] Such audiences would evaluate speeches by the rhetorical sensitivity the historian displays with regard to speakers and situations.[20]

Even within the genre of Greco-Roman historiography, there is a range of writers with differing levels of concern for historical verisimilitude when composing speeches, from self-professed critical historians such as Thucydides or Polybius, to more rhetorically minded historians like Dionysius or Josephus, who are known to make frequent and blatant inventions. For this reason, although the identification of the genre of Acts is important for understanding its contents, the fact that Acts resembles the writings of the ancient historians in style and content is largely inconsequential to the question of historicity;

---

15. Gempf, "Public Speaking", p. 259. See also Merle Bland Dudley, "The Speeches in Acts," *EvQ* 50 (1978): 147-55.

16. Charles W. Fornara, *The Nature of History in Ancient Greece and Rome* (Berkeley: University of California Press, 1983), pp. 154-68.

17. Keener, *Acts*, p. 309.

18. James D. G. Dunn, *The Acts of the Apostles* (Harrisburg, Pa.: Trinity Press International, 1996) pp. xvii-xviii.

19. F. W. Walbank, *Speeches in Greek Historians* (Oxford: Blackwell, 1965), p. 19.

20. Keener, *Acts*, p. 309.

depending on the author, speeches found in ancient historiography could be broadly historical or entirely fictitious.[21]

Luke's Literary Style

Arguments surrounding the historicity of Peter's speeches also often depend on observations pertaining to the literary features in the speeches. There is a general consensus that there is a literary unity to the speeches but that they also contain numerous peculiarities, leading scholars to different conclusions.

It is generally acknowledged that when composing a work of history the ancient historian will write in his own literary style,[22] and espouse his own perspective on the events he reports;[23] therefore, uniformity in style and language in a single work, despite its dependence on sources, is not the exception but the norm.[24] However, it must also be acknowledged that the common structure and theological unity found across the speeches of different speakers and situations in Acts[25] have led some scholars to question their authenticity.[26] Is it merely a coincidence that Paul's sermon in 13:16-41 shares so many similarities with Peter's speeches in the preceding chapters? And does not the fact that Peter essentially preaches the same message regardless of his audience or situation (2:14-40; 3:12-26; 10:34-43) suggest that Luke is not concerned with what Peter actually said on those occasions?

Marion Soards suggests that the repetition of common themes is an important literary device employed by Luke to create analogies that allow the audience to perceive the unity and emphasis of the story he tells, while instilling in them a sense of expectation concerning an ongoing mission toward

21. See also Keener, *Acts,* p. 8.

22. For example, the speeches all begin with "men, brothers" regardless of who is speaking (e.g., Acts 1:16; 2:29; 7:2; 13:15; 15:7; 22:1; 23:1; 28:17).

23. Keener, *Acts,* p. 304.

24. Ben Witherington III, *The Acts of the Apostles: A Socio-Rhetorical Commentary* (Grand Rapids: Eerdmans, 1997), p. 117; Keener, *Acts,* p. 308.

25. See the analysis of the Petrine speeches by Herman N. Ridderbos, *The Speeches of Peter in the Acts of the Apostles* (London: Tyndale, 1956); Eduard Schweizer, "The Concept of the Davidic 'Son of God' in Acts and Its Old Testament Background," in *Studies in Luke-Acts: Essays Presented in Honour of Paul Schubert,* ed. Leander E. Keck and J. Louis Martyn (Nashville: Abingdon, 1966), pp. 208-16; Soards, *Speeches in Acts;* and Richard F. Zehnle, *Peter's Pentecost Discourse: Tradition and Lukan Interpretation in Peter's Speeches of Acts 2 and 3* (Nashville: Abingdon, 1971), pp. 19-24.

26. Keener, *Acts,* pp. 304-11.

the Jews.[27] Despite the disparate narrative settings in which they are found, the components of Peter's message within the speeches attributed to him are essentially the same: a presentation of the early Christian proclamation that consists of the death of Jesus at the hands of Israel (2:23, 36; 3:15; 4:10; 5:30; 10:39), Jesus' resurrection (2:24; 3:15, 26; 4:10; 5:30; 10:40) and exaltation at the hands of God (2:33; 3:13; 4:11; 5:31; 10:42), an emphasis on the function of the apostles as witnesses to these realities (2:32; 3:15; 5:32; 10:41; cf. Luke 24:48), and an exhortation to repentance and an offer of forgiveness or salvation (forgiveness: 2:33; 3:19; 5:31; 10:43; repentance: 2:38; 3:19, 26; 5:31; salvation: 2:21, 40; 4:12). Several of these elements are also found in Jesus' postresurrection speech in Luke 24:44-49, including the suffering and resurrection of the Messiah (Luke 24:46), the proclamation of repentance and forgiveness (Luke 24:47), and the charge to be witnesses of these things (Luke 24:48), connecting the message of Peter in Acts with Jesus' commission in Luke.

While it is possible that the stylistic unity found in the speeches is merely a literary device Luke imposes on the speeches at the expense of authenticity, an alternative interpretation may also explain the data. Luke may be employing repetition to emphasize the usage and significance of tradition in the proclamation of the early church. The reason the various missionary speeches are so similar may well be that the leaders of the early church focused on preaching, and perhaps did so in the manner Luke describes.[28] An analogy might be seen in Luke's inclusion of Jesus' parables that are unique to his Gospel.[29] While it is possible Luke invented these parables to convey his own theological concerns without regard for authenticity, it is equally plausible that the parables are authentic; they could be a genuine reflection of an early Christian tradition that was aware of Jesus' parabolic teachings.[30] Similarly, Luke's use of repetition in Peter's speeches need not be a literary invention de novo; it might also reflect the content of a typical missionary speech by the leaders of the early church.[31]

---

27. Soards, *Speeches in Acts,* pp. 204-8.

28. Keener suggests that the similarities in the speeches may "reflect the common gospel preached by early Christians not only in Acts but in most of our earliest Christian sources." *Acts,* pp. 306-7. See Mark 1:14-15; 1 Cor. 11:23-25; 15:1-11; Gal. 1:7-8; 2:7-8. See also Dodd, *Apostolic Preaching,* p. 27.

29. Luke 7:36-50; 10:25-37; 12:16-21; 13:6-9; 15:3-7, 8-10, 11-32; 16:1-13, 19-31; 18:1-8, 9-14; 19:11-27.

30. On the authenticity of Jesus' parables in the Gospels, see Klyne R. Snodgrass, "Parable," in *Dictionary of Jesus and the Gospels,* ed. Joel B. Green and Scot McKnight (Downers Grove, Ill.: InterVarsity Press, 1992), pp. 591-601.

31. I. Howard Marshall, *Luke: Historian and Theologian* (Grand Rapids: Zondervan, 1989), p. 55.

Moreover, despite the repetition in the structure and content of the Petrine speeches, it is noteworthy that Luke primarily attributes these speeches to Peter and not to another speaker,[32] even if Peter is portrayed as speaking on behalf of the apostles in some instances (2:14; 3:12; 4:19; 5:29).[33] An examination of the text of Acts will reveal that although there is a succinct kerygmatic framework within Peter's speeches, Luke often provides shorter summary statements of the apostles' messages in his narration, namely that "Jesus is the Messiah" (5:42; 8:5; 9:22; 18:5, 28; 28:23), that "Jesus is the Son of God" (9:20), that this is "the kingdom of God" (8:12; 19:8; 20:25; 28:23, 31), and also simply that there is a "resurrection from the dead" (4:2, 33; 17:18, 32; 23:6; 24:21; 26:23), namely, Jesus' resurrection (e.g., 1:22; 4:2; 23:6). Furthermore, Peter is not the sole evangelist of Acts — proclamations are also attributed to Stephen (chapters 6–7), Philip (chapter 8), "Saul" (chapter 9), and of course Paul in the rest of Acts — but the gospel message as it appears in the missionary speeches of Peter is unique, with the exception of Paul's speech in Pisidian Antioch in Acts 13. This observation demonstrates that Luke's use of repetition with respect to the structure and content of Peter's speeches does not appear in all of the speeches, but only in Peter's. In this regard, Luke's repetition is focused on describing the proclamation of Peter as a leader of the early church.

The major difficulty with this approach is Paul's speech in Acts 13, which has many similarities with the structure and content of the Petrine speeches.[34] After presenting a summary of Israel's history, beginning with their days in Egypt and leading up to the ministry of John the Baptist, Paul's presentation includes many of the elements of the Petrine speeches: an emphasis on the continuation of Israel's story (13:27), Israel's complicity in Jesus' death on a cross (13:28-29), God raising Jesus from the dead (13:30), and the reference to the apostles as witnesses (13:31). The expression "witness" (μάρτυς), as it pertains to witnessing Jesus' resurrection, is used predominantly by Peter as a self-reference in his speeches.[35] When Paul uses the expression in 13:31, he applies it to Peter and the apostles but not to himself: "for many days he appeared to those who came up with him *from Galilee to Jerusalem*, the very ones who are now his witnesses to the people." To be sure, Paul is also to become a witness for Jesus in Acts, but in a slightly different sense — he is

---

32. Paul's speech in Acts 13:16-41 closely resembles the Petrine speeches, but this point will be discussed further below.

33. C. H. Dodd attributes the recurring content of the speeches to the kerygma of the Jerusalem church. *Apostolic Preaching*, pp. 20-21.

34. See also M. D. Goulder, *Type and History in Acts* (London: SPCK, 1964), p. 83.

35. Ridderbos, *Speeches*, p. 17.

to be a witness of the things he has "seen and heard" and also of the things that "will be revealed to him" (22:15; 26:16). Admittedly, this is a slight distinction, but it can help explain the function of Paul's speech in 13:16-41: Paul is different from the apostles who followed Jesus from Galilee, but he is proclaiming the same gospel message that the Twelve preached.[36] For Luke, Paul's sermon to the Jews among the gentiles might function as a hinge that establishes the continuity between Peter and Paul's ministry in his narrative about the early church.

Be that as it may, it should be noted that although Paul's speech in Acts 13 resembles the Petrine speeches, it is manifestly dissimilar to Paul's other speeches in Acts. In none of Paul's speeches in Lystra (14:15-17), the Areopagus (17:22-31), Corinth (18:5), Miletus (20:18-35), or Jerusalem (22:17-21) does he present the gospel in the way he does in Acts 13. Neither do his speeches before the Jewish council (23:6), Felix (24:10-21), Festus (25:8-11), or Agrippa (26:4-23) contain these Petrine elements. There are several common themes, such as the mention of Moses and the prophets and Jesus' death and resurrection (26:22-23), but the presentation of the gospel in the pattern found in the Petrine speeches simply does not characterize the majority of Paul's speeches in Acts; on the contrary, in light of the evidence above, the content of the Petrine speeches seems to be specifically attributed to Peter and his function as one who faithfully receives the commission of the risen Jesus.

Besides the element of literary unity in the speeches, the peculiarities observed in them have also been debated. Richard Zehnle's study of the Pentecost discourse raises some interesting questions regarding certain irregularities in Peter's speech in Acts 3 that can also be observed in the other Petrine speeches.[37] These literary oddities exhibit characteristics that are distinct from the material found outside of the Petrine speeches.

For example, scholars have observed Semitisms in the Petrine speeches,[38] noticing a sharp contrast with Luke's normally polished Greek.[39] A. T. Robert-

36. Josef Pichler, "Das theologische Anliegen der Paulusrezeption im lukanischen Werk," in *The Unity of Luke-Acts*, ed. J. Verheyden (Leuven: Leuven University Press, 1999), pp. 742-43.

37. Zehnle, *Peter's Pentecost Discourse*, pp. 136-37.

38. Max Wilcox, "A Foreword to the Study of Speeches in Acts," in *Christianity, Judaism, and Other Greco-Roman Cults: Studies for Morton Smith at Sixty*, ed. Jacob Neusner (Leiden: Brill, 1975), vol. 1, pp. 220-25; Dodd, *Preaching*, pp. 19-20.

39. Gasque, "Speeches," pp. 248-49; F. F. Bruce, *The Acts of the Apostles: The Greek Text with Introduction and Commentary* (Grand Rapids: Eerdmans, 1951), p. 18. However, Keener advises caution because of the overlap between Koine, Semitic, and translation Greek. *Acts*, p. 311.

son and J. de Zwaan allow the possibility of Luke's usage of Aramaic sources in the first twelve chapters of Acts.[40] C. H. Dodd also notes that Peter's speeches in Acts contain a high degree of Aramaisms, particularly in the speech to Cornelius in Acts 10.[41] C. K. Barrett agrees with Dodd, saying, "The language of [10:36, 38] . . . is so difficult as to be untranslatable."[42] Ward Gasque adds that "the speeches of the early chapters are often extremely awkward in style. To suggest this awkwardness is due to Luke's literary ability . . . is scarcely plausible."[43] Proponents of this perspective hold a high view of Luke's literary ability, attributing unpolished grammar to a primitive source that Luke has not entirely adapted into his own style. Taking Luke's use of Mark in the Gospel of Luke as an example, Luke attempts to improve the grammar of his source material, removing foreign loanwords and replacing Mark's frequent parataxis with more complex sentence structures.[44] However, since no sources have been identified for Acts, conclusions drawn from observing literary tendencies in the Gospel remain speculative.

Others have claimed that the use of obscure phrases and awkward grammar is a result of Luke's application of "ethopoeia," the rhetorical practice whereby a writer composes speeches "in the character" of the speaker, using language appropriate to that speaker's education, social class, values, and even regional characteristics.[45] Luke may not be drawing on primitive Judean sources, but rather purposely using archaizing language to depict an earlier period. For example, the speeches include obscure phrases containing ideas uncharacteristic of Luke, which are not revisited outside of these speeches. "Times of refreshing" (καιροὶ ἀναψύξεως) in 3:20 is an unusual expression generally understood to mean "the final era of salvation."[46] The term "relief" (ἀνάψυξις), for example, occurs exclusively here. Similarly, the phrase "times of the restoration of all things/men" (χρόνων ἀποκαταστάσεως πάντων) in 3:21 is

40. A. T. Robertson, *Grammar of the New Testament in Light of Recent Research,* 3rd ed. (London: Hodder & Stoughton, 1919), p. 105; J. de Zwaan, "The Use of the Greek Language in Acts," in *The Beginnings of Christianity,* vol. 1, part 2, *The Acts of the Apostles,* ed. F. J. Foakes Jackson and K. Lake (London: Macmillan, 1922), pp. 30-65.

41. Dodd, *Preaching,* p. 20.

42. C. K. Barrett, *The Acts of the Apostles* (London: T&T Clark, 1994), 1:521.

43. Gasque, "Speeches," p. 249.

44. Helmut Koester, *Introduction to the New Testament* (Philadelphia: Fortress, 1982), 1:108.

45. Keener, *Acts,* pp. 284-86. Larry W. Hurtado suggests that the designation "the Nazarene" for Jesus is used to convey the "linguistic colour" of a Jewish setting. "Christology in Acts: Jesus in Early Christian Belief and Practice," in Adams and Pahl, *Issues in Luke-Acts,* pp. 217-37.

46. I. Howard Marshall, *Acts* (Leicester, U.K.: Inter-Varsity Press, 1980), p. 93.

enigmatic and distinctive.[47] In 10:36 Peter proclaims: "God sent the word to the sons of Israel, *preaching peace through Jesus Christ*" (εὐαγγελιζόμενος εἰρήνην διὰ Ἰησοῦ Χριστοῦ). These phrases only appear in the Petrine speeches and are not repeated in the rest of Acts. Dibelius calls such phenomena "old-fashioned phrases,"[48] while Luke Timothy Johnson calls them "narrative filler."[49] G. H. R. Horsley justifies their inclusion because they are literary devices intended to "vivify the narrative."[50] But according to Ward Gasque and F. F. Bruce, they are vestiges of an earlier tradition.[51]

Whether one holds the opinion that Luke fails to remove primitive elements from his sources or that he intentionally mimics an older style of expression, the question of the authenticity of the speeches remains unanswered. Those who maintain that these peculiar elements derive from a primitive source must consider that ethopoeia was a valid and common literary device within the genre of ancient historiography, especially when sources were unavailable.[52]

Luke's intentional archaizing of his speeches does not render it a priori inauthentic. Rather, it demonstrates Luke's knowledge of an earlier period and its language, and his ability to differentiate it from his own context; Luke is able to reproduce an effective and satisfying imitation for his audience.[53] Hence, even if Luke lacks a specific source for a particular speech, he may have had access to the historical tradition of the content, style, and manner of the types of speeches given by early evangelists.

Christology

Scholarly debates on the historicity of the speeches also rely on arguments based on their Christology,[54] especially in areas where it appears that the

---

47. Barrett, *Acts,* pp. 206-7.

48. Dibelius, *Book of Acts,* p. 67.

49. Johnson, *Acts of the Apostles,* p. 10.

50. G. H. R. Horsley, "Speeches and Dialogues in Acts," *NTS* 32 (1986): 609-14; see also J. C. O'Neill, *The Theology of Acts in Its Historical Setting* (London: SPCK, 1970), p. 145.

51. Gasque, "Speeches," pp. 247-49; Bruce, *Acts,* p. 18.

52. Soards, *Speeches in Acts,* p. 140.

53. Keener similarly claims that Luke's "ability to archaize presupposes his knowledge of earlier Christian language." *Acts,* p. 312; see also p. 286.

54. For a recent discussion of the Christology of Acts, see Hurtado, "Christology," pp. 229-37.

speeches contain a Christology uncharacteristic of Luke.[55] For example, Luke's most common designations for Jesus are "Lord" and "Christ";[56] however, the Petrine speeches refer to Jesus by obscure titles. The designation of Jesus as "God's Servant" in 3:13 and 26 (τὸν παῖδα αὐτοῦ) is not used again in Acts apart from the prayer of the apostles in 4:24-30, where Jesus is referred to as "your holy servant" (τὸν ἅγιον παῖδά σου), possibly in reference to the Davidic servant motif at the start of the prayer (4:25). Outside of Acts, the designation παῖς is only used with regard to Jesus in Matthew 12:18, where Jesus is identified with the servant of Isaiah 42, and in Luke 2:43, where Jesus is described as a youth. The term παῖς does not appear in Paul, either in relation to Jesus or otherwise. Zehnle contends that the usage of παῖς reflects a Mosaic rather than Davidic typology,[57] but in view of the importance of the Isaianic servant songs (especially Isa 42 and 49) in Acts, an Isaianic servant typology is also possible. The designation of Jesus as Servant occurs in prayers that appear in other early Christian literature, including 1 Clement 59.2-3 and Didache 9.2-3 and 10.2, and may reflect earlier liturgical traditions. Larry Hurtado suggests that the expression was used by the earliest Jewish Christians in Acts to denote a royal-messianic status that may have fallen into disuse in later Christianity.[58] Similarly, other obscure titles for Jesus, such as "the Just" (ὁ δίκαιος), "the author of life" (ἀρχηγὸς τῆς ζωῆς), and "the Son of Man" (ὁ υἱός τοῦ ἀνθρώπου) might also be allusions to christological titles of an earlier period.[59]

The speeches frequently refer to Jesus "of Nazareth" (2:22; 3:6; 4:10; 10:38) and tend to emphasize details from the earthly ministry of Jesus, a focus mostly absent outside of the Gospel narratives. Peter's speeches mention the baptism of John the Baptist (10:37; 11:16), Jesus being anointed by the Holy Spirit (10:38), the progression of his ministry from Galilee to Jerusalem (10:37, 39), and Jesus' ministries of healing and exorcism (10:38). Furthermore, Jesus is described as a "man" appointed by God (2:22), whom God "made Lord and Christ" (2:36). In view of these emphases, some perceive a primitive Christology in the speeches that is irreconcilable with the more developed Christology of later Christianity, thus betraying hints of an earlier tradition.[60] However,

55. Marshall, Luke, p. 54.

56. Hurtado, "Christology," pp. 221-23.

57. Zehnle, Peter's Pentecost Discourse, pp. 48-49.

58. Hurtado, "Christology," pp. 217-37.

59. For an exhaustive survey of christological titles and language in Acts, as well as other NT works, see Larry W. Hurtado, Lord Jesus Christ: Devotion to Jesus in Earliest Christianity (Grand Rapids: Eerdmans, 2003).

60. E.g., Wilfred L. Knox, The Acts of the Apostles (Cambridge: Cambridge University

such a view is inherently flawed, because as Hurtado has convincingly argued,[61] high Christology does not indicate a later tradition because many of the earliest Christians already held Jesus in the highest regard at the very outset of the Christian movement (e.g., Phil 2:6-11). Furthermore, Keener observes that high Christology appears even in the earliest speeches,[62] while elements that have been associated with primitive Christology, such as God's exaltation and enthronement of Jesus, appear in arguably later Christian writings, such as the book of Hebrews or Paul's letter to the Ephesians.[63] This supposed tension is resolved if one takes Hurtado's approach of understanding the resurrection of Jesus as an event that projects Jesus into heavenly glory as well as retrojects his divine status back into his earthly life in the recollections of his followers.[64] While there is continuing debate concerning how best to reconcile the various strands of Christology found in the speeches, there is good reason to believe that Luke was aware of the language, if not also some of the ideas of earliest Christianity.[65]

Isolating a distinctive Petrine theology in Acts is a difficult task because the entire work, including the speeches Luke adapts, is used to communicate his own theological message. Attempts to isolate a Petrine theology from the speeches must also consider the function of the speeches in the literary and theological structure of Acts;[66] Luke's work is not a biography of the first apostles, but a theological description of the historical spread of the gospel from its earliest days in Jerusalem. However, Luke's inclusion of primitive christological language and ideas into his narrative demonstrates that his own views are not incompatible with the proclamation of the earlier Christian tradition.

Press, 1948), pp. 75-78; C. F. D. Moule, "The Christology of Acts," in Keck and Martyn, *Studies in Luke-Acts,* pp. 159-85; Stephen S. Smalley, "The Christology of Acts," *ExpTim* 73 (1962): 358; John A. T. Robinson, "The Most Primitive Christology of All?" *JTS* 7 (1956): 177-89.

61. Hurtado notes that "devotion to Jesus as divine erupted suddenly and quickly, not gradually and late, among first-century circles of followers. . . . The origins lie in Jewish Christian circles of the earliest years." *Lord Jesus Christ,* p. 650.

62. Keener, *Acts,* p. 312.

63. Keener, *Acts,* pp. 312-13.

64. Hurtado, "Christology," pp. 228-29.

65. Hurtado suggests that "Luke may have been more concerned to reflect his sources of information about early Christological statements than to assert some distinctive Christological teaching of his own." "Christology," p. 226.

66. Ridderbos, "Speeches," p. 5.

Conclusion

After surveying the three areas that inform discussions about the historicity of the Petrine speeches, it has become clear that the evidence is inconclusive at best. However, several additional factors in the speeches support the hypothesis that the issue of historicity was more important to Luke than scholars have previously acknowledged. First, the length of the speeches in Acts is considerably shorter than those found in other works of ancient history, suggesting that the speeches in Acts are not vehicles for Luke to demonstrate his rhetorical ability through expansion, but rather succinct summaries of lengthier addresses.[67] Second, a significant factor in determining the historicity of the speeches is whether the historian had access to traditional materials, and his proximity to the events he describes. It is generally acknowledged that Luke was closer in temporal proximity to the events he describes than Thucydides or Livy were to their subject matter.[68] It is also likely that Luke was acquainted with Paul and other characters in his narrative.[69] Finally, Luke's use of the Gospel of Mark in his Gospel proves to be remarkably instructive for understanding how the evangelist adapts a known source. Luke contains about half of the Gospel of Mark,[70] but when he uses Mark as a source he follows it closely and rarely expands Mark's text. In comparison with Matthew's more extensive use of Mark, Luke includes more Markan details, though he presents them in his own style and language. Luke's usage of Mark may show that Luke can be a reasonably faithful redactor of existing traditions.[71]

Did Peter really say the things attributed to him in the speeches in Acts? It appears as though there may well be historical value to the Petrine speeches in Acts, but the definition of historicity must be carefully nuanced to reflect the expectations of Luke's audience.[72] Audiences of ancient historiography simply did not expect to find verbatim reports of speeches, and therefore it was likely

---

67. Keener, *Acts,* pp. 260, 300.

68. Joseph A. Fitzmyer, *The Acts of the Apostles,* AB 31 (New York: Doubleday, 1998), p. 105.

69. Keener contends that Luke relies on oral eyewitnesses for most of the events in Acts and may personally have been present for others. *Acts,* p. 318. See also Darrell L. Bock, *Acts,* BECNT (Grand Rapids: Baker Academic, 2007), p. 21.

70. Only 53 percent of Mark appears in Luke, while 92 percent of Mark can be found in Matthew.

71. Bock, *Acts,* p. 23.

72. See also Osvaldo Padilla, "The Speeches in Acts: Historicity, Theology, and Genre," in Adams and Pahl, *Issues in Luke-Acts,* pp. 171-93.

not Luke's intention to reproduce what Peter literally said on any particular occasion. Even though Peter may not have said all the things that Luke includes in the speeches, the words of Peter in Acts confirm the identification of the historical Peter as a prominent figure in the early church — as the witness par excellence of Jesus' resurrection,[73] as the speaker and representative of the Twelve, and as the evangelist depicted as faithfully receiving and carrying out the commission of the risen Jesus to preach the gospel.

73. In 1 Cor. 15:5, Peter is listed as first of the apostles to see the risen Jesus; in 1 Pet. 5:1, the writer claims to be "a witness [μάρτυς] to the sufferings of Christ"; Luke's resurrection narrative emphasizes Peter's role as a key witness of Jesus' resurrection: "The Lord has risen indeed, and he has appeared to Simon!" (Luke 24:34; cf. 24:12); see also Larry R. Helyer, *The Life and Witness of Peter* (Downers Grove, Ill.: IVP Academic, 2012), p. 72.

CHAPTER 6

"Another Shall Gird Thee":
Probative Evidence for the Death of Peter

Timothy D. Barnes

The present essay develops an argument I first advanced in a lecture at the University of Jena in November 2008, then refined in a seminar at New College, Edinburgh, in 2009 and published in 2010 in a book on early Christian hagiography and the history of the Roman Empire.[1] Unfortunately, the book was published too late to be taken into account by Ernst Dassmann in his thorough and able survey of the long scholarly debate over the question, "Was Peter ever in Rome?" which was published in the following year.[2] Fortunately, however, in 2012 Markus Bockmuehl expressly drew attention to my thesis that Peter was burned alive, not crucified.[3]

At the conference "Peter in Earliest Christianity" in July 2013 I delivered a lecture with the deliberately provocative title "'Another Shall Gird Thee': New Testament 'Scholarship' and Ancient Evidence," which included the polemical discussion of some matters extraneous to Peter.[4] My conclusions about the

1. T. D. Barnes, *Early Christian Hagiography and Roman History*, Tria Corda, Jenaer Vorlesungen zu Judentum, Antike und Christentum/Jena Lectures on Judaism, Antiquity and Christianity 5 (Tübingen: Mohr Siebeck, 2010), pp. 5-9.

2. E. Dassmann, "Petrus in Rom? Zu den Hintergründen eines alten Streites," in *Petrus und Paulus in Rom: Eine interdisciplinäre Debatte*, ed. S. Heid, with R. von Haehling, V. M. Strocka, and M. Vielberg (Freiburg: Herder, 2011), pp. 13-31.

3. Markus Bockmuehl, *Simon Peter in Scripture and Memory: The New Testament Apostle in the Early Church* (Grand Rapids: Baker Academic, 2012), p. 4 n. 2.

4. The lecture contained a digression on John M. Rist, "Luke 2:2: Making Sense of the Date of Jesus' Birth," *JTS*, n.s. 56 (2005): 489-91, which I characterized as a piece of pseudo-scholarship. Rist argued that the name Quirinius (Κυρηνίου) in Luke 2:2 is a mistake for Quintilius (Κοιντιλίου), proposed that we "read ἐπαρχίαν (province) for οἰκουμένην (world)"

date, place, and mode of Peter's death met with greater acceptance from my audience than I had expected. To be sure, a skeptic in the audience confidently reasserted the hypercritical (and Protestant) view that there is no evidence earlier than the late second century that Peter ever set foot in Rome.[5] On the other hand, Peter Lampe and Markus Bockmuehl significantly strengthened my conclusion by emphasizing the relevance of supporting evidence that I had deliberately left out of account in the lecture, which I based exclusively on the evidence of John's Gospel and the Roman historian Tacitus, while Tobias Nicklas introduced evidence for Peter's death that I had overlooked. The structure of the present essay accordingly reflects the contribution of these three scholars to the lively discussion that followed my lecture.

I. John's Gospel and Tacitus

For the death of the apostle Peter, there is precisely one, and only one, item of direct and explicit evidence that is both early and reliable. It is found in the New Testament, in the last chapter of the Gospel according to John (21:18-19), a chapter that many have judged to be an addition to the original draft of the Gospel.[6]

ἀμὴν ἀμὴν λέγω σοι, ὅτε ἦς νεώτερος, ἐζώννυες σεαυτὸν καὶ περιεπάτεις ὅπου ἤθελες· ὅταν δὲ γηράσῃς, ἐκτενεῖς τὰς χεῖράς σου, καὶ ἄλλος σε ζώσει καὶ οἴσει ὅπου οὐ θέλεις. τοῦτο δὲ εἶπεν σημαίνων ποίῳ θανάτῳ δοξάσει τὸν θεόν. καὶ τοῦτο εἰπὼν λέγει αὐτῷ, Ἀκολούθει μοι.

This passage of John proves beyond all possible doubt that Peter did not undergo a normal crucifixion. More than a century ago Theodor Mommsen,

---

in Luke 2:1, that Luke or his source, as rewritten in this way, dated Jesus' birth to late 7 or early 6 BC when P. Quintilius Varus was governor of Syria — and that this date is historically correct. In support of these arresting claims Rist quoted Tertullian, *Adversus Marcionem* 4.19.10: *sed et census constat actos sub Augusto tunc in Iudaea per Sentium Saturninum, apud quos genus eius* [sc. of Christ] *inquirere potuissent.* I remarked that Rist's arguments reminded me of Humpty Dumpty's treatment of verbs in *Alice in Wonderland,* since he makes the evidence say what he wants it to say rather than what it actually says.

5. For a list of such naysayers, see Bockmuehl, *Simon Peter,* p. 4 n. 2.

6. The compositional problems of this chapter are intelligently discussed by William Barclay, *The Gospels and Acts,* vol. 2, *The Fourth Gospel and the Acts of the Apostles* (London: SCM, 1976), pp. 73-83. It is argued to be "integral to the Gospel" by Richard Bauckham, *Jesus and the Eyewitnesses: The Gospels as Eyewitness Testimony* (Grand Rapids: Eerdmans, 2006), esp. p. 396.

who has rarely, if ever, been cited in recent New Testament scholarship, set out the main evidence for how different crimes were defined and punished by the Roman state.[7] There are three essential facts about crucifixion in the Roman Empire. First, only men were crucified: to the best of my knowledge, there is no example at all of a woman being crucified in the ancient world. Second, crucifixion was a degrading form of execution reserved for slaves and for antisocial criminals such as rebels and brigands. Jesus was crucified, according to the Gospels, together with two brigands, and the placard Pilate placed above his head stated explicitly that he was being executed as a rebel.[8] Third, men who were crucified were stripped of their clothes before being crucified completely naked. In the case of Jesus, the Gospel of Matthew reports that when the Roman soldiers had nailed him to the cross, they cast lots for his clothes, which they had previously removed (Matt. 27:35, quoting Ps. 22:18). Matthew means precisely what he says: the soldiers removed Jesus' clothes, all of them; they had not merely removed his robe leaving his private parts decently covered with a loin cloth. In this they were following normal practice, as Matthew's original readers would have known full well.[9] To suppose that Jesus' genitals were decently covered by a loin cloth, as they are on crucifixes and in almost all artistic depictions of his crucifixion, both

7. For more recent discussion of crucifixion as a penalty in Roman law, see Peter Garnsey, *Social Status and Legal Privilege in the Roman Empire* (Oxford: Oxford University Press, 1970), pp. 126-29; H.-W. Kuhn, "Die Kreuzesstrafe während der frühen Kaiserzeit. Ihre Wirklichkeit und Wertung in der Umwelt des Christentums," *Aufstieg und Niedergang der römischen Welt* 2.25.1 (Berlin: de Gruyter, 1982), pp. 648-793; Jeanne Robert and Louis Robert, *Fouilles d'Amyzon en Carie,* vol. 1, *Exploration, Histoire, Monnaies et Inscriptions* (Paris: Commission des fouilles et missions archéologiques au Ministère des relations extérieures, 1983), pp. 259-63; J.-J. Aubert, "A Double Standard in Roman Criminal Law? The Death Penalty and Social Structure in Late Republican and Early Imperial Rome," in *Speculum Iuris: Roman Law as a Reflexion of Social and Economic Life in Antiquity,* ed. J.-J. Aubert and B. Sirks (Ann Arbor: University of Michigan Press, 2002), pp. 110-30.

8. W. Eck, *Rom und Judaea: Fünf Vorträge zur römischen Herrschaft in Palaestina,* Tria Corda 2 (Tübingen: Mohr Siebeck, 2007), pp. 160-61; cf. J. Geiger, "Titulus crucis," *Scripta Classica Israelica* 15 (1996): 202-8; P. L. Maier, "The Inscription on the Cross of Jesus of Nazareth," *Hermes* 124 (1996): 58-75.

9. So, briefly, Helen K. Bond, *The Historical Jesus: A Guide for the Perplexed* (London: T&T Clark, 2012), pp. 162-64. For a full discussion, see H. Fulda, *Das Kreuz und die Kreuzigung. Eine antiquarische Untersuchung* (Breslau: Koebner, 1878), pp. 144-47, who duly cited Artemidorus, *Oneirocritica* 2.53 (quoted below) and included at the end of his book a lithograph of the "Wahrscheinlichste Kreuzigung des Erlösers," which depicts Christ from the left side and without a loin cloth, his hands nailed and his feet tied by a rope to a tree trunk without a crosspiece (tab. 1).

contradicts the Gospels and entails the impossible corollary that the Roman soldiers who crucified Jesus made a unique exception for him because they knew that he was the Son of God in the full Christian sense before they started to fix him to the cross.

One item of evidence not quoted by Mommsen is even more clear-cut than those he did adduce. The second-century writer Artemidorus of Daldis composed a work on the interpretation of dreams, whose hermeneutical approach is the antithesis of Sigmund Freud's: whereas Freud found the meaning of dreams in the psyche and the past experiences of the individual dreamer, Artemidorus interpreted dreams according to the objective reality of the dreamer's social and economic status on the assumption that dreams could predict the future of the individual dreamer either directly or allusively and symbolically.[10] Hence Artemidorus interpreted dreams in a way that has similarities to Joseph's interpretation of the Egyptian Pharaoh's dreams of seven beautiful and well-nourished cows emerging from the Nile only to be eaten by seven ugly and emaciated cows and of seven sheaves of choice, fully grown grain being consumed by seven sheaves of empty husks as indicating seven years of plenty followed by seven years of famine (Genesis 41). Toward the end of his second book Artemidorus considered what significance it might have to dream of dying in various different ways (2.49-66). His discussion of dreaming of being crucified proceeds as follows:

> Being crucified is auspicious for all seafarers. For the cross, like a ship, is made of wood and nails, and a ship's mast resembles a cross. It is also auspicious for poor men. For a crucified man is raised high and his substance suffices to feed many <birds>.[11] But it also means the revelation of secrets, since a crucified man can be seen by all. On the other hand, it signifies harm for rich men, since the crucified are stripped naked and

10. S. R. F. Price, "The Future of Dreams: From Freud to Artemidorus," *Past and Present* 113 (1986): 3-37; see also the index of the specific dreams elucidated in Artemidorus books 1-4 in D. E. Harris-McCoy, *Artemidorus' Oneirocritica: Text, Translation, and Commentary* (Oxford: Oxford University Press, 2012), pp. 571-74.

11. The noun οἰωνούς ("birds") must be inserted as the object of the verb τρέφει as in the Teubner editions of R. Hercher (Leipzig, 1864) and R. Pack (Leipzig, 1963). The insertion was first proposed by Hercher in an article preparatory to his edition, "Lectiones Artemidoreae," *Rheinisches Museum* 17 (1862): 81-98, 407-423, which adduced the parallel phrase at 4.49, where Artemidorus also argues that for a poor man to dream of being crucified presages future wealth because a crucified man "nourishes many birds" (διὰ τὸ πολλοὺς τρέφειν οἰωνούς). The French translation by A.-J. Festugière, *Artémidore: La Clef des Songes* (Paris: Vrin, 1975), p. 166, renders the clause as "nourit beaucoup de rapaces."

lose their flesh (γυμνοὶ γὰρ σταυροῦνται καὶ τὰς σάρκας ἀπολλύουσιν οἱ σταυρωθέντες).[12]

Artemidorus could hardly be more explicit: those who were crucified were crucified naked, and when they expired their bodies were normally left on the cross for their flesh to be pecked away by vultures and other such birds. In Judea of course the Roman authorities respected Jewish religious taboos: hence after Jesus expired Pilate acted on the request of the Jewish leaders and ordered the legs of the two criminals crucified with Jesus to be broken so that they died quickly and the bodies of the three executed men could be taken down from the cross before sunset as Jewish law required (John 19:31-37; cf. Deut. 21:23).[13]

The allusion to Peter's execution in John's Gospel cannot refer to a death by crucifixion because it states that Peter died clothed, not naked. The allusion dovetails perfectly with what Tacitus reports about the emperor Nero's execution of Christians in Rome in the year 64. Regrettably, New Testament scholars who have written about Peter have failed to make a crucial distinction between two similar but in fact different methods of execution employed in the Roman Empire; indeed, Martin Hengel's supposedly authoritative book on crucifixion, to which appeal has so often been made, systematically confuses them.[14] Crucifixion was a long, slow, and excruciatingly painful form of execution, in which death normally came from asphyxiation as the crucified man gradually became too exhausted and too feeble to be able to hoist his body up

---

12. Modified very slightly from the translation by R. J. White, *The Interpretation of Dreams: The Oneirocritica by Artemidorus: Translation and Commentary* (Park Ridge, N.J.: Noyes, 1975), p. 127, whose commentary correctly adduces Matt. 27:35 (p. 153 n. 127). (I have not been able to consult either of the two later versions of White's book, published respectively by Original Books [Torrance, Calif., 1990] and Barton Press [Largs, 1992].)

The translation of the passage by Harris-McCoy, *Artemidorus'* Oneirocritica, p. 237, is unsatisfactory and also untrue to the original in several respects, though not on the central point at issue here: "To be crucified is good for all who are sailing. For in fact the crucifix is made from wood and nails just like a ship, and its mast is like a crucifix. And it is also good for poor men. For in fact a man who has been crucified is 'lofty' and nourishes many birds. And it exposes secrets. For a man who has been crucified is visible. And it harms the rich. For people are crucified in the nude and those who are crucified lose their flesh."

13. Bond, *Historical Jesus*, p. 164. As so often, John has superior historical information to the Synoptic Gospels, which omit this episode and pass directly from the death of Jesus to the recovery of his body by Joseph of Arimathea and his burial, which is recorded in all four Gospels (Matt. 27:57-61; Mark 15:42-47; Luke 23:50-56; John 19:38-42).

14. Martin Hengel, *Crucifixion in the Ancient World and the Folly of the Message of the Cross* (London: SCM, 1977); cf. Barnes, *Early Christian Hagiography*, pp. 331-42.

by pressing on his feet or ankles so that he could breathe and supply oxygen to his lungs. In contrast, burning alive brought death quickly because, before they were set on fire, victims were normally, though not invariably, clothed in a special tunic that, in Seneca's words to Lucilius, had been "smeared and interwoven with inflammable materials" (*Letter* 14.5).[15] Moreover, it is well attested that later Christians suffered martyrdom by being burned alive tied to a stake or upright post, sometimes with their arms splayed wide as if they were being crucified.[16]

In July 64 a large part of the city of Rome was destroyed by fire: of the fourteen districts *(regiones)* into which Augustus had divided the city, only four were completely untouched; three were leveled to the ground and "in the other seven there survived a few traces of housing, mauled and charred" (*Ann.* 15.40.2, trans. A. J. Woodman).[17] There were persistent rumors that Nero himself had ordered the fire to be started in order to build a new palace for himself, and when normal measures failed to quell the rumors, the emperor sought a scapegoat. He fixed on the tiny community of Christians in Rome, whom he accused of starting the fire, an accusation that derived plausibility from the fact that at this time the Christians of Rome were probably concentrated in the modern Trastevere, a quarter that had remained unscathed by the conflagration because it lay across the River Tiber from the main part of the city.[18] All who could be identified as Christians were arrested, and their admission that they were Christians was treated as tantamount to a confession of arson. They were then handed over to the imperial authorities so that Nero could exercise his talents as a provider of spectacles for the people while diverting suspicion from himself.

Like the great Mikado in Gilbert and Sullivan, Nero decided to make the punishment fit the alleged crime by devising novel methods of execution that would advertise the guilt of his victims, who were presented as both arsonists and inveterate enemies of the whole human race. Tacitus provides the only detailed account of this episode to survive (*Ann.* 15.44), and its historicity has

---

15. For execution by this *tunica molesta,* see also Martial 4.86.8, 10.25.5; Juvenal 8.235.

16. Barnes, *Early Christian Hagiography,* pp. 338-41, noting that, according to the *Acts of Carpus, Papylus, and Agathonice* (*BHG*[3] 293; *BHLAMA* 1622m), both Carpus and Papylus suffered a mock crucifixion by being hoisted upright on a cross and then burned alive — just like Peter and other victims of Nero.

17. On the fire and its consequences, see now E. J. Champlin, *Nero* (Cambridge, Mass.: Harvard University Press, 2003), pp. 48-49, 121-26, 178-200.

18. Peter Lampe, *From Paul to Valentinus: Christians at Rome in the First Two Centuries,* trans. M. Steinhauser, ed. M. D. Johnson (Minneapolis: Fortress, 2003), pp. 19-24, 47-58.

withstood ferocious critical attacks.[19] In accordance with his normal stylistic habits, however, Tacitus is brief and allusive. Moreover, the text of the relevant passage is corrupt in the only independent manuscript of books 11-16 of the *Annals,* so that many modern discussions have proceeded on the basis of a false reading.[20] The recent editions by Franz Römer and Heinz Heubner, however, accept the diagnosis of the textual problems offered by Georg Andresen nearly a century ago and print the passage as follows:

> et pereuntibus addita ludibria, ut ferarum tergis contecti laniatu canum interirent aut crucibus adfixi [aut flammandi atque] ubi defecisset dies in usum nocturni luminis urerentur.[21]

> And, as they perished, mockeries were added, so that, covered in the hides of wild beasts, they expired from mutilation by dogs, or were burned fixed to crosses for use as nocturnal illumination on the dwindling of daylight.[22]

Tacitus emphasizes that mockeries were added to the normal modes of execution *(pereuntibus addita ludibria),* and Edward Champlin has definitively identified what these were.[23] Nero's innovation with the first group of Christians was to replace the normal punishment of exposure to wild beasts by dressing the Christians in animal skins as if they themselves were wild beasts, and then setting savage hunting dogs on them to maul them to death. The second group of Christians were set alight as torches after being clothed in inflammable tunics: the splaying of their arms alluded to the crucifixion of Jesus, while their use as human torches after dark represented a symbolic revenge for their alleged burning of the temple of Luna Noctiluca (that is, "Luna Light of the Night") on the Palatine, which had previously been illuminated at night. Such a punishment was not a modified form of crucifixion, but a

19. Tacitus provides the only independent ancient account: Tertullian names Tacitus as his authority and his account is completely dependent on him (*Apol.* 5.3), while Eusebius derived his knowledge of the episode from a Greek translation of Tertullian's *Apologeticum* (*H.E.* 2.25.4; cf. 2.2.4-6).

20. For example, H.-W. Kuhn, *Aufstieg und Niedergang der römischen Welt* 2.25.1 (Berlin: de Gruyter, 1982), pp. 698-701.

21. F. Römer, *P. Corneli Taciti Annalium libri XV-XVI* (Vienna, Cologne, and Graz: Böhlau, 1976), p. 67; H. Heubner, *P. Corneli Taciti libri quae supersunt,* 1² (Leipzig: Teubner, 1994), p. 369.

22. A. J. Woodman, *Tacitus: The Annals* (Indianapolis: Hackett, 2004), p. 326 (with modifications).

23. Champlin, *Nero,* pp. 122-23, 302 n. 29.

modified form of burning alive, in German "ein Feuerstod." Indeed, there is no reliable evidence that Christians were ever crucified for being Christians unless they were slaves, except perhaps in the last paroxysm of pagan violence and sadism at the very end of the "Great Persecution" in the early fourth century.[24] One of Nero's victims in 64 was the apostle Peter, whose charred and perhaps unrecognizable body was presumably thrown into the River Tiber.[25]

II. The Traditional Exegesis of John 21:18

In the words of the venerable Authorized Version of the Bible, the risen Christ appeared to Peter and said to him:

> "Verily, verily, I say unto thee, When thou wast young, thou girdest thyself, and walkedst whither thou wouldest; but when thou shalt be old, thou shalt stretch forth thy hands, and another shall gird thee, and carry thee whither thou wouldest not." This spake he, signifying by what death he should glorify God.

Despite the archaic language, this is overall a more accurate translation than most modern and supposedly more scholarly versions of the original Greek. The New Revised Standard Version, for example, gives the crucial Greek verb ζώννυμι a much more restricted sense:

> "Very truly, I tell you, when you were younger, you used to fasten your own belt and go wherever you wished. But when you grow old, you will stretch out your hands, and someone else will fasten a belt around you and take you where you do not wish to go." (He said this to indicate the kind of death by which he would glorify God.)

24. Barnes, *Early Christian Hagiography*, pp. 340-42.

25. It cannot be excluded a priori that Christians of Rome rescued some relics of Peter and buried them (or gave them a symbolic burial) on the Vatican Hill, where a shrine of Peter was constructed a century later (§ III). However, the bones stolen by Mgr. Ludwig Kaas from the official excavations under the Vatican in 1941 and later proclaimed to be those of Saint Peter by Pope Paul VI on June 27, 1968, are more likely those of either Silvester or Julius, who were bishops of Rome from 314 to 335 and from 336 to 352 respectively: see Barnes, *Early Christian Hagiography*, p. 406, with appeal to H. G. Thümmel, *Die Memorien für Petrus and Paulus in Rom. Die archäologischen Denkmäler und die literarische Tradition* (Berlin: de Gruyter, 1999), p. 70; A. H. B. Logan, "Constantine, the Liber Pontificalis and the Christian Basilicas of Rome," *Studia Patristica* 50 (2010): 31-53, at pp. 44-48.

TIMOTHY D. BARNES

Similarly the Jerusalem Bible, which prints Jesus' words as Hebrew-style verse, offers:

"I tell you most solemnly,/when you were young
you put on your own belt/and walked where you liked;
but when you grow old/you will stretch out your hands,
and somebody else will put a belt around you
and take you where you would rather not go."

In these words he indicated the kind of death by which Peter would give glory to God.

Both the New Revised Standard Version and the Jerusalem Bible take the Greek verb, ζώννυμι, which occurs in this passage both in the second-person singular of the imperfect tense and in the third-person singular of the future tense, in a much narrower sense than the Authorized Version. But the original and primary meaning of the verb ζώννυμι was "to gird," "to clothe," or "to put on clothing," and the verb was used especially in the context of preparation for a pugilistic conflict, an athletic contest or battle.[26] John sets Jesus' words to Peter in the context of the risen Christ's appearance to several of his disciples near Tiberias. When the disciples espy Jesus on the seashore from their fishing boat, Peter puts on a tunic[27] and dives into the Sea of Galilee while the others beach their boat in the normal way before they all eat together (John 21:1-14). Here the King James translators render τὸν ἐπενδύτην διεζώσατο, ἦν γὰρ γυμνός (John 21:7) as "he girt his fisher's coat unto him (for he was naked)," where the New Revised Standard Version has the prosaic "he put on some clothes, for he was naked" and the Jerusalem Bible lapses into inaccurate colloquialism when it offers "Simon Peter, who had practically nothing on, wrapped his clothes around him." These verbal quibbles matter little, however, since whatever the precise nuances of the Greek phrases ἐζώννυες σεαυτόν and ἄλλος σε ζώσει may be, the risen Jesus tells Peter that, whereas he used to dress himself as a boy, another will dress him when he is put to death.

What have recent New Testament scholars made of the risen Christ's

26. H. G. Liddell and R. Scott, revised by H. S. Jones, *A Greek-English Lexicon,* 9th ed. (Oxford: Clarendon, 1940), p. 759. The *Supplement* (Oxford: Clarendon, 1968), p. 68, adds the sense "for walking," adducing John 21:18; Acts 12:8.

27. The Greek noun ἐπενδύτης is rarely found in literary texts: it normally means "tunic" and refers specifically to a man's tunic or an outer tunic worn over an inner one: see, e.g., Julius Pollux, *Onomasticon* 7.12.45.

words to Peter? The answer is simple: without exception, they have failed to understand the words' precise significance, even though they are not unanimous on how to interpret them. There is no point in attempting to compile an exhaustive list of modern commentators and exegetes. It will suffice to cite a representative sample of the most respected, widely used, and scholarly commentaries. The Anchor Bible insists that the two phrases in which the Greek verb ζώννυμι occurs must mean "you used to fasten your own belt" and "another will fasten a belt around you," and asserts that the words "you will stretch out your hands" must refer to crucifixion.[28] C. K. Barrett stated, correctly enough, that stretching out the hands often refers to crucifixion, but he badly misinterpreted the significance of the crucial verb ζώννυμι when he observed that "criminals were always fastened to the cross in part, and sometimes wholly, by ropes."[29] Rudolf Bultmann, whose opinion was endorsed by Oscar Cullmann, correctly saw that the Greek verb ζώννυμι means "to gird" and not "to bind," but he argued that the phrase "you will stretch out your hands" refers not to Peter's manner of death but to the aged Peter being led to execution by another, since "the picture paints the helplessness of the old man who stretches out his hands to feel for support or for someone to lead him."[30] Ernst Haenchen rightly took issue with Bultmann's ad hoc postulate that a proverb about the helplessness of the aged lies behind the words that John puts into Christ's mouth, but then went on to claim quite wrongly that the author introduced the phrases "you girded yourself" and "another shall gird you" in order to "indicate crucifixion" as the kind of death that Peter would suffer, and he held, following Walter Bauer, that the phrase "the outstretched hands" refers to the criminal's carrying of the crossbar of the cross "to the place of execution with his arms outstretched and bound to the cross-beam."[31] This interpretation

---

28. Raymond E. Brown, *The Gospel according to John (xiii-xxi)*, AB 29A (Garden City, N.Y.: Doubleday, 1970), pp. 1101, 1107-8.

29. C. K. Barrett, *The Gospel according to St John: An Introduction with Commentary and Notes on the Greek Text* (London: SPCK, 1955), p. 487.

30. Rudolf Bultmann, *Das Evangelium des Johannes*, 11th ed. (Göttingen: Vandenhoeck & Ruprecht, 1950), p. 552 = *The Gospel of John: A Commentary*, trans. G. R. Beasley-Murray (Oxford: Blackwell, 1971; trans. from *Das Evangelium des Johannes*, 18th ed. [Göttingen: Vandenhoeck & Ruprecht, 1964]), pp. 713-14 nn. 7-8; cf. Oscar Cullmann, *Petrus: Jünger, Apostel, Märtyrer: Das historische und das theologische Petrusproblem*, 2nd ed. (Zürich: Zwingli-Verlag, 1960), p. 79 = *Peter: Disciple, Apostle, Martyr*, trans. Floyd V. Filson, 2nd ed. (London: SCM, 1962), p. 88, who asserted that "it is not entirely certain whether the 'stretching out of the hands' in John 21:18 is intended to indicate a special manner of execution, by crucifixion."

31. E. Haenchen, *Das Johannesevangelium. Ein Kommentar*, ed. U. Busse (Tübingen: Mohr, 1980), pp. 589-91 = *John*, vol. 2, *A Commentary on the Gospel of John Chapters 7-21*, trans.

of the outstretched arms was also espoused by George Beasley-Murray, who argued that, since "by the time that this chapter was written" Peter had been crucified, "the obscurity of the saying was clarified by the event, and thereby it becomes the earliest witness we possess to the death of Peter by crucifixion."[32] Markus Bockmuehl, who is not strictly speaking a biblical commentator or exegete, has discussed the death of Peter at length twice. In 2007 he asserted, with appeal to Foakes Jackson, that there is a "surprising lack of direct evidence for Peter's fate," as if John 21:18 were not direct evidence, then accepted Richard Bauckham's argument that "to 'stretch out the hands' would be readily recognized as alluding to crucifixion."[33] And in his recent monograph on the traditions about Peter, Bockmuehl consistently assumes that John 21:18 indicates that Peter will suffer "crucifixion in old age, an interpretation well understood in sources as early as the mid-second century."[34]

The recent study of the literary texts relating to Peter in Rome by Otto Zwierlein unfortunately represents a nadir in historical criticism.[35] Zwierlein made his reputation as an editor of classical texts, and his critical edition of the second-century *Martyrdom of Peter*, which includes an account of the death of Paul, "on a fresh manuscript basis" is truly excellent.[36] But Zwierlein

---

Robert W. Funk (Philadelphia: Fortress, 1984), pp. 226-27, citing Walter Bauer, *Das Johannesevangelium*, 3rd ed. (Tübingen: J. C. B. Mohr, 1933), pp. 238-39, who in turn appeals to Fulda, *Das Kreuz und die Kreuzigung*, pp. 119-26, 137-42, 209-29.

32. G. R. Beasley-Murray, *John*, WBC 36, 2nd ed. (Nashville: Thomas Nelson, 1999), 407-9.

33. Markus Bockmuehl, "Peter's Death in Rome? Back to Front and Upside Down," *SJT* 60 (2007): 1-23, at p. 21 = *The Remembered Peter in Ancient Reception and Modern Debate*, WUNT 1/262 (Tübingen: Mohr Siebeck, 2010), pp. 114-32 (chap. 6. "Peter's Death in Rome?"), at p. 131, adducing F. J. Foakes Jackson, *Peter, Prince of Apostles: A Study in the History and Tradition of Christianity* (London: Hodder & Stoughton, 1927), p. vii; Richard J. Bauckham, "The Martyrdom of Peter in Early Christian Literature," *Aufstieg und Niedergang der römischen Welt* 2.26.1 (Berlin: de Gruyter, 1992), pp. 539-95, at pp. 546-50.

34. Bockmuehl, *Simon Peter*, p. 66, citing the *Acts of Andrew* 20; Tertullian, *Scorpiace* 15.3: *tunc* (sc. in Rome in 64 CE) *Petrus ab altero cingitur, cum cruci adstringitur*. Bockmuehl's index has eight entries under the rubric "Peter: crucifixion of" (p. 222). Tertullian's words (let it be noted) are consistent with the hypothesis argued above that Peter was burnt alive fixed to a cross.

35. See trenchant criticisms in the volume *Petrus und Paulus in Rom: Eine interdisziplinäre Debatte*, ed. S. Heid et al. (Freiburg: Herder, 2011), esp. the refutations by R. Riesner, "Apostelgeschichte, Pastoralbriefe, 1. Clemensbrief unde die Martyrien der Apostel in Rom" (pp. 153-79); H. E. Lona, " 'Petrus in Rom' und der erste Clemensbrief" (pp. 221-46); C. Gnilka, "Philologisches zur römischen Petrustradition" (pp. 241-82).

36. O. Zwierlein, *Petrus in Rom. Die literarischen Zeugnisse. Mit einer kritischen Edition der Martyrien des Petrus und Paulus auf neuer handschriftlicher Grundlage*, Untersuchungen

is essentially an *Altphilolog*, and like many of that ilk he goes badly astray when he attempts to use literary texts as historical evidence. Zwierlein argues that John's Gospel refers not to the clothing of Peter before he was led to death, but to his being shackled in fetters before being "led to prison or, more generally, to martyrdom," perhaps to death in the arena to be mauled to death by wild animals, and he continues: "to deduce from John 21:18 that the author of this added chapter knew about the death of Peter by crucifixion, seems reckless."[37] That exegesis of John's words can only be described as perverse, while the second argument is clumsily expressed. Zwierlein writes of "*the* death of Peter by crucifixion" (emphasis added: the German reads "vom Kreuzestod Petri") as if Peter had in fact been crucified, whereas he ought to have spoken of "a presumed death by crucifixion" ("von einem vermütlichen Kreuzestod Petri"). On wider historical matters, Zwierlein enthusiastically embraces historical opinions that are both hypercritical and certainly erroneous: for example, in addition to denying that Peter ever set foot in Rome, he asserts that the letters of Ignatius of Antioch cannot be dated any earlier than the first decade of the reign of Marcus Aurelius, that is, between 161 and 170, and are in fact a pseudonymous confection from around 170.[38] Strangest of all, though he cites the passage several times, Zwierlein avoids any substantive discussion of Tacitus's account of Nero's execution of Christians in Rome in 64, of whose relevance to Peter he seems blissfully unaware.[39]

III. Peter in Rome

The preceding discussion has of set purpose concentrated on the two items of evidence that, by the normal criteria employed in historical scholarship, decisively establish that Peter was burned to death in Rome in the autumn of the year 64. This conclusion can be reinforced by consideration of other evidence I have so far deliberately not deployed lest its comparative imprecision

---

zur antiken Literatur und Geschichte 96 (Berlin: Walter de Gruyter, 2009; 2nd ed., 2010), pp. 337-449.

37. Zwierlein, *Petrus in Rom* (2009), p. 121: "Das laüft . . . auf die Vorstellung, daß Petrus in Fesseln in ein Gefängnis oder — im allgemein — zum Martyrium geführt wird. . . . Aus Joh 21.18 abzuleiten, daß der Verfasser dieses Zusatzkapitels Kenntnis vom Kreuzestod Petri gehabt habe, scheint mehr als kühn."

38. Zwierlein, *Petrus in Rom*, pp. 183-237.

39. Tacitus, *Ann.* 15.44, is adduced by Zwierlein, *Petrus in Rom*, pp. 24 n. 71, 29 n. 82, 119 n. 238, 309 n. 174, 311, 312.

detract or distract from the compelling force of the inferences drawn from John's Gospel and Tacitus set out above.

There is ample archaeological, liturgical, and literary evidence for a cult of Peter on the Vatican Hill from the second half of the second century onward, which Peter Lampe masterfully surveyed in his lecture at the Edinburgh conference, which is printed in this volume.[40] From this varied evidence it is clear that the Christians of Rome a century after Peter's death firmly believed that Peter had died in Rome, since a shrine was built around 160 on the Vatican Hill over the place where either Peter's body or at least some relic of Peter was believed to be. However, the traditional inference from this abundant later evidence to the middle of the first century is invalid. First, it is extremely doubtful whether the Christians of the late second century possessed any authentic evidence for Christianity in the age of the apostles beyond what they could read in the New Testament. The clearest example of their ignorance is provided by Irenaeus, who dated the book of Revelation a whole generation too late, after the death of Domitian in 96, even though internal criteria prove that it was written between the death of Nero in June 68 and victory of Vespasian, who had become master of the whole of the Roman Empire by the end of the year 69.[41] Second, Christians from the late second century onward believed that Peter had not only been crucified (Tertullian, *Praescr.* 36.3: *habes Romam . . . ubi Petrus passioni dominicae adaequatur; Scorpiace* 15.3), but that he had been crucified upside down (Eusebius, *H.E.* 3.1.2, quoting Origen's lost commentaries on Genesis), and the pious legend that he was crucified upside down was invented before the end of the second century (*Martyrdom of Peter* 8.3/-4.1 Zwierlein).[42]

There is also literary evidence from the late first century, namely, the *Letter of the Church of Rome to the Church of Corinth,* otherwise known as the first epistle of Clement, whose relevance to Peter has long been recognized.[43] Commenting on my lecture in Edinburgh, Markus Bockmuehl eloquently reiterated the relevance of this letter to the death of Peter, and his comments have encouraged me to advance a new interpretation here. The letter passes

40. Chapter 18.

41. Barnes, *Early Christian Hagiography,* pp. 36-40.

42. R. A. Lipsius, *Acta Apostolorum Apocrypha* (Leipzig, 1891), 1:92-97: translated into English by J. K. Elliott, *The Apocryphal New Testament: A Collection of Apocryphal Christian Literature in an English Translation* (Oxford: Oxford University Press, 1993), pp. 424-26.

43. The fullest and most incisive treatment of the date remains the classic discussion by J. B. Lightfoot, *Apostolic Fathers,* 1^2, *S. Clement of Rome* 1 (London: Macmillan, 1890), pp. 346-58; for a sensible brief outline of the parameters of the problem, see Bart D. Ehrman, *The Apostolic Fathers* 1 (Cambridge, Mass.: Harvard University Press, 2003), pp. 23-25.

in review a series of examples of those who have been killed or persecuted for their devotion to God because of "jealousy and envy" (*1 Clement* 3–6). First come some examples from the Old Testament (*1 Clement* 4) — Cain's murder of Abel (Gen. 4:3-8), Jacob ordered by his mother to flee the wrath of Esau (Gen. 27:41-42), the enslavement of Joseph (Gen. 37:12-36), the flight of Moses after he killed an Egyptian (Exod. 2:11-15), Aaron and Miriam (Num. 12:1-15), Dathan and Abiram, who were punished by God when they opposed Moses (Num. 16:12-15, 23-33), and David, whom Saul tried to kill (1 Sam. 18:10-11; 19:9–24:22). The writer then turns to the recent past:

> But so that we may stop giving ancient examples, let us come to those who became athletic contenders recently and take the noble examples of our own generation. Because of jealousy and envy the greatest and most upright pillars were persecuted and contended even unto death. Let us set before our eyes the good apostles. There is Peter, who because of unjust jealousy endured not one or two hardships, but many, and having thus borne witness he travelled to the place of glory that he deserved. Because of jealousy and strife Paul showed a prize for endurance. Seven times he bore chains, he was sent into exile and stoned, he became a herald both in the East and in the West, and he received a noble reputation for his faith. He taught righteousness to the whole world, he went to the limits of the West, he bore witness before the authorities, and thus he was released from this world and taken up to the holy place, having become the greatest example of endurance. (*1 Clement* 5)

The writer starts with Peter, who "contended even unto death" and "bore witness" before he "travelled to the place of glory that he deserved"; that is, Peter was put to death after he had confessed that he was a Christian, for in this passage the Greek aorist participle μαρτυρήσας must still have its primary etymological meaning of "having borne his testimony," since at the time when the letter was written, the concept of "martyrdom" had not yet been invented.[44] The letter, therefore, may and must be construed as direct evidence that Peter was put to death as a Christian, although the passage quoted does not explicitly locate his death in Rome.

---

44. Barnes, *Early Christian Hagiography,* pp. 12-19, developing the arguments of G. W. Bowersock, *Martyrdom and Rome* (Cambridge: Cambridge University Press, 1995), pp. 41-57, and with reference to earlier discussions of this passage, esp. Lightfoot, *Apostolic Fathers,* 1², *S. Clement of Rome* 2, pp. 26-27.

For Paul the letter confirms the evidence of the so-called Muratorian Canon and some apocryphal *Acts of the Apostles* that Paul went to Spain after being released from the two years of house arrest in Rome with which the canonical *Acts of the Apostles* concludes (Acts 28:30-31). The Muratorian Canon, which was compiled in Rome before the end of the second century,[45] states that

> Luke, <addressing> the "most excellent Theophilus," includes the individual events which were done in his own presence, as he makes manifestly clear by omitting the passion of Peter and also the departure of Paul as he set out from the city to Spain.[46]

Two apocryphal *Acts of the Apostles* also preserve memories of Paul's journey to Spain.[47] The *Letter of the Church of Rome to the Church of Corinth* confirms their testimony. For when a letter written in Rome to addressees in Corinth states that Paul went to "the boundaries of the West," these boundaries must lie to the west of Italy, and imply that Paul did indeed at some date proceed from Rome to Spain, as he had told the Christians of Rome that he intended to do before he came to the imperial city (Rom. 15:28). The letter also says that, after traveling to "the boundaries of the West," Paul bore witness before the Roman authorities, that is, before a Roman provincial governor in Spain.[48] It does not

45. Everett Ferguson, review of *The Muratorian Fragment and the Development of the Canon*, by Geoffrey Mark Hahnemann, *JTS*, n.s. 44 (1993): 691-97.

46. My translation from the diplomatic transcript by E. S. Buchanan, "The Codex Muratorianus," *JTS* 8 (1907): 537-45, at pp. 540-41, which reads: *Lucas obtime theofile conprindit quia sub praesentia eius singula gerebantur sicute et semote passionē petri evidenter declarat. Sed profectionē pauli au (corrected to "ab" by a later hand) urbes ad spaniā proficescentis* (Milan, Ambrosianus I 101 sup. fol. 10 verso, lines 4-8). The canon is an overly literal translation from a Greek original (*CPL* 83a = *CPG* 1862): for a critical edition, see H. Lietzmann, *Das Muratorische Fragment und die monarchischen Prologe zu den Evangelien* (Bonn: Marcus und Weber, 1902; 2nd ed. 1908), pp. 5-11. The English translation by G. Ogg in E. Hennecke and W. Schneemelcher, *New Testament Apocrypha*, ed. R. McL. Wilson (London: Lutterworth, 1963), 1:43, renders the German of E. Hennecke and W. Schneemelcher, *Neutestamentliche Apokryphen in deutscher Übersetzung* 1³ (Tübingen: J. C. B. Mohr [P. Siebeck], 1959), p. 19, not the Latin of the Muratorian Fragment itself.

47. *Actus Petri cum Simone* (*BHL* 6656) 1, 6; *Martyrium sanctorum apostolorum Petri et Pauli* (*BHG* 1491) 1, ed. Lipsius, *Acta Apostolorum Apocrypha* 1, pp. 45.8-15, 51.25-28; 118.2-3. The first two passages are translated into English by G. C. Stead, *New Testament Apocrypha*, ed. Wilson 2, pp. 279, 286; Elliott, *Apocryphal New Testament*, pp. 499, 503.

48. The traditional translation of ἐπὶ τῶν ἡγουμένων as "before the rulers" is seriously misleading, since at this period the phrase normally designates governors of Roman provinces: see the passages collected by H. J. Mason, *Greek Terms for Roman Institutions: A Lexicon and Analysis*,

follow, however, as I incautiously deduced before, that Paul was executed in Spain rather than in Rome.[49] Rather, the very strong tradition that both Peter and Paul died in Rome implies that the provincial governor in Spain before whom Paul appeared sent him, as a Roman citizen, to Rome either to be executed there or for his case to be reviewed by the emperor:[50] nearly fifty years later the younger Pliny, as governor of Bithynia around 110, executed most of those accused before him of being Christians who admitted the charge on the spot, but dispatched to Rome confessed Christians who were Roman citizens, apparently according to normal practice (*Epistula* 10.96.2-4).[51]

The letter continues by describing the deaths of numerous others besides Peter and Paul who are presented as having perished with them:

> These men who conducted themselves in a holy fashion were accompanied by a great multitude of the elect, who by suffering many indignities and tortures because of jealousy became an excellent example among us. Because of jealousy women were persecuted as Danaids and Dircae and suffered terrible and unholy indignities. But they confidently completed the race of faith and, though weak in body, received a noble reward. Jealousy estranged wives from their husbands and nullified the saying of our father Adam: "This now is bone from my bone and flesh from my flesh" (Genesis 2:23). Jealousy and strife have overturned great cities and uprooted great nations.[52]

The reference to "Danaids and Dircae" (Δαναΐδες καὶ Διρκαί) has appeared so puzzling to many scholars that it has sometimes been emended away. In the

---

American Studies in Papyrology 13 (Toronto: Hakkert, 1974), p. 52, to which add Dio 72(71).22.2 (3, p. 264.3 Boissevain), Eusebius, *H.E.* 3.33.3; 4.2.2, 8.6, 15.19; 6.3.3, 19.15, 41.21; 7.11.25; 9.1.2.

49. Barnes, *Early Christian Hagiography,* p. 35.

50. For the two possibilities, see F. Millar, *The Emperor in the Roman World (31 BC-AD 337)* (London: Duckworth, 1977), pp. 323, 507 n. 4, 557.

51. Trajan expressed his complete approval of both these actions: *actum quem debuisti, mi Secunde, in excutiendis causis eorum qui Christiani ad te delati sunt, secutus es* (Pliny, *Ep.* 10.97.1).

52. My translation, modified from Kirsopp Lake, *The Apostolic Fathers* 1 (London: Heinemann; New York: Macmillan, 1912), p. 19; Ehrman, *Apostolic Fathers* 1, pp. 45-47. For the crucial phrase τούτοις τοῖς ἀνδράσιν . . . συνηθροίσθη πλῆθος πολύ Ehrman offers the colorless and misleading "to these men . . . has been added a great multitude." Lake comes closer to the original with "to these men . . . was gathered a great multitude of the chosen." But even that attenuates the meaning of the verb, which elsewhere is normally used of people gathered together in the same place at the same time (e.g., LXX Joshua 22:12; 1 Kingdoms 7:7; 3 Kingdoms 11:14; Diodorus Siculus 14.77.3; 16.21.3; Josephus, *J.W.* 1.330; 2.513; *Ant.* 17.254).

middle of the nineteenth century the classical scholar Christopher Wordsworth, in his commentary on the Alexandrian bucolic poet Theocritus, proposed to read νεανίδες, παιδίσκαι after γύναικες[53] and in his first edition of the
letter Bishop Lightfoot printed his emendation,[54] though in his second edition
he merely obelized the transmitted words.[55] But the problematic words have
now been explained by Edward Champlin as conveying a specific allusion to
Nero's "fatal charades."[56] Why Danaids? Because the temple of Apollo on the
Palatine, dedicated in 28 BCE, had been destroyed in the fire of Rome, and the
portico surrounding the sacred area in front of the temple contained statues
of the fifty mythical daughters of King Danaus. Why Dircae? The mythical
Dirce, wife of the king of Thebes, was tied by her hair to a bull, which then
trampled and gored her to death. One of the buildings burned down in 64
was the amphitheater in the Campus Martius built by Statilius Taurus in 26
BCE, known as the amphitheater of Taurus or the amphitheater of the Bull
(Cassius Dio 62.18.2).

The *Letter of the Church of Rome to the Church of Corinth* thus states not
only that both Peter and many women perished in Nero's entertainments in
64, but also that Paul too was put to death in the immediate aftermath of the
great "Fire of Rome" in 64, though he, as a Roman citizen, was presumably
beheaded and thus spared the more prolonged and painful death to which
both Peter and the women were subjected.

IV. Apocryphal Evidence for the Death of Peter

Two passages in early Christian apocrypha are relevant to the death of Peter.
The *Ascension of Isaiah,* which survives wholly or partially in Ethiopic, Coptic,
Greek, Latin, and a Slavonic version identified as "Proto-Bulgarian,"[57] contains
a passage in which the Old Testament prophet Isaiah predicts that one of Jesus'
twelve original disciples will be killed by Nero:

53. C. Wordsworth, *Theocritus. Codicum manuscriptorum ope recensuit* (Cambridge:
Cambridge University Press, 1844), p. 213.

54. J. B. Lightfoot, *S. Clement of Rome: The Two Epistles to the Corinthians* (London and
Cambridge: Macmillan, 1869), pp. 51-52.

55. Lightfoot, *Apostolic* Fathers 1².1, pp. 32-33.

56. Champlin, *Nero,* pp. 123-25.

57. E. Norelli , with L. Perrone, P. Bettiolo, C. Leonardi, and G. Kossova, *Ascensio Isaiae.*
Textus. Corpus Christianorum, Series Apocryphorum 7 (Turnhout: Brepols, 1995).

Now, therefore, Hezekiah and Josab my son, these are the days of the completion of the world. And after it is completed, Beliar will descend, the great ruler, the king of this world, which he has ruled ever since it existed. He will descend from his firmament in the form of a man, a lawless emperor, a matricide — this is the king of this world — and he will persecute the plant which the Twelve Apostles of the Beloved will have planted, and one[58] of the Twelve will be delivered into his hands. This ruler will come in the form of that emperor, and with him will come all the powers of this world, and they will obey him in all that he desires. (4.1-4)[59]

The reference to Nero is clear,[60] and Champlin's discussion of Nero's posthumous reputation duly quotes the passage.[61] No Roman emperor other than Nero killed his mother, still less was any other Roman emperor famous precisely for killing his mother.[62] Moreover, this passage of the *Ascension of Isaiah* not only alludes to Nero's persecution of the Christians of Rome in 64 but also reflects the belief, widespread in the East in the decades after his death in 68, that Nero would reappear on earth restored to life again and usher in the end of the world.[63] Historical considerations, including this allusion to Nero redi-

---

58. The Greek has "one" (εἷς), the Ethiopic version "some": perhaps the original had "one or two" (εἷς ἢ δύο). Instead of "ruler" (ἄρχων) the Ethiopic version also has "angel."

59. Modified slightly from the translation by M. A. Knibb, "Martyrdom and Ascension of Isaiah (Second Century B.C.–Fourth Century A.D.): A New Translation and Introduction," in *Old Testament Pseudepigrapha*, ed. J. H. Charlesworth (London: Darton, Longman & Todd, 1985): 2:143-76, at p. 161, in the light of Knibb's notes, the earlier English translation by R. H. Charles, *The Ascension of Isaiah Translated from the Ethiopic Version* (London: Black, 1900), pp. 24-26, and the re-edition by Norelli, *Ascensio Isaiae*, p. 145, of *P. Amherst* 1, cols. XIII-XIV (*BHG*³ 957), first published by B. P. Grenfell and A. S. Hunt, *The Amherst Papyri* (London: Egypt Exploration Society, 1900), 1:1-22, and reprinted in parallel with the Ethiopic version by Charles, *Ascension of Isaiah*, p. 95.

60. E. Norelli, *Ascensio Isaiae. Commentarius*, Corpus Christianorum, Series Apocryphorum 8 (Turnhout: Brepols, 1995), pp. 243-44.

61. Champlin, *Nero*, p. 17, quoting Knibb's translation verbatim.

62. By far the fullest extant account of the assassination of Agrippina in 59 is Tacitus, *Ann.* 14.3-13, though some additional details are supplied by Suetonius, *Nero* 34.2-4; Cassius Dio 62(61).13-14; see E. Koestermann, *Cornelius Tacitus: Annalen* (Heidelberg: Winter, 1968), 4:20-50; Champlin, *Nero*, pp. 86-89.

63. False Neros appeared in the East in 68/69, in the reign of the emperor Titus (79-81) and around 88 or 89, and at a slightly later date Dio of Prusa, *Oration* 21.10, asserted that everyone wanted Nero still to be alive and that "most people" thought that he was: see C. Tuplin, "The False Neros of the First Century," in *Studies in Latin Literature and History*, ed. C. Deroux, Collection Latomus 206 (Brussels: Éditions Latomus, 1989), 364-404; Champlin, *Nero*, pp. 9-19.

vivus, indicate a date "about the end of the first century" for the composition of this section of the work (3.13–4.22).[64] As the apostle whom Nero killed, Peter is the obvious and inevitable candidate.

Similar cosmological beliefs underlie the *Apocalypse of Peter*, which survives in full only in an Ethiopic version whose accuracy and reliability have been questioned.[65] Two important fragments, however, are preserved of a Greek codex datable to the second half of the fifth century. In one of them Jesus talks about the conflagration that will consume the world at the end of time and continues:

> Look Peter, I have manifested to you and expounded all this [sc. the Last Judgment after the destruction of the world]. And go into the city that rules over the West and drink the cup that I promised you at the hand of the son of the one who is in Hades, so that his destruction may have a beginning and you, the receiver of the promise. . . . (14.4-6)[66]

Presumably "the son of the one who is in Hades" means "the son of the devil" and denotes Nero. More significant, the passage alludes to Jesus' private prayer in the garden of Gethsemane that the cup of death be taken from him (Matt. 26:39, 42, 44; Mark 14:36, 39; Luke 22:42), so that "the cup that I promised you"

---

64. Knibb, "Martyrdom and Ascension," p. 149; cf. Champlin, *Nero*, p. 17: the passage "can be dated with rough certainty to the very late first century AD."

65. There is a preliminary edition by P. Marrassini, "L'Apocalisse di Pietro," in *Etiopia e oltre. Studi in onore di Lanfranco Ricci*, ed. Y. Beyene, Studi africanistici 1, Serie etiopica (Naples: Istituto universitario orientale, Dipartimento de studi e ricerche su Africa e paesi arabi, 1994), 171-232. On the date and probable Alexandrian provenance of the original work, see T. Nicklas, "Insider und outsider: Überlegungen zum historischen Kontext der Darstellung jenseitiger Orte in der Offenbarung des Petrus," in *Topogaphie des Jenseits. Studien zur Geschichte des Todes in Kaiserzeit und Spätantike*, ed. W. Ameling, Altertumswissenschaftliches Kolloquium 21 (Stuttgart: Steiner, 2011), 35-48.

66. Modified from the translation of *P. Vindob. G* 39756, fol. 2 recto 8 — verso 13 by T. J. Kraus and T. Nicklas, *Das Petrusevangelium und die Petrusapokalypse. Die griechischen Fragmente mit deutscher und englischer Übersetzung*, GCS, n.f. 11: Neutestamentliche Apokryphen 1 (Berlin: de Gruyter, 2004), p. 128. Kraus and Nicklas render δεκτὸς τῆς ἐπαγγελίας as "acceptable to (or excepted of) the promise . . ." taking account of the reading δ' εκτὸς τῆς ἐπαγγελ[ίας . . . proposed by P. van Minnen, "The Greek *Apocalypse of Peter*," in *The Apocalypse of Peter*, ed. J. N. Bremmer and I. Czachesz, Studies on Early Christian Apocrypha 7 (Leuven: Peeters, 2003), pp. 15-39, at p. 39. Although δεκτός normally has a passive meaning and is found with the dative of the person or group to whom the individual is acceptable, as in the Septuagint (Deut. 33:24; Prov. 12:22; 14:35), it is surely better in this context to take δεκτός plus the genitive in an active sense.

must refer to the future death of Peter: Peter will go to Rome, "the city that rules over the West," where he will drink the cup promised to him by Jesus; that is, he will be executed as a follower of Christ. The date of the *Apocalypse of Peter*, which may have been composed in Alexandria or Egypt, can hardly be later than the Bar Kokhba revolt of 132-135, though it could well be earlier.[67] Moreover, Jesus' words in this text are completely compatible with the hypothesis that the writer knew that Peter was burned alive in a posture of crucifixion.

V. Conclusion

The results of the present inquiry can be summed up simply and very briefly: there exists relatively abundant early evidence that the apostle Peter was burned alive in Rome in 64, so that it is perverse and ignorant to assert that he never set foot in the city.[68]

---

67. For discussion, see E. Norelli, "Situation des apocryphes pétrininens," *Apocrypha* 2 (1991): 31-83; Richard Bauckham, "The *Apocalypse of Peter*: A Jewish Christian Apocalypse from the Time of Bar Kokhba," *Apocrypha* 5 (1994): 7-111, reprinted in his *The Fate of the Dead: Studies on the Jewish and Christian Apocalypses,* New Testament Studies 93 (Leiden: Brill, 1998), pp. 160-258; J. N. Bremmer, "The *Apocalypse of Peter*: Christian or Jewish?" *The Apocalypse of Peter*, ed. J. N. Bremmer and I. Czachesz, Studies on Early Christian Apocrypha 7 (Leuven: Peeters, 2003), pp. 1-14; T. J. Kraus, "Die griechische Petrus-Apokalypse und ihre Relation zu ausgewählten Überlieferungsträgen apokalyptischer Stoffe," *Apocrypha* 14 (2003): 73-99.

68. I hope that it will be obvious how much I owe to both Markus Bockmuehl and Tobias Nicklas, neither of whom I had ever met before the conference, and especially to the latter for informing me about evidence of which I was previously unaware.

Peter in the New Testament

Reassessing Peter's Imperception in Synoptic Tradition

John R. Markley

Introduction

Peter's prominence in the Synoptic Gospels and his importance for Christianity have not always been matched by the amount of scholarly literature focused on him. Prior to Oscar Cullmann's 1952 book, *Petrus: Jünger, Apostel, Märtyrer,*[1] there were very few historical-critical studies of Peter. Cullmann's work was a watershed in this regard, and as Markus Bockmuehl has noted, it led to something of a renaissance in Petrine studies.[2] Although Cullmann had produced a credible biographical sketch of Peter, his study did not devote any sustained attention to analyzing the redactional tendencies of the Synoptic evangelists. He simply concluded that "it is impossible to discern in any of the Synoptic Gospels a bias for or against Peter."[3]

Cullmann's conclusion on this point was soon contradicted by redaction critics who set about describing the biases of the evangelists regarding the figure of Peter. Toward this end, it became customary for redaction critics to classify data concerning Peter into categories such as "positive" and "negative," "favorable" and "unfavorable," "pro-" and "anti-Petrine."[4] For example, Georg Strecker concludes his redactional analysis of Peter in Matthew by say-

1. Oscar Cullmann, *Petrus: Jünger, Apostel, Märtyrer* (Zürich: Zwingli-Verlag, 1952); ET: *Peter: Disciple, Apostle, Martyr,* trans. Floyd V. Filson (London: SCM, 1953).
2. Markus Bockmuehl, *Simon Peter in Scripture and Memory: The New Testament Apostle in the Early Church* (Grand Rapids: Baker Academic, 2012), p. xiii.
3. Cullmann, *Peter,* p. 26.
4. See Ernest Best, "Peter in the Gospel According to Mark," *CBQ* 40, no. 4 (1978): 547-

ing that the juxtaposition of positive and negative elements in the portrait of Peter indicates that Matthew portrays him as a type for the individual disciple in the Matthean community, whose discipleship was likewise characterized by the combination of positive and negative elements.[5] The most significant redaction-critical study of Peter in the Gospels — the 1973 ecumenical work of Raymond E. Brown, Karl Donfried, and John Reumann — concludes that the Markan Peter has a dark side;[6] the Matthean Peter is variegated, with both strengths and weaknesses underscored;[7] and the Lukan Peter is presented favorably.[8]

This manner of classifying the Synoptic data related to Peter into "positive" and "negative" rubrics was an element of redaction criticism that has carried over into narrative criticism. In an influential 1979 article, Jack Kingsbury reaffirmed Strecker's conclusion about the positive and negative dimensions of the Matthean Peter, though he also added that Peter is portrayed as having salvation-historical primacy among the disciples.[9] Kingsbury's conclusions have been followed in one form or another in the important works of Michael Wilkins, Pheme Perkins, Kari Syreeni, and (to a lesser degree) Timothy Wiarda.[10]

58; Martin Hengel, *Saint Peter: The Underestimated Apostle,* trans. Thomas H. Trapp (Grand Rapids: Eerdmans, 2010), p. 28.

5. Georg Strecker, *Der Weg der Gerechtigkeit,* Forschungen zur Religion und Literatur des Alten und Neuen Testaments 87, 2nd ed. (Göttingen: Vandenhoeck & Ruprecht, 1971), p. 204.

6. Raymond E. Brown, Karl P. Donfried, and John Reumann, eds., *Peter in the New Testament* (Minneapolis: Augsburg, 1973), p. 61.

7. Brown, Donfried, and Reumann, *Peter in the New Testament,* p. 107.

8. Brown, Donfried, and Reumann, *Peter in the New Testament,* p. 127.

9. Jack D. Kingsbury, "The Figure of Peter in Matthew's Gospel as a Theological Problem," *JBL* 98 (1979): 67-83, here p. 80. Kingsbury's general conclusions and method are followed by Michael J. Wilkins, *The Concept of Disciple in Matthew's Gospel: As Reflected in the Use of the Term* μαθητής, NovTSup 59 (Leiden: Brill, 1988), pp. 212, 215; Pheme Perkins, *Peter: Apostle for the Whole Church* (Columbia: University of South Carolina Press, 1994), pp. 66, 72; Kari Syreeni, "Peter as a Character and Symbol in the Gospel of Matthew," in *Characterization in the Gospels: Reconceiving Narrative Criticism,* ed. David Rhoads and Kari Syreeni, JSNTSup 184 (Sheffield: Sheffield Academic, 1999), pp. 149, 149-50 n. 80. See also Timothy Wiarda, *Peter in the Gospels: Pattern, Personality, and Relationship,* WUNT 2/127 (Tübingen: Mohr Siebeck, 2000), pp. 42-45, 98-99; Hengel, *Saint Peter,* p. 25 n. 76.

10. Wilkins's graphic representation of Peter's portrayal along a positive/negative axis illustrates how many narrative critics organize the data. Wilkins, *Concept of Disciple,* p. 240; cf. Arlo J. Nau, *Peter in Matthew: Discipleship, Diplomacy, and Dispraise — with an Assessment of Power and Privilege in the Petrine Office,* GNS 36 (Collegeville, Minn.: Liturgical Press, 1992), p. 25.

As scholars continue to use these categories — positive, negative, favorable, unfavorable — it has become routine to classify as "negative" those portions of the tradition where Peter appears to exhibit imperception regarding Jesus' teaching or mission. My purpose in this essay is to challenge the validity of this classification, since I think it fails to account for the significance of human imperception in early Jewish and Christian apocalyptic literature. I will argue that Peter's imperception represents the appropriation of an apocalyptic motif in the Synoptic tradition. This motif can be referred to as *human imperception in the face of divinely revealed mysteries.*[11] If Peter's imperception is an expression of this motif, then its purpose was probably not to cast him in a negative light or to undercut his reputation among the earliest Christian communities, as many scholars conclude. Instead, the purpose was to assert his status as a recipient of revelation, which was a positive status in the Second Temple period.

Scenes of Imperception

There are five scenes in the Synoptic Gospels where scholars normally see Peter expressing imperception: (1) Peter's request in Matthew 15:15 that Jesus explain his parable about the true source of defilement; (2) Peter's proposal to build three tents during the transfiguration, which Mark 9:6 and Luke 9:33 say arises from his confusion; (3) Peter's rebuke of Jesus' passion prediction, for which Jesus rebukes Peter as "satan" in Mark 8:33 // Matthew 16:23; (4) Peter's question in Mark 10:28 // Matthew 19:27 // Luke 18:28 about the eschatological rewards that await the disciples in exchange for what they have left in order to follow Jesus; (5) Peter's deficient proposal in Matthew 18:21 of a sevenfold limit to forgiveness, which Jesus greatly expands.[12] Due to space constraints, this essay will only address the first three scenes, since these seem to be the most determinative for evaluations of Peter's imperception.[13]

11. For a full treatment of this motif in Jewish and Christian apocalypses, see John R. Markley, *Peter — Apocalyptic Seer: The Influence of the Apocalypse Genre on Matthew's Portrayal of Peter,* WUNT 2/348 (Tübingen: Mohr Siebeck, 2013), pp. 78-113.

12. In addition to these scenes, some scholars view the Markan version of Peter's confession as an expression of Peter's imperception (e.g., James D. G. Dunn, *Jesus Remembered,* Christianity in the Making 1 [Grand Rapids: Eerdmans, 2003], pp. 648-49, who suggests that "the command to silence functions more to indicate a messianic misunderstanding [i.e., the popular understanding of Jesus as a Davidic Messiah] than a messianic secret").

13. For a discussion of the scenes 4 and 5, see Markley, *Peter — Apocalyptic Seer,* pp. 186-87, 207-9.

Peter's Request for Explanation in Matthew 15:15

Matthew 15:1-21 describes Jesus' conflict with the scribes and Pharisees from Jerusalem over the issue of eating with unwashed hands. At the conclusion of the conflict, Jesus teaches the crowds that "nothing entering into the mouth of a person makes him or her unclean; rather it is what comes out of the mouth that makes one unclean" (Matt. 15:11). As is normally the case, this parabolic saying is not immediately understood by the disciples. In the Markan version of the episode, the disciples request an explanation from Jesus while in the private setting of a house (see Mark 7:17). Matthew makes a significant redactional alteration at this point, placing the request for explanation on the lips of Peter. Thus, in Matthew 15:15, Peter asks Jesus to "explain this parable to us." Jesus responds to Peter's request with a statement that seems to reflect a negative evaluation of Peter: Jesus says, "Are you still without understanding?" (ἀκμὴν καὶ ὑμεῖς ἀσύνετοί ἐστε; [Matt. 15:16; cf. Mark 7:18]). Although Jesus' response is directed to the group of disciples, as the second-person-plural subject and verb indicate, it would appear that Matthean redaction draws Peter especially into the line of fire here. Thus, Wilkins says, "Peter is the obtuse one who brings on Jesus' rebuke."[14] Wilkins goes on to conclude that "Peter receives prominence as the representative for the disciples, but it is a negative prominence."[15]

However, Jesus' response to Peter is not necessarily negative when understood in the context of apocalyptic literature. Occasionally in apocalyptic texts, angelic mediators of revelation respond very similarly when a human seer requests explanation. For example, in Zechariah 4, an angelic mediator asks the prophet what he sees (Zech. 4:2). Zechariah responds by describing a golden lampstand and two olive trees (4:2-3). Zechariah then asks, "What are these, my lord?" (4:4). The angel answers Zechariah's question by asking in return, "Do you not know what these are?" (οὐ γινώσκεις τί ἐστιν ταῦτα [4:5]). After the angel explains the vision, Zechariah asks for an explanation of the two olive trees. The angel again responds by asking in return, "Do you not know what these are?" (οὐκ οἶδας τί ἐστιν ταῦτα [4:13]), and then he proceeds to explain their significance to Zechariah.

Similar angelic responses are found elsewhere in apocalyptic literature. In the *Testament of Abraham*, Abraham asks the angelic mediator about the identity of a figure he sees in his vision. The angel responds by asking, "Do you not know who he is?" (*T. Ab.* 8.8 [B]). In the *Shepherd of Hermas*, the seer's inability

---

14. Wilkins, *Concept of Disciple*, p. 184.
15. Wilkins, *Concept of Disciple*, p. 185. Cf. Nau, *Peter*, p. 25.

to recognize the Shepherd provokes a similar response from the mediator of revelation: "Do you not recognize me?" (Herm. 25.3). In Revelation 17, when John is struck with astonishment while seeing the vision of the woman and beast, the angelic mediator responds by saying, "Why are you astonished? I will explain to you the mystery of the woman and the beast" (Rev. 17:7).

These texts illustrate that angelic mediators sometimes respond with puzzlement or surprise when a seer is unable to understand some aspect of what is being revealed. The function of these angelic responses in apocalyptic literature is not to construct a negative view of the human seer. Instead, such responses are designed to identify the limits of the seer's unaided human comprehension while he encounters divine revelation. They have the effect of escalating the otherworldly quality of what is about to be explained to the seer, while reinforcing the idea that the revealed content does not arise from the seer's own thinking. When such responses occur, they are simply part of the rhetorical interplay between the human perception of the seer and the divine perspective revealed by the mediator. This rhetorical interplay between human seers and heavenly mediators of revelation is part of a larger motif found throughout apocalyptic literature: a motif of *human imperception in the face of divinely revealed mysteries*. This motif reflects the duality in apocalyptic thought between what humans are capable of perceiving on their own and what must be divinely revealed and explained to them.

It is likely that this motif is present in Peter's request for explanation in Matthew 15:15 and Jesus' response to his request in verse 16. If this is the case, then Matthew seems to be portraying Peter in the role of a seer and Jesus in the role of a mediator of revelation, albeit in a different genre of literature, and with a different flavor of revelatory content. Peter's request and Jesus' response are designed to signal that the explanation of this parable constitutes divine revelation about the issue of defilement, which is delivered to Peter and the disciples in a private setting. The disciples are thus presented as exclusive recipients of revelation who stand in contradistinction to the scribes and Pharisees of Jerusalem, whom Jesus indicts for replacing the word of God with traditions that are merely human in origin (Matt. 15:6, 8-9).

This conclusion is corroborated by other episodes in Matthew's Gospel that assert the disciples' status as recipients of revelation, particularly with regard to receiving explanations of Jesus' parables. In 13:11 Jesus tells them, "To you it has been granted to know the mysteries of the kingdom of heaven, but to them it has not been granted." Additionally, Matthew and Luke each include a statement from Q where Jesus says, "Blessed are your eyes because they see and your ears because they hear. For truly I tell you that many prophets and righteous people longed to see what you see, but did not see, and to hear what you hear, but did not hear" (Matt. 13:16-17; Luke 10:23-24). In light of these statements, it is not a stretch to conclude that Peter's interaction with Jesus in Matthew 15:15-16 is analogous to the interaction between seers and mediators of revelation in apocalyptic texts. If this is correct, then the point of verses 15-16 is not that Peter was an idiot; the point is that Peter engages in revelatory interaction with Jesus, which would seem to be something positive.

Peter's Proposal to Build Three Tents (Mark 9:5-6; Matt. 17:4; Luke 9:33)

The transfiguration includes another expression of Peter's imperception that scholars normally view as a "negative" aspect of his portrayal. Peter is one of three disciples who receive a privileged disclosure of Jesus transfigured to his heavenly glory, and they hear the voice of God confirm Jesus' divine sonship. Moreover, they see Jesus in the company of the righteous dead, who are represented by Moses and Elijah. Peter expresses his imperception in this episode through his proposal to build three tabernacles for each of the glorious figures who appear on the mountain. Mark and Luke both include a narratorial comment that Peter's proposal arose from his confusion. Mark says that "he did not know what to say, for they were afraid" (Mark 9:6), and Luke says that Peter spoke this proposal "not knowing what he said" (Luke 9:33).

Ernest Best, for example, views Peter's proposal and the following narratorial comment as reflecting the "stupidity of Peter," which was already a part of the tradition that Mark drew from.[16] Terence Smith, on the other hand, views the narratorial comment about Peter's confusion as Mark's own negative evaluation of Peter's proposal; though Smith likewise concludes that the episode was designed to demonstrate "Peter's stupidity."[17] Brown, Donfried, and Reumann

---

16. Ernest Best, *Disciples and Discipleship: Studies in the Gospel according to Mark* (Edinburgh: T&T Clark, 1986), p. 216; Best, "Peter," p. 550.

17. Terence V. Smith, *Petrine Controversies in Early Christianity: Attitudes towards Peter in Christian Writings of the First Two Centuries,* WUNT 15 (Tübingen: Mohr Siebeck, 1985), pp. 171-72. Joel Marcus concludes that 9:6 "is probably the evangelist's editorial insertion into a preexisting narrative in order to highlight the obtuseness of the disciples and the fallacy of Peter's suggestion" (Joel Marcus, *Mark 8–16,* AB 27A [New York: Doubleday, 2009], 635). Bubar's admitted polemic against the institutional church causes him to grossly misconstrue Peter's expression of imperception: "Peter babbles unintelligibly when he attempts to speak" (Wallace W. Bubar, "Killing Two Birds with One Stone: The Utter De(con)struction of Matthew and His Church," *BibInt* 3 [1995]: 144-57, here p. 148).

conclude that Peter's confusion supports the "dark side" of the Markan Peter,[18] and Wiarda says that "Peter serves as a negative role model" in this scene.[19]

But again with this episode, there are reasons to conclude that Peter's proposal, and Mark's (and Luke's) comment about his confusion, do not represent negative evaluations of Peter. Instead, as I have suggested with reference to Matthew 15:15-16, these features represent a motif that is common in apocalyptic literature: *human imperception in the face of divinely revealed mysteries.* In apocalyptic texts, human seers are regularly portrayed as being profoundly confused by the otherworldly realities they observe during visions and epiphanies. The venerable figure of Daniel, for example, cannot perceive the significance of his visions apart from divine explanation, despite his unrivaled qualities of wisdom and understanding. In Daniel 8:27, after Daniel has received an explanation of his vision, he comments that he did not understand it. Similarly, following the historical review of chapters 10-12, Daniel says, "I heard but could not understand" (12:8). Daniel is therefore portrayed as expressing confusion and imperception when confronted with the eschatological mysteries revealed to him, but there is no indication that his confusion is designed to reflect negatively on him. It merely plays into the duality between God's plan for the righteous, expressed as otherworldly mysteries, and the ability of finite humans such as Daniel to grasp this mainly ominous plan.

Fourth Ezra is another text where a venerable seer is confused by the otherworldly mysteries he observes. In *Fourth Ezra* 10, Ezra sees a vision of a woman who then changes into the heavenly Jerusalem. As a result of what he observes, Ezra narrates that he is "deprived of his understanding" (10:30).[20] In his subsequent dialogue with the angelic mediator, Uriel, Ezra says that he has seen what he is unable to explain (10:31), and he reiterates that he is incapable of understanding the vision: Ezra says, "I have seen what I did not know, and I have heard what I do not understand" (10:35). Lest we jump to the conclusion that Ezra's confusion reflects a negative evaluation of him in the apocalypse, it is important to note that the angelic mediator's response highlights Ezra's venerable status as an exclusive recipient of revealed mysteries: the angel says, "Listen to me and I will inform you, and tell you about the things which you fear, for the Most High has revealed many secrets to you. For he has seen your righteous conduct" (10:38-39a).

18. Brown, Donfried, and Reumann, *Peter in the New Testament*, p. 61.

19. Wiarda, *Peter in the Gospels*, pp. 155-56.

20. Translations of *Fourth Ezra* are from Bruce M. Metzger, "The Fourth Book of Ezra," in *The Old Testament Pseudepigrapha*, vol. 1, *Apocalyptic Literature and Testaments*, ed. James H. Charlesworth (New York: Doubleday, 1983), pp. 515-59.

There are many other examples of human confusion in the apocalypses,[21] but these examples from the books of Daniel and *Fourth Ezra* are sufficient to show that Mark's (and Luke's) comment that Peter was confused should probably not be viewed as a negative evaluation of him. Peter's imperception and fear during this revelatory moment are the natural responses of a human seer when witnessing the mysteries of the divine realm. As John Paul Heil observes, Peter's response triggers the divine voice, which then interprets the epiphany and corrects Peter's imperception.[22] The voice exalts Jesus and his teaching above the figures of Moses and Elijah by saying, "This is my beloved Son; listen to him!" (Mark 9:7). Listening to Jesus in this context means listening to his passion predictions, because the time for dwelling in the company of the glorious Messiah has not yet come, despite Peter's conclusion that "it is good for us to be here" (Mark 9:5 // Luke 9:33).

In the transfiguration we again see the interplay between Peter's human imperception and the divine perspective on Jesus' mission and teaching. That Peter was confused simply means he responded to this revelatory moment in a fitting and appropriate manner.

Peter's Rebuke of Jesus' Passion Prediction (Mark 8:32-33; Matt. 16:22-23)

Peter's imperception is most evident in his rebuke of Jesus' passion prediction that the Son of Man must suffer and die. After Peter takes Jesus aside and rebukes him, Jesus then rebukes Peter in return saying, "Get behind me, adversary/satan, for you do not have in mind divine things, but human things" (Mark 8:32-33 // Matt. 16:22-23; absent from Luke's Gospel). Based on Jesus' reference to Peter as σατανᾶς, scholars are quick to point out the very negative implications of this rebuke for the portrayal of Peter. Rudolf Bultmann concludes that Mark has "introduced a polemic against the Jewish-Christian point of view represented by Peter,"[23] and Smith agrees that this episode exhibits Mark's "anti-Petrine stance."[24] Commenting on Matthew's version, Wilkins

---

21. See Markley, *Peter — Apocalyptic Seer,* pp. 78-113.

22. John P. Heil, *The Transfiguration of Jesus: Narrative Meaning and Function of Mark 9:2-8, Matt 17:1-8 and Luke 9:28-36,* AnBib 144 (Rome: Editrice Pontificio Istituto Biblico, 2000), pp. 132-43.

23. Rudolf Bultmann, *History of the Synoptic Tradition,* trans. John Marsh, rev. ed. (1963; repr., Peabody, Mass.: Hendrickson, 1994), p. 258.

24. Smith, *Petrine Controversies,* p. 169.

says that "Peter functions as a negative example of what happens when a believer, even a leader, ceases to listen to the voice of God the Father."[25] Although I will not argue that Peter is here presented as a neutral or even positive figure, I do think there are reasons to qualify our conclusions about the degree to which this episode reflects a negative view or portrait of Peter.

Fourth Ezra may provide a helpful analogy for understanding Peter's rebuke of Jesus, and Jesus' subsequent rebuke of Peter. In this apocalypse, Ezra questions whether God is just since the righteous suffer at the hands of the unrighteous. Occasionally, Ezra presumes to possess a point of view that is superior to the one represented by his angelic mediator, Uriel. For this reason, Uriel takes a biting tone with Ezra at points. He claims that a human like Ezra cannot understand the ways of God (*4 Ezra* 4:2, 10-11, 21; 5:35-37, 40); he questions whether Ezra believes that he loves Israel more than God does (5:33; cf. 4:34; 8:47a); and he is critical of Ezra for considering the present rather than what is yet to come (7:15). When Ezra queries if the fate of the wicked is just, Uriel sharply rebukes him: "You are not a better judge than God, or wiser than the Most High!" (7:19). Uriel's antagonistic tone must be interpreted against the backdrop of the glowing statements made about Ezra elsewhere in the apocalypse (e.g., 6:32-33; 7:[67]-[77]; 8:47b-54; 10:38-40, 55-58; 13:53-56), the direct comparison of him with Moses (14:1-6, 37-48), and his removal from the earth before death (14:9). In light of these, it does not seem likely that the apocalypse reflects a negative or ambivalent view of Ezra himself; rather, it seems that Uriel's tone is directed toward Ezra's human point of view, which is fundamentally different from the divine point of view that is required to grapple faithfully with the problems of gentile hegemony, sin, and divine justice. The revelations then granted to Ezra recalibrate his point of view, supplying him with a divine perspective on the present age.[26]

Ezra's human perspective is continually contrasted with the divine perspective that the angel Uriel discloses, much like Peter's rebuke of Jesus' passion prediction is designed to sharply contrast his human perspective with the divine perspective Jesus discloses. Indeed, just as the angel Uriel criticizes Ezra's limited human perspective, Jesus says that Peter is thinking "human things," τὰ τῶν ἀνθρώπων, rather than "divine things," τὰ τοῦ θεοῦ.[27] This emphasis on Peter's human point of view suggests that "adversary" is perhaps the

---

25. Wilkins, *Concept of Disciple*, p. 203.

26. Portions of this paragraph appear in Markley, *Peter — Apocalyptic Seer*, p. 93, and have been reproduced with permission from the publisher.

27. Paul uses this same phrase in 1 Cor. 2:11 to connote the secret purposes of God, which might not be far from what is intended by its use in Mark 8:33 and Matt. 16:23.

best translation for σατανᾶς, although the evangelists may intend to signal that Peter's human point of view is ultimately aligned with Satan's opposition to the work of God. Regardless of the translation used, it should not be overlooked that Jesus' comments focus on the human perspective that Peter represents.

The main purpose of this episode, therefore, may not be to construct a negative view of Peter, or to undercut a positive view of Peter. Its purpose is probably not to use Peter as an example of faulty discipleship. Instead, Peter performs the somewhat stereotyped function of a seer, who voices the human perspective that the divine revelation is designed to correct.

Conclusions

My purpose has not been to argue that Peter's expressions of imperception reflect positively on his portrait or memory in Synoptic tradition. Instead, I have argued against the common, almost habitual conclusion that Peter's imperception is designed to portray him in a negative light. My thesis is that Peter's imperception represents the appropriation of an apocalyptic motif in the Synoptic tradition. I have referred to this motif as *human imperception in the face of divinely revealed mysteries*. If this is correct, then Peter's imperception is meant to portray him as performing the standard functions that seers in apocalyptic literature usually perform.

In Matthew 15:15, Peter requests the explanation of a parable, and thereby secures divine revelation from the Messiah about the issue of cleanliness. In this way Peter receives revelation that stands in contrast with the human teaching of the scribes and Pharisees. During the transfiguration, Peter's individual proposal and confusion represent standard responses of a human seer when encountering otherworldly mysteries. His confused response escalates the otherworldly nature of what he observes and highlights the importance of listening to Jesus, who is elevated above Moses and Elijah. Peter's rebuke of Jesus' passion prediction is the human point of view that provides the backdrop against which Jesus' suffering can be projected as the revealed will of God for the Messiah. In each of these cases, Peter's imperception flags the transferal of revelation from Jesus or about Jesus.

CHAPTER 8

The Centrality of Discipleship
in the Johannine Portrayal of Peter

Jason S. Sturdevant

In the last two decades of Johannine scholarship, opinions on two key characters, Peter and the Beloved Disciple, have undergone a significant change. That
is, many have come to see the Beloved Disciple and Peter as complementary
figures, rather than in contrast to or in competition with one another.[1] This
change overturned a long-standing assumption by many that the Fourth Gospel had an anti-Petrine bias, since Peter in this earlier view seemed to come
off rather negatively when compared with the Beloved Disciple.[2] At points,

---

1. Richard Bauckham, "The Beloved Disciple as Ideal Author," *JSNT* 49 (1993): 21-44.
Following in Bauckham's wake are D. Francois Tolmie, "The (Not So) Good Shepherd: The
Use of Shepherd Imagery in the Characterisation of Peter in the Fourth Gospel," in *Imagery
in the Gospel of John: Terms, Forms, Themes, and Theology of Johannine Figurative Language*,
ed. Jörg Frey, J. G. Van der Watt, and Ruben Zimmermann (Tübingen: Mohr Siebeck, 2006),
pp. 353-67; Bradford Blaine, *Peter in the Gospel of John: The Making of an Authentic Disciple*
(Atlanta: Society of Biblical Literature, 2007); Cornelis Bennema, *Encountering Jesus: Character Studies in the Gospel of John* (Colorado Springs, Colo.: Paternoster, 2009), pp. 176-77;
R. Alan Culpepper, "Peter as Exemplary Disciple in John 21:15-19," *PRSt* 37 (2010): 165-78. See
also Kevin Quast, *Peter and the Beloved Disciple* (Sheffield: Sheffield Academic, 1989), which
predates Bauckham, though Bauckham's formulation of the relationship between Peter and
the Beloved Disciple has proved by far more influential.
2. E.g., Raymond E. Brown, Karl P. Donfried, and John Reumann, eds., *Peter in the New
Testament: a Collaborative Assessment by Protestant and Roman Catholic Scholars* (Minneapolis: Augsburg, 1973), pp. 135-39; Raymond F. Collins, "Representative Figures of the Fourth
Gospel," *DRev* 94 (1976): 127-28, 130-32; R. Alan Culpepper, *Anatomy of the Fourth Gospel: A
Study in Literary Design* (Philadelphia: Fortress, 1983), p. 122; Pheme Perkins, *Peter: Apostle for
the Whole Church* (Columbia: University of South Carolina Press, 1994), pp. 96-97, 100-101.

some even suggested that Peter's negative portrayal was born from the Johannine community finding itself at odds with so-called Petrine Christianity.[3] But thanks in large part to the work of Richard Bauckham, recent scholarship has reappraised Peter's portrayal in John as generally positive. Peter's character simply responds *differently* to Jesus than does the Beloved Disciple, but both respond appropriately. Whereas the Beloved Disciple will serve as the ideal witness, Peter will become Jesus' successor as the caretaker of the flock.[4]

Despite the strengths of this reading of Peter's character in John, the discourse nevertheless requires a corrective, as it overlooks a key component of Peter's portrayal. To survey some accounts of the Johannine Peter, one might be inclined to think that, as far as Peter's character development is concerned, he reaches his maturity inevitably, albeit with difficulty.[5] That is, the present discourse on Peter implicitly assumes that, thanks to the pressure from history and tradition, Peter's character in the Gospel simply evolves into Jesus' successor. This way of understanding Peter's character development seems, however, to ignore almost completely his primary role as a disciple, that is, one who is formed by his teacher. This failure to appreciate Peter's path of discipleship arises primarily from the framing of Peter's characterization, which occurs almost always vis-à-vis the character of the Beloved Disciple. Yet in the Gospel narrative the Beloved Disciple is not the character who most determines Peter's development. Rather, the character who tells us the most about the Peter of the Fourth Gospel is none other than Jesus. When viewed in relation to Jesus, Peter's character and narrative arc become less about memory or history or intra-Christian debates, and more about his progression under Jesus' educative and discipling work.

Throughout this discipleship process, Jesus guides Peter with the same approach he uses with others, adapting to their needs and according to his aims.[6] The Fourth Evangelist portrays Jesus as an adaptable guide, similar to

3. E.g., Arthur H. Maynard, "The Role of Peter in the Fourth Gospel," *NTS* 30 (1984): 531-48; Martin Hengel, *The Johannine Question* (Philadelphia: Trinity Press International, 1989), pp. 78, 125; Arthur J. Droge, "The Status of Peter in the Fourth Gospel: a Note on John 18:10-11," *JBL* 109 (1990): 307-11; Christopher W. Skinner, *John and Thomas — Gospels in Conflict? Johannine Characterization and the Thomas Question* (Eugene, Ore.: Pickwick, 2009), pp. 78-138.

4. Bauckham, "Beloved Disciple."

5. An example of such a view is Culpepper (*Anatomy*, p. 121), who characterizes Peter's development almost entirely in verbs that refer to Peter, rather than Jesus. Bauckham ("Beloved Disciple," p. 36) is a little more careful, recognizing that in John 21 Peter is a disciple who "through failure and grace is enabled *by Jesus* to become the chief pastor of the church" (emphasis added). Even so, Jesus' role in Peter's formation is minimally addressed in Bauckham's influential study.

6. Jason S. Sturdevant, "Incarnation as Psychagogy: The Purpose of the Word's Descent

other moral philosophers of his era, who make use of various methods to instruct a variety of potential students. Sometimes he speaks with harsh words, at other times gentle; he uses metaphors to guide people from the lowly to the lofty; and he treats different people differently. The Johannine Jesus does this with many interlocutors: Nicodemus, the Samaritan woman, Martha and Mary (to name a few). Most significantly, as argued below, Jesus also accommodates to Peter. By considering Peter's formation under the guidance of the Johannine Jesus, Peter's character development will come into clearer focus, as will the nature of these interactions. Exploring Peter's character in this light will reveal that his successful transformation from denying disciple to capable successor is not in the Gospel narrative merely a reflection of history, but results from Jesus' adaptable guidance. In this way, the centrality of discipleship will emerge distinctly as a key way to understand Peter's character, and will highlight his larger role in the Fourth Gospel's narrative.

Peter's Call: Forced into Form (John 1:40-42)

The disciple's first encounter with Jesus entails no initiative on Peter's part. He hears about Jesus from his brother, who then brings him to Jesus (1:41-42). In the exchange that ensues, Peter says not a word, but is only spoken to. Jesus begins by revealing his supernatural knowledge of Peter: "'You are Simon, the son of John; you will be called Cephas' (which means 'Peter')" (1:42b).[7] Nowhere does the evangelist suggest that Jesus had already met Simon or that he was acquainted with him. On the contrary, Andrew's claim to have found the Messiah (1:41) suggests that neither he nor Peter had any prior awareness of Jesus. Jesus' acknowledgment of Simon's name and family indicates that Jesus is here demonstrating his preternatural abilities (as he does with Nathanael in 1:47, 49) in order to effect some positive response from Simon, namely, discipleship. Jesus further establishes his authority over Simon by renaming him, something characteristically done by God in the Jewish Scriptures.[8]

The evangelist ends the scene there, withholding the result of Jesus' revelation on Simon, but the presumptive outcome is obvious: on the basis of this

---

in John's Gospel," *NovT* 56 (2014): 24-44; Jason S. Sturdevant, *The Adaptable Jesus of the Fourth Gospel: The Pedagogy of the Logos* (NovTSup 162; Leiden: Brill, 2015).

    7. This interpretation follows Rudolf K. Bultmann, *The Gospel of John: a Commentary*, trans. G. R. Beasley-Murray, R. W. Hoare, and J. K. Riches (Philadelphia: Westminster, 1971), pp. 101-2.

    8. As in, e.g., Gen. 17:4-5; 32:28-29.

meeting, Simon Peter begins to follow Jesus. Notably, in this scene Peter has remained completely passive (not even the subject of a verb), and this passivity in 1:41-42 has much more in common with the prophecy of what his future life *will be* (21:18b-19). But first, Peter will appear more impulsive and self-determined, in stark contrast to this initial appearance. For this reason, in the remainder of the Gospel Jesus will have to find some way to bring Peter back to this starting point, to form the disciple into one whose life is determined by God's will rather than his own.

Misunderstanding and Misguided Promises: John 13

Peter's next significant engagement with Jesus in John occurs in chapter 13 (the confession in 6:68-69 notwithstanding). Jesus is sharing his last moments with the Twelve before his death. Yet in these final hours, Jesus will engage in some of the most challenging teaching and shaping of Peter to guide him toward maturity, primarily the gesture of servitude in washing his disciples' feet, the giving of the "new commandment," and his prediction of Peter's denial. In particular, his dialogues with Peter challenge the disciple's understanding of and commitment to him, which must be reformed if Peter is to succeed Jesus as the chief shepherd.

Misunderstanding: The Washing of the Disciples' Feet (13:1-18)

The evangelist's narration of the footwashing evokes the portrayal of the Good Shepherd.[9] Jesus lays down (τίθησιν) his outer garment and takes up (λαβὼν) a towel — just as he "lays down" and "takes up" his life — and begins washing the feet of his disciples (13:4-5). Jesus will explain the significance of this act, but in the act itself a conflict arises between Jesus and Peter about its appropriateness. The disciple objects, "Do *you* wash my feet?" (13:6). Peter cannot accept that Jesus, his lord and teacher, much less "the Holy One of God" (6:69), should debase himself by taking on a slave's errand. His words suggest that he does not comprehend Jesus' mission on earth. Jesus responds to him, "Right now,

---

9. See 10:17-18. Cf. C. K. Barrett, *The Gospel according to St. John* (2d ed., London: SPCK, 1978), p. 366; Craig S. Keener, *The Gospel of John: A Commentary* (Peabody, Mass.: Hendrickson, 2003), 2:902; Andrew T. Lincoln, *The Gospel according to Saint John* (Peabody, Mass.: Hendrickson, 2005), p. 306.

you do not understand what I am doing, but you will understand after these things" (13:7).[10] He does not rebuke Peter for failing to understand, because he knows that such understanding will come with time.[11] Indeed, Peter's lack of comprehension is understandable. So Jesus only invites Peter to trust.

Peter rejects this out of hand. For him, it is too great an impropriety, and so he says: "May you never, ever wash my feet!" (13:8a).[12] Faced with Peter's stubbornness, Jesus must make use of an alternate method. To draw Peter toward a clearer understanding, he reveals that only in allowing him to perform this service will Peter have a "portion" with him (13:8b). He makes the choice clear: either Peter allows him to wash his feet, or else Peter will effectively deny his relationship with Jesus. In order to follow Jesus, Peter must submit to Jesus' will rather than impose his own on Jesus. Yet Peter responds with another attempt to control Jesus. He responds with a request that Jesus wash also his hands and his head (13:9). The disciple, lacking understanding, refuses to submit fully, and Jesus carefully rebukes him again by answering, "Someone who has bathed does not need to wash anything but his feet, since he is entirely clean" (13:10a). Jesus, not Peter, will decide what does and does not need to be washed, and thus rebuffs Peter's attempt to commandeer his activity.

After washing the disciples' feet, Jesus then explains his actions, and in so doing provides instruction on what it means to follow him. "I have given you an example, so that you might also do as I have done for you" (13:12, 15). He did not wash their feet simply as an act of service, but to instruct them in the way they should treat one another. The footwashing scene is thus an extension of his action as the Good Shepherd, who lays down his life for the sheep (10:17-18), and ties in with the love command he will offer shortly. Somewhat ironically, the one who resisted this exemplary act of service, Peter, is the one whom Jesus will choose to be the future shepherd. So Jesus will need to continue his efforts to transform the self-determined man into one whose life is determined by God.

Misguided Promises: Peter's Avowal of Love (13:31-38)

Later in John 13, Jesus engages in much more direct and thorough instruction of Peter. Among other things, he promises his disciples that his departure

10. "These things" refer almost certainly to Jesus' death and resurrection, as noted by, e.g., Bultmann, *John*, p. 467; Barrett, *St. John*, p. 367.

11. See Blaine, *Peter*, p. 65.

12. Peter's statement that Jesus will by no means wash his feet "ever," or εἰς τὸν αἰῶνα, is filled with irony, since what Jesus offers in this act is in part a share (μέρος, 13:8b) in eternal life.

is near and they will not be able to go with him (13:33). Yet he follows this prediction with the new commandment, phrased in a way that recalls the command for the footwashing: "Just as I have loved you, so also you should love one another" (13:34).[13] As noted, the footwashing was to be understood as an expression of the disposition of the Good Shepherd, to lay down his life for others, motivated by the very love highlighted in 13:34, a connection Jesus will make even more explicit in the statement about "no greater love" (15:13).[14] If any disciple wants to fulfill Jesus' commandment, he will need to follow in the path set out by Jesus himself. Any presumptive successor to Jesus cannot take on this role without a willingness to part with his life.

Peter ignores the command altogether, however, and instead asks Jesus about his impending departure (13:36a). Peter does not yet understand Jesus' destiny, much less what he is calling his disciples to do. Peter's focus is on the anticipated absence.[15] But Jesus reassures him, "You cannot follow[16] me where I am going now — but you *will* follow later on" (13:36b). Jesus tries to point Peter in the right direction, to underscore his future role as the next shepherd of the sheep, and consequently, to urge him to lay down his life for them — but not yet. Peter must first be formed in order to offer himself for others.

Peter then insists that he will follow with Jesus to the very end, even claiming he will lay down his life for his master (13:37), perhaps evoking the ethic of the Good Shepherd.[17] Peter overestimates his commitment, however, and mischaracterizes the exact form of the love that Jesus himself will show in death. In the arrest scene in John 18, Peter will attempt to carry out his promise by risking his life in a violent struggle, but this reflects a failed understanding of the nature of the self-sacrifice Jesus desires.[18]

---

13. καθὼς ἐγώ ἐποίησα ὑμῖν καὶ ὑμεῖς ποιῆτε (13:15); καθὼς ἠγάπησα ὑμᾶς ἵνα καὶ ὑμεῖς ἀγαπᾶτε ἀλλήλους (13:34).

14. 15:13: μείζονα ἀγάπην οὐδεὶς ἔχει, ἵνα τις *τὴν ψυχὴν αὐτοῦ θῇ ὑπὲρ* τῶν φίλων αὐτοῦ. This mirrors Jesus' statement about the Good Shepherd in 10:11, where he identifies the shepherd as one who lays down his life for the sheep.

15. See Eva Krafft, "Die Personen des Johannesevangeliums," *EvT* 16 (1956): 18-32, here p. 24.

16. See Wayne A. Meeks, "The Man from Heaven in Johannine Sectarianism," *JBL* 91 (1972): 64. There, Meeks notes the equivalence of discipleship and death in Jesus' statement.

17. Meeks ("Man from Heaven," p. 65) notes that Peter rightly perceives what Jesus means by "departing."

18. Lincoln (*John*, p. 388) characterizes this exchange thus: "[Peter] has not understood the crucial distinction between 'now' and 'later' in Jesus' words. Not until Jesus' hour has been completed and his love demonstrated in death will Peter have the resources for living out Jesus' model (cf. 21.18-19)."

Jesus' response to Peter's vow does not address this failure to understand, however, but rather Peter's inability to carry it out. Jesus tells him directly not only that his claims are vain, but also that Peter will deny him three times that very night (13:38). Despite Peter's grand claims of devotion, he will soon deny his association with his master outright. Jesus does not say this simply to deflate Peter's ego. Rather, he challenges the adequacy of Peter's discipleship, a matter Peter himself might seriously take up once the denial has taken place.[19] The rebuff, then, is above all intended for Peter's formation so that "later" (13:36) he might follow Jesus with greater understanding. But not yet; first he must pass through the trial Jesus has forewarned.

Peter's Double Betrayal: John 18

In two scenes, the garden arrest and the interrogation before Annas, Jesus and his disciples become separated from one another, causing a crisis of discipleship, as Jesus' followers find their commitment to him tested. For no one in the Gospel is this crisis greater than for Peter, who appears in stark relief to Jesus on several levels throughout these two scenes. Though Jesus' arrest provides the major focal point of John 18, the secondary focus of this chapter is Peter's plunge into a double betrayal of Jesus: first through his failed attempt to circumvent Jesus' death, and second through his denial of his identity as Jesus' disciple. Yet even this betrayal can serve as an important stage in Peter's transformation from self-determination to submission to his master.

In the Garden (18:1-11)

The scene opens in a garden, and Judas, together with troops from the Jewish authorities, arrives to arrest Jesus (18:3). After Jesus affirms his identity as the man for whom they are searching — twice he replies, ἐγώ εἰμί (18:5, 8) — he then pleads for the release of his disciples (18:8) to fulfill his own words in 17:12 (18:9), themselves echoing the actions of the Good Shepherd (10:28; cf. 10:10). He thus exemplifies once more that the Good Shepherd lays down his life for the sheep, protecting them from those who would seek their harm.

Peter's actions run contrary to this ideal, however, though he fails to rec-

19. This is made explicit in the Synoptics (Mark 14:72 and pars.), though not in the Fourth Gospel, where Peter's grief is displaced to the scene of his "rehabilitation" in 21:15-17.

ognize it. He unsheathes his sword and cuts off the ear of the slave of the high priest (18:10).[20] Peter demonstrates in this one act the height of his misunderstanding of Jesus' mission: whereas Peter wants to defend Jesus through violence, Jesus will defend Peter (and the rest of the Twelve) by *succumbing* to violence in his death (see 10:11, 15; 18:8). Peter acts, moreover, to circumvent that very hour to which Jesus' entire career has been driving. He has betrayed the very essence of Jesus' mission.[21]

The teacher does not mince words with his wayward follower: "Put the sword in its sheath! Am I not to drink the cup the Father has given me?" (18:11).[22] We should note here that Jesus is not on a suicide mission, but he is submitting to the plan of the Father — the very posture Jesus has worked to inculcate within Peter. So he puts the question to Peter, in effect: "Will you resist God's plans in pursuit of your own?" Peter thus unwittingly values his own ideals and will rather than submitting to God. Such a posture will not serve if Peter is to follow Jesus as the next shepherd.

In the Courtyard (18:18-27)

After Peter's violent act and Jesus' rebuke of it, Jesus and Peter part ways, and they remain parted until after the resurrection. Jesus is bound and led to Annas (18:12-13), while Peter follows at a distance, together with "another disciple" (18:15). Despite their physical separation, however, this scene is still a part of Jesus' formation of Peter, since it functions as an outworking of Jesus' guidance up to this point. Having tried to shape Peter with little positive result, Jesus must allow Peter to pass through this trial if the disciple is to make progress. Peter can only begin to understand what Jesus wants of him once he sees the poor fruits of his own discipleship.

20. Krafft, "Personen," p. 24; Régis Burnet, "Pierre, Apôtre entre Judas et le disciple bien-aimé," *ETR* 77 (2002): 105-11, here p. 109.

21. Blaine (*Peter*, pp. 88-89) claims that Peter is here only trying to protect Jesus, to keep his master from harm. He may be right, but this view in no way diminishes the fact that Peter betrays Jesus' very mission in this misguided endeavor.

22. Barrett (*St. John*, p. 436) stresses the use of ποτήριον here as an adaptation of the Synoptic tradition (cf. Mark 10:38; 14:36), now stressing Jesus' "calm determined acceptance" of his fate, which is "the work appointed him by the Father." See also Francis J. Moloney, *The Gospel of John* (Collegeville, Minn.: Liturgical Press, 1998), p. 484; J. Ramsey Michaels, *The Gospel of John* (Grand Rapids: Eerdmans, 2010), pp. 895-96. Droge ("Status," p. 311) connects this rebuke also to 18:36 ("If my kingdom were of this world, my subjects would fight"), which constitutes "a devastating indictment" of Peter's actions.

Once inside the courtyard, Peter's trial begins, as Jesus' trial unfolds nearby. The servant girl watching the courtyard door asks him, "You aren't also one of this man's disciples, are you?"[23] Peter responds simply: "I am not [οὐκ εἰμί]" (18:17).[24] This completely reverses the situation in the garden, where when questioned about his identity, Jesus said, "I am (ἐγώ εἰμι)" (18:5, 8). Whereas Jesus affirmed his identity, Peter denies it and his relationship to Jesus.

After a brief interlude describing Jesus' interrogation before Annas (18:19-24), the evangelist returns to Peter, who makes every attempt to hide his association with his teacher. For the second time, someone asks Peter if in fact he was a disciple of Jesus, and Peter again utters the anticonfession οὐκ εἰμί (18:25). The third denial recalls Peter's initial violent betrayal: "One of the slaves of the high priest, a relative of *the man whose ear Peter cut off,* said, 'Didn't I see you *in the garden* with him?' And again Peter denied it" (18:26-27).[25] Peter's promise to go with Jesus even to death (13:37) has been proved hollow, and his betrayal of Jesus is complete.[26] Even so, this failure is not the end of Peter's journey, but rather the nadir of his discipleship. Peter cannot continue as he is, and must change his way of understanding his relationship to Jesus.

The Commissioning of the Shepherd (John 21)

Space does not permit a full discussion of the relationship between John 21 and the rest of the Gospel, though I think Bauckham and Paul Minear are right to note that in many ways the Gospel is incomplete without this chapter.[27] Certainly this can be said of Peter's own character arc, which reaches its culmina-

---

23. Barrett (*St. John*, p. 439) considers this μή to indicate a tentative statement, not unlike the question of the Samaritan woman in 4:29.

24. See Culpepper, *Anatomy*, p. 120: "Significantly, what Peter denies in John is not that Jesus is Lord but that he is his disciple (18:17, 25, 27)." See also Krafft, "Personnen," pp. 24-25; Droge, "Status," p. 311.

25. Readers of John must be on guard not to import Synoptic accounts of Peter's reaction to his triple denial (Mark 14:72 and pars.). The evangelist does not describe Peter as stricken with grief or weeping. He simply describes the rooster's crow, and proceeds with the account of Jesus' trial. Nevertheless, the real moment for Peter's grief will not come until he sees Jesus again (21:17). See Lincoln, *John*, p. 456.

26. Michaels (*John*, p. 901) notes the irony here: Jesus has already ensured that his disciples will be safe from harm (18:9), and so Peter proves himself unfaithful even when his security is assured.

27. Paul S. Minear, "The Original Functions of John 21," *JBL* 102 (1983): 85-98; Bauckham, "Beloved Disciple," pp. 27-28.

tion in this last scene of the Gospel.[28] Though Peter has seen the empty tomb (20:8-9), and though he has (presumably) been among the disciples whom the resurrected Jesus visited and commissioned (20:19-29), Peter and some of his fellow disciples do not immediately go and fulfill their duties, but instead go fishing. The expedition reveals that Peter has not yet fully realized his potential as a disciple. Jesus must lead him along the final leg of his journey. So Jesus arrives on the shore, and makes himself known to the disciples via a miraculous catch of fish. Once aware of Jesus' presence on the shore, Peter shows his characteristic impetuousness: he puts on his outer garment and swims for shore, while the rest of the disciples bring in the boats (21:7b-8). Once on shore, they see a coal fire (ἀνθρακιὰν, 21:9), an image that appeared only once earlier in the Gospel, during the courtyard scene where Peter warmed himself with the guards (18:18), priming the reader to connect the two scenes.

After sharing a meal, Jesus turns his attention to Peter. Here he urges him to accept the role of shepherd, with the attitude appropriate for such a leader.[29] He begins, "Simon, son of John," which is only the second time he calls Peter by this title. The other time he did so was at their first meeting (1:42). In that encounter, we should recall, Peter remained completely passive, exhibiting submission to Jesus rather than self-determination. Jesus elicits that first meeting and allows Peter to start again, only now possessing greater knowledge and experience. Having gone through his betrayal and denial of Jesus and seeing how *not* to be a disciple, Peter can start afresh.

Jesus uses this past experience, particularly the triple denial, to guide Peter along the last steps of his journey. He asks him, "Do you love me more than these?" (21:15).[30] Raising this question of Peter's love for Jesus enables Peter to think seriously about his relationship to his master. He invites Peter to reform: "Do you love me?" Peter answers with a humble, "Yes, Lord, you know that I love you" (21:15).[31] Jesus responds with a simple command: "Feed my lambs"

28. See, e.g., Beverly Roberts Gaventa, "The Archive of Excess: John 21 and the Problem of Narrative Closure," in *Exploring the Gospel of John: In Honor of D. Moody Smith,* ed. R. Alan Culpepper and C. Clifton Black (Louisville: Westminster John Knox, 1996), pp. 240-52.

29. C. M. Conway notes that "rehabilitation" is not the best word to describe this scene, but rather simply that "Peter's character takes on a new dimension in chapter 21, which seems to compensate for his earlier portrayal." *Men and Women in the Fourth Gospel: Gender and Johannine Characterization* (Atlanta: Society of Biblical Literature, 1999), pp. 174-75.

30. Culpepper's understanding of the meaning of "more than these [πλέον τούτων]" is the least controversial, and raises the most appropriate aspect of this question: where does Peter's loyalty lie? ("Peter," pp. 172-73). See also Blaine, *Peter,* p. 164.

31. While some have wondered if there are two kinds of love referenced by the different verbs here, the variation does not seem to accord with the evangelist's overall style. For exam-

(21:15). If Peter loves Jesus (as he says), then he will do what Jesus has done in taking care of the flock. Peter's love will be measured only by his willingness to fulfill this command.

This interaction takes place three successive times, mirroring the triple denial, to which Peter responds with grief (21:17), signaling his full recognition of the prior failures.[32] He responds, "Lord, you know all things; you know that I love you" (21:17). So Peter has come to embrace the humility and love necessary to serve as the shepherd of the sheep in Jesus' stead, though Jesus has had to guide the man with sometimes sharp rebuke and even allowing him to fail utterly as a disciple.

Having given the final command to tend his flock, Jesus tells Peter most vividly how he will play a part in the divine drama, how he will live out his life in submission to God's plans rather than his own. "When you were younger, you used to dress yourself and go wherever you wanted. But when you grow old, you will extend your hands, and someone else will clothe you and take you where you do not want to go" (21:18). This, the evangelist says, signified "the death by which [Peter] would die" (21:19). For Peter to accept the role as the shepherd, then he, like the Good Shepherd, would have to lay down his life.[33] Knowing this, when Jesus gives him the final invitation: "Follow me!" (21:19), Peter does as he is bidden.

Summary and Conclusion

In his first scene, Peter was passive to all, and submitted to Jesus. In the last scene, he appears similarly, only now with an understanding of the task Jesus has set before him. Having learned what sort of discipleship Jesus truly desires, he has set aside his violent and self-determined ways of following. Instead, he adopts a posture of submission to God's will, even if it means laying down his life. Yet Peter does not come to such maturity on his own. At every step, Jesus has prepared him, challenged him, and led him so that he could fulfill the role Jesus had in store for him. Only through Jesus' instruction does Peter become fully realized as a disciple.

---

ple, "the disciple Jesus loved" is described with φιλέω in 20:2, though elsewhere with ἀγαπάω. See Culpepper, "Peter," p. 175; Barrett, *St. John*, p. 486.

32. So T. Wiarda, who observes that in this exchange Jesus "confronts Peter . . . , upsetting his equilibrium and challenging him to make decisions and take new action." "John 21.1-23: Narrative Unity and Its Implications," *JSNT* 46 (1992): 53-71, here p. 53.

33. Cf. Bennema, *Encountering Jesus*, p. 60.

This leads to the real focus of Peter's characterization: Peter's story is not only, or even principally, his own. To be sure, the evangelist presumes Peter to be the right man for the job of the chief shepherd.[34] But the one who selected him and equipped him for his future role in the church — Jesus — is the most crucial character in Peter's story, because without Jesus, Peter has no story. Jesus' adaptability, his concern for Peter, his concern for his disciples after his departure and the community they will lead, all find expression in Peter's story, and reveal several things the evangelist affirms about Jesus' character. Peter's function in the Gospel is to provide an example (among several) of Jesus' pedagogy and formative work among his followers. What is more, this provides the Gospel's readers with some insight about their own discipleship: if Peter can be so radically transformed to serve God so nobly, then so can they.

This observation allows for a reappraisal of the question of the portrayal of Peter and the reconstruction of early Christian history. The debate mentioned at the beginning of this essay regarding Peter's portrayal implied an anti-Petrine bias in John, even suggesting a rift with Petrine Christianity, while the more recent consensus considers the Johannine Peter as a memorialization of a faithful leader in the church's memory. Yet, while this latter view has many strengths, the centrality of Peter's discipleship in the Gospel indicates that his portrayal has less to do with the historical Peter or even "Petrine Christianity" than it does with the Johannine understanding of discipleship. In this way, the Johannine Peter serves to illustrate one key facet of the community's memory of the historical Peter: principally as one who becomes equipped to lead only by means of Jesus' guidance and care, the same guidance and care by which they believed themselves to be transformed.

34. Bauckham, "Beloved Disciple," p. 36.

CHAPTER 9

Moving the People to Repentance: Peter in Luke-Acts

Finn Damgaard

Introduction

Luke's portrayal of Peter is probably the most positive portrayal in the New Testament Gospels. According to Luke, Peter has already grasped Jesus' true identity at his call, and he is therefore turned into a much more positive figure than in Mark (and Matthew and John for that matter). Luke specifies already at the outset that Peter leaves everything in order to follow Jesus (Luke 5:11),[1] and in rewriting the earlier Gospel portrayal of Peter, Luke removes almost every sign of Peter's failing and even omits passages in which Peter turns out badly. The Lukan Peter does not protest against Jesus' passion predictions (Luke 9:21-22), so Jesus has no need to reprimand him. Luke also comes to Peter's rescue in the transfiguration story by claiming that the disciples fell asleep; as a consequence, Peter could not have known of the previous conversation between Jesus, Moses, and Elijah when he suggested making three dwellings, and in case a former reader of Mark or Matthew might hold Peter responsible for such an ill-timed remark, Luke explains that Peter was still heavy with sleep, clarifying that Peter "did not know what he said" (Luke 9:33). Luke also whitewashes Peter at the Mount of Olives. While Peter is singled out by Jesus and reproached for his sleeping in the Gethsemane story in both Mark and Matthew (Mark 14:37; Matt. 26:40), the Lukan Jesus, by contrast, reproaches the disciples as a group,

---

1. In Mark and Matthew, the fact that Peter left everything in order to follow Jesus is pointed out much later (Mark 10:28; Matt. 19:27).

and the reproach is softened by the note that the disciples were "sleeping because of grief" (Luke 22:45).

The same tendency to soften the characterization of Peter can also be found in the denial scene. Luke's Peter neither swears an oath nor invokes a curse upon himself to strengthen his vow that he does not know Jesus (in contrast to Mark 14:71; Matt. 26:72, 74), and he never promises that he will not become a deserter (Luke 22:33) as the Peter of Mark and Matthew does (Mark 14:29; Matt. 26:33). The readers also already know that Peter will turn again, since it is anticipated in Jesus' words in Luke 22:32. One might wonder, however, why Luke did not simply omit the denial story when his recasting of the scene demonstrates that it was problematic for him that Peter makes a poor show. The fact that the denial story was part of the Gospel tradition does not seem to be a sufficient reason for Luke to include the story. Luke apparently did not hesitate to omit Peter's protest against Jesus' passion predictions — which is also an important element in Mark's Gospel. It seems therefore highly relevant to ask for what reason Luke included an account of the denial. I shall argue that the scene provided Luke with an opportunity to show that Peter, just as Paul, had experienced a change or reversal prior to his new ministry as a preacher of repentance. As we shall see, Luke's recasting of Peter's denial and subsequent turning reflects the people's involvement in Jesus' crucifixion and their subsequent repentance and returning. Luke thus turns Peter's denial and turning into a paradigmatic experience for repentance and "conversion" similar to Paul's "conversion." Although Peter himself never explicitly recalls the circumstances of his own turning in order to appeal to his listeners to recognize the need for repentance (such as Paul does in Acts 26:19-20), Luke emphasizes that it is only Peter's turning that enables him to become a preacher of repentance.

The Turning of Peter and the People

So why did Luke include an account of the denial? The answer to the puzzle, I believe, can be found in Luke's version of Jesus' prediction of Peter's denial. Once Peter has turned back, he is admonished by Jesus to "strengthen your brothers" (στήρισον τοὺς ἀδελφούς σου, Luke 22:32). Jesus' appeal to Peter is normally seen as referring to the disciples or the Twelve only.[2] Luke, however,

2. Such as Gerhard Schneider, " 'Stärke deine Brüder!' (Lk 22,32). Die Aufgabe des Petrus nach Lukas," in *Lukas, Theologe der Heilsgeschichte. Aufsätze zum lukanischen Doppelwerk,* ed. Gerhard Schneider (Bonn: Hanstein, 1985), pp. 148-49.

never explicitly tells *when* Peter strengthens the other disciples (in contrast to Paul, who is explicitly said to have strengthened the disciples in Acts 14:21; 15:41; 16:5; 18:23).[3] Perhaps we have been looking in the wrong direction when we assume that the Lukan Jesus here refers to the disciples. Given the fact that Peter himself refers to the *people* as brothers in Acts 2:29 and 3:17, we should probably presuppose a wider understanding of ἀδελφοί in Luke 22:32. Add to this the fact that Luke never depicts the other disciples as stumbling (in contrast to Mark 14:27, 50), it seems rather strange that it would be the disciples who are in need of Peter to strengthen them. A wider understanding of ἀδελφοί in Luke 22:32 would mean that Luke does actually portray Peter as fulfilling Jesus' commission to strengthen his brothers when he moves the people to repentance at the beginning of Acts.

This would also explain why Luke has emphasized that it is only Peter's *turning* (ἐπιστρέψας as the conjunctive participle to στήρισον) — and implicitly his previous denial — that enables him to strengthen the brothers.[4] Luke seems to imply that Peter, as a preacher of repentance, had to pass through the same crisis as the people. Peter's denial seems thus to be a foil to the people's sudden involvement in Jesus' crucifixion. As Richard Ascough has shown, there are some striking similarities between the denial scene and Luke's account of the people in the passion narrative and the beginning of Acts.[5] Thus just as Peter went out and wept bitterly immediately after his denials (Luke 22:62), so too Luke claims that the people (ὄχλοι)[6] returned home "beating their breasts" (τύπτοντες τὰ στήθη, Luke 23:48), which is a sign of grief and repentance (see Luke 18:13). The people's rejection of Jesus was accordingly short-lived, similar to Peter's rejection, and they therefore responded readily to Peter's missionary speeches summoning them to repentance in the beginning of Acts (Acts 2:38; 3:19). According to Acts 2:37, the people "were cut to the

---

3. Readers of Acts have often looked in vain for Luke's account of Peter strengthening his brothers. The copyist of Codex Bezae Cantabrigiensis has — presumably on his own initiative — added a lengthy paragraph before Acts 11:2 in order to solve the problem: "Now Peter had wanted for a long time to go to Jerusalem. He called the brothers and strengthened them."

4. As also noted by Wolfgang Dietrich, *Das Petrusbild der lukanischen Schriften* (Stuttgart: Kohlhammer, 1972), pp. 133-34; and Markus Bockmuehl, *Simon Peter in Scripture and Memory: The New Testament Apostle in the Early Church* (Grand Rapids: Baker Academic, 2012), p. 156.

5. Richard S. Ascough, "Rejection and Repentance: Peter and the People in Luke's Passion Narrative," *Biblica* 74 (1993): 349-65, here p. 357.

6. There is no consistent pattern in Luke's use of ὄχλος, ὄχλοι, and λαός. Here ὄχλοι should probably be taken as a synonym for λαός; see also Ascough, "Rejection and Repentance," p. 364; J. Kodell, "Luke's Use of Laos, 'People,' especially in the Jerusalem Narrative (LK 19,28-24,53)," *CBQ* 31 (1969): 327-43.

heart" (κατενύγησαν τὴν καρδίαν) by Peter's Pentecost speech and three thousand were baptized (Acts 2:41), and later five thousand more were added (Acts 4:4; see also 2:47; 5:14). In order to effect repentance Peter accuses the people of having killed Jesus (ἀνείλατε, Acts 2:23; ἀπεκτείνατε, 3:15), fastening him to the cross (προσπήξαντες, Acts 2:23), crucifying him (ἐσταυρώσατε, Acts 2:36), and handing him over (παρεδώκατε, Acts 3:13). In the mouth of Peter, the crucial term is of course his accusation that they *denied* Jesus (ἠρνήσασθε, Acts 3:13-14) just as he himself had done (ἠρνήσατο, Luke 22:57; cf. ἀπαρνήσῃ, Luke 22:34, 61).

Ascough also calls attention to several similarities between Luke's account of Peter's denial and the people's call for Jesus' crucifixion. In each of these cases Luke uses a triadic structure in which the issue at hand becomes more and more intense with each element of the triad.[7] Thus in the third instance, a man emphatically insists (διϊσχυρίζετο) that he is sure (ἐπ' ἀληθείας) that Peter was with Jesus, because Peter is a Galilean (Luke 22:59). The same intensity can be found in the third instance of the people's response to Pilate in which they desire more urgently (οἱ δὲ ἐπέκειντο), demanding with loud shouts (φωναῖς μεγάλαις αἰτούμενοι) that Jesus should be crucified (Luke 23:23). Both Peter and the crowd respond to the challenge by ignoring the evidence: Peter ignores that he is a Galilean and offers no evidence to the contrary ("Man, I do not know what you are talking about!" Luke 22:60), and the crowd does not respond to Pilate's challenge to produce evidence ("Why, what evil has he done? I have found in him no ground for the sentence of death," Luke 23:22), but keeps demanding that Jesus should be crucified.[8]

The aim of Ascough's article is to explain why Luke suddenly involves the people in Jesus' death when he hitherto has been careful to indicate that the people were not in any way in opposition to Jesus. In Ascough's view, "the comparison of the account of Peter's denials with the [people's] call for Jesus' crucifixion helps the reader to see more clearly why the people become involved in Jesus' condemnation in Luke's gospel,"[9] namely, in order "to prepare the way for the repentance and conversion of many of the people in the book of Acts."[10] The influence does, however, work both ways, and Luke's presentation of the people in the passion narrative has probably also influenced his account of Peter's denials or perhaps even been the actual reason why Luke preserved

7. Ascough, "Rejection and Repentance," p. 357.
8. Ascough, "Rejection and Repentance," p. 358.
9. Ascough, "Rejection and Repentance," p. 357.
10. Ascough, "Rejection and Repentance," p. 365.

the account in his Gospel. Though Peter does not himself refer explicitly to his denial and repentance in his missionary speeches in Acts, readers of Luke-Acts know from Luke 22:32 that it is precisely his own denials that enable Peter to strengthen the people and take up a leading position in the church. When Peter commands the people to "turn" (ἐπιστρέψατε, Acts 3:19) it might also be read as Luke's subtle reference to Peter's own turning (see σύ ποτε ἐπιστρέψας, Luke 22:32).[11] Peter's denial and subsequent turning thus reflect the people's involvement in Jesus' crucifixion and their subsequent repentance and returning. Like Peter, the people fail in the passion narrative, but both before and after the passion narrative Luke is keen on portraying them positively. He stresses their openness to Jesus in his introduction to Jesus' public work in Jerusalem (Luke 19:48), and in the beginning of Acts he emphasizes that the believers had "all" the people's goodwill (χάρις, Acts 2:47; see also 4:21) and were held in high esteem (Acts 5:13). Luke also claims that they are devout (εὐλαβεῖς, Acts 2:5), and Peter's reference to them as "brothers" in the middle of his Pentecost speech is a sign to the reader that Peter views his audience as responsive (which is also confirmed by the people's response in Acts 2:37 ["*Brothers,* what should we do?" (emphasis added)]). And, as we have seen, the people also embraced the gospel message in large numbers. Although the parallels between Peter's denial and the people's involvement in Jesus' crucifixion do not completely exculpate the people of responsibility (compare Peter's accusations of the people above), they do, however, take the edge off their responsibility, for just as the disciples did not understand Jesus' passion predictions, since "its meaning was concealed from them" (Luke 9:45; see also 18:34), so Peter claims that the people and their leaders acted "in ignorance" (κατὰ ἄγνοιαν, Acts 3:17).[12]

Actually, it may not come as a surprise to the reader that the people are sorely tried during the passion narrative, since Jesus had informed Peter that "Satan demanded to have you [ὑμᾶς] that he may sift you like wheat" (Luke 22:31). Although the plural probably refers to the Twelve (cf. Luke 22:14-30), it seems reasonable to suppose that the people's sudden involvement in the death of Jesus was also part of the supernatural conflict attending Jesus' ministry. In

11. On ἐπιστρέψας in Luke 22:32, see also Benedetto Prete, "Il senso di ἐπιστρέψας in Luca 22:32," in *San Pietro: Atti della XIX Settimana Biblica,* ed. Associazione biblica italiana (Brescia: Paideia, 1967), pp. 113-35.

12. The ignorance motif is, however, much more insignificant in Codex Bezae as noted by Eldon Jay Epp long ago. The variations in Codex Bezae put more emphasis on the Jews' responsibility for Jesus' death and on their more direct and hostile action against him. See Epp, *The Theological Tendency of Codex Bezae Cantabrigiensis in Acts* (Cambridge: Cambridge University Press, 1966), pp. 41-64.

light of Luke 22:31 the reader would expect the evangelist to demonstrate how the Twelve were sifted. In fact, quite to the contrary, Luke omits to mention that the disciples deserted Jesus and fled (Mark 14:50, 27; Matt. 26:56, 31). Thus, immediately before his prediction of Peter's denial, Luke's Jesus even says to the Twelve: "You are those who have stood by me in my trials" (Luke 22:28). Except for his accounts of Judas' betrayal and Peter's denial, Luke does not focus on the Twelve being "sifted". He seems to be more interested in presenting another example of Satan's sifting, namely the people's sudden involvement in Jesus' death.

Peter and Paul as Preachers of Repentance

As often noted, the concept of repentance (μετανοεῖν/μετάνοια) plays a crucial role in Luke-Acts.[13] In the Gospel, the call to repentance occurs frequently in the preaching and teaching of Jesus. While Jesus in Mark and Matthew claims that he has "not come to call the righteous, but sinners" (Mark 2:17; Matt. 9:13), Luke significantly adds that Jesus has come to call the sinners "to repentance [εἰς μετάνοιαν]" (Luke 5:32). This undoubtedly programmatic statement (see also Luke 24:47) has a crucial impact on the way Luke recasts the figure of Peter. While Mark's portrayal of Peter time and again focuses on Peter's misunderstanding of Jesus' person and mission (Mark 1:35-38; 8:31-33; 9:5-7) and his weakness and fear (Mark 14:37-41, 54, 66-72) and only hints at his remorse and perhaps repentance at the end (Mark 14:72; 16:7), Luke has moved Peter's "conversion" and acknowledgment of Jesus' holiness forward to his call as a disciple, as Peter's words indicate: "Go away from me, Lord, for I am a sinful man" (Luke 5:8). Luke's portrayal of Peter focuses accordingly on Peter's life *after* his "conversion," and this might explain why he writes an embellished version of the Peter narrative. Thus while in Mark's Gospel Peter's denial was the last incident in a long line of failings, the denial is the only occasion when Peter is portrayed in a poor light in Luke's Gospel.[14] As I have argued in this es-

---

13. On repentance in Luke-Acts, see especially Guy D. Nave Jr., *The Role and Function of Repentance in Luke-Acts* (Atlanta: Society of Biblical Literature, 2002), pp. 145-224.

14. Luke seems to have transferred Mark's portrayal of Peter as a person who misjudges situations and is perplexed and confused to his account of Peter and Cornelius in Acts. Here Peter resists (presumably thrice) the voice that commands him to get up and kill and eat, although he himself identifies the voice as being his Lord's voice (Acts 10:14). As Luke Timothy Johnson has rightly stressed, Luke here uses Peter's perplexity and confusion to communicate to the reader how "the Church tries to catch up to God's initiative." See Johnson, *The Acts of the Apostles* (Collegeville, Minn.: Liturgical Press, 1992), p. 187. Just as in Mark's Gospel, Luke's

say, the account of Peter's denials was probably included in order to emphasize Peter's paradigmatic role in repentance and "conversion." Peter is, however, not the only figure in Acts that is paradigmatic for repentance and "conversion."

As often noted,[15] there is a parallel portrayal of Peter and Paul in Acts.[16] They are both led by the Holy Spirit (*Peter:* Acts 2:4; 4:8; 10:19, 44-46; *Paul:* Acts 13:4, 9; 16:6-7; 20:22), and learn about God's plan through visions (*Peter:* Acts 10:3, 17; *Paul:* Acts 16:9-10; 18:9). Their gospel message is very similar and they believe that the Jews as well as the gentiles are coheirs (*Peter:* Acts 10:34-48; 15:7-11; *Paul:* 13:46; 17:22-31). They speak with παρρησία (*Peter:* Acts 2:29; *Paul:* Acts 9:28; 13:46; 14:3; 26:26; 28:31), are successful (*Peter:* Acts 2:41; 4:4; *Paul:* Acts 13:42-43), and act courageously before the Jewish council (*Peter:* Acts 5:26-33; *Paul:* Acts 23:1-10). They have a miraculous aura (*Peter:* Acts 5:15; *Paul:* 19:11-12), perform miracles (*Peter:* Acts 3:1-11; 5:12-16; *Paul:* 14:3, 8-10; 28:3-6), resurrections (*Peter:* Acts 9:32-43; *Paul:* Acts 20:7-12), exorcisms (*Peter:* Acts 5:16; *Paul:* 16:16-18), and miracles of punishment (*Peter:* Acts 5:1-11; *Paul:* Acts 13:6-12). They are imprisoned (*Peter:* Acts 4:3; 5:18; 12:3-5; *Paul:* 16:19-24; 21:33), experience a miraculous release (*Peter:* Acts 5:19-25; 12:6-19; *Paul:* 16:25-40), and have a tense relationship with parts of the church in Jerusalem at some point in their career (*Peter:* Acts 11:2-3; *Paul:* 15:1-6).[17] For our purpose, the

---

portrayal of the perplexed Peter does not mean that the readers dissociate themselves from him. On the contrary, the readers cannot help but sympathize with Peter's struggle. Interestingly, when Peter later justifies his baptism of Cornelius and his household to the circumcised believers in Jerusalem, he claims that he "remembered [ἐμνήσθην] the word of the Lord" (Acts 11:16). Just as in the Gospel of Mark, remembrance thus plays an important role for Luke's figure of Peter. When Peter remembers, he stops failing (cf. also Luke 22:61-62).

15. For recent studies of the parallels between Peter and Paul in Acts, see Susan Marie Praeder, "Miracle Worker and Missionary: Paul in the Acts of the Apostles," in *Society of Biblical Literature Seminar Papers 1983*, ed. Kent Harold Richards (Chico, Calif.: Scholars Press, 1983), pp. 114-20; Andrew C. Clark, "The Role of the Apostles," in *Witness to the Gospel: The Theology of Acts*, ed. I. Howard Marshall and David Peterson (Grand Rapids: Eerdmans, 1998), pp. 185-89; and Jürgen Becker, *Simon Petrus im Urchristentum*, 2nd ed. (Neukirchen-Vluyn: Neukirchener Verlagsgesellschaft, 2011), pp. 115-22. In Codex Bezae, there is even a tendency to enhance the parallels between Peter and Paul as argued by Epp, *Theological Tendency*, pp. 156-57; and Carlo M. Martini, "La Figura di Pietro secondo le variant del Codice D negli atti degli apostolic," in Associazione biblica italiana, *San Pietro*, pp. 279-89, here p. 285.

16. This paragraph on the parallel portrayal of Peter and Paul in Acts reproduces parts of a paragraph in my article, "Persecution and Denial — Paradigmatic Apostolic Portrayals in Paul and Mark," in *Mark and Paul: Comparative Essays*, Part II, *For and Against Pauline Influence on Mark*, ed. Eve-Marie Becker, Troels Engberg-Pedersen, and Mogens Müller (Berlin: de Gruyter, 2014), pp. 295-310, here pp. 306-7.

17. Most of these parallels are also conveniently listed in Becker, *Simon Petrus*, pp. 120-21.

most significant parallel is, however, that they both act as preachers of repentance (*Peter:* Acts 2:38; 3:19-26;[18] 5:31; 8:22; 11:18; *Paul:* Acts 13:24, 38-39; 17:30; 20:21; 26:20), and just as Peter experienced a change or reversal prior to his new ministry as a preacher of repentance, so did Paul. They are even addressed by Jesus in a similar way when he twice calls them with their former name in the crucial narratives about their "turning" (*Peter:* "Simon, Simon," Luke 22:31; *Paul:* "Saul, Saul," Acts 9:4; 22:7; 26:14).

By focusing on the transformation of Paul, his change from persecutor to persecuted, Luke also turns Paul into a paradigmatic figure. Paul's journey of "conversion" becomes "representative of the conversion of all believers"[19] when, for instance, he recalls the circumstances of his own "conversion" in order to appeal to his listeners to recognize the need for repentance (Acts 26:19-20). By emphasizing Paul's role as the great persecutor in each account of his "conversion," Luke draws a contrast between Saul the ideal persecutor and Paul the ideal missionary (Acts 9:4, 6, 13-14; 22:7-8; 26:14-15). Paul's persecution is here used as a foil to display God's miraculous intervention. With his portrayal of Paul as a paradigmatic figure, Luke probably exploits Paul's self-portrayal as a persecutor of the church. Though Paul himself claims to have persecuted the church in order "to destroy it" (ἐπόρθουν αὐτήν, Gal 1:13; see also 1:23),[20] he is not as specific as Luke concerning the nature of the persecutions. According to Luke, Paul was engaged in acts of violence against his victims. He had Christians imprisoned (Acts 8:3; 22:4; 26:10) and voted for the death penalty against them (Acts 9:1; 26:10). Luke seems, however, to exaggerate Paul's brutality, probably in order to emphasize God's transforming power and highlight all the more his later missionary activity. As rightly stressed by Arland Hultgren, Paul probably did "not understand persecution as a procedure which ends in the death of the victim";[21] his persecution should rather be seen within the framework of "the Jewish system of discipline pre-

18. According to Robert C. Tannehill, Peter's speech in Solomon's portico is "the repentance speech *par excellence.*" See Tannehill, "The Function of Peter's Mission Speeches in the Narrative of Acts," *NTS* 37 (1991): 400-414, here p. 406 (emphasis original).

19. Jean-François Landolt, "'Be Imitators of Me, Brothers and Sisters' (Philippians 3.17): Paul as an Exemplary Figure in the Pauline Corpus and the Acts of the Apostles," in *Paul and the Heritage of Israel,* ed. David P. Moessner, Daniel Marguerat, Mikeal C. Parsons, and Michael Wolter (London: T&T Clark, 2012), pp. 290-317, here p. 307.

20. For Paul's use of πορθεῖν, see Philippe H. Menoud, "Le sens du verbe Πορθεῖν," in *Apophoreta: Festschrift für Ernst Haenchen,* ed. Walther Eltester et al. (Berlin: Töpelmann, 1964), pp. 178-186.

21. Arland J. Hultgren, "Paul's Pre-Christian Persecutions of the Church: Their Purpose, Locale, and Nature," *JBL* 95 (1976): 97-111, here p. 108.

vailing at the time, i.e., the judicial flogging and imprisonment, both of which were designed to bring the offender back into line."[22] By exaggerating Paul's brutality Luke creates a greater contrast between Saul the persecutor (Acts 9:1-2) and Paul the persecuted (Acts 9:23-29). Paul is now persecuted for the same reasons that he himself became a persecutor.

Luke's portrayal of Paul seems to develop the contrast between "then" and "now" — between Paul as persecutor and Paul as preacher — which is a crucial idea in the letter to the Galatians. Given the fact that Luke portrays both Peter and Paul as preachers of repentance in Acts, I would hypothetically suggest that Luke's portrayal of Peter might have been written under the influence of Paul's letters. Luke might not only have written a "Pauline" speech for Peter at the Jerusalem council (Acts 15:7-11), he may even have rewritten Peter narratives such as the denial narrative under the influence of Paul's letters — in this case Paul's self-portrayal as a persecutor of the church. Just as Luke turns Paul into a paradigmatic figure for repentance and "conversion," so he presents Peter's denial and subsequent repentance and returning as a paradigmatic experience similar to the people's sudden involvement in Jesus' crucifixion and their subsequent repentance and turning.

Although Luke never explicitly mentions Peter's repentance after the denial scene (with the exception of his bitter weeping), much of the later story in Luke and Acts actually depends on this incident. Luke accordingly picks up Mark's figure of Peter at the moment when he breaks down outside the high priest's palace (Mark 14:72). While Mark left his figure in the courtyard and only indicated that Peter got the better of his fear (Mark 16:7), Luke takes on the mantle of Mark and demonstrates what the figure would look like upon leaving the courtyard. In Luke's view, Peter would of course be present at Jesus' crucifixion (οἱ γνωστοὶ in Luke 23:49 implies that Peter was present, along with the other disciples), would later run to the tomb (Luke 24:12), and would be the first to meet the risen Lord (Luke 24:34). But most importantly, he would carry on Jesus' mission in Luke's Gospel by moving the people to repentance (see also Luke 24:47).

22. Hultgren, "Paul's Pre-Christian Persecutions," p. 110.

CHAPTER 10

The Tradition of Peter's Literacy: Acts, 1 Peter, and Petrine Literature

Sean A. Adams

One of the main observations of Markus Bockmuehl's recent work is that the picture presented of Peter in the New Testament is surprisingly vague and incomplete, particularly in terms of biographical details.[1] In the following investigation, however, I am not concerned with the reconstruction of the historical Peter, nor do I attempt to determine his level of literacy.[2] Rather, I seek to trace the literary development and characterization of Peter as literate in both canonical and parabiblical literature.[3] Nevertheless, assumptions about the historic Peter's literacy have influenced the debate regarding the authorship of 1 Peter and his later depictions. How one views the literary world of first-century Galilee and Peter's involvement (or lack thereof) within it directly affects one's response to the question of Peter's literacy. This in turn frames one's view of the authorship and interpretation of the Petrine letters and the reception of Peter in Christian literature. The viewpoint offered here is that the perception of Peter as a literate figure helped shaped the constructed portraits of Peter in subsequent literature.

---

1. Markus Bockmuehl, *Simon Peter in Scripture and Memory: The New Testament Apostle in the Early Church* (Grand Rapids: Baker Academic, 2012), p. 32.

2. The name Peter will be used to refer to both the literary and historical figure of Peter. This is not because I do not recognize that there is a difference, but because using quotation marks for Peter's name throughout the work is tedious and distracting.

3. A theme surprisingly absent in most books and articles on Peter. E.g., Fred Lapham, *Peter: The Myth, the Man and the Writings*, JSNTSup 239 (Sheffield: Sheffield Academic, 2003); Lutz Doering, "Apostle, Co-Elder, and Witness of Suffering: Author Construction and Peter Image in First Peter," in *Pseudepigraphe und Verfasserfiktion in frühchristlichen Briefen*, ed. J. Frey et al., WUNT 246 (Tübingen: Mohr Siebeck, 2009), pp. 645-81.

In this essay I begin by looking briefly at Acts 4:13 and what Luke's presentation of Peter's literacy contributes to modern and ancient discussions. Following this we turn to the question of the authorship of 1 Peter and how its attribution to Peter began the literary presentation of Peter as someone with reading and writing competencies. The main body of my discussion identifies the representations of Peter as a literate teacher. In this section I argue that, although there are no explicit claims to Peter's formal education, Peter is presented as competently handling and interacting with texts in a way that is consistent with that of what we may call a "text-broker." Overall, the goals of this paper are twofold. First, I seek to identify and trace references and depictions of Peter as literate; and second I argue that the assertion of literacy in the letter of 1 Peter and the early church's acceptance of Peter's authorship, regardless of whether or not Peter was the actual author, provided the foundation for later writers to construct a portrait of a literate Peter.

One final comment on terminology is warranted before we continue, although insufficient space does not allow for a full discussion. It is important to highlight at the outset that I do not ascribe to a literate/illiterate dichotomy, but recognize that many gradations of literacy existed in the ancient world.[4] Accordingly, when I use the terms *literate* or *illiterate* I am not making an either/or distinction, but employ these terms as convenient representations of broad concepts.

Acts 4:13 and Peter as ἀγράμματος

Before turning to the Petrine corpus, we need to evaluate briefly the one verse in the New Testament that appears to address explicitly Peter's level of education, namely Acts 4:13. In this scene (Acts 4:1-22) Luke narrates an encounter between Peter and the Jewish leaders in which the rulers, elders, scribes, and the high priest marvel at Peter and John's speaking prowess and attribute their ability to their time with Jesus.[5] The reason for the Jewish leaders' shock is

4. For example, a person's ability to write could range from "signature literate" to the ability to craft high-level prose or poetry. For a more thorough discussion, see William V. Harris, *Ancient Literacy* (Cambridge, Mass.: Harvard University Press, 1989), pp. 3-24; Raffaella Cribiore, *Gymnastics of the Mind: Greek Education in Hellenistic and Roman Egypt* (Princeton: Princeton University Press, 2001), pp. 160-84.

5. On Peter in Acts, see Sean A. Adams, *The Genre of Acts and Collected Biography*, SNTSMS 156 (Cambridge: Cambridge University Press, 2013), pp. 212-18; Osvaldo Padilla, *The*

that Peter and John were known to them to be "uneducated and untrained" (ἄνθρωποι ἀγράμματοί εἰσιν καὶ ἰδιῶται).

Substantial debate has ensued over the interpretation of ἀγράμματος and ἰδιώτης, their meaning in Luke's narrative, and their impact on the reconstruction of the historical Peter and John. Speaking purely on the narrative level, the event in Acts is understood by Richard Pervo to represent the fulfillment of Luke 21:12-15 and the promise of supernatural wisdom and ability when the disciples are before their accusers.[6] This is an insightful connection with the Lukan narrative and provides one reason for the inclusion of the statement in 4:13. The implications of this reading, however, still need to be teased out for the development of Peter's character in Luke-Acts and the debate surrounding the (possible) representativeness of the person of Peter in this two-volume work.

In Greek literature, the term ἀγράμματος describes one who is "without letters," that is, illiterate (Xenophon, *Mem.* 4.2.20; Plutarch, *Reg. imp. apophth.* 186A).[7] This understanding continued throughout the Hellenistic and Roman eras and is by far the most common way of understanding this term.[8] Interestingly, a number of commentators are reticent to accept this general interpretation for ἀγράμματος and argue that a lack of theological training was in view. For example, David Peterson interprets "unlettered" in the sense that "they were not trained as interpreters of Scripture and rabbinic tradition."[9] In his interpretation of Acts, C. K. Barrett contrasts ἀγράμματος, not with γραμματικός, but with γραμματεύς, in order to reach the interpretation that Peter was "a man without scribal training in the law."[10] Other scholars reject the interpretation of "illiterate" due to their assumption of widespread literacy among the population of Jewish Palestine.[11]

Speeches of Outsiders in Acts: Poetics, Theology and Historiography, SNTSMS 144 (Cambridge: Cambridge University Press, 2008), p. 112.

6. Richard I. Pervo, *Acts,* Hermeneia (Minneapolis: Fortress, 2009), p. 117.

7. See the discussion in n. 4 regarding levels of "illiteracy."

8. As the extant papyri amply demonstrate, being unable to read or write was not stigmatized in ancient times as it is today. Thomas J. Kraus, "'Uneducated,' 'Ignorant,' or even 'Illiterate'? Aspects and Background for an Understanding of ΑΓΡΑΜΜΑΤΟΙ (and ΙΔΙΩΤΑΙ) in Acts 4.13," *NTS* 45 (1999): 434-49.

9. David G. Peterson, *The Acts of the Apostles,* PNTC (Grand Rapids: Eerdmans, 2009), p. 194.

10. C. K. Barrett, *Acts 1–14,* ICC (Edinburgh: T&T Clark, 1994), p. 234. Contra Ernst Haenchen, *The Acts of the Apostles: A Commentary* (Oxford: Blackwell, 1971), p. 218 n. 1; Christian Grappe, *Images de Pierre aux deux premiers siècles,* EHPR 71 (Paris: Presses universitaires de France, 1995), p. 206.

11. E.g., L&N §27.23. Contra Meir Bar-Ilan, "Illiteracy in the Land of Israel in the First

Part of this confusion is based on the assumption that ἀγράμματος and ἰδιώτης are synonymous. For example, Josep Rius-Camps and Jenny Read-Heimerdinger argue that the scribe of Codex Bezae held such a view and so deleted the superfluous καὶ ἰδιῶται.[12] The problem with this reading for their argument, however, is that it suggests that the other text traditions most likely understood ἀγράμματος in its traditional way of "uneducated" and so included καὶ ἰδιῶται to indicate something else, possibly their lack of theological training (i.e., that they were laymen).[13]

Thomas Kraus has argued, I think convincingly, that the term ἰδιώτης, although related to ἀγράμματος, has a distinct semantic range.[14] An ἰδιώτης was someone without formal training. This could refer to a specific skill, such as speaking (Josephus, *Ant.* 2.274), or, more generally, it could indicate that the person was not a professional (Thucydides 2.48.2; Plato, *Laws* 830A). The term ἰδιώτης may include or imply a lack of reading and writing ability, but it is much more encompassing and speaks to a person's general training for a profession. As a result, it appears that the Acts narrative presents Peter as both uneducated *and* as a layperson.[15] Accordingly, Barrett does not totally miss the mark when comparing Peter with the scribes, as the scribes were understood to be literate and the text-brokers for the community. A contest of mediating authoritative interpretations is clearly in view in Acts 4:13, and Peter is presented by Luke as challenging the hegemony of the Jewish leadership. That Peter is unlettered undermines (in their view) both his claim to this position and his ability to interpret the scriptural text authoritatively, which results in their agitation.[16]

Centuries C.E.," in *Essays in the Social Scientific Study of Judaism and Jewish Society,* ed. S. Fishbane et al. (Hoboken, N.J.: Ktav, 1992), 2:46-61; Catherine Hezser, *Jewish Literacy in Roman Palestine,* TSAJ 81 (Tübingen: Mohr Siebeck, 2001), pp. 496-504.

12. Josep Rius-Camps and Jenny Read-Heimerdinger, *Message of Acts in Codex Bezae: A Comparison with the Alexandrian Tradition,* vol. 1, *Acts 1.1–5.42: Jerusalem,* JSNTSup 257 (London: T&T Clark, 2004), pp. 250, 262. Challenged by Kraus, "Uneducated," pp. 444-46.

13. Rius-Camps and Read-Heimerdinger, *Message,* pp. 250, 262. Others, such as Barrett (*Acts,* pp. 233-34) and Darrell L. Bock, *Acts* (BECNT; Grand Rapids: Baker, 2007), p. 195, assert that Codex D omitted ἰδιώτης, not because it was superfluous, but because it was disrespectful for the disciples.

14. Kraus, "Uneducated," pp. 444-46.

15. Martin Hengel, *Saint Peter: The Underestimated Apostle,* trans. T. H. Trapp (Grand Rapids: Eerdmans, 2006), p. 13.

16. For a similar discussion regarding the comparison of Jesus and the scribes and for a discussion of the nature of text-brokers, see Chris Keith, *The Pericope Adulterae, the Gospel of John, and the Literacy of Jesus,* NTTSD 38 (Leiden: Brill, 2009), pp. 116, 201.

In addition to the modern interpretations of Acts, of importance for my discussion is the way that early Christian writers understood Acts 4:13 and how they may have viewed Peter's education level. Unfortunately, few texts or extant commentaries on Acts from the first centuries specifically address our passage, although what we do have supports our presentation above. For example, in *Recognitions* 1.62 Pseudo-Clement alludes to Acts 4:13 and presents Peter himself as claiming that he is both uneducated and unlearned, highlighting his rural upbringing and lowly profession as a fisherman. Origen, in *Contra Celsum* 1.62, contrasts Jesus' disciples with philosophers and sect leaders, claiming that if Jesus had chosen men who were wise according to the world's standards he could be accused of employing artifice.[17] Moreover, Origen describes the fishermen who were called by Jesus as those "who had not acquired even the merest elements of learning." John Chrysostom (*Hom. Act.* 10), in addition to reading ἀγράμματος and ἰδιώτης as differing — "For one can be unlearned, yet not a common or private man, and a common man, yet not unlearned" — presents the transformation of Peter and John into learned speakers in Acts 4:13 as a miracle, implying that they had not previously received formal training.

According to these early Christian writers, Peter is thus presented in Acts as not formally educated or theologically trained. Rather, his ability to speak was a result of his empowerment by God to present and defend the gospel in his time of challenge. From this discussion it is clear that the Acts narrative did not initiate the tradition of a literate Peter, but rather was an obstacle for this understanding. Where, then, did this tradition arise from? To begin to answer this question we turn now to the Petrine letter corpus.

Peter's Literacy and the Authorship of 1 Peter

As has been highlighted by John H. Elliott, the position that one takes on the question of authorship affects one's reading of 1 Peter.[18] In this study, I am less concerned with the discussion of authorship or the criteria by which one comes to a conclusion, and more interested in evaluating the consequences of the early Christian attribution of the authorship of 1 Peter to Peter and how

17. A similar perspective is provided by Bede (*Com. Acts* 4.13; trans. Lawrence T. Martin, CS 117 [Kalamazoo, Mich.: Cistercian Publications, 1989], 50), who compared Peter and John against the educated of 1 Cor 1:17.

18. John H. Elliott, *1 Peter: A New Translation with Introduction and Commentary*, AB 37B (New York: Doubleday, 2000), p. 118.

this resulted in a claim of Peter's literacy in the subsequent body of literature around the figure of Peter.

Notwithstanding my focus in this essay, the criterion of literary style typically employed to refute Petrine authorship requires brief discussion, as this involves explicit claims regarding the historical Peter's presumed level of Greek education. The argument typically runs thus: The quality of Greek exhibited in 1 Peter outstrips the expected level of education that a Jewish fisherman in rural Galilee would have received; therefore, 1 Peter could not have been written by the historical Peter.[19] The question of the literary style and quality of Greek in 1 Peter, however, was barely broached by early commentators. In fact, near unanimity existed among early church writers in asserting Petrine authorship for 1 Peter.[20] This is not to say that ancients did not use stylistic analysis to determine authorship. They did; and there are a number of examples both in wider Greco-Roman literature and in early Christian writings.[21] However, there is little discussion regarding the quality of Greek in 1 Peter. In fact, the primary example is that of Jerome (*Vir. ill.* 1), who pointed out that many have questioned the attribution of 2 Peter to Peter because of its stylistic differences from 1 Peter.

Although debate over the authorship of 1 Peter will no doubt continue, it is actually a nonissue for my purpose as it does not have any bearing on the later presentations of Peter as literate. The most important feature here is the early church's endorsement of Petrine authorship. Granted, the writing of letters for people who were illiterate or semiliterate was not uncommon in the ancient world, as the standard illiteracy formula employed by scribes attest: "I wrote on his/her behalf because he/she does not know letters [*agrammatos*]."[22] Although this formula was not required for personal letters, the absence of such a formula in 1 Peter provides the basis for the idea that Peter actually penned the letter himself and did not require assistance. Moreover, once Pe-

---

19. See Elliott, *1 Peter*, pp. 118-30; Karen H. Jobes, *1 Peter*, BECNT (Grand Rapids: Baker Academic, 2005), pp. 14-19. For a substantial critique of the amanuensis theory for 1 Peter, see Elliott, *1 Peter*, pp. 123-24; E. Randolph Richards, *Paul and First-Century Letter Writing: Secretaries, Composition and Collection* (Downers Grove, Ill.: IVP Academic, 2004), pp. 33-35.

20. 2 Pet. 3:1; (use of 1 Peter in) Polycarp, *Phil.* 1.3; 2.1-2; 5.3; 7.2; 8.1-2; 10.2; Irenaeus, *Adv. haer.* 4.9.2; 4.16.5; 5.7.2; Eusebius, *H.E.* 3.25.2; Jerome, *Vir. ill.* 1.

21. E.g., Dionysius of Halicarnassus, *Dinarchus* 5; *On Thucydides; Lysias;* Aulus Gellius, *Noct. att.* 3.3; Philostratus, *Vit. Apoll.* 7.35; Jerome, *Vir. ill.* 25 (on Theophilus of Antioch); Origen in Eusebius, *H.E.* 6.25 (on Pauline nonauthorship of Hebrews); Dionysius of Alexandria in Eusebius, *H.E.* 7.25.7 (on Johannine nonauthorship of Revelation).

22. For discussion and examples, see Harris, *Literacy*, pp. 141-42; Kraus, "Uneducated." Cf. Quintilian, *Inst.* 1.1.28-29.

ter's authorship was established in early church tradition, the literacy claim in 1 Peter 5:12, "I wrote" (ἔγραψα), could be directly conferred to him. It is my suggestion that 1 Peter, both its attribution to Peter and the grapho-literacy claim in 5:12, created sufficient basis and space for a tradition of a literate Peter to form.[23] Although 1 Peter is the first literary work (to our knowledge) attributed to Peter, it is most certainly not the last. It is to this literary tradition and corpus that we now turn.

Subsequent Petrine Literature and Depictions of Peter's Literacy

In this section we will evaluate the works that describe the life and ministry of Peter, especially those that present him as the author/narrator or main character. In these works there are various portraits of Peter — preacher, prophet, debater, miracle worker, seer — none of which is entirely dependent on his ability to read or write. Nevertheless, in these documents we can identify specific instances in which Peter is also presented as reading, writing, or interacting with texts. Such a proficiency for Peter is not supported by the Gospels and appears to be undermined by the Acts narrative, but it forms part of the larger tradition regarding Peter. From this investigation a consistent picture will emerge of Peter as competent to handle and interpret texts. This is not a dominant theme, but is prominent, and provides intriguing evidence of the reception history of Peter in the authors and communities that revered his name.[24] My goal here is not to provide a detailed exegesis of each passage, but to trace this theme as it weaves its way through the tapestry of Petrine literature. Following this we will attempt to tease out the rationale for the inclusion of this theme and discuss the implications of such a presentation of a literate Peter.

The best-known example of this tradition is 2 Peter, which, despite concerns over authorship expressed by some early church writers, found its way into the canon.[25] This skepticism is still held by a majority of modern scholars, who are incredulous at the thought of Petrine authorship of 2 Peter.[26] Never-

---

23. This claim does not speak to the intentionality of the person(s) who penned 1 Peter (assuming it was not Peter himself). Rather, the resultant view of Peter as literate is a secondary, (possibly) unforeseen by-product of the writing and acceptance of 1 Peter.

24. Markus Bockmuehl, *The Remembered Peter in Ancient Reception and Modern Debate*, WUNT 1/262 (Tübingen: Mohr Siebeck, 2010), p. 82.

25. The best examples are Eusebius, *H.E.* 3.3.1-2; 6.25.8 (from Origen); Jerome, *Vir. ill.* 1; Didymus the Blind, *PG* 39 1774A.

26. See Richard Bauckham, *Jude, 2 Peter*, WBC 50 (Waco: Word, 1983), pp. 158-62.

theless, the author of 2 Peter makes repeated claims to Petrine authorship and, correspondingly, asserts a level of literary ability for Peter. The letter opens (1:1) with an attribution to Simon Peter by using the standard letter-opening formula, which is reinforced by the clear claim of authorship and of literacy in 3:1 — "This is now, friends, the second letter I am writing to you." Finally, in 3:16 the author of 2 Peter briefly discusses Paul's letters and the difficulty in understanding their content. Peter expresses awareness of Paul's manner of composition; that Paul's style is consistent among his epistles and that his content is difficult to understand. Though this last passage does not provide an explicit claim for Peter's literary ability, its importance for the theme of interacting with and commenting authoritatively and knowledgeably on texts will become apparent. In 2 Peter itself, however, Peter is presented as handling and interpreting Scripture with authority (see 2 Pet. 2:4-10) and acting as a text-broker for the letter addressees (see 2 Pet. 1:12-16).

One of the earliest noncanonical works attributed to Peter is the *Gospel of Peter.* The extant portion of this text focuses on the passion narrative, beginning with Pilate washing his hands and ending with the disciples in mourning and returning to their homes. In this narrative Peter is presented as the narrator of the work through the use of the first-person singular (v. 26) and an explicit introduction in verse 60: "But I, Simon Peter, and my brother Andrew. . . ." Its fragmentary nature precludes our knowing with certainty whether the writing of the work is attributed to someone other than Peter. Nevertheless, the text as we have it presents Peter not only as a character but also as the first-person narrator, with the implication that he is understood to be the "author" of the work.[27] This, therefore, is a tacit claim of Petrine literacy and is an example of the outworking of this tradition.

A similar case is found in the *Apocalypse of Peter,* of which we have two textual traditions.[28] In the Greek version of the Akhmim text Peter is not explicitly named, although the narrative is set in the context of the canonical transfiguration story. The work begins with the use of the first-person plural, explicitly identified as "we, the twelve disciples" (v. 5); however, beginning at verse 9 the text adopts the first-person singular perspective. The

27. Paul Foster, *The Gospel of Peter: Introduction, Critical Edition and Commentary,* TENTS 4 (Leiden: Brill, 2010), p. 91; Tobias Nicklas, "Erzähler und Charakter zugleich. Zur literarischen Funktion des 'Petrus' in dem nach ihm benannten Evangelienfragment," *VC* 55 (2001): 318-26.

28. For a brief introduction to the texts and related issues, see J. K. Elliott, *The Apocryphal New Testament: A Collection of Apocryphal Christian Literature in an English Translation* (Oxford: Clarendon, 1993), pp. 593-95; Lapham, *Peter,* pp. 195-97.

most likely candidate for this speaker is Peter, although he is not explicitly named. Conversely, the Ethiopian text explicitly identifies Peter as the author ("I, Peter," v. 2), although he is still grouped with the disciples throughout the narrative. Again, though there is no specific mention of Peter's literacy, the use of the first-person singular implies that he is the author of the text. This understanding is made more explicit in a later addition to the Ethiopic text, in which Peter orders Clement to hide the revelation in a box so that foolish people may not see it. The text provides no explicit rationale for introducing the Clement character. It could be that Peter is presented as having dictated his apocalypse to Clement and so was not the implied author, or there could be a desire to give the work further credibility through association. That this section is clearly a later addition in the Ethiopic version does not undermine its value as it provides evidence of how early readers reacted to the text and how some developed the notion of Peter as author.

The Acts of Peter, another second-century document, also presents Peter as literate, although this time in a much more explicit fashion. The narrative recounts a series of interactions between Peter and Simon Magus in which Peter consistently reveals to the crowds that Simon is a deceiver and that his god and gospel message are false. The majority of the work centers on debates, miracles, and speeches, providing only a few instances in which reading and writing are mentioned. There is one scene between confrontations (*Acts Pet.* 20), however, in which Peter claims the ability to write. The narrative is as follows:

> When Peter came into the dining-room he saw that the gospel was being read. And rolling it up he said, "Men, who believe in Christ and hope in him, you shall know how the Holy Scriptures of our Lord must be explained. What we have written down according to his grace."[29]

Although Peter here does not display an ability to read, his claim of writing is unmistakable and so contributes to the tradition of his literacy. Moreover, this passage presents Peter as a mediator of textual traditions and one who acts with authority in explaining Jewish and Christian(!) Scripture.

The connection between Clement and Peter mentioned above is further witnessed in Clement's many references to a work known as the *Preaching of Peter* (*Strom.* 1.29; 2.15; 6.5, 6, 15). In one of these instances Peter claims to have read the Scriptures for references to Jesus: "Peter in the *Preaching,* speaking of the apostles, says, 'But, having opened the books of the prophets which

---

29. In *The Epistle of the Apostles* 2 Peter is part of the authorial, apostolic "we."

we had, we found, sometimes expressed by parables, sometimes by riddles, and sometimes directly and in so many words the name Jesus Christ . . .'" (6.15.128). Again, Peter is presented as handling texts and as competent to provide authoritative interpretations for the community. Moreover, Peter is included in a group of readers and, though he is not singled out as reading, his inclusion provides supporting evidence of a literacy claim. This association is all the more significant coming from Clement, a person with whom Peter is reported to have interacted at length.

These references to the *Preaching of Peter* in the work of Clement were likely instrumental for the construction of the *Homilies* and *Recognitions* that have come down to us today under Clement's name.[30] Regarding their transmission history, the *Recognitions* were transmitted separately, in two codices (*Parisinus Graecus* 930; *Vaticanus Ottobonianus* 443), whereas the *Homilies* were prefaced by two pseudonymous epistles (*Epistula Petri* and *Epistula Clementis*) and the "Instructions" for the right use of the book.

Both of the letters are of interest for this present discussion. First, the *Epistula Petri* claims to be a letter written by Peter to James (1.1).[31] This supports the view of Peter as a letter writer and provides explicit evidence of the impact of 1 Peter on the literary Petrine tradition. In the beginning of the letter body (1.2) Peter informs James of the enclosed books of his preaching and asks him to keep them safe (see 2.1; 3.1). This attribution of books to Peter reaffirms the claim of Peter's literacy and provides support for a recurring theme in the *Recognitions*. In the *Epistula Clementis,* a letter reported to have been sent from Clement to James, there is another reference to the books that Peter sent to James (20.1). Outside of this reference little in the letter contributes to our discussion except for the comment by Clement that Peter specified being "learned" as one of the key characteristics of being a bishop (2.3), the mantle that Peter passes to Clement (2.1–4.4). These two letters provide the introductory framework for reading the *Homilies.*

The *Homilies* and *Recognitions* of Pseudo-Clement provide us with an extended narrative of Peter's ministry.[32] Unlike the other books we have noted in

---

30. For the critical editions, see B. Rehm and G. Strecker, eds., *Die Pseudoklementinen: Homilien,* 3rd ed., GCS 42 (Berlin: Akademie, 1992); B. Rehm and G. Strecker, eds., *Die Pseudoklementinen: Rekognitionen in Rufins Übersetzung,* 2nd ed., GCS 51 (Berlin: Akademie, 1994).

31. See the *Letter of Peter to Philip,* in which Peter is also presented as the letter's author.

32. B. Rehm, "Zur Entstehung der pseudoklementinischen Schriften," *ZNW* 37 (1938): 77-184, here 155; Johannes Irmscher and Georg Strecker, "The Pseudo-Clementines," in *New Testament Apocrypha,* ed. W. Schneemelcher, trans. R. McL. Wilson, rev. ed. (Louisville: Westminster John Knox, 1992), pp. 2:483-541, here 484-85; Lapham, *Peter,* pp. 101-3.

which Peter is reported to be the author, the *Recognitions* present "Clement" as the first-person narrator (1.1-7, passim). Throughout this work we witness Peter as a great preacher/teacher of truth and a personal mentor to the character of Clement. A majority of the text takes the form of dialogue and extended speeches, and the author provides many scenes in which Peter reads or interacts with texts. One of the first instances occurs in 1.17, where we are told that an account of Peter's sayings and doings has been sent to Pseudo-Clement's interlocutor (see 3.75). It is clear in this passage that Peter did not write the sent account but, rather, that it was composed by Clement. However, in 1.72 (prior to the meeting of Peter and Clement), Peter is told by James the bishop to submit an account in writing of his activities: "Now be sure that you send me in writing every year an account of your sayings and doings, and especially at the end of every seven years." Again, it is not explicit in this passage that Peter has the ability to write, but the narrative as a whole exploits this ambiguity and presents Peter as capable of doing so.

This perspective is strengthened by the passages in the *Recognitions* that imply that Peter could read. For example, in 1.21 Peter speaks to Clement about the teachings by the true Prophet and the struggles in interpreting texts:

> Which things were indeed plainly spoken [by the true Prophet], but are not plainly written; so much so, that when they are read, they cannot be understood without an expounder, on account of the sin which has grown up with men, as I said before. Therefore I shall explain all things to you, that in those things which are written you may clearly perceive the mind of the Lawgiver.[33]

Here Peter claims that he can read the text and also provide authoritative interpretations of it based on his teaching from the true Prophet.[34] A similar scene is presented in *Recognitions* 10.42, in which Peter speaks about reading the law of God.[35] Again, Peter is not presented explicitly as reading, but as one who

---

33. In other places (e.g., *Rec.* 2.1.6) Peter speaks primarily of memory recollection for the teaching of Jesus. Translation is adapted from Irmscher and Strecker, "The Pseudo-Clementines."

34. A potential counterexample to this presentation is found in *Rec.* 3.74, in which Peter has a letter read to the crowd and does not read it himself. The rationale for Peter's not reading the letter is not provided, and so it does not counter the trend of presenting Peter as literate. Nevertheless, this would have been a great opportunity to reinforce the presentation of a literate Peter.

35. See also *Rec.* 1.21-23 for references to Peter's memory regarding the law.

instructs those wishing to read the law about its pitfalls. The conclusion of this passage affirms the value of having a liberal education for the interpretation of Scripture; however, the educated one must first reject the false teaching/doctrine that he has learned. The author of the text, moreover, has Peter claim the need for outsiders to have an expounder to understand the text properly. In presenting Peter in this manner, he is established as a gatekeeper and guide for correctly interpreting the Scriptures.

This is not the only time that the author of the *Recognitions* broaches the topic of a literary education. As mentioned above, *Recognitions* 1.62 clearly alludes to Acts 4:13.[36] Peter is presented as an unlearned and uneducated fisherman in contrast to Caiaphas, the "wise," well-educated high priest. Explicitly denying any claim to "long learning," Peter informs Caiaphas that his understanding is a result of supernaturally given knowledge.[37] This rejection of "long learning" by Peter as a basis for his knowledge reinforces the claim in the Acts narrative while concurrently providing a reasonable answer for how Peter could read and write in the current text. Here we witness the colliding of the two contrary traditions and an attempt by an early author to provide an explanation that accounts for both the Acts text and the view of Peter's literacy (i.e., 1 Peter).

The first comparison between Peter and Clement occurs in *Recognitions* 1.25, where Peter praises Clement for his ability to recall what Peter has taught, exclaiming, "You have stated these things more clearly than I myself explained them." Clement's reply to this is illuminating: "Liberal learning has conferred upon me the power of orderly narration, and of stating those things clearly for which there is occasion."[38] Clement attributes his ability to summarize and rephrase to his education, which recalls the opening of the *Recognitions* where we were told that Clement began studying philosophy, but did not complete his schooling (see 1.3; 7.9). Implicit in Clement's response is the view that Peter did not have a liberal education and so could not express his thoughts as clearly as he would have been able to do if he had a formal education.

A similar impression is given in books 8 and 10 of *Recognitions,* where people other than Peter provide extended rebuttals to Greek philosophical

36. For the use of Acts in the *Recognitions,* see F. S. Jones, *An Ancient Christian Source on the History of Christianity: Pseudo-Clementine* Recognitions *1.27.71* (Atlanta: Scholars, 1995), pp. 140-42.

37. Clement of Alexandria interestingly contrasts faith and the knowledge of letters in *Paed.* 3.11.78.

38. For other church leaders expressing the benefit of a liberal education, see Basil, *Address to Young Men on Reading Greek Literature* 1.5; 4.1.

ideas. The first example begins in *Recognitions* 8.7 with a discussion of studies undertaken by the two brothers of Clement, Niceta and Aquila (see *Hom.* 13.7; 15.4). This is followed by an extended discussion of Greek philosophy by Niceta (*Rec.* 8.9-34). A similar event occurs in *Recognitions* 10.30-34, in which Peter allows Niceta to discourse on Greek literature, specifically the works written by Orpheus and Hesiod. After this, Peter acknowledges that Niceta is well-versed in gentile literature (10.40). In both of these scenes Peter is shown to defer to Niceta and his knowledge of Greek philosophy and literature, suggesting that this was an area in which Peter was lacking. The only contradiction to this understanding is *Recognitions* 10.28 and Peter's comment on Greek literature and the rationale for why Greeks worship false gods: "The ancients have left these things skillfully composed in their writings, and elegantly engrafted in their verses." Although this passage does not directly claim an education for Peter, it does present him as knowledgeable about Greek literary texts.

In contrast to this downplaying of Peter's level of formal education, particularly through contrasting portraits with Clement and his brothers, the narrative portrays him as having substantial faculty in handling texts. This is constantly reinforced by Peter's exposition of Jewish Scripture (particularly the books of Moses; e.g., 1.27-38) as well as by having him employ the phrase "It is written . . ." (*Rec.* 2.41, 42; 4.5; 5.2, 11). Moreover, in *Homilies* 19.3 Peter chastises Simon for going beyond the written text and challenges him to point to places in the text as support for his position. These scenes present Peter as knowledgeable of texts and mediating the literary tradition, something that is typically associated with someone who is literate.

What we see in the *Recognitions* and the *Homilies* of Pseudo-Clement is a complex portrait of Peter's literacy. Throughout the work Peter consistently references, expounds on, and interacts with written texts. There are also times when he is presented as reading and is asked to make written reports. On the other hand, it is clear that the author does not claim a formal education for Peter. In *Recognitions* 1.62 the character of Peter claims that his knowledge is divinely bestowed and did not come from extensive learning (although in *Rec.* 6.1 he does talk about personal study). Likewise, Peter acknowledges that others (esp. Clement, Niceta) have expertise in Greek literature and philosophy and so allows them to take the initiative in the debate (e.g., *Rec.* 10.40). In short, the depiction of Peter's literacy in Pseudo-Clement's *Recognitions* is that of a literate Peter, one who can read and potentially write, but who did not have an extensive, formal Greek education. Nevertheless, despite this ambiguity and inferiority with regard to Greek literature, Peter is presented as the highest authority when expositing the Scriptures.

Implications

What we have seen in the Petrine literary tradition is Peter consistently being presented as one who interprets texts with authority. Not only does he occasionally handle, read, and write texts, but he also regularly cites texts and his interpretations and expositions are considered to be definitive.[39] In such presentations Peter is shown to be a leading authority within the community and a "text-broker" disseminating the Jesus tradition. Gregory Snyder rightfully notes that "in groups where written texts were central, individuals able to serve as text-brokers accordingly occupied a position of power and prestige."[40] In the Greco-Roman and Jewish communities, the people who were text-brokers were those who could read (and potentially write) and act as gatekeepers, mediating access to and knowledge of important and/or sacred texts.[41] For example, in Jewish communities the Pharisees and scribes functioned as intermediaries between the uneducated populace and their religious texts.[42] Chris Keith, employing the models outlined by Snyder and Anthony Saldarini (with some modifications), highlights the usefulness of the concept of text-broker for understanding Jewish and Christian book culture. He claims:

> Without demanding particularities such as precise literary rates or sharp differentiation between different Jewish groups, it recognizes the core mechanism behind the importance and power of sacred literacy: on the one hand was a group of individuals for whom a particular text held intrinsic and identity-forming value; on the other hand was the text itself, which was all but inaccessible to the vast majority of those individuals. Between these two entities was a group (or multiple groups) of individuals who mediated that relationship, providing points of access to the text.[43]

It is very unlikely that the ancients had a category for an uneducated or illiterate text-broker, as this job almost always involved some type of mediation by

39. A visual representation of this understanding is the *traditio legis*, a scene that depicts Jesus handing a scroll to Peter. I thank Peter Lampe for bringing this to my attention.

40. H. Gregory Snyder, *Teachers and Texts in the Ancient World: Philosophers, Jews and Christians*, RFCC (New York: Routledge, 2000), p. 3.

41. Carr correctly highlights the difference in prestige between a general scribe and a person who held a mastery of holy texts. See David M. Carr, *Writing on the Tablet of the Heart: Origins of Scripture and Literature* (New York: Oxford University Press, 2005), p. 13.

42. Anthony J. Saldarini, *Pharisees, Scribes and Sadducees in Palestinian Society: A Sociological Approach*, BRS (Grand Rapids: Eerdmans, 2001), p. 58; Keith, *Pericope*, pp. 100-101.

43. Keith, *Pericope*, p. 101.

a trained specialist.[44] Rather, the public impression of such people (as part of a specialized group) would be to assume that they were literate.

In all of the texts studied above, Peter functions as a text-broker and is presented as doing what text-brokers do. That the historical Peter likely did not have a formal education therefore has little to do with the perception of him in these texts, as the role that he assumes is one of authority and acting as a person mediating the interpretation of Scripture. The presentation of a literate Peter is consistent with 1 Peter and the claim of grapho-literacy in 5:12. Explicit claims of Peter "writing" a letter, moreover, appear throughout the Petrine literary tradition and are likely based on 1 Peter's presentation of Peter as both literate and a letter writer.[45]

The perception of Peter as literate also fits well with the general second- and third-century Christian responses to pagan criticisms of Christian illiteracy. Along with the other traditions highlighting Peter's intellectual capabilities, the Petrine tradition also asserts Peter's literary knowledge. Although it is true that no document claims that Peter received an elite or even a formal education, it is also true that none of the above noncanonical works questions his ability to read or write. Rather, he is assumed to have these skills. As a result, Peter fits well within the intellectual tradition begun by Jesus,[46] whose depiction in the Gospels is one who has supernatural knowledge (e.g., Matt 17:27; Luke 6:8; John 1:48), a tradition continued by his disciples in Acts (e.g., Acts 5:1-10; 27:10).

Continuing questions regarding Peter's level of literacy are present, if subtle, in the Petrine tradition. Some ancient writers, responding to the claims in Acts 4:13, felt the need to argue for, rather than just assume, Peter's ability to read and write. This suggests that there was some debate over how Peter should be portrayed, at least from those with knowledge of the Acts narrative. This is especially important when one considers the growing significance of Peter in the early church and his role as a leading holder and disseminator of Jesus tradition. This role required an ability to engage and interpret the Jewish Scriptures authoritatively. The texts that struggle with Acts 4:13 provide an answer for why Peter could do what he is portrayed as doing if he did not have a formal education. The answer is simple: God gave him the ability. It is through

---

44. Snyder, *Teachers*, p. 11.

45. David G. Meade *Pseudonymity and Canon* (Tübingen: Mohr, 1986), pp. 186-88, comes close to this perspective when he suggests that 1 Peter may have had a role in construction of later Petrine literature, including the *Gospel of Peter* and the *Apocalypse of Peter*.

46. For a recent discussion of Jesus' (il)literacy, see Chris Keith, *Jesus' Literacy: Scribal Culture and the Teacher from Galilee*, LNTS 413 (London: T&T Clark, 2011).

this justification that the Acts narrative and the literary claims of 1 Peter are reconciled and the tradition of a literate Peter is born.

Conclusion

Overall, this paper maps the tradition of Peter as a literate individual. We began by looking at the contrary representations of Peter's literacy in the New Testament. In the Acts narrative Peter is presented as ἀγράμματος and as an ἰδιώτης; whereas 1 Peter portrays Peter as literate and makes a specific writing claim for him (1 Pet 5:12). In later, extracanonical literature Peter is primarily presented as a preacher, miracle worker, and debater; however, he also reportedly handles, reads, and writes texts. In addition, Peter regularly cites texts, and his interpretations and expositions are depicted as authoritative. In this way Peter is a text-broker and mediator of the Christian tradition. A person in this position can hardly be understood to be illiterate, and so the tradition and the depiction of his literacy are adopted into the subsequent body of literature on the figure of Peter. The initial basis or impetus of this depiction of him is 1 Peter. Accordingly, whether or not Peter was the actual author of 1 Peter, it is his accepted authorship of this letter that subsequently provided authoritative support for Peter's literacy. This perspective was assumed in later traditions, which depicted Peter as literate and competent both to handle and to interpret Scripture authoritatively.

CHAPTER 11

Why Are There Some Petrine Epistles Rather Than None?

Matthew V. Novenson

Introduction

It was Leibniz who famously posed that question to trump all questions: *Pourquoi il y a plutôt quelque chose que rien?* "Why is there something rather than nothing?" (*Principes de la nature et de la grâce fondés en raison §7*).[1] In this essay I pose an analogous question about the small corpus of ancient letters attributed to the apostle Peter: Why are there some Petrine epistles rather than none? This question might seem strange inasmuch we experience the existence of the Petrine epistles as a given, and we have a picture of the production of apostolic pseudepigrapha in late antiquity that tempts us to think of Petrine epistles as a naturally occurring species. In fact, however, the production of this genre of literature in the name of this apostle was not at all inevitable. Closer examination reveals that the Petrine epistles are not a naturally occurring species but an anomaly. Explaining why any were written at all turns out to be an instructive exercise in the study of early Christian history and literature.[2]

---

1. The standard edition is G. W. Leibniz, *Die philosophischen Schriften*, ed. ed. C. I. Gerhardt (Berlin: Weidmann, 1875-1890), 6:598-606.

2. I received valuable comments on the conference version of this essay from Sean Adams, David Horrell, Larry Hurtado, Peter Lampe, and Tobias Nicklas. The essay is much improved for their feedback, and any remaining deficiencies are entirely my own fault. All translations are my own unless otherwise noted.

Apostolic Epistles

Although one might imagine (and we sometimes speak in terms of) a general explosion of apostolic pseudepigrapha — gospels, acts, epistles, apocalypses, dialogues, homilies, and so on — from the late first century onward,[3] in fact the distribution of such texts by genre is quite uneven. In particular, epistles attributed to apostles are actually quite rare. As Montague Rhodes James noted in 1924,

> This form [viz. the epistle] did not find much favour with the makers of apocrypha. . . . Apart from [some exceptions], it does appear that the Epistle was on the whole too serious an effort for the forger, more liable to detection, perhaps, as a fraud, and not so likely to gain the desired popularity as a narrative or an Apocalypse. Certain it is that our apocryphal Epistles are few and not impressive.[4]

James did not live to see the discovery of the Nag Hammadi codices, but that corpus bears out his observation. For all the Nag Hammadi gospels, apocalypses, and dialogues attributed to apostles,[5] there are only two epistles so attributed: the *Apocryphon of James* and the *Epistle of Peter to Philip* (on which more anon). Indeed, granting an exception for the ostensibly coauthored *Epistula Apostolorum*,[6] we have no ancient epistles at all attributed to Simon the Zealot, Judas Iscariot, James son of Zebedee, James son of Alphaeus, Andrew, Philip, Bartholomew, Thomas, Matthew, Thaddeus, Nathanael, Matthias, Apollos, Andronicus, Junia, Silas, Timothy, or Mary.

---

3. E.g., Bart D. Ehrman, *Forgery and Counterforgery: The Use of Literary Deceit in Early Christian Polemics* (New York: Oxford University Press, 2012), p. 1: "Arguably the most distinctive feature of the early Christian literature is the degree to which it was forged. . . . Only two authors named themselves correctly in the surviving literature of the first Christian century. All other Christian writings are either anonymous, falsely ascribed (based on an original anonymity or homonymity), or forged. Matters begin to change with the second Christian century, even though orthonymity continues to be the exception rather than the rule."

4. M. R. James, *The Apocryphal New Testament* (Oxford: Clarendon, 1960 [1st ed. 1924]), p. 476. A similar point is made in greater detail by Richard Bauckham, "Pseudo-Apostolic Letters," *JBL* 107 (1988): 469-94.

5. Viz. *Prayer of the Apostle Paul, Apocryphon of John, Gospel of Thomas, Gospel of Philip, Book of Thomas the Contender, Apocalypse of Paul, (First) Apocalypse of James, (Second) Apocalypse of James, Acts of Peter and the Twelve Apostles, Apocalypse of Peter, Gospel of Mary,* and *Acts of Peter.*

6. On which see Manfred Hornschuh, *Studien zur Epistula Apostolorum* (Berlin: de Gruyter, 1965).

The obvious counterexample to James's claim are the pseudo-Pauline epistles, which are, if not legion, at least ample: as many as six within the New Testament (2 Thessalonians, Colossians, Ephesians, 1 Timothy, 2 Timothy, and Titus, although one or more of these might be authentic), to which may be added 3 Corinthians, Laodiceans, and the Correspondence of Paul and Seneca (in which six of the fourteen individual missives ostensibly come from Paul).[7] The author of the Muratorian Canon (lines 64-65) mentions a certain Epistle of Paul to the Alexandrians, which he ascribes to a Marcionite propagandist, but this work has not survived even in part.[8] Clement of Alexandria (Protr. 9) mentions a letter of Paul to the Macedonians, but this is probably a reference to canonical Philippians.[9] (From Nag Hammadi, we have a Prayer of Paul and another Apocalypse of Paul, but no epistles attributed to Paul.)[10]

Paul, then, can claim a respectable portfolio of pseudonymous epistles, but he represents the exception rather than the rule. And, given Paul's unique position as the letter-writing apostle par excellence, this is perhaps not surprising. Once there existed a nucleus of reasonably well-known Pauline epistles (see 2 Pet. 3:15-16), there was a pretext for the production of pseudo-Pauline epistles. Someone wrote an apocryphal 3 Corinthians because of the precedent of the several authentic letters of Paul to the Corinthians.[11] Someone wrote

---

7. See the recent studies of Vahan Hovhannessian, Third Corinthians: Reclaiming Paul for Christian Orthodoxy (New York: Lang, 2000); and Philip L. Tite, The Apocryphal Epistle to the Laodiceans: An Epistolary and Rhetorical Analysis, TENTS 7 (Leiden: Brill, 2012); and the older but still valuable J. N. Sevenster, Paul and Seneca (Leiden: Brill, 1961).

8. Therefore about it one can only speculate, as do Theodor Zahn, Geschichte des neutes-tamentlichen Kanons (Leipzig: Deichert, 1892), 2.2:586-92; and Adolf von Harnack, Marcion: Das Evangelium vom fremden Gott, 2nd ed. (Leipzig: Hinrichs, 1924), 2:134.

9. Clement quotes from an epistle in which "the apostle of the Lord [viz. Paul] exhorts the Macedonians, saying, "The lord is near; take care that we not be overtaken empty-handed [ὁ κύριος ἤγγικεν, εὐλαβεῖσθε μὴ καταληφθῶμεν κενοί]" (Protr. 9 [Greek text from G. W. Butterworth, ed., The Exhortation to the Greeks. The Rich Man's Salvation. To the Newly Baptized, LCL 92 (Cambridge, Mass.: Harvard University Press, 1919)]). In light of the Macedonia connection and the verbal parallels with Philippians (ὁ κύριος ἐγγύς [Phil. 4:5]; ἐφ' ᾧ καὶ κατελήμφθην ὑπὸ Χριστοῦ [Phil. 3:12]; καύχημα ἐμοὶ εἰς ἡμέραν Χριστοῦ, ὅτι οὐκ εἰς κενὸν ἔδραμον οὐδὲ εἰς κενὸν ἐκοπίασα [Phil. 2:16]), this is almost certainly a paraphrase of bits of that letter rather than a fragment of a lost epistle. (Here and throughout, for the New Testament I follow the Greek text of NA[27]).

10. On these texts see Michael Kaler, "The Prayer of the Apostle Paul in the Context of Nag Hammadi Codex I," JECS 16 (2008): 319-39; Michael Kaler, Louis Panchaud, and Marie-Pierre Bussières, "The Coptic Apocalypse of Paul, Irenaeus' Adversus Haereses 2.30.7, and the Second-Century Battle for Paul's Legacy," JECS 12 (2004): 173-93.

11. See 1 Cor. 5:9: Ἔγραψα ὑμῖν ἐν τῇ ἐπιστολῇ μὴ συναναμίγνυσθαι πόρνοις, "I wrote to

an apocryphal *Epistle of Paul to the Laodiceans* because Col. 4:16 mentions a letter of Paul addressed to that city.[12] And so on. An analogy is provided by the apocryphal epistles of Jeremiah and Baruch (viz. *Epistle of Jeremiah; 1 Baruch;* 4Q389; *2 Baruch* 78-87; and *Paraleipomena Jeremiou* 6-7), which derive their literary conceit from the precedent of the letter of Jeremiah in Jeremiah 29 and the scroll of Baruch in Jeremiah 36.[13] The same is true of Isocrates, Plato, Demosthenes, Seneca, Apollonius of Tyana, Ignatius of Antioch, the emperor Julian, and other ancient letter writers who had letters forged in their names. Paul himself had been a letter writer; so when others wrote in his name they were naturally attracted to the genre of letter.[14]

For apostles other than Paul, however, we have not so much as a single undisputed letter, much less a corpus on which enterprising forgers could easily piggyback. In fact, on closer inspection, we do not even have very many properly pseudo-apostolic letters. The epistle to the Hebrews, the first epistle of John, the *Epistle of Barnabas,* and the late ancient *Epistle of Titus* (N.B. not the canonical epistle of Paul to Titus) are all formally anonymous and were attributed to apostolic authors in later traditions. Only marginally different is the case of 2 John and 3 John, which are not entirely anonymous, since both claim authorship by "the elder," but lack an author's personal name, and so became associated with the name of the apostle John.[15] The epistle of James (like the canonical Apocalypse of John) has a named author who is homonymous with an apostle but who does not straightforwardly claim to be that apostle.[16] Contrast this with the epistle of Jude, the first and second

---

you in the letter not to associate with immoral people"; 1 Cor. 7:1: Περὶ δὲ ὧν ἐγράψατε, "Concerning the things about which you wrote"; 2 Cor. 7:8: εἰ καὶ ἐλύπησα ὑμᾶς ἐν τῇ ἐπιστολῇ, οὐ μεταμέλομαι, "If indeed I grieved you by the letter, I do not regret it"; 2 Cor. 10:9: ἵνα μὴ δόξω ὡς ἂν ἐκφοβεῖν ὑμᾶς διὰ τῶν ἐπιστολῶν, "Lest I seem to be frightening you with my letters."

12. Col. 4:16: ὅταν ἀναγνωσθῇ παρ᾽ ὑμῖν ἡ ἐπιστολή, ποιήσατε ἵνα καὶ ἐν τῇ Λαοδικέων ἐκκλησίᾳ ἀναγνωσθῇ, καὶ τὴν ἐκ Λαοδικείας ἵνα καὶ ὑμεῖς ἀναγνῶτε, "When this epistle has been read among you, see that it is also read in the church of the Laodiceans, and that you read the one from Laodicea."

13. See Lutz Doering, *Ancient Jewish Letters and the Beginnings of Christian Epistolography,* WUNT 298 (Tübingen: Mohr Siebeck, 2012), pp. 104-8, 154-60, 190-94, 241-62.

14. To be sure, there are also ancient pseudonymous letters that have no authentic counterparts, especially imagined letters to or from famous characters, such as the letter of Dido to Aeneas in Ovid's *Heroides,* the *Letters of Jesus and Abgar,* and the *Letters of Pilate and Herod.*

15. See Judith M. Lieu, *I, II, and III John: A Commentary,* NTL (Louisville: Westminster John Knox, 2008), pp. 1-14.

16. So rightly Todd C. Penner, *The Epistle of James and Eschatology,* JSNTSup 121 (Sheffield: Sheffield Academic, 1996), p. 48 n. 2: "It is church tradition which makes this claim [apostolic authorship] for the epistle, not the epistle itself." James claims neither apostleship

epistles of Peter, and the *Epistula Apostolorum,* which (in like manner to the deutero-Pauline letters) do press claims to have been written by that Jude, that Peter, and those apostles.

Which brings us to the Petrine epistles. Apropos of the preceding discussion, there is nothing at all in the first-century accounts of Peter in the Pauline corpus, the canonical Gospels, or the Acts of the Apostles to suggest that Peter wrote letters. (Of course, there is nothing in the Acts of the Apostles to suggest that Paul wrote letters either, which is an instructive reminder.) The only even indirect hint is the story of the apostolic council in Acts 15, in which the apostles and elders draft an epistle to the church in Antioch. Peter is named as a participant in the council (Acts 15:7-11), but the narrator presents James as the primary impetus behind the letter (Acts 15:13-21).[17] Nor, again, is Peter associated with epistolography in any of the later Petrine apocrypha (*Gospel of Peter, Apocalypse of Peter,* Nag Hammadi *Apocalypse of Peter, Kerygma Petrou, Kerygmata Petrou, Act of Peter, Acts of Peter and Andrew, Acts of Peter and Paul, Acts of Peter and the Twelve*), with the exception of the few Petrine epistles themselves.[18] Later ecclesiastical writers (e.g., Eusebius, *H.E.* 3.1.2; Jerome, *Vir. ill.* 1) remember Peter as a preacher, a tradent of Jesus tradition, and a leader of the church, which accords with the portrait of Peter in the first-century Gospels and Acts and explains the proliferation of Petrine apocrypha in the form of homilies, dialogues, and revelations.

Petrine Epistles

The first indication we have that Peter might have written an epistle is, fittingly enough, the first epistle of Peter. In fact, in all of early Christian literature there are only four epistles attributed to Peter, plus one doubtful mention of another. In his treatise *On the Schism of the Donatists,* Optatus, the late-fourth-century bishop of Milevis in North Africa, mentions and quotes from a certain "Epistle of the Apostle Peter": "We have read in the Epistle of the Apostle Peter, 'Be unwilling to judge your brother on a conjecture [Nolite per opinionem judicare fratres vestros]'" (Optatus, *de Schism. Donat.* 1.5 [PL 11:893]). Har-

---

(cf. the Petrine epistles) nor membership in the family of Jesus (cf. Jude). He only identifies himself as Ἰάκωβος θεοῦ καὶ κυρίου Ἰησοῦ Χριστοῦ δοῦλος, "James, a slave of God and of the lord Jesus Christ" (Jas. 1:1).

17. See the treatment in Hans-Josef Klauck, *Ancient Letters and the New Testament* (Waco: Baylor University Press, 2006), pp. 420-29.

18. See Paul Foster, "Peter in Noncanonical Traditions," in the present volume.

nack noted, however, that the citation looks rather like a paraphrase of James 2:1 and 4:11, and suggested that Optatus mistakenly attributed it to Peter.[19] Alternatively, as Wilhelm Schneemelcher proposed, it could conceivably be a fragment of an otherwise unknown Petrine apocryphon that happens to overlap with the content of the epistle of James;[20] but Harnack's explanation is the more economical.

If so, then we have a corpus of four ancient Petrine letters: 1 Peter, 2 Peter, the *Epistle of Peter to James,* and the *Epistle of Peter to Philip.* All four are arguably pseudonymous, but in quite different ways. It will be heuristically helpful to discuss the later examples first. The *Epistle of Peter to James* (perhaps third century) is not a freestanding letter but a composite part of the preface to the pseudo-Clementine *Homilies.*[21] Together with the *Contestatio* (an account of the reception of Peter's letter) and an *Epistle of Clement to James,* the *Epistle of Peter to James* purports to explain why these homilies of Peter (our *Kerygmata Petrou*), supposedly epitomized by Clement of Rome, are only appearing publicly long after the events. The letter comprises just fifteen verses and begins as follows:

> Peter to James, the lord and bishop of the holy church: Peace be with you always from the father of all through Jesus Christ. Knowing well that you, my brother, eagerly take pains about what is for the mutual benefit of us all, I earnestly beseech you not to pass on to any one of the Gentiles the books of my preachings which I (here) forward to you, nor to any one of our own tribe before probation. But if some one of them has been examined and found to be worthy, then you may hand them over to him in the same way as Moses handed over his office of a teacher to the seventy. (*Epistle of Peter to James* 1.1-2)[22]

---

19. Adolf von Harnack, *Geschichte der altchristlichen Literatur bis Eusebius* (Leipzig: Hinrichs, 1893-1904), 1.2:788. See Jas. 2:1: Ἀδελφοί μου, μὴ ἐν προσωπολημψίαις ἔχετε τὴν πίστιν, "My brothers, keep the faith without partiality"; Jas. 4:11: Μὴ καταλαλεῖτε ἀλλήλων, ἀδελφοί. ὁ καταλαλῶν ἀδελφοῦ ἢ κρίνων τὸν ἀδελφὸν αὐτοῦ καταλαλεῖ νόμου καὶ κρίνει νόμον, "Do not speak evil against one another, brothers. The one who speaks evil against a brother or judges a brother speaks evil against the law and judges the law."

20. See W. Schneemelcher, "Apostolic Pseudepigrapha: Introduction," in *New Testament Apocrypha,* ed. E. Hennecke, W. Schneemelcher, and R. McL. Wilson (Philadelphia: Fortress, 1965), 2:91.

21. See François Bovon, "En tête des Homélies clémentines: La Lettre de Pierre à Jacques," in *Nouvelles intrigues pseudo-clémentines,* ed. Frédéric Amsler et al., Publications de l'Institut romand des sciences bibliques 6 (Prahins, Switzerland: Éditions du Zèbre, 2008), pp. 329-36.

22. Trans. from Hennecke-Schneemelcher, *New Testament Apocrypha,* 2:111.

This very brief epistle is functionally analogous to the stereotyped angelic command to "seal up the book," which we find in some apocalypses attributed to ancient sages (Dan. 8:26; 12:4, 9; 2 Bar 20:3; cf. Rev. 22:10).[23] Its obvious purpose is to justify the untimely publication of the apocryphon to which it is attached, in this case, a collection of Petrine homilies, which is not coincidentally a better-attested genre of Petrine apocrypha.

In a similar way, the *Epistle of Peter to Philip* (perhaps second or third century), attested in Nag Hammadi Codex VIII and now also in the Tchacos Codex, is a brief epistolary preface to what is actually a dialogue of the apostles with the heavenly Jesus.[24] Per the colophon in Nag Hammadi Codex VIII, the whole dialogue is transmitted under the title *Epistle of Peter to Philip*, but the actual epistle itself (comprising just the first four sentences of the work) reads in full as follows:

> Peter the apostle of Jesus Christ, to Philip our beloved brother and our fellow apostle and (to) the brethren who are with you: greetings! Now I want you to know, our brother, [that] we received orders from our Lord and the Savior of the whole world that [we] should come [together] to give instruction and preach in the salvation which was promised us by our Lord Jesus Christ. But as for you, you were separate from us, and you did not desire us to come together and to know how we should organize ourselves in order that we might tell the good news. Therefore would it be agreeable to you, our brother, to come according to the orders of our God Jesus? (*NHL* VIII 132-133)[25]

The text continues with an account of the reception of and response to the letter: "When Philip had received these, and when he had read them, he went to Peter rejoicing with gladness. Then Peter gathered the others also. They

23. On which see Ithamar Gruenwald, *Apocalyptic and Merkavah Mysticism*, AGJU 141 (Leiden: Brill, 1980), p. 12: "This belief belongs to the heart of apocalypticism as a pseudonymous literary genre. The secrets had been disclosed to the legendary sages of antiquity who in turn put them into books which were sealed away, and in that condition they were preserved till the eschatological time came to open them."

24. See Hans-Gebhard Bethge, "Der sogennante 'Brief des Petrus an Philippus,'" *TLZ* 103 (1978): 161-70; Bethge, *Der Brief des Petrus an Philippus: Ein neutestamentliches Apokryphon aus dem Fund von Nag Hammadi (NHC VIII,2)*, TUGAL 141 (Berlin: Akademie, 1997); Michael Kaler, "The *Letter of Peter to Philip* and Its Message of Gnostic Revelation and Christian Unity," *VC* 63 (2009): 264-95.

25. Trans. Frederik Wisse in *The Nag Hammadi Library in English*, ed. James M. Robinson (San Francisco: HarperSanFrancisco, 1990).

went upon the mountain which is called 'the (mount) olives' " (*NHL* VIII 133). On the mountain, Jesus appears in the form of a great light and discourses with the disciples about the deficiency of the aeons, the descent of the divine *plēroma,* and the conflict with the heavenly archons. Thus informed, the disciples return to Jerusalem and go forth to preach. Like the *Epistle of Peter to James,* the *Epistle of Peter to Philip* purports to be a very short Petrine epistle but is really an artificial framing device for a different genre of apocryphon, in this case a dialogue.

Canonical 1 Peter and 2 Peter, by contrast, are freestanding epistles, the former parenetic and the latter testamentary. First Peter is certainly the earliest of all the Petrine letters, since it is known to Papias (per Eusebius, *H.E.* 3.39.16) and Polycarp (*Phil.* 1.3; 2.1-2; 5.3; 7.2; 8.1-2; 10.2) in the early second century and perhaps already to the author of *1 Clement* in the 90s CE, although this lattermost connection is debatable.[26] In contrast to the case of the deutero-Pauline letters, we have no undisputed letters of Peter with which to compare the language and theology of 1 Peter and so to make a judgment regarding its authenticity. Numerous features of the letter, however — the use of the name Babylon for Rome (1 Pet. 5:13), the use of the name Christians for the recipients (1 Pet. 4:16), and the presence of established churches throughout Asia Minor (1 Pet. 1:1), among other things — suggest a date after 70 CE, which is to say, after the death of Peter. The epistle's possible provenance in Rome, its likely late-first-century date, and its preservation of motifs elsewhere associated with Peter (cf. 1 Pet. 2:4-8 with Matt. 16:18; 1 Pet. 5:1-5 with Matt. 26:37-75 and John 21:16) suggest that it may not be too remote in time or in tradition history from the figure of the apostle.[27] On the other hand, 1 Peter has so much in common with other early Christian traditions (not only Paul but also the Synoptic Gospels and James), and so little that can be identified as specifically Petrine, that provenance in a Petrine circle in Rome, while not implausible, is hard to sustain.[28]

---

26. Cf. *1 Clem.* 4.8 with 1 Pet. 3:6; *1 Clem.* 8.1 with 1 Pet. 1:11; *1 Clem.* 16.17 with 1 Pet. 2:21; *1 Clem.* 30.2 with 1 Pet. 5:5; *1 Clem.* 49.5 with 1 Pet. 4:8; *1 Clem.* 57.1 with 1 Pet. 5:1-5; *1 Clem.* 59.2 with 1 Pet. 2:9.

27. So especially John H. Elliott, "Peter, Silvanus and Mark in 1 Peter and Acts: Sociological-Exegetical Perspectives on a Petrine Group in Rome," in *Wort in der Zeit: Neutestamentliche Studien,* ed. W. Haubeck and M. Bachmann (Leiden: Brill, 1980), pp. 250-67.

28. So rightly David G. Horrell, "The Product of a Petrine Circle? A Reassessment of the Origin and Character of 1 Peter," *JSNT* 86 (2002): 29-60. On 1 Peter's debt to a wide range of early Christian traditions, see C. Spicq, "La Iᵃ Petri et le témoignage évangélique de saint Pierre," *ST* 20 (1966): 37-61.

The epistle addresses itself as an encyclical to Christians in five neighboring provinces of Anatolia: "Peter, an apostle of Jesus Christ, to the elect exiles of the diaspora in Pontus, Galatia, Cappadocia, Asia, and Bithynia" (1 Pet. 1:1). Although the writer identifies himself as the apostle Peter in 1:1, the authorial "I" is notably muted throughout the letter. He comes to the fore only in the final chapter: "Therefore I exhort the elders among you, as a fellow elder and a witness of the sufferings of Christ and a sharer in the glory that is about to be revealed. Shepherd the flock of God that is with you" (5:1-2). And again at the very close of the letter, this time mentioning co-senders: "Through Silvanus, whom I regard as a faithful brother, I have written briefly to you, exhorting and testifying that this is the true grace of God. Stand in it. The co-elect one in Babylon greets you, and so does my son Mark" (5:12-13). Silvanus and Mark are names elsewhere closely associated with the Pauline mission.[29] Acts, however, places them in Jerusalem and Antioch for the events surrounding the apostolic council (Acts 15:7, 22, 27, 32, 37, 39, 40), and some such tradition may help explain their association with Peter here.

Of course, if 1 Peter is pseudonymous, then its provenance in Rome and, for that matter, its audience in Asia Minor may be contrived as well.[30] But there is no positive evidence that they are in fact contrived, and it is therefore at least plausible that in 1 Peter we have a group of Roman Christians, either Petrine (so John Elliott) or broadly catholic (so David Horrell), relaying a posthumous exhortation from the martyred apostle to their coreligionists in Asia Minor. If so, then at a literary level, we might think of 1 Peter doing for Peter what Ephesians does for Paul. It is a product of followers of the apostle within a few decades of his death. It comprises their version of his message, preserved for and relayed to a subsequent generation.[31] The difference between Ephesians and 1 Peter is that, whereas Ephesians epitomizes Pauline teaching from existing Pauline epistles (especially Colossians), 1 Peter draws on an array of early Christian traditions but is itself the first text that claims to speak in the voice of this apostle.

By all accounts, 1 Peter circulated very efficiently, being attested early and often in the second century and quite securely thereafter.[32] One important

29. Silvanus in 2 Cor. 1:19; 1 Thess. 1:1; 2 Thess. 1:1; and cf. Acts 15–18; Mark in Philem. 24; Col. 4:10; 2 Tim. 4:11; and cf. Acts 12:12, 25; 15:37-39.

30. As rightly noted by N. Brox, "Zur pseudepigraphischen Rahmung des ersten Petrusbriefes," *BZ* 19 (1975): 95.

31. On this aspect of Ephesians, see Nils A. Dahl, "The Letter to the Ephesians: Its Fictional and Real Setting," in *Studies in Ephesians,* WUNT 141 (Tübingen: Mohr Siebeck, 2000), pp. 451-59.

32. So rightly Charles Bigg, *The Epistles of St. Peter and St. Jude,* ICC (Edinburgh: T&T

consequence of this early reception history was the establishment of precedent for the idea of a Petrine epistle. With the reception of 1 Peter, the apostle Peter effectively became a letter writer.[33] It is not insignificant that 2 Peter, written in the late first or early to mid-second century, justifies its existence by appealing to an earlier letter of Peter:[34] "Beloved, I write to you now this second letter, in both of which I am rousing your sincere mind by way of reminder" (2 Pet. 3:1). Because 2 Peter does not cite any part of the previous letter to which he refers, interpreters have wondered whether it might be another, otherwise unknown Petrine letter (cf. 1 Cor. 5:9).[35] But in light of the strong attestation of 1 Peter and the absence of evidence for any other candidates, the chances of this being the case are virtually nil. On analogy to the deutero-Pauline letters discussed above, 2 Peter exists because 1 Peter provided it an occasion.[36]

Being the particular kind of pseudepigraphon that it is, 2 Peter presses its claim to Petrine authorship more strenuously than its predecessor does. The writer introduces himself as the apostle Simeon Peter and addresses a maximally catholic audience: "Simeon Peter, a slave and apostle of Jesus Christ, to those who have obtained an equally precious faith with us, in the righteousness of our God and savior Jesus Christ: Grace and peace be multiplied to you in the knowledge of God and of our lord Jesus" (2 Pet. 1:1-2). He purports to give an eyewitness recollection of the transfiguration of Jesus, reporting the words of the heavenly voice in a form very much like that in the transfiguration scene in the Gospel of Matthew: "When he received honor and glory from God the father and such a voice was borne to him by the majestic glory, 'This is my beloved son, in whom I am well pleased,' we heard this voice borne from heaven, because we were with him on the holy mountain" (2 Pet. 1:17-18; cf. Matt. 17:1-8).[37] Just here, despite its epistolary genre, 2 Peter has a key feature

---

Clark, 1901), p. 7: "There is no book in the New Testament which has earlier, better, or stronger attestation."

33. On this point, see further Sean A. Adams, "The Tradition of Peter's Literacy," in the present volume.

34. Regarding the date of 2 Peter, the crucial question is whether the *Apocalypse of Peter* (likely 130s CE) is dependent on 2 Peter or vice versa. In favor of the former, see Richard Bauckham, "2 Peter and the Apocalypse of Peter," in *The Fate of the Dead: Studies on the Jewish and Christian Apocalypses,* NovTSup 93 (Leiden: Brill, 1998), pp. 290-303.

35. So, e.g., John H. Elliott, "Peter, First Epistle of," *ABD* 5:269.

36. See G. H. Boobyer, "The Indebtedness of 2 Peter to 1 Peter," in *New Testament Essays: Studies in Memory of T. W. Manson,* ed. A. J. B. Higgins (Manchester: Manchester University Press, 1959), pp. 34-53.

37. See Jerome H. Neyrey, "The Apologetic Use of the Transfiguration in 2 Peter 1:16-21," *CBQ* 42 (1980): 504-19.

in common with the more numerous and more typical Petrine apocrypha (gospel, apocalypses, acts, etc.). Like those apocrypha, 2 Peter gets its rhetorical power by directly invoking the traditional image of Peter the companion of Jesus. The effect of this literary device stands out when we compare 1 Peter, which largely abstains from using it and consequently is less overtly "Petrine."

Perhaps the most striking feature of 2 Peter is its self-presentation as the testament of the apostle.[38] So, in the first chapter we read,

> I am always going to remind you of these things, though you know them and are strong in the truth that is with you. I think it right, for such a time as I am in this tent, to rouse you by way of reminder, since I know that the putting off of my tent will be soon, as our lord Jesus Christ made clear to me. And I will see to it that after my departure you are able always to recall these things. (2 Pet. 1:12-15)

Early Christian writers, like their ancient Israelite spiritual forebears and their Jewish contemporaries, sometimes wrote deathbed exhortations from their own founding fathers, who for Christians were the apostles.[39] (Interestingly, however, early Christian testaments are actually very few, perhaps because they were effectively supplanted as a genre by the martyr *acta*.) Most pertinent to the case of 2 Peter is the testament of Paul in 2 Timothy. The Paul of 2 Timothy writes, "I am already being poured out as a libation; the time of my departure has come. I have fought the good fight, I have finished the race, I have guarded the faith. Finally there is stored away for me the crown of righteousness, which the lord, the righteous judge, will reward me on that day" (2 Tim. 4:6-8).[40] As 2 Timothy does for Paul, so 2 Peter allows Peter to take stock of his apostolic legacy and to give a last warning to the faithful about the false teachers who will come after he is gone (see also the *Epistle of Peter to James* in this respect). It is not impossible that, as Markus Bockmuehl has recently suggested, 2 Peter

---

38. Mark D. Mathews ("The Genre of 2 Peter: A Comparison with Early Jewish and Christian Testaments," *BBR* 21 [2011]: 55-68) rightly notes that 2 Peter lacks certain textbook features of ancient testaments (e.g., narrative frame, deathbed scene). But it does have the final exhortation (albeit transposed into epistolary format), which is the decisive point of commonality.

39. But not only the apostles. In some instances, early Christian writers adopt ancient Israelite worthies as their founding fathers. The upshot is that some apparently Jewish pseudepigrapha are actually probably Christian pseudepigrapha (see James R. Davila, *The Provenance of the Pseudepigrapha: Jewish, Christian, or Other?* JSJSup 105 [Leiden: Brill, 2005], pp. 74-119).

40. On 2 Timothy as a testament of Paul, see Raymond F. Collins, *I and II Timothy and Titus: A Commentary*, NTL (Louisville: Westminster John Knox, 2002), pp. 181-85.

can perhaps be traced back, as 1 Peter is on Elliott's account, to Petrine circles, who took it upon themselves to pass on their version of Petrinism in letter form.[41] But on this question one can only speculate, since 2 Peter yields not even the few meager hints of provenance, audience, and date that its predecessor 1 Peter does. Indeed, by its very refusal to name any place or any time, 2 Peter positions itself as an address to all places and all times.[42]

Conclusion

So, to return to the question with which we began: Why are there some Petrine epistles rather than none? If not for the late-first-century catholic writer who penned 1 Peter to relay an exhortation from the martyred apostle, there might be no Petrine epistles. Very probably 2 Peter would not have been written, since it justifies itself on the precedent established by 1 Peter (2 Pet. 3:1) and adds to the literary record surrounding the apostle a deathbed testament (2 Pet. 1:12-15), as 2 Timothy does for Paul (2 Tim. 4:6-8). It is conceivable that the *Epistle of Peter to James* and the *Epistle of Peter to Philip* might have been written even if 1 Peter and 2 Peter never had been. Neither of the letters to individuals gives any clear indication that it knows either of the general letters. Their perfunctory literary purposes in their respective texts (the former a collection of homilies, the latter a dialogue with Jesus) might be sufficient to account for their composition, although we cannot exclude the possibility that they, too, were inspired by the precedent set by 1 Peter. Either way, a close examination of the primary sources demonstrates that there was nothing inevitable about the production of this small corpus of Petrine letters. Peter was otherwise remembered in antiquity almost exclusively as a disciple, a preacher, and a church leader, not a letter writer. Other disciples in the same situation (e.g., Thomas, Philip, Andrew) attracted pseudonymous gospels and acts, but not epistles. The Petrine epistles are therefore an anomaly in early Christian literature, a happy accident.

41. See Markus Bockmuehl, *The Remembered Peter in Ancient Reception and Modern Debate*, WUNT 1/262 (Tübingen: Mohr Siebeck, 2010), p. 26: "It remains in my view perfectly plausible that the author [of 2 Peter] issues such encouragement on the basis of first-hand acquaintance with the apostle and his circle."

42. So rightly Ernst Käsemann ("An Apologia for Primitive Christian Eschatology," in *Essays on New Testament Themes*, trans. W. J. Montague, SBT 41 [Naperville, Il.: Allenson, 1964], pp. 169-95), who, however, harbored a dogmatic hostility to the theology of 2 Peter.

Peter in Later Christian Traditions

CHAPTER 12

Images of Peter in the Apostolic Fathers

Todd D. Still

Throughout my academic writing career, I have robbed Peter (and most every other New Testament character and writer for that matter) to pay Paul. In this paper, however, I would like to begin to pay back Peter, even as I begin to incline my mind toward things Petrine in preparation for the writing of a commentary on 1 Peter.[1] In this essay I will consider the figure of Peter in the Apostolic Fathers. This topic is of inherent to Petrine scholars; moreover, I have been working of late in the Apostolic Fathers.[2] We all have to begin somewhere, I gather, in our quest for the "historical Peter."

In his recently published volumes on Peter, Markus Bockmuehl has noted, "The primary-source material at our disposal [for the study of Peter as a historical and historic figure] is woefully thin."[3] What is true of the record in general is no less the case with the collection of documents we know as the Apostolic Fathers in particular. Be that as it may, in this essay I will note and comment on nine passages in this corpus where Peter (or in one instance, Cephas) appears.[4] Although my treatment of these texts will be necessarily

---

1. This commentary on 1 Peter will appear in due course in the socio-rhetorical commentary series published by Eerdmans.

2. Todd D. Still and David E. Wilhite, eds., *The Apostolic Fathers and Paul,* Pauline and Patristic Scholars in Debate 2 (London: T&T Clark, forthcoming).

3. So Markus Bockmuehl, *The Remembered Peter in Ancient Reception and Modern Debate,* WUNT 1/262 (Tübingen: Mohr Siebeck, 2010), p. 3. See similarly, Markus Bockmuehl, *Simon Peter in Scripture and Memory: The New Testament Apostle in the Early Church* (Grand Rapids: Baker Academic, 2012), p. 3.

4. These texts are as follows: *1 Clem.* 5.1-4; 47.1-3; *2 Clem.* 5.1-4; Ignatius *Smyrn.* 3; *Rom.* 4.3;

brief, this study will offer a valuable glimpse into how Peter was being perceived and presented by certain Christian writers and leaders from the late first through the mid-second century CE, a timeframe sometimes referred to as the "postapostolic period."[5]

First Clement 5.1-4; 47.1-3

The first text to consider is *1 Clement* 5.1-4. In this protracted, deliberative letter (see 58.2), seemingly composed near the end of the first century CE, Christian leaders in Rome through a certain Clement write to the Corinthian church with a view to calling the fractious fellowship there to "peace and concord" (εἰρήνης καὶ ὁμονοίας, 63.2). In so doing, the Roman Christians enjoin the Corinthian assembly to embrace humble unity and to eschew divisive jealousy.

Near the beginning of the letter, the author denounces the deleterious effects of jealousy. After decrying "unrighteous and ungodly jealousy" (3.4), in chapter 4 Clement cites seven illustrations that he culls from biblical history. Then, in chapters 5-6, he addresses contemporary casualties of "jealousy and envy" (ζῆλον καὶ φθόνον, 3.2). In chapter 5 in particular, he names Peter and Paul. Depicting them as "athletic contenders," "noble examples," and "the greatest and most upright pillars," Clement admonishes Roman and Corinthian believers to "set before [their] eyes the good apostles" (5.1-3).

With respect to Peter in particular, who notably and understandably (given the audience, a Pauline church) gets rather less press than Paul, *1 Clement* indicates that Peter bore up under not just one or two hardships, but many trials. In keeping with the holy life he led and the holy way he trod (6.1), "having borne witness [μαρτυρήσας] [Peter] entered into the appointed place of glory" (5.4). Here the literary context makes clear that Peter bore witness not only with his lips but also with his very life (see also 5.2, 7). In seeking to impress upon the Corinthians, then, that "jealousy and strife" (ζῆλον καὶ ἔρις, 6.4) can reduce individuals, couples, cities, and even nations to ruin, Clement appeals to two prominent and recent examples — Peter and Paul. In the process, he extols Peter, whom he pairs with Paul, as an exemplar, an athlete, a pillar, an apostle, and a steadfast sufferer, indeed a martyr.

---

and Papias 2; 3.15; 5; 12.1 (as numbered in Bart D. Ehrman, ed. and trans., *The Apostolic Fathers*, vol. 2, LCL 25 [Cambridge, Mass.: Harvard University Press, 2003]).

   5. So, e.g., Michael W. Holmes, ed. and trans., *The Apostolic Fathers in English*, 3rd ed. (Grand Rapids: Baker Academic, 2006), p. 17.

Later in the letter, Peter appears again (this time as "Cephas" [Κηφᾶ, 47.3]) alongside the "blessed apostle Paul" (τοῦ μακαρίου Παύλου τοῦ ἀποστόλου, 47.1). In admonishing the Corinthians to take up (Ἀναλάβετε, 47.1) Paul's letter now known as 1 Corinthians lest they continue to be rent asunder by "partisanship" (πρόσκλισις, 47.2), Clement recalls the earlier, and to his mind less egregious, congregational division over "reputable apostles" (ἀποστόλοις μεμαρτυρημένοις, 47.4) (i.e., Paul and Peter) and "a man approved by them" (i.e., Apollos) (see Paul's comments in 1 Cor. 1:12). As we will see, the Apostolic Fathers regularly refer to "Peter."[6] This, however, is the only occasion within the collection where Peter, in keeping with Pauline parlance, is called by his Aramaic nickname Cephas.[7]

Second Clement 5.1-4

In the anonymous homily known as 2 *Clement*, Peter makes a cameo appearance in chapter 5. To buttress an admonition set forth in 5.1 to "do the will of the one who called us and not fear departing from the world," in 5.2 the presbyter appeals to a saying of Jesus closely akin to both Matthew 10:16 and Luke 10:3: "You will be like sheep in the midst of wolves." This generates an otherwise unknown question from Peter: "What if the wolves rip apart the sheep?" (5.3). In a response to Peter partially paralleled in Matthew 10:28 and Luke 12:4-5, Jesus reasons that even as dead sheep should no longer fear wolves, his followers (the "you" is plural) ought not "fear those who kill you and then can do nothing more to you." Rather, they should "fear the one who, after you die, has the power to cast your body and soul into the hell of fire" (2 *Clem.* 5.4).

The author proceeds to encourage believers to recognize that, whereas their stay in the flesh is "brief and short-lived," Christ's promise of "rest in the coming kingdom and eternal life" is "great and astounding" (5.5). Therefore, they should conduct themselves "in a holy and upright way" and jettison "worldly affairs foreign to [them]" (5.6).

Although it would be imprudent to read too much into this truncated dialogue between Jesus and Peter in 2 *Clement*, we may reasonably posit that this passage presumes that the sermon's recipients will readily recognize Peter

---

6. So also 1 *Clem.* 5.3; Ignatius *Rom.* 4.3; Papias 2; 5; 12.1.

7. In contrast with the Apostolic Fathers, Paul employs "Cephas" in 1 Cor. 1:12; 3:22; 9:5; 15:5; Gal. 1:18; 2:9, 11, 14 (cf. John 1:42) and "Peter" only in Gal. 2:7-8. On the use of "Cephas" and "Peter" in Paul, see now, e.g., Martinus C. de Boer, *Galatians: A Commentary*, NTL (Louisville: Westminster John Knox, 2011), pp. 119-21.

as one of Jesus' principal followers, if not as the leading spokesperson for the apostolic band. It is also possible that this purported exchange prompted recipients of 2 *Clement* to remember Peter as a pastoral shepherd and an apostolic martyr (see esp. John 21:15-19; cf. 1 Pet. 5:1-4).

Ignatius, *To the Smyrnaeans* 3; *To the Romans,* 4.3

An early gospel tradition regarding Jesus' bodily resurrection to which Ignatius appeals in his letter to the Smyrnaeans also portrays Peter as a pivotal leader among Jesus' followers. In the course of insisting on Jesus' resurrection and countering "unbelievers" who maintain that Jesus Christ "suffered only in appearance" (2), Ignatius declares, "For I know and believe that [Jesus] was in the flesh even after the resurrection" (3.1). The Antiochene bishop then reports in terms akin to Luke 24:39 that Jesus came to those with Peter (πρὸς τοὺς περὶ Πέτρον) and said, "Reach out, touch me and see that I am not a bodiless *daimonion*" (3.2).

The bishop, bound and en route to martyrdom, continues his account of this encounter of Peter and his companions with the risen Jesus by reporting that they "touched him and believed" and that the Lord "ate and drank with them as a fleshly being" (3.2-3). "Having been intermixed [or closely united] with his flesh and blood," Ignatius maintains, "they also despised death, for they were found to be above death" (3.2).

Taken together, this passage in Ignatius's letter to the church in Smyrna recalls and represents Peter as the leader of the disciples and as an eyewitness of and believer in the resurrected Jesus. It also strongly suggests that for Ignatius "the memory of Peter, quite possibly as an apostolic martyr ('despising even death'), underpins the apostolic gospel and guards it from misinterpretation."[8] The only other text in the middle recension of Ignatius's letters that mentions Peter is *To the Romans* 4.3.[9] In writing to the church in Rome prior to his arrival, Ignatius implores Roman believers not to intervene in his impending martyrdom. Instead, he enjoins them to "petition Christ on [his] behalf that [he] might be found a sacrifice through these instruments of God [i.e., the wild beasts]" (4.2). In offering them instruction, however, Ignatius does not

---

8. So Bockmuehl, *Simon Peter,* pp. 47-48.

9. As Bockmuehl (*Simon Peter,* p. 48 n. 16) notes, the longer recension of Ignatius's letters has a fair bit more to say about Peter. See, e.g., pseudo-Ignatius, *Trall.* 7.4; *Magn.* 10.2; *Tars.* 3.3; and *Letter to Mary* 4.1.

place himself on a par with Peter and Paul. Instead, he regards their status as apostles and their teaching ministry (in Rome?) to be categorically different from his own (4.3).

Papias 2; 3.15; 5; 12.1

Having examined, albeit briefly, five relevant texts from *1 Clement, 2 Clement,* and Ignatius, we are now in a position to consider four fragments from Papias that are pertinent to this study of Peter. Unfortunately, the writings of Papias, bishop of Hierapolis in Phrygia in the early to mid-second century CE, do not survive independently. Later church fathers do, however, occasionally cite Papias. For our part, we will note two Papian passages in Eusebius's *Ecclesiastical History,* one in Jerome's *Lives of Illustrious Men,* and one in Philip of Side's *Ecclesiastical History.* Given space constraints, I will not seek to reconstruct the respective literary contexts in which these Papian quotations appear. Even if Eusebius was accurate in describing Papias as a "man of exceedingly small intelligence" (*H.E.* 3.39.3), his various and sundry remarks regarding Peter aid our investigative process.

In Papias 2 (= Eusebius, *H.E.* 2.15.1), Peter is presented as a divinely inspired and illuminating teacher of the gospel.[10] So gifted was he that those he taught wanted to hear more. Therefore, we are told that unspecified Petrine auditors prevailed upon Mark, a follower of Peter (ἀκόλουθον ὄντα Πέτρου), to "leave behind a written record of the teaching that had been given to them orally [by Peter]." Having learned of this development through the Spirit's revelation, the apostle Peter is said to have been delighted by his audiences' eagerness and to have authorized the reading of Mark's Gospel in the churches. Eusebius also reports that Papias indicates that Peter mentions Mark in his first letter (1 Pet. 5:13), which Papias maintains was written in Rome.

Although this fragment is marked by anachronism and stands at some remove from the historical fisherman from Bethsaida, it is teeming with putative recollections and claims regarding Peter. According to Papias 2, the apostle Peter was an illuminating teacher/preacher who was accompanied and aided by one Mark, who in turn responded to the demands of Peter's listeners and

---

10. The Papias fragments are given in the *Apostolic Fathers* in the LCL (ed. and trans. Ehrman), 2:85-119. I employ the fragment numbers that Ehrman uses. For differences in contents and numbering of the fragments of Papias, see the useful chart in Holmes, *Apostolic Fathers,* p. 307.

wrote a Gospel based on Peter's oral instruction. What is more, this literary snippet states that Mark was in Rome when Peter wrote his first letter.

With further regard to Mark's connection with Peter and Peter with Mark's Gospel, Papias 3.15 (= Eusebius, *H.E.* 3.39.15) reports that Mark served as a ἑρμηνευτής and companion of Peter (who is portrayed here as an adaptive teacher). Given Helen Bond's contribution to this volume, it is unnecessary to linger here. I would like to note in passing, however, that Eusebius also reports that Papias "made use of the testimonies (μαρτυρίαις) found in . . . the epistle of Peter" (Papias 3.17 = Eusebius, *H.E.* 3.39.17).

We may deal even more rapidly with Papias 5 and 12.1 respectively. For our purposes, the importance of Papias 5 (= Jerome, *Vir. ill.* 18) is its pairing of Andrew with Peter. To the best of my knowledge, this is the only passage in the Apostolic Fathers that mentions Andrew. In so doing, it places Andrew prior to Peter as in John 1:40, 44. Since he does not explicitly say so, it may well be that Papias assumed his readers would know that Andrew and Peter were brothers. Finally, Papias 12.1 (in Philip of Side, *H.E.*) refers to Peter as an "apostle" and pairs him with John, as does Acts 3–4.

Conclusions

Taken together, a rather full portrait of Peter emerges from the pages of the Apostolic Fathers. Not only is the so-called underestimated apostle[11] repeatedly portrayed as a "good and faithful" apostle (*1 Clem.* 5.3; Ignatius, *Rom.* 4.3; Papias 2; 5; 12), but he is also depicted as an "athletic contender," "noble example," "upright pillar," and "steadfast witness" (*1 Clem.* 5.1-4; *2 Clem.* 5.1-4; note, too, Ignatius, *Smyrn.* 3.2). Additionally, "Cephas" (*1 Clem.* 47.3) is remembered in this corpus of writings as the spokesman for and leading representative of the disciples (so *2 Clem.* 5.3; Ignatius, *Smyrn.* 3.2), an eyewitness of Jesus' bodily resurrection (Ignatius, *Smyrn.* 3), teacher of the (Roman) church (Ignatius, *Rom.* 4.3; Papias 2; 3.15), mentor of Mark (Papias 2; 3.15), wellspring of the Gospel of Mark (Papias 2; 3.15), letter writer (Papias 2; 3.17; cf. 1 Pet. 1:1; 2 Pet. 1:1; 3:1), Spirit-illumined guide (Papias 2), and authority for the church(es) (Papias 2; 5), whom the Apostolic Fathers pair with Paul (*1 Clem.* 5.1-7; Ignatius, *Rom.* 4.3), Andrew (Papias 5), and John (Papias 12.1).

Despite this impressive array of attributes, there are other facets of the

---

11. Thus Martin Hengel, *Saint Peter: The Underestimated Apostle*, trans. Thomas Trapp (Grand Rapids: Eerdmans, 2010).

New Testament Peter that do not appear in the Apostolic Fathers. Among these, one might note that the images of Peter as "rock" (Matt. 16:18), "keeper of the keys" (Matt. 16:19), "elder" (1 Pet. 5:1), "missioner" (e.g., Acts 9:32; 10:45; 1 Cor. 9:5; Gal. 2:7-8), "miracle worker" (e.g., Acts 3:1-10; 5:15; 9:40), "fisher" (Mark 1:16; Matt. 4:18), "shepherd" (John 21:15-17; cf. 1 Pet. 5:1-4), and "denier" (e.g., Luke 22:34) are absent from the collection. Frankly, I find the omission of these roles (minus "denier") rather surprising, as I do the fact that Peter does not feature even more fully than he does in the Apostolic Fathers. But I find it no less surprising that scholars of early Christian studies have seldom examined the various ways these particular early Christian writers portray Peter.

It is sometimes suggested that the apostle Paul is well described as a "round character," a term coined by E. M. Forster to depict a complex, multidimensional individual within a story.[12] If nothing else, this short study has shown that the Peter of the Apostolic Fathers is no "flat," monodimensional character himself. Indeed, so round is he that it is challenging to get one's mind around how pivotal a figure he seemingly was for numerous Christians living in the postapostolic period. Peter served as a paragon of, and paradigm for, the faith they had come to embrace. What was true for some believers then is still true for other Christ followers now, albeit at some remove in time from the Apostolic Fathers.

12. So, e.g., John B. Polhill, *Paul and His Letters* (Nashville: Broadman & Holman, 1999), p. 440. See E. M. Forster, *Aspects of the Novel* (London: Edward Arnold, 1927).

CHAPTER 13

Peter in Paul's Churches: The Early Reception of Peter in *1 Clement* and in Polycarp's *Philippians*

Paul A. Hartog

At first glance, the topic of the reception of Peter within *1 Clement* and Polycarp's *Epistle to the Philippians* may seem ill-advised, as Peter is never actually mentioned in Polycarp's *Philippians*. In addition, the name Peter is found only once in *1 Clement,* although the name Cephas appears once as well. One mention of "Peter" and another mention of "Cephas" may not seem to merit the proposed study of these two letters. Nevertheless, the combined evidence of *1 Clement* and Polycarp's *Philippians* demonstrates that the early reception of Peter goes beyond the explicit references to Peter. Moreover, as one scratches under the surface, one discovers an interesting phenomenon. Within these two letters written to Pauline churches (in Corinth and Philippi), the imaging of Peter is framed within a more fundamental imaging of Paul. Readers may be familiar with the concept of a Russian matryoshka doll, in which carved, wooden figures fit within one another in descending order of size. The "matryoshka principle" or "nested doll principle" serves as a fitting analogy to the reception of Peter *nested within* the overt reception of Paul as found in *1 Clement* and especially Polycarp's *Philippians.*

As an initial datum, one notes that Paul's own letter to the Philippians never mentions Peter. But Paul's correspondence with the Corinthians, like his letter to the Galatians, refers several times to Peter under the appellation of Cephas. First Corinthians 15:5 notes that the risen Christ appeared to Cephas and then to the Twelve. First Corinthians 9:5 mentions that Cephas took along his wife as he traveled. More importantly, for our present investigation, 1 Corinthians 1:12 and 3:22 highlight a Corinthian factionalism, centered on parties loyal to Paul, Apollos, and Cephas, and perhaps a "Christ" faction as well.

Among works now appearing among the "Apostolic Fathers" are letters written to the Pauline-founded faith communities in Corinth *(1 Clement)* and Philippi (Polycarp's *Philippians*).[1] The explicit reference to Cephas in *1 Clement* 47 (a text not discussed in Markus Bockmuehl's recent *Simon Peter in Scripture and Memory*) may serve as an entry point.[2] The passage states,

> Take up the epistle of the blessed Paul the apostle. What did he first write to you in the beginning of the gospel? Truly he wrote to you in the Spirit about himself and Cephas and Apollos, because even then you had split into factions. Yet that splitting into factions brought less sin upon you, for you were partisans of highly reputed apostles and of a man approved by them.[3]

Several interpretive points are immediately evident: First, *1 Clement* approvingly references "the epistle of the blessed Paul the apostle," which (in this context) obviously refers to Paul's letter now titled 1 Corinthians.[4] Andrew Gregory maintains, "Such clear testimony to 1 Corinthians means that this conclusion is secure, even without any significant verbatim parallels at this point."[5] Second, *1 Clement* affirms that Paul wrote this epistle πνευματικῶς ("spiritually" or "in the Spirit"). Third, *1 Clement* 47 alludes to 1 Corinthians 1:12 and/or 3:22. Fourth, the purpose of the allusion is to discourage a resurfacing factionalism. Fifth, *1 Clement* calls both Paul and Cephas (or Peter) "reputed apostles," and labels Apollos as "a man approved by them."[6]

---

1. On the Pauline founding of the churches, see *1 Clem.* 47.2 and Polycarp, *Phil.* 11.3.

2. Markus Bockmuehl, *Simon Peter in Scripture and Memory* (Grand Rapids: Baker Academic, 2012); cf. Markus Bockmuehl, *The Remembered Peter in Ancient Reception and Modern Debate,* WUNT 1/262 (Tübingen: Mohr Siebeck, 2010). Perhaps the passage was overlooked because of its use of "Cephas" rather than "Peter."

3. English translations of the Apostolic Fathers come from Michael W. Holmes, *The Apostolic Fathers: Greek Texts and English Translations,* 3rd ed. (Grand Rapids: Baker Academic, 2007).

4. Andrew Gregory surmises that the author of *1 Clement* knew 1 Corinthians because "there were ongoing relationships between the churches in the imperial capital and in one of its major colonies." Andrew F. Gregory, "*1 Clement* and the Writings That Later Formed the New Testament," in *The Reception of the New Testament in the Apostolic Fathers,* ed. Andrew F. Gregory and Christopher M. Tuckett (Oxford: Oxford University Press, 2005), pp. 129-57, here p. 157. See also Horacio E. Lona, "'Petrus in Rom' und der Erste Clemensbrief," in *Petrus und Paulus in Rom,* ed. Stefan Heid (Freiburg: Herder, 2011), pp. 221-46.

5. Gregory, "*1 Clement* and the Writings," p. 144. See also Oxford Society of Historical Theology, *The New Testament in the Apostolic Fathers* (Oxford: Clarendon, 1905), pp. 40-41.

6. See Otto Knoch, "Im Namen des Petrus und Paulus: Der Brief des Clemens Romanus und die Eigenart des römischen Christentums," in *Aufstieg und Niedergang der römischen Welt* 2.27.1, ed. Wolfgang Haase (Berlin: de Gruyter, 1992), pp. 3-54.

The "apostles" (without the naming of specific examples) appear as a group in *1 Clement* 42 and 44: "The apostles received the gospel for us from the Lord Jesus Christ; Jesus the Christ was sent forth from God. So then Christ is from God, and the apostles are from Christ" (42.1-2). "Our apostles likewise knew, through our Lord Jesus Christ, that there would be strife over the bishop's office. For this reason, therefore, having received complete foreknowledge, they appointed the leaders mentioned earlier and afterwards they gave the offices a permanent character" (44.1-2). These two passages do not mention Peter or Paul specifically, but they do project a general apostolic image in three specific ways: The apostles received their commission from Jesus Christ, they appointed church leaders, and they foresaw that there would be strife over ecclesiastical leadership.

A spirit of dissension had resurfaced in the Corinthian church. After gathering examples of jealousy from the Hebrew Scriptures, *1 Clement* 5 exclaims,

> Let us consider the noble examples that belong to our own generation. Because of jealousy and envy the greatest and most righteous pillars were persecuted and fought to the death. Let us set before our eyes the good apostles. There was Peter, who because of unrighteous jealousy endured not one or two but many trials, and thus having given his testimony went to his appointed place of glory.

Echoing the language of Galatians, *1 Clement* describes these "good apostles" as "righteous pillars" (cf. the reputed "pillars" of James, Cephas, and John in Gal. 2:7-9).[7] *1 Clement* 5 affirms that the apostles were persecuted and eventually executed due to jealousy and envy, which fits the argument of the wider context and the epistle as a whole. The text then highlights Peter's endurance of suffering and states that he "went to his appointed place of glory."[8]

The material immediately following in *1 Clement* 5.5 continues with a similar description of Paul:

7. See also Boudewijn Dehandschutter, "Some Notes on *1 Clement* 5,4-7," in *Fructus Centesimus*, ed. A. A. R. Bastiansen, A. Hilhorst, and C. H. Kneepkens, Instrumenta Patristica 19 (Dordrecht: Kluwer, 1989), pp. 83-89; Helmut Löhr, "Zur Paulus-Notiz in *1 Clem* 5,5-7," in *Das Ende des Paulus: Historische, theologische, und literaturgeschichtliche Aspekte*, ed. Friedrich Wilhelm Horn (Berlin: de Gruyter, 2001), pp. 197-213.

8. See Bockmuehl, *Simon Peter*, pp. 108-11; Morton Smith, "The Report about Peter in I Clement V:4," *NTS* 7 (1960): 86-88. Smith argued that everything *1 Clement* says about Peter comes from Acts. Contrast Stanislas Giet, "Le témoignage de Clément de Rome, I: sur la venue à Rome de saint Pierre," *RevScRel* 29 (1955): 123-36.

Because of jealousy and strife Paul showed the way to the prize for endurance. After he had been seven times in chains, had been driven into exile, had been stoned, and had preached in the east and in the west, he won the genuine glory for his faith, having taught righteousness to the whole world and having reached the farthest limits of the west. Finally, when he had given his testimony before the rulers, he thus departed from the world and went to the holy place, having become an outstanding example of endurance.

In a continuation of the topic of jealousy, the text highlights Paul's teaching of δικαιοσύνη ("righteousness") and his personal ὑπομονή ("endurance"), which appears twice.[9] The passage emphasizes Paul's experience of persecution in a manner that goes beyond the materials of 2 Corinthians 11:22-28, by the enumeration of seven imprisonments and by the notoriously puzzling reference to the "farthest limits of the west." As encouragement, *1 Clement* stresses Paul's reception of "the prize" and "genuine glory" as he went to "the holy place." Clearly, Paul is paralleled with Peter as one who suffered at jealous hands and who received his appointed reward. In fact, the two passages in *1 Clement* that explicitly mention Peter by name (as "Peter" in chapter 5 and as "Cephas" in chapter 47) are also the only two passages that explicitly mention Paul by name.[10] The author self-consciously writes to the Pauline-founded church at Corinth, and he openly employs Paul's own Corinthian correspondence in his appeals (*1 Clement* 47).[11]

By contrast, as mentioned in my introductory remarks, Polycarp's *Philippians* (hereafter *Philippians*) never directly mentions Peter (or "Cephas"). Multiple similarities, however, parallel *1 Clement* 5 with *Philippians* 9, which states:

I urge all of you, therefore, to obey the teaching about righteousness and to exercise unlimited endurance, like that which you saw with your own eyes

9. See Andreas Lindemann, "Paul's Influence on 'Clement' and Ignatius," in *Trajectories through the New Testament and the Apostolic Fathers*, ed. Andrew F. Gregory and Christopher M. Tuckett (Oxford: Oxford University Press, 2005), pp. 9-24, here pp. 10-12.

10. Thomas Herron used these materials in the development of his minority view that *1 Clement* should be dated to around 70. See Thomas J. Herron, *Clement and the Early Church of Rome: On the Dating of Clement's First Epistle to the Corinthians* (Steubenville: Emmaus Road, 2010), pp. 82-83.

11. On Paul being more important than Peter in *1 Clem.* 5, see Lindemann, "Paul's Influence," p. 10; contra Karlmann Beyschlag, *Clemens Romanus und der Frühkatholizismus: Untersuchungen zu I Clemens 1-7*, BHT (Tübingen: Mohr Siebeck, 1966), p. 280.

not only in the blessed Ignatius and Zosimus and Rufus but also in others from your congregation and in Paul himself and the rest of the apostles. Be assured that all these did not run in vain but with faith and righteousness, and that they are now in the place due them with the Lord, with whom they also suffered. For they did not love the present world but the one who died on our behalf and was raised by God for our sakes.

These similarities are heightened by *1 Clement*'s influence elsewhere on Polycarp's epistle.[12] B. H. Streeter believed that Polycarp knew *1 Clement* almost "by heart," adding that *Philippians* was "more influenced by the language of Clement than by any book of the New Testament, except perhaps 1 Peter."[13] Nevertheless, one must caution against overstatement. Kenneth Berding has recently reassessed Polycarp's use of *1 Clement* and has reached a more tempered conclusion: "Polycarp knew and used *1 Clement,* but his familiarity with this early Christian document should not be exaggerated."[14]

In both *1 Clement* 5 and *Philippians* 9, the apostles serve as *paradeigmata* ("models") to follow, in view of their personal endurance in suffering.[15] The specific similarities between *1 Clement* 5 and *Philippians* 9 include (1) the reappearance of "righteousness" (twice); (2) the reappearance of "endurance"; (3) the similar references to events appearing before the "eyes" of the recipients; (4) the apostolic reputation of "faith"; (5) similar references to the "appointed place of glory" and "the holy place" *(1 Clement)* and "the place due them with the Lord" *(Philippians)*;[16] and (6) somewhat similar otherworldly

---

12. See Johannes B. Bauer, *Die Polykarpbriefe,* Kommentar zu den Apostolischen Vätern (Göttingen: Vandenhoeck & Ruprecht, 1995), pp. 28-30.

13. B. H. Streeter, *The Four Gospels* (London: Macmillan, 1924), p. 528; Streeter, *The Primitive Church* (London: Macmillan, 1929), p. 159. Cf. Otto Bardenhewer, *Geschichte der altkirchlichen Literatur,* 2nd ed. (Freiburg: Herder, 1913), 1:166.

14. Kenneth Berding, "Polycarp's Use of *1 Clement:* An Assumption Reconsidered," *JECS* 19 (2011): 127-39, here p. 139. Berding's monograph lists three "probable" dependences of Polycarp, *Philippians* on *1 Clement* and seven "possible" dependences. Kenneth Berding, *Polycarp and Paul,* Supplements to Vigiliae Christianae 62 (Leiden: Brill, 2002), p. 202. Holmes's apparatus cites four of these ten parallels and adds a parallel between Polycarp, *Phil.* 4.3, and *1 Clem.* 21.3 (Holmes, *Apostolic Fathers,* pp. 280-97). With this addition, one might speak of a small cluster of reminiscences of *1 Clement* in Polycarp *Phil.* 4.2-3 (as noted in Berding, *Polycarp and Paul,* pp. 151-53).

15. This fact may help explain the seeming contradiction between Polycarp, *Phil.* 9 and 13. See Paul Hartog, *Polycarp and the New Testament,* WUNT 134 (Tübingen: Mohr Siebeck, 2002), pp. 161-65; Paul Hartog, *Polycarp's Epistle to the Philippians and the Martyrdom of Polycarp,* Oxford Apostolic Fathers (Oxford: Oxford University Press, 2013), pp. 37-40.

16. *1 Clement* 5 also references "genuine glory" and "the prize."

sentiments (although using different vocabulary), as Paul "departed from the world [ἀπαλλαγὴ τοῦ κόσμου]" in *1 Clement* 5.7, and the martyrs did not "love the present world [οὐ τὸν νῦν ἠγάπησαν αἰῶνα]" in *Philippians* 9.1. William Schoedel noted such parallels and maintained that Peter is the implied "leader of the 'rest of the apostles'" in *Philippians* 9.[17]

Of course, differences between *1 Clement* 5 and *Philippians* 9 are also evident: (1) Polycarp adds kerygmatic material about "the one who died on our behalf and was raised by God for our sakes" (*Phil.* 9.2); (2) Polycarp emphasizes the sufferings of later contemporaries, such as Ignatius, Zosimus, Rufus, and other Philippians (*Phil.* 9.1); (3) *1 Clement* is more explicit in its nomenclature about the various examples serving as ὑποδείγματα ("patterns") and Paul being a ὑπογραμμός ("model/example") (*1 Clem.* 5.1, 6); and (4) Polycarp does not explicitly mention "Peter" (although he is undoubtedly included among "the rest of the apostles") (*Phil.* 9.1). Andreas Lindemann, for instance, found it striking that Peter is not mentioned by name in *Philippians* 9.1, although similar materials in *1 Clement* 5.3-7 (as well as Ignatius, *Rom.* 4.3) mention Peter along with Paul.[18]

Taras Khomych's recent study of the diverse notions of "apostolicity" in the Apostolic Fathers does not examine *Philippians*.[19] The "apostolic"/"apostle" word group appears only twice in *Philippians* (in 6.3 and 9.1). In *Philippians* 6.3, as in *1 Clement* 42, the apostles received or preached the gospel. In *Philippians* 9.1, as in *1 Clement* 5 (see above), the apostles suffered persecution with "endurance." Yet the tenor of *Philippians* portrays Polycarp (in his authorial role)

---

17. William R. Schoedel, *Polycarp, Martyrdom of Polycarp, Fragments of Papias,* The Apostolic Fathers 5 (London: Nelson, 1967), p. 29.

18. Andreas Lindemann, *Paulus im ältesten Christentum,* BHT 58 (Tübingen: Mohr Siebeck, 1979), p. 89. Holmes discusses Ignatius, *Eph.* 12 (Paul); *1 Clem.* 5.5-7 (Paul); 47.1 (Paul); Ignatius, *Eph.* 12.2 (Paul); *Smyrn.* 3.2 (Peter); *Rom.* 4.3 (Peter and Paul): "In light of these parallels, in letters that Polycarp used as sources for his own letter, much of what Polycarp says about Paul appears rather derivative and conventional, even stereotyped" (Michael W. Holmes, "Paul and Polycarp," in *Paul and the Second Century,* ed. Michael F. Bird and Joseph R. Dodson, LNTS 412 [London: T&T Clark, 2011], pp. 57-69, here p. 65). Perhaps, however, Polycarp's use of the figure of Paul does not reflect literary dependence on texts such as *1 Clement* and the Ignatian letters, but rather a general respect for Paul in the circles represented by Polycarp and the recipients.

19. Taras Khomych, "Diversity of the Notion of Apostolicity in the Writings of the Apostolic Fathers," in *Heiligkeit und Apostolizität der Kirche,* ed. Franz Mali, Theresia Hainthaler, and Gregor Emmenegger (Innsbruck: Tyrolia, 2010), pp. 63-81. Khomych examined the *Didache, 1 Clement,* the Ignatian correspondence, and the *Shepherd of Hermas,* and he highlighted the "complex picture" of the "differences between the individual views of apostolicity and apostolic authority" (Khomych, "Diversity," pp. 69, 81).

as faithful to apostolic traditions, or as Hans Lohmann notes, as a "guardian of apostolic tradition."[20]

Paul is the only apostle explicitly referenced throughout Polycarp's epistle (3.2; 9.1; 11.2; 11.3).[21] Having examined *Philippians* 9.1, I turn now to the remaining three passages. In *Philippians* 3.2, Polycarp explains,

> For neither I nor anyone like me can keep pace with the wisdom of the blessed and glorious Paul. When he was with you in the presence of the people of that time, he accurately and reliably taught the word concerning the truth. And when he was absent he wrote you letters; if you study them carefully, you will be able to build yourselves up in the faith that has been given to you.

Chapter 11 addresses the avarice of Valens, a fallen elder, and explicitly mentions Paul twice:[22] "Or do we not know that the saints will judge the world, as Paul teaches? But I have not observed or heard of any such thing among you, in whose midst the blessed Paul labored, and who are praised in the beginning of his letter." Thus, within Polycarp's epistle, Paul is apostolically imaged as a blessed and glorious martyr, as a teacher of truth and righteousness, as a letter writer, and as a church planter.

Furthermore, Polycarp's counsel is filled with Pauline quotations and allusions.[23] For example, in Berding's perspective, besides Polycarp's "almost certain" knowledge of Paul's epistle to the Philippians, the following qualify as

20. Hans Lohmann, *Drohung und Verheißung,* Beihefte zur Zeitschrift für die neutestamentliche Wissenschaft und die Kunde der alteren Kirche 55 (Berlin: de Gruyter, 1989), p. 178.

21. Some have theorized that the Latin translator added *sicut Paulus docet* into the text. See Édouard Massaux, *The Influence of the Gospel of Saint Matthew on Christian Literature before Saint Irenaeus,* ed. Arthur J. Bellinzoni, New Gospel Studies 5/2 (Macon, Ga.: Mercer University Press, 1990), 2:3; Lindemann, *Paulus im ältesten Christentum,* pp. 90 n. 113, 228. Berding responds, "If one takes away the *sicut Paulus docet* in 11.2, the appearance of Paul's name in the following verse is not as contextually smooth (though it cannot be said to be impossible)" (Berding, *Polycarp and Paul,* p. 111). Donald Hagner maintained that the Latin translator may have harmonized Polycarp, *Phil.* 11.2 to parallel with 1 Cor. 6:2 (Donald A. Hagner, *The Use of the Old and New Testaments in Clement of Rome,* NovTSup 34 [Leiden: Brill, 1973], p. 284 n. 3). Holmes argues, "The question as to whether this phrase *(sicut Paulus docet)* is an addition by the Latin translator is unimportant to the present discussion, inasmuch as it does not add anything additional to the portrait drawn by the other three mentions of Paul" (Holmes, "Paul and Polycarp," p. 64 n. 28).

22. Assuming the Latin faithfully represents the original Greek.

23. David K. Rensberger, "As the Apostle Teaches: The Development of the Use of Paul's Letters in Second-Century Christianity" (Ph.D. diss., Yale University, 1981), p. 116.

"almost certain quotations" or "almost certain allusions": the use of Romans 14:10, 12, in *Philippians* 6.2; the use of 1 Corinthians 6:2 in *Philippians* 11.2; the use of 1 Corinthians 6:9-10 in *Philippians* 5.3; the use of 2 Corinthians 6:7 in *Philippians* 4.1; the use of Galatians 6:7 in *Philippians* 5.1; the use of Ephesians 2:5, 8-9, in *Philippians* 1.3; the use of 1 Timothy 6:7, 10, in *Philippians* 4.1; and the use of 2 Timothy 4:10 in *Philippians* 9.2.[24] If one appends Berding's classifications of "possible" allusions, another twenty-five allusions to Pauline literature are added. Berding contrasts his own "middle approach" with the "thin" reading of Michael Holmes, my own tempered "thin" reading, and the "thick" readings of P. N. Harrison and Charles Hill.[25] While some (like myself) may not agree with *all* of Berding's conclusions, scholarship universally agrees that *Philippians* repeatedly draws from Pauline literature.

On the other hand, *Philippians* is unmistakably influenced by 1 Peter as well, a fact already noted by Eusebius: "Polycarp, in his above-mentioned letter to the Philippians, which is still extant, has made some quotations from the first Epistle of Peter" (Eusebius, *H.E.* 4.14.9).[26] Harrison gushed that Polycarp knew 1 Peter "intimately," and Massey Shepherd labeled 1 Peter as Polycarp's "special favorite."[27]

Berding classifies the following uses of 1 Peter within *Philippians:* An "almost certain loose citation" of 1 Peter 1:8 and a probable allusion to 1 Peter 1:12 in *Philippians* 1.3; a "probable allusion" to 1 Peter 1:13 and a "probable loose allusion" to 1 Peter 1:21 in *Philippians* 2.1; an "almost certain true citation" of 1 Peter 3:9, a "probable allusion" to 1 Peter 1:13, and a "probable loose citation" of 1 Peter 1:21 in *Philippians* 2.1-2; a "probable loose citation" of 1 Peter 2:11 in *Philippians* 5.3; a "probable loose citation" of 1 Peter 4:7 in *Philippians* 7.2; an

---

24. See Berding, *Polycarp and Paul,* pp. 199-201. The recurrence of introductory formulas especially highlights the inclusion of Pauline materials. Cf. Hartog, *Polycarp and the New Testament,* pp. 177-79, 191, 195.

25. Berding, "Polycarp's Use," p. 131.

26. English translation from Eusebius, *The Ecclesiastical History,* ed. Kirsopp Lake, LCL (Cambridge, Mass.: Harvard University Press, 1965), 1:339. According to Boudewijn Dehandschutter, Polycarp's *Philippians* may be the only example of a usage of 1 Peter before the end of the second century: Boudewijn Dehandschutter, *Polycarpiana: Collected Essays,* ed. Johan Leemans, BETL 205 (Leuven: Leuven University Press, 2007), p. 162 n. 38. Contrast Bockmuehl, *Simon Peter,* pp. 30, 106 n. 11.

27. P. N. Harrison, *Polycarp's Two Epistles to the Philippians* (Cambridge: Cambridge University Press, 1936), p. 296; Massey Hamilton Shepherd, "The Letter of Polycarp, Bishop of Smyrna, to the Philippians," in *Early Christian Fathers,* ed. Cyril C. Richardson (New York: Collier, 1970), p. 125. Polycarp arguably accepted Petrine authorship of 1 Peter; but cf. John A. Lawson, *Theological and Historical Introduction to the Apostolic Fathers* (New York: Macmillan, 1961), p. 159.

"almost certain loose citation" of 1 Peter 2:24, an "almost certain true citation" of 1 Peter 2:22, a "probable allusion" to 1 Peter 2:21, and a "possible allusion" to 1 Peter 4:16 in *Philippians* 8.1-2; an "almost certain loose citation" of 1 Peter 2:12, a "possible allusion" to 1 Peter 2:17 or 3:8, and a "possible loose citation" of 1 Peter 5:5 in *Philippians* 10.1-2.[28]

Berding claims that "Polycarp does not always cluster his references, as his use of 1 Peter illustrates," and the Petrine references do not follow any "identifiable pattern" but rather are "sprinkled randomly throughout the letter."[29] Nevertheless, Berding's own monograph does note Petrine clustering.[30] Berding's statistical analysis reveals an ambiguous, small clustering of Petrine materials in *Philippians* 10; a more probable, small clustering of Petrine materials in *Philippians* 2; and a distinct clustering of multiple Petrine materials in *Philippians* 8.[31] In comparable fashion, Berding has demonstrated a "marked" tendency in *Philippians* "to cluster Pauline citations and allusions after each of the three references to the apostle" (in 3.2; 9.1; and 11.2-12.1).[32] Other clusters in *Philippians* include the materials from *1 Clement* gathered in *Philippians* 4.2-3 and the materials from 1 John coalesced in *Philippians* 7.1-2.[33]

Charles Nielsen argued that Polycarp was an incipient Marcionite because of his strategic dependence on Paul, who alone is mentioned by name.[34] But the repeated role of 1 Peter and the clear use of 1 John belie this simplistic, "Marcionite" caricature. The influence of 1 Peter has been dutifully acknowledged by Richard Stuckwisch as well as by Berding. In a 1997 article Stuckwisch noted, "Alongside the Pauline Epistles, it is also a well-known fact that 1 Peter plays a prominent role in the epistle of Polycarp. 1 Peter is, in fact, the single most prominent writing of our New Testament in Polycarp."[35] Stuckwisch concluded, "Perhaps it would be best, therefore, in the final analysis, to regard

28. Berding, *Polycarp and Paul,* pp. 201-2.

29. Kenneth Berding, "Polycarp of Smyrna's View of the Authorship of 1 and 2 Timothy," *VC* 53 (1999): 349-60, here p. 357.

30. Berding, *Polycarp and Paul,* pp. 94-97.

31. Berding, *Polycarp and Paul,* 44-48, 95-97, 106-7, 201-2. See also Michael W. Holmes, "Polycarp's *Letter to the Philippians* and the Writings That Later Formed the New Testament," in Gregory and Tuckett, eds., *Reception of the New Testament,* pp. 220-23.

32. Berding, "Polycarp of Smyrna's View," pp. 349, 360.

33. Berding, "Polycarp of Smyrna's View," p. 357.

34. Charles M. Nielsen, "Polycarp and Marcion: A Note," *TS* 47 (1986): 297-99.

35. D. Richard Stuckwisch, "Saint Polycarp of Smyrna: Johannine or Pauline Figure?" *CTQ* 61 (1997): 113-25, here p. 122. Whereas Christian tradition linked Polycarp with the apostle John, Stuckwisch leaned toward the view that Irenaeus confused "John the Apostle" with a "John the Elder" (Stuckwisch, "Saint Polycarp," pp. 119, 124-25).

Polycarp as neither a 'Johannine' figure nor a 'Pauline' figure, but simply as the truly apostolic figure that he was."[36] While addressing "the theological questions and issues of his day," he "consciously stood on the foundation of the apostles — Peter, Paul, and John."[37]

In a 2008 article, Berding tackled the same topic.[38] After addressing Pauline connections in *Philippians* and the role of 1 John in chapter 7, Berding noted that *Philippians* "draws regularly" on 1 Peter. "Of course," explained Berding, "when compared with the frequency with which he quotes from the letters of Paul, his employment of 1 Peter is significantly less."[39] One might remark, however, that if one compares *individual works* rather than *corpora,* then the use of 1 Peter stands head and shoulders above evidence of *any* other single New Testament work in *Philippians* (including any *individual* Pauline epistle), even though the Pauline corpus carries the day.

According to Boudewijn Dehandschutter, 1 Peter has the same functional authority in *Philippians* as the Pauline writings do, "but Polycarp does not mention Peter explicitly, because that apostle has no particular authority with the Philippians."[40] One could add a further explanation: Just as Polycarp's use of Pauline materials may be tied to the particular audience (a Pauline congregation) and a particular occasion (the transgression of an elder through avarice), even so his extensive use of 1 Peter may be tied to a particular purpose (parenetic summoning to endurance and forgiveness in the midst of suffering).[41] Perhaps Polycarp was also drawn to 1 Peter (like the Pastorals) because of interest in the topic of elders, incited by the Valens case.[42] Nevertheless,

---

36. Stuckwisch, "Saint Polycarp," p. 125.

37. Stuckwisch, "Saint Polycarp," pp. 124-25.

38. Berding mentioned Stuckwisch's earlier work in passing: Kenneth Berding, "John or Paul? Who Was Polycarp's Mentor?" *TynBul* 59 (2008): 135-43, here p. 137 n. 11. Berding noted the "explicit historical link" to the apostle John in various patristic sources, including Irenaeus, Tertullian, Eusebius, Jerome, and the Harris Fragments. See the addenda at the end of the text of the *Martyrdom of Polycarp.* Berding himself pled ignorance concerning whether Polycarp had personal contact with the apostle John or a certain John the Elder or neither (Berding, "John or Paul?" p. 139).

39. Berding, "John or Paul?" p. 142.

40. Dehandschutter, *Polycarpiana,* p. 162. Cf. Otto Knoch, "Petrus und Paulus in den Schriften der Apostolischen Väter," in *Kontinuität und Einheit,* ed. Franz Mussner, Paul-Gerhard Müller, and Werner Stenger (Freiburg: Herder, 1981), pp. 240-60.

41. See Peter Oakes, "Leadership and Suffering in the Letters of Polycarp and Paul to the Philippians," in Gregory and Tuckett, *Trajectories,* pp. 353-73.

42. On Polycarp and the Pastorals, see Hartog, *Polycarp and the New Testament,* pp. 228-31.

the use of 1 Peter 5:5 in *Philippians* 10.1-2 (as discussed by Berding) seems ultimately indemonstrable.[43]

In any case, Polycarp seems to borrow from 1 Peter because of his parenetic intent, and his use especially accentuates the "ethical dimensions" of 1 Peter.[44] Overall, "Polycarp frequently uses paraenetic material, such as 1 Peter, the dominical sayings, Paul's moral exhortations, and *1 Clement,* because they fit his purpose."[45] Berding further notes that *Philippians* reflects "one almost certain loose citation of Acts 2:24." Although the case remains debatable, it may be relevant for our purposes that Acts 2:24 appears in a Petrine speech.[46]

Berding deduced, "Polycarp is not *merely* in a stream of any one apostle or another. He is willing to draw from any of a number of different streams of God-given authority, including a Pauline stream, a Petrine stream, a Johannine stream, the words of the Lord (both in oral and written form), and the Old Testament Scriptures. His writings clearly demonstrate that he understands himself to be in continuity with these authorities, not opposed to any of them."[47] Therefore, two scholars (Stuckwisch and Berding) who began their investigation by wondering whether Polycarp was in a Johannine or Pauline stream concluded that he is actually a key figure in the reception history of Petrine traditions as well.

Thus, on the one hand, *1 Clement* twice references Peter (once as Peter and once as Cephas), but does not feature Petrine traditions. Writing to a Pauline-founded community, the author highlights the apostle Paul's teaching addressed to them (*1 Clem.* 47, 49). On the other hand, Polycarp's *Philippians* never mentions Peter by name but does include multiple quotations or allusions from 1 Peter. Undoubtedly, this anonymity relates to Polycarp's stated and implied purposes. His stated purpose, as he wrote to a Pauline-founded

43. See Berding, *Polycarp and Paul,* p. 105 (which cites 1 Pet. 5:15 but clearly intends 1 Pet. 5:5).

44. Dehandschutter, *Polycarpiana,* p. 162. Dehandschutter adds, "Some passages could rely on a liturgical tradition on which *1 Peter* is also dependent."

45. Hartog, *Polycarp and the New Testament,* p. 194; cf. Holmes, "Paul and the Letter," p. 69.

46. Berding, "John or Paul?" p. 142, 142 n. 28. I have classified the use of Acts as "possible" rather than "almost certain" (Hartog, *Polycarp and the New Testament,* pp. 185, 195). Holmes has classified Acts with a "D" rating (Holmes, "Polycarp's Letter," p. 226, see also pp. 199-201). Bruce Metzger does not discuss the possible influence of Acts on Polycarp's *Philippians.* Bruce Metzger, *The Canon of the New Testament* (Oxford: Oxford University Press, 1987), pp. 59-63.

47. Berding, "John or Paul?" p. 143, italics his. In a recent article, Berding concludes that "Polycarp's primary literary influences should be ranked as follows: (1) Paul, (2) 1 Peter, (3) *1 Clement,* (4) 1 John" (Berding, "Polycarp's Use," p. 139).

church, was to address "righteousness" while pointing them to Paul's own materials (*Phil.* 3.2; cf. 11.2).[48] His implied objective, as discussed by Berding, was to appeal in a Pauline style and manner, in the perceived spirit of Paul.[49] Nevertheless, Polycarp's epistle quotes from 1 Peter far more than any other single source and includes a definite "clustering" of Petrine quotations (*Phil.* 8). This use of material from 1 Peter fits Polycarp's parenetic purposes, especially his exhortations to forgiveness and righteous endurance in the midst of suffering (themes also found in 1 Peter).

Scholars have insisted on various distinctions in the reception of Paul (Paul as epistolary author vs. Paul as authoritative figure, etc.). For example, Lindemann has cautioned that one must carefully distinguish between the influence of Paul's image *(Paulusbild),* the influence of his writings, and the influence of a genuine understanding of Pauline theology.[50] Applying similar notions to our study, *1 Clement* receives Peter by name as an authoritative and exemplary figure alongside Paul. Polycarp's *Philippians* never mentions Peter by name but is a conduit of Petrine traditions (especially parenetic materials from 1 Peter), yet within a Pauline framework. These phenomena ultimately cause us to reconsider the debated "apostolic" nature or imaging of Polycarp himself. While early traditions emphasized a Johannine connection, and while modern scholars have often mined the text for Pauline quotations and allusions, Petrine influences run deep within Polycarp's *Philippians,* although Peter himself never appears by name.

In conclusion, both *1 Clement* and Polycarp's *Philippians,* two letters written to Pauline-founded churches, purposefully reflect a Pauline focus in view of their targeted Pauline audiences. Yet they both also incorporate the image

---

48. On Polycarp and "justification" as well as "righteousness," see Michael Theobald, "Paulus und Polykarp an die Philipper: Schlaglichter auf die frühe Rezeption des Basissatzes von der Rechtfertigung," in *Lutherische und neue Paulusperspektive,* ed. Michael Bachmann and Johannes Woyke (Tübingen: Mohr Siebeck, 2005), pp. 349-88.

49. See Berding, *Polycarp and Paul,* pp. 26-27.

50. Lindemann permitted the identification of Pauline concepts and terminology within early Christian texts only if they appeared as *Fremdkörper* ("foreign bodies") that could not be explained through alternative sources (Lindemann, *Paulus im ältesten Christentum,* pp. 17-18); cf. Martinus C. de Boer, "Comment: Which Paul?" in *Paul and the Legacies of Paul,* ed. William S. Babcock (Dallas: Southern Methodist University Press, 1990), pp. 45-54. Holmes, following Daniel Marguerat, differentiates between "Paul as Writer," "Paul as Remembered," and "Paul as Theologian." "The first offers an opportunity to survey Polycarp's knowledge and use of the Pauline letters; the second, Polycarp's knowledge of Paul's biography; and the third, Paul's theological influence on Polycarp" (Holmes, "Paul and the Letter," p. 58). For a recent survey, see Bird and Dodson, *Paul and the Second Century.*

of Peter or Petrine traditions within a wider sense of apostolicity. Overall, similar to the "matryoshka principle," both *1 Clement* and, especially, Polycarp's *Philippians* seem to "nest" their receptions of Peter within their overt receptions of Paul. However, *1 Clement* explicitly mentions the figure of Peter, while *Philippians* manifests an anonymous usage of Petrine traditions. In this manner, "Peter" has a role to play in each of these two epistles written to Pauline churches, yet the explicit and implicit Petrine roles in the two remain fascinatingly distinct, reflecting divergent modes of the reception of "Peter."

CHAPTER 14

On the Trail of the Scribal Peter:
Petrine Memory, Hellenist Mission, and
the Parting of the Ways in *Peter's Preaching*

William Rutherford

Among the repertoire of traditional images of the apostle Peter, one most captures my imagination. A well-represented stream of texts attests the perception of a complex transformation in the person of Peter, not simply in role but in literary and scribal competence as well.[1] Consider an episode from the pseudo-Clementine *Recognitions*.[2] In debate with priests at the Jerusalem temple, the apostles proclaim Jesus to be the messianic "prophet like Moses." The high priest Caiaphas directs his gaze to Peter and admonishes him: "Do you dare act in the office of teacher, though you are an untrained, rustic fisherman?" Peter had arrogated to himself the public office of teacher, and his lack of pedigree rendered suspect his messianic reading of Scripture. In response, Peter reaffirms the problematic nature of his life story: "If, as you claim, I am

---

1. E.g., Origen, *C. Cels.* 8.47; Justin, *1 Apol.* 39.3; Chrysostom, *Hom. Act.* 4.

2. There is general consensus that a source underlies *Rec.* 1.27-71. Robert E. Van Voorst identifies the source with *Ascents of James* mentioned by Epiphanius (*The Ascents of James: History and Theology of a Jewish-Christian Community,* SBLDS 112 [Atlanta: Scholars Press, 1989). F. Stanley Jones critiques his thesis (review of *The Ascents of James: History and Theology of a Jewish-Christian Community,* in *Pseudoclementina Elchasaiticaque inter judaeochristiana: Collected Studies* [Leuven: Peeters, 2012], pp. 279-82) and suggests the source offers a Jewish Christian "acts of the apostles" that revises the Lukan Acts ("An Ancient Jewish Christian Rejoinder to Luke's Acts of the Apostles: pseudo-Clementine *Recognitions* 1.27-71," in *Pseudo-clementina,* pp. 207-29).

I wish to thank Tobias Nicklas, Chris Keith, and Larry Hurtado for helpful comments and suggestions.

an ignorant and uneducated man, a fisherman and rustic, and I confess that I know more than the sages, this ought to alarm you greatly." This exchange frames Peter's complex identity through a homologous series of antitheses — fisherman: sage; learner: teacher; uneducated: educated — designed to raise one question: How could a simple, uneducated fisherman of humble Galilean origins declaim with such eloquence and appeal to Scripture so persuasively as to resist learned scribes?

The *Recognitions* resolve the tensions of this "Peter problem" by appeal to the dynamism of Israel's God. Peter continues: "If we had obtained instruction and then refuted you sages, this would be a work of time and diligence that is of natural disposition and not of God's power. Yet since we untrained men refute you who are wise, who would not realize that our abilities come . . . from the will of God?"[3] Sheer divine empowerment vanquishes Peter's educational deficit. The Acts of the Apostles offers a similar solution by attributing to Peter — an "illiterate" and "nonspecialist" — a filling of the messianic spirit.[4] Yet through intertextual allusion the author of Luke and Acts weaves a more intriguing possibility. The epilogue of the Lukan Gospel (Luke 24:13-49) and the prologue of Acts (Acts 1:3-8) relate how the risen Jesus instructed his disciples in Scripture.[5]

The supposition that the disciples, and preeminently Peter, received divine empowerment and/or education in a post-Easter context offers an elegant attempt to resolve the Peter problem. It is not the only solution offered in antiquity; nor did the problem of Peter's transformed identity and authority remain uncontested.[6] One of our earliest texts to mention Peter outside the New Testament affirms his proficiency as interpreter of Scripture and yet situates this in Peter's pre-Easter competencies. In the *Preaching of Peter,* Peter puts the very logia of the risen Jesus to the test of Scripture! In this study I trace *Preaching*'s image of Peter as scribe, root it in a Petrine strand of Hellenist mission, and comment on its significance for the "parting of the ways."

---

3. Pseudo-Clement, *Rec.* 1.62.2, 5-7. Translated from the Latin text in Bernhard Rehm, *Die Pseudoklementinen II: Rekognitionen in Rufins Übersetzung,* GCS 51,2 (Berlin: Akademie, 1965).

4. Acts 4:8-13. Thomas J. Kraus, "'Uneducated,' 'Ignorant,' or Even 'Illiterate'? Aspects and Background for an Understanding of ΑΓΡΑΜΜΑΤΟΙ (and ΙΔΙΩΤΑΙ) in Acts 4.13," *NTS* 45, no. 3 (1999): 434-49, surveys evidence from the documentary papyri relevant to the social background of Acts 4:13.

5. A variant in Codex Bezae at Luke 24:34 (λέγοντες, not ας) offers the intriguing reading that Jesus met Peter on the Emmaus road; Joseph H. Crehan, "St. Peter's Journey to Emmaus," *CBQ* 15 (1953): 418-26.

6. Several "gnostic" texts contest Peter's authority and hence his transformational narrative (e.g., *Gos. Thom.* 13, 114; *Gos. Mary,* BG 17.16-22).

Recovering the Scribal Peter from *Preaching*'s Gnostic Puzzle

Preaching is preserved as a series of fragments in Clement of Alexandria's *Stromata*, with two parallel fragments in Origen's *Commentary on John*.[7] It was very likely composed in Alexandria, Egypt,[8] in the first quarter of the second century.[9] Propriety bids us to exercise humility when reading it. We face the task of assembling a puzzle. A few handfuls of pieces lie before us. We have no box cover with a picture to measure or guide our progress, only pieces without context. Some are missing. We are not sure how many. Yet, as with any puzzle, we anticipate that all the pieces, if we had them, would fit to constitute a coherent image, for they were cut from the same patterned form. Curiosity summons us to attempt to set the pieces in a framework.

The confluence of three citations in Clement secures our first piece (figure 1). *Preaching* describes Jesus as "Law and Word" (frags. 1a, b, c).[10] As we sift, sort, and piece together the pieces, several clusters emerge. Four pieces fit nicely (2-5),

7. I adopt Ernst von Dobschütz's enumeration (*Das Kerygma Petri kritisch untersucht*, TU 11,1 [Leipzig: Hinrichs, 1893], pp. 18-27) and Michel Cambe's Greek text (*Kerygma Petri. Textus et commentarius*, CCSA 15 [Turnhout: Brepols, 2003], pp. 150-61). From Clement's *Stromata* are fragments 1a (1.29.182.3), 1b (2.15.68.2), 2a (6.5.39.2-3), 2b (6.7.58.1), 3a (6.5.39.4-40.2), 4a (6.5.41.2-3), 5 (6.5.41.4-6), 6 (6.5.43.3), 7 (6.6.48.1-2), 8 (6.6.48.6), 9 (6.15.128.1-2), and 10 (6.15.128.3); frag. 1c appears in his *Prophetic Eclogues* 58. Frags. 3b and 4b are in Origen, *Comm. Jo.* 13.17.104.

8. The evidence for Egypt is compelling. *Preaching* shares thematic concerns with Christian and Jewish literature from Egypt (e.g., mention of zoolatry, fixation on knowledge, programmatic scriptural interpretation) and enjoyed a vigorous Alexandrian reception. Aside from Heracleon (n. 9), Clement, and Origen (n. 7), an anonymous (Alexandrian?) commentator on the first Psalm (in Clement, *Strom.* 2.15.68.1-2) and the anonymous Alexandrian author of the Berlin Coptic Book (see Gesine Schenke Robinson, *Das Berliner "Koptische Buch" (P20915): Eine wiederhergestellte frühchristlich-theologische Abhandlung*, CSCO 611 [Louvain: Peeters, 2004], pp. xiv-xv, 245) cite it. *Preaching* also shares affinities with another work of Egyptian provenance, *Sibylline Oracles*, book 3 (Cambe, *Kerygma*, pp. 225-26).

9. Heracleon (ca. 180 CE) cites *Preaching* as *authoritative* in his commentary on John (Origen, *Comm. Jo.* 13.17.104), so a date in the first half of the second century is plausible (Wolfgang Grünstäudl, *Petrus Alexandrinus. Studien zum historischen und theologischen Ort des Zweiten Petrusbriefes*, WUNT 2/353 [Tübingen: Mohr Siebeck, 2013], p. 91: "zur Mitte des zweiten Jahrhunderts"; my thanks to Dr. Grünstäudl for sharing materials in advance of publication). I am now convinced the author of Aristides' *Apology* (ca. 124-125 CE) adapted *Preaching*; for scholarly opinions see my "Reinscribing the Jews: The Story of Aristides' *Apology* 2.2-4 and 14.1b-15.2," HTR 106, no. 1 (2013): 61-91, here p. 89 n. 75. *Kerygma* may have been composed prior to the Jewish uprising in 115-117 CE, after which Egyptian Judaism lost substantial political clout. Alternatively, a date in the 120s might suggest that *Preaching* responds to the proto-gnostic Basilides.

10. According to Clement *Preaching* described *Kyrios* (frags. 1ab) and "the Savior himself" (frag. 1c) as "Law and Logos," indicating the identification of Jesus and *Kyrios* in frag. 1.

Figure 1. The Gnostic Puzzle of *Peter's Preaching*

joined in a single argument by literary style, thematic coherence, self-reference, and theological trajectory. Michel Cambe labels this unit *Peter's Exhortation to Christians.*[11] Pieces three and four are independently attested by Clement (3a, 4a) and Origen (3b, 4b), and piece two finds an abbreviated counterpart elsewhere in Clement (2b). *Exhortation* embarks on a classification strategy that indexes human groups by their respective "knowledge," or gnosis, of God.[12] This unit assumed a vital role in *Preaching*'s argument and warrants an entire corner. Another three pieces (6-8) fit together by shared form and content.[13] Peter transmits sayings of the risen Jesus that authorize apostolic mission. In the final

11. Cambe, *Kerygma.*

12. The terms *gnosis* and "gnostic" designate a conceptual space shared by a broad assemblage of early Christian texts, including *Preaching*, which display a fascination with "knowledge" of God. It is not meant to suggest a genetic link between *Preaching* and any of the groups more commonly labeled "gnostic" in scholarly and popular parlance (e.g., Sethian or Valentinian gnosticism).

13. E.g., "without excuse" (frags. 6, 7); "repentance" (frags. 6, 8); "the/one God" (frags. 6, 7, 8).

two fragments (9-10) Peter secures the scriptural authority for his message. As we will see, these two fragments more clearly orient us to the puzzle frame. They link the other clusters in an argument at the heart of *Preaching*.

As a framework takes shape, we see what appears to be a map showing the way to knowledge of God. This impression, while incomplete, is not distorted. Knowledge assumes a privileged place in the logic that binds *Exhortation,* and the remaining fragments reprise a veritable lexicon of gnosis.[14] As we extrapolate interconnections we see that what first suggested a map to gnosis now more clearly reveals the apostle Peter. On his every word hangs a "Christian" audience. Peter is preaching an in-house sermon on the knowledge of God (frag. 2):

> Therefore know there is one God, who created the beginning of all things and possesses authority over (their) end. And (this is) the unseen (God), who sees all things; is uncontained, who contains all things; is in need of nothing, of whom all things have need, and through whom they exist; incomprehensible, everlasting, incorruptible, uncreated, who created all things by his potent word.[15]

This stylistically elegant passage opens with a call to recognize a single, supremely transcendent creator God, uncontingent and unconstrained by anything in the cosmos. A vital logic underpins Peter's message. God is independent; creatures, dependent. Human worship reveals "knowledge" of God insofar as it accurately showcases God's transcendence and humanity's dependence. All subsequent references to God in *Preaching* refer to this God. The apostle next distinguishes three human groups — Hellenes, Judeans, and Christians — and assesses each group in light of its relationship to God (figure 2).[16] Peter construes each group as a "way" (γένος) of piety (θεοσέβεια), an at-

---

14. Cognates and synonyms: (ἐπι-)γινώσκω (frags. 2a, 4a, 7, 9), ἐφίστημι (3a, 4a, 4b), οἶδα (8), πιστεύω/πιστός/πίστις (6, 7), εὑρίσκω (5, 9), μανθάνω/μαθητής (5, 7). Antonyms: ἀγνοέω/ἄγνοια (3a, 4b, 8). Frag. 1 makes no explicit appeal to "knowledge," though mention of "Law and Word" suggests discursive modes of knowledge that reinforced *Preaching*'s gnostic framework.

15. All translations of *Preaching* are mine.

16. The translation "Judeans" emphasizes the Judeo- and temple-centric orientations in the literary image of the fragments. *Preaching*'s fictive setting is first-century Roman Judea, where οἱ Ἰουδαῖοι connotes an ethno-national polity whose cultic center is the Jerusalem temple — "Judeans." The messianic events that shape the world occur in Jerusalem (frags. 9; 1c: *out of Sion*), and the apostolic mission goes out after twelve years from "Israel" (a chorographic genitive) into "the world" (= lands outside the temple environs) (frag. 6; cf. frag. 7). Even the globalizing taxonomic project (frags. 2-5), which encompasses practices within and without

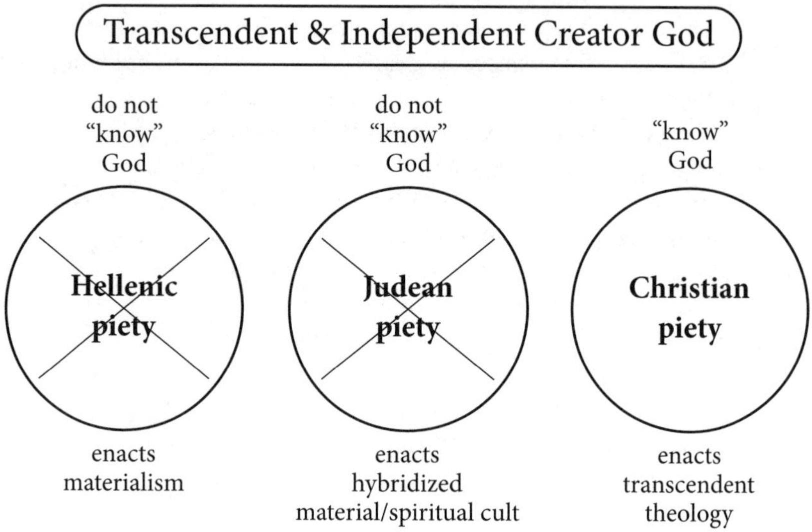

Figure 2. Three Ways of Piety

tempt to enact human dependence on God. In Peter's judgment, Hellenic ritual culture performs a pervasive materiality (frag. 3). Hellenes sacrifice created things to fabricated idols in ritual practices that amount to ungratefulness for God's gifts and denial of God's existence. Judean rites enact an angelo-lunar cult, a hybridization of material and spiritual elements slightly more ethereal than base Hellenic piety (frag. 4). Both, however, display ignorance of the spiritual nature of God. Christians alone practice transcendent theology (frag. 5).

Peter also invokes narrative elements (frags. 6-8). He recounts how the risen Jesus commissioned him and his confreres to proclaim the gospel in apostolic ministry (frag. 7):

> I have chosen you twelve, having adjudged (you) disciples worthy of me. And because I have considered you faithful apostles, I send you . . . to preach the gospel to people throughout the entire inhabited world, so they might know there is one God through faith in me, and to explain the future (to them), so those who hear and believe might be saved, while those who do not believe might testify that they understood and may have no excuse to say, "We have not heard."

Judea, envisions "the Judean practices" (τὰ Ἰουδαίων; frag. 5γ) associated with the festival cycles of the Jerusalem temple (frag. 4γ) (see discussion below).

Jesus tasks the apostles with making known the gospel of repentance from ignorance to knowledge. The reference to one God alludes to *Exhortation*. The content of the apostolic commission resonates with that of the homily. We see the popular and early image of Peter transformed into a dynamic preacher following his commission by the risen Jesus.

Fragment nine offers further insight into Peter's transformation, as he relates the events that transpired between his commission and subsequent preaching ministry:

ᵃ Now we (apostles) unfolded the book rolls that were in our keeping[17] from the prophets, who sometimes in illustrative types, sometimes in riddles, and sometimes with specific phrasing and perfect clarity designate Jesus as Messiah. And we discovered (in them) his advent, death, cross, and all the rest of the punishments the Judeans did to him, and his resurrection and ascension into heaven before Jerusalem is established. (We discovered) how everything he had to endure and that would take place after him had (already) been written.

β So once we ascertained these things we placed our trust in God, because of what stands written about him [= Messiah].

Peter's story transitions from commission to proclamation by way of scribal culture. We are observing a textual community at work.[18] The band of apostles assembles together, the air thick with anticipation. Much lies at stake as they search the traditional sources of divine gnosis. Will Israel's Scriptures authenticate Jesus' messianic identity? Failure to produce a positive verdict would deliver a devastating blow to the character of divine knowledge revealed in Jesus and invalidate their apostolic mission. Note the following markers of scribal culture:

1. Mention of textual storage, handling, and regular consultation emphasizes scribal technologies. This reading community houses a sacred deposit of texts transmitted from ancient Israelite "prophets," a circumlocution for all Israel's Scriptures perceived as redolent with prophetic potential. The

---

17. The imperfect tense (εἴχομεν) indicates the book rolls remained in the community's possession for regular consultation.

18. Brian Stock, "Textual Communities: Judaism, Christianity, and the Definitional Problem," in *Listening for the Text: On the Uses of the Past* (Baltimore: Johns Hopkins University Press), pp. 140-58.

"unfolding" of texts signals scrolls, and *Preaching*'s citations and allusions to extended portions of Israel's Scriptures envision large scrolls, requiring a lectern for reading.[19]

2. The community harbors assumptions and expectations about the nature of these texts. They partake of canonical privilege and contain the locus of divine prognosis. They are objects for careful scrutiny, reservoirs of semantic potential and encoded meaning. Some lexical and syntagmatic codes are simple, unassuming, plain to the sense. Others, like ciphers, shroud their message in illustrative type and riddle. All are communicative, housing divine gnosis. The apostles anticipate that the texts will speak proleptically of Christian kerygma. Like literary archaeologists they excavate linguistic strata, and they strike it rich. The scrolls "clearly designate" Jesus, by name no less. They confirm the events of his career and his last days, and foretell the establishment of a new Jerusalem.

3. The community formulates its shared identity in view of these texts. The knowledge ascertained through scribal practice produces apostolic belief in the transcendent God as revealed through Jesus (frag. 9β). From scribal activity springs a new faith, and with it an alternative vision of the Judean past (see below).

4. We also perceive the function of textual practice in this community. Scribalism generates and performs gnosis. Textuality and knowledge are mutually constitutive — a hendiadys of practice. Fragment ten unequivocally weds the search of Scripture with the apostolic and gnostic preaching mission: "For we (apostles) have come to know [ἔγνωμεν] that God really did decree these things. And so we speak [λέγομεν] nothing without reference to scripture."

We cannot be absolutely certain of the placement and sequence of these pieces in *Preaching*'s literary fabric. We can say they reveal a discursive flow, an inner logic that generates the schema shown in figure 3. The risen Jesus' pronouncements institute the apostolic and gnostic mission (no. 1). A search of Scripture confirms the gnosis revealed in Jesus (no. 2). And Peter preaches this gnosis on behalf of the other apostles (no. 3). In *Preaching*'s fictive setting, the commission and scriptural search (nos. 1-2) take place in Roman Judea

19. Roger Bagnall, "Jesus Reads a Book," *JTS* 51, no. 2 (2000): 577-88, notes that ἀναπτύσσω means "to unfold," yet his attempt to link the action with the codex form is unpersuasive; see Peter van Minnen, "Luke 4:17-20 and the Handling of Ancient Books," *JTS* 52, no. 2 (2001): 689-90.

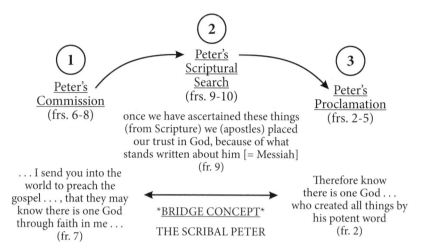

Figure 3. Peter's Story in Literary Image

following Jesus' resurrection and prior to the destruction of the Jerusalem temple in 70 CE, though Peter's proclamation (no. 3) may be situated in a non-Judean missional context. The entire narrative, of course, is Peter's. Remember our puzzle. Peter recounts this story to a "Christian" audience. In short, Peter as apostolic preacher of gnosis only emerges from Peter as scribal literate, and the scribal Peter offers the key link that binds the discursive logic of the extant fragments.[20] The fragments project Peter as scribe par excellence, head and spokesman of an interpretive community of apostolic tradents in scriptural gnosis, and as patron apostle of the community that commissioned or produced *Preaching*.

The Scribal Peter's Strategies of Difference

Preaching provides our most ancient attestation of the name Christian in Alexandria, and the scribal Peter employs this ascription in a discourse that frames the difference from "the Judeans." A sketch of Peter's strategies of Jewish and Christian difference yields insights into notional and taxonomic processes at work in early-second-century Roman Egypt, and may also help situate the image of Peter as scribe in a Petrine strand of Hellenist mission.

20. The fragments image Peter's reading literacy, not grapho-literacy. They do not indicate whether *Preaching* presented Peter as its author.

In his description of God the scribal Peter adopts the *via negationis*,[21] a rhetoric that laid claim to the divine nature through what could *not* be asserted of it. God is *un*knowable, *un*created, *in*effable, *in*corruptible, and so on. The tendency to abstract the supreme divinity through such (and similar) rhetoric had left its distinctive mark on segments of Alexandrian Jewry, most famously Philo. The scribal Peter's use of transcendent theology would have had a certain cachet among Alexandrian auditors, yet Peter employs it in a controversial claim, namely, that the Jerusalem temple cult institutionalized an inadequate gnosis of the transcendent God.

To make this conceptual move Peter constructs a narrative of sacred history in fragment five:

α So then, as for you, as you learn the things we (apostles) are handing down to you, observe (them) with holiness and justice by worshiping God in a new manner through Messiah. For we have discovered in the Scriptures how *Kyrios* (= God)[22] says:

β "Behold I establish a new covenant with you, not like the covenant I established[23] with your ancestors at Mount Choreb."

γ The covenant he established with you is new. Indeed, Hellenic and Judean practices are obsolete [παλαιά], but it is you Christians who worship him in a new manner, in a third way [τρίτῳ γένει].

Peter adapts the text of Jeremiah 31:31-32 (= LXX 38:31-32) to claim that Christians alone enact transcendent theology. His hermeneutic envisions in Jesus a new way to worship God. It also envisions an age before the new arrived, when there were but two ways of piety — one Hellenic, rooted in stark materialism; another Judean, directed legitimately toward God. For the prophet states that the same God (= *Kyrios*) who presently makes the new covenant with Messiah's community formerly established the old one with their "ancestors." Mention of Mount Choreb as site of former revelation signals Mosaic law (frag. 5). Yet

---

21. A.-J. Festugière, "La doctrine Platonicienne de la transcendance divine au IIᵉ siècle," in *La Révélation d'Hermès Trismégiste*, vol. 4, *Le Dieu Inconnu et la Gnose* (Paris: Lecoffre, 1954), pp. 92-140.

22. The identification of Jesus and *Kyrios* at frag. 1 (see n. 10) is not operative in frag. 5.

23. ὡς διεθέμην: ὡς modifies the inner accusative of διεθέμην and highlights the covenant's novel quality, as the subsequent clause explains (Νέαν ὑμῖν διέθετο), rather than the novel mode of revelation ("not in the way [ὡς] I covenanted").

reference to cycles of Sabbath, new moons, and festivals in the critique against contemporary Judean worship (frag. 4γ) suggests a narrower field of halakah — Torah's festal regulations enshrined in tabernacle rites. Peter's invocation of the tabernacle also envisions the Jerusalem temple as the subsequent institutional embodiment of the tabernacle, for he situates his story (see figure 3) in the vicinity of Jerusalem in the days following Jesus' death, resurrection, and ascension.[24] In these events, Peter claims, God has obviated the prior covenant with the "ancestors" instantiated in the tabernacle-temple complex. Jesus is the fulcrum of sacred history, who introduces a "messianic shift" that reorients humanity to a new, nonlocalized means of performing gnosis.

Peter's sacred history intertwines the covenant at Choreb with what he alleges is a contemporary Judean angel cult: "While the Judeans suppose they alone have gnosis [γινώσκειν] of God, they do not understand [ἐπίστανται] that they render cult to angels and archangels, to month and moon" (frag. 4β).[25] The claim that Judeans worship angels makes no accusation of intentional and widespread sidereal worship. Peter does not cite angelic hierarchies in their role as agents tasked with administering planetary and starry hosts in a complex cosmic architecture. The only heavenly body in view is the moon, "and so if the moon should not appear they do not observe the Sabbath called 'First,' and neither do they observe the new moon," and so on (frag. 4γ). A fascinating conclusion emerges. Because of the messianic shift the temple now functions as an angelo-lunar cult, quite without Judean recognition. When Judeans worship at the temple, they intend to worship the one transcendent God. In fact, however, naive to the messianic shift, they practice a cult to angelic hierarchies and lunar cycles.

Peter does not explain how observance of time-honored Judean festivals exemplified in temple rites enacts angel veneration.[26] A popular theologoumenon may provide the missing link. A number of ancient Jewish texts refer

---

24. See n. 16.

25. Cambe punctuates frag. 4a: "while supposing they alone have gnosis of God, they do not understand [God], since they render cult to angels," etc. (*Kerygma*, p. 155); this agrees with the shape of frag. 4b in Origen — "they do not have gnosis of him, since they worship angels." My proposed reading has the advantage of being attested in an early adaptation of *Preaching* (Aristides' *Apology* 14.4 Sy = "they think in their minds they are offering service to God, but in the methods of their practices their service is to angels"; see n. 9). The antitemple argument remains valid in either reading.

26. During the first century CE, temple rites followed the lunar calendar; see Hanan Eshel, "4Q390, the 490 Years of Prophecy and the Calendrical History of the Second Temple Period," in *Enoch and Qumran Origins*, ed. G. Boccaccini (Grand Rapids: Eerdmans, 2005), pp. 102-10, here p. 110.

to the notion that an angel or angels mediated Torah at Mount Sinai/Choreb.[27] Assuming that *Preaching* used (implicitly or explicitly) the Sinai angelophany trope, the following reconstruction of Peter's sacred history becomes plausible.

Through the mediation of angels God instituted tabernacle rites tied to lunar motion. These rites still operate in the temple of *Preaching*'s first-century Judean literary setting. Yet a centralized ritual apparatus could never encompass the fullness of the transcendent God, and God had intended it only as a timely means of enacting imperfect gnosis. God had always planned for its eventual obsolescence. Through Jesus' death, resurrection, and ascension, God effected that obsolescence and offers Messiah as a more immediate locus of revelation. Temple worship is now obsolete. Having formerly been mediated *through* angelic hierarchies to God, it is now reduced to a liturgy *to* angelic hierarchies; and knowledge of the divine nature finds its most substantive expression through the ethical "holiness and justice" proclaimed by the prophets, ratified in Jesus, and enacted by Christians (frag. 5a).

Peter's claim that Judeans worship angels is more firmly rooted in a constructed narrative of sacred history than empirical observation.[28] It does not critique an intentional sectarian angelolatry, as sometimes suggested, but marks a more universalizing strategy directed against the central economic and cultic center of first-century Judea. There is no reason why such a narrative history could not have developed prior to the temple's destruction in 70 CE. The Sinai angelophany appears already in the third century BCE, and Philo in the early first century CE laments Alexandrians whose approach to Scripture leads them to eschew Sabbath, festival observance, and the temple's sanctity.[29]

The confluence of these traditions appears in the Lukan idealization of pre-70 Jewish Hellenists in the person of Stephen (Acts 6–7). Stephen's accusers claim that he disparages temple and law (Acts 6:13), and Stephen's speech merges traditions of Sinai angelophany (7:38, 53) with a critique of the tabernacle-temple complex (esp. 7:37-53). *Preaching* weds these ancient traditions too, yet presumably not in dependence on Acts, for Acts nowhere cites the Jeremianic language of new covenant but, instead, invokes the Greek text of Amos 5:25-27 and Isaiah 66:1-2. *Preaching* independently attests a strand

---

27. E.g., LXX Deut. 33:2-4; *Jub.* 1.27-29; Josephus, *Ant.* 15.136; Heb. 2:2; Gal. 3:19; 5 Ezra 2.33, 44-48.

28. See Marcel Simon, "Remarques sur l'Angélolâtrie Juive au Début de l'Ère Chrétienne," in *Le Christianisme antique et son contexte religieux. Scripta Varia*, WUNT 23 (Tübingen: Mohr Siebeck, 1981), 2:450-64, here 459: "l'accusation d'angélolâtrie, lorsqu'elle s'applique non plus à des phénomènes sectaires, mais au judaïsme orthodoxe, est d'origine livresque."

29. Philo, *Migr.* 89-93.

of Hellenist thought that valorizes Peter, not Stephen. Why? Surely its author could have chosen another apostle. Or could he?

Peter's Scribal Strategies and Preaching's Missional Roots

Perhaps the lionization of Peter has historical moorings in a Petrine strand of Jewish Hellenist mission. In his study of early Petrine apocrypha, Enrico Norelli makes a proposal that dovetails nicely with mine.[30] Norelli argues that the early Petrine apocrypha, including *Preaching,* emerged from a "shared patrimony" in groups of Jewish Hellenists at Antioch. Missionaries sponsored by these groups transported Petrine memories and independently developed them to meet the needs of communities in nearby Palestine and in more remote settings such as Egypt and Rome. Under this construct, we may imagine the following scenario.

Jewish Hellenist missionaries, possibly from Antioch or more likely Jerusalem,[31] came to Alexandrian synagogues, possibly before 70 CE, and preached a message of divine gnosis. The risen Jesus, they claimed, has announced a new covenant rooted in a vision of God's radical transcendence. In Jesus God has obviated all former modes of worship, including festival halakot institutionalized in the Judean temple cultus. To perpetuate Torah's festal demands now amounts to an angelo-lunar cult that falls short of the spiritual worship befitting the ineffable God. Jesus has entrusted this message to twelve apostles who certified that Israel's prophets had foretold his passion and resurrection. The Hellenist missionaries received this message from Peter's associates who claimed to remember him as faithful spokesman for the Twelve and competent expositor and interpreter of Scripture. And they have come to Egypt to preach Peter's gospel.

Some Jews and gentile God-fearers, like the Bereans, "eagerly welcomed the message and examined the Scriptures daily to see whether these things were so" (Acts 17:11). To them, the tradition these missionaries preached made compelling sense of the prophets and God's transcendence. They adopted the new covenant and abandoned traditional Jewish festival rites as too intimately wed to the material realities of the old covenant. They established their own community that favored the ethical injunctions of Israel's prophets and Jesus,

---

30. Enrico Norelli, "Situation des apocryphes Pétriniens," *Apocrypha* 2 (1991): 31-83, here 75-77.

31. In light of *Preaching*'s Judeo-centrism; n. 16.

which they regarded as spiritual and gnostic. Yet they retained the textual culture they had known from the synagogues and had received in the model of their patron apostle. The group adopted as its own the story and mission of the remembered Peter, whom it had never met.

Like its eponymous apostle this community now preaches a superior knowledge of God and a new way to worship God in Jesus, and it valorizes scribal culture. In memory of the scribal Peter the group's literary specialists continue to search the prophetic rolls for connections to Jesus. The group pays homage to its apostolic lodestar and its origins in Hellenist mission by commissioning *Preaching,* in which the community enshrines the living memory of its foundation narrative by merging an antitemple tradition and the image of Peter as scribe. In the context of *Preaching*'s post-70 composition, when the temple no longer functioned, the informed readership (with "gnosis" of this remembered tradition) would have treated Peter's critique of Judean temple cult as applicable to all forms of Sabbath and festival observance, whether practiced in synagogal or sectarian settings, within Judea or elsewhere.

Such reconstructions are tentative. Yet they spark the imagination, and the historiographic task is largely to reimagine the past in light of available evidence. Insofar as my proposal conforms to the evidence in the fragments of *Preaching,* I believe I have recovered a lost voice of Jewish Hellenists in an Alexandrian milieu.

The Scribal Peter and the Parting of the Ways in Roman Egypt

We should take care not to regard the representation of the scribal Peter's (emic) strategies of difference as decisive evidence for an early "parting of the ways" in Egypt. To do so might artificially suggest too early a partition of "Judaism" and "Christianity" in Egypt, for Peter's strategies conceal proximities. A nuanced reading, sensitive to *Preaching*'s genesis in a Petrine strand of Hellenist mission, yields a different (etic) picture, against the text's own "Christian" ascriptive claims. Several identity markers root the community that commissioned *Preaching* in the cultural milieu of Alexandrian Jewry. The community has missional roots in a strand of Hellenist Judaism that emphasizes the absolute transcendence of one God; it uses a popular (pre-Christian) Jewish discourse of Sinai angelophany; it centers its own identity on Israel's Scriptures in Greek; it argues from sacred history for a particular approach to festival halakot; and it employs technologies and reading practices suggestive of Diaspora synagogues.

From a wider perspective, we are witnessing a thoroughly inner-Jewish dispute about the nature of the universal God and the value of festival halakot for knowing God. The community's claim to possess superior gnosis is best understood not vis-à-vis *the* Jews, or Judeans, as the text claims, but against *other* Jews. Try as it might to forge a new identity marked by a novel name, Christian, the community that commissioned *Preaching* has not yet escaped the gravity of its rootedness in the ambit of Alexandrian Jewry.

CHAPTER 15

"Gnostic" Perspectives on Peter

Tobias Nicklas

In the 2012 volume of the journal *Studien zum Neuen Testament und seiner Umwelt* Wilhelm Pratscher has given an excellent and detailed overview on the topic "Die Bedeutung des Petrus in gnostischen Texten" ("The significance of Peter in gnostic texts").[1] Pratscher's survey of many, somewhat different writings concludes as follows:

> The relevance of Peter is deemphasized in various gnostic texts: in the apocryphal Letter of James (NHC I,2), in the Gospel of Thomas (NHC II,2), in the Gospel of Mary (BG 1), and in the Pistis Sophia. The reason for this is the lower appreciation of Peter in comparison with other personalities. In contrast, according to the Kerygmata Petrou (a source of the pseudo-Clementines), the Letter of Peter to Philip (NHC VIII,2), the Apocalypse of Peter (NHC VII,3), as well as the Acts of Peter and the Twelve Apostles (NHC VI,1) and the Manichaeans, Peter holds the central position in early Christianity in regard to administration and theology. From the gnostic point of view, Peter is the true disciple of Jesus, and in this function, he is responsible for the correct interpretation of the beginnings of Christianity.

1. W. Pratscher, "Die Bedeutung des Petrus in gnostischen Texten," *SNTU* 37 (2012): 111-50. Regarding the topic see also K. Berger, "Unfehlbare Offenbarung: Petrus in der gnostischen und apokalyptischen Offenbarungsliteratur," in *Kontinuität und Einheit: Festschrift Franz Mußner*, ed. P. G. Müller and W. Stenger (Freiburg: Herder, 1981), pp. 261-326; and Th. Baumeister, "Die Rolle des Petrus in gnostischen Texten," in *Acts of the Second International Congress of Coptic Studies, Rome 22-26 Sept. 1980*, ed. T. Orlandi and F. Wisse (Rome: C.I.M., 1985), pp. 3-12.

This makes him the decisive guarantor of the identity of the gnostic groups concerned, who are opposing the growing Catholic church.[2]

Pratscher's article makes it difficult to justify another essay regarding "gnostic" perspectives on Peter. I will try nevertheless. My own approach, however, differs from Pratscher's in a few points: Whereas Pratscher uses a very broad idea of "gnosis" and "gnosticism," and includes texts from quite different groups and contexts, I would like to distinguish between (1) texts of different groups usually labeled "gnostic" and (2) different perspectives on their works. As is well known, in recent years, the use of terms such as *gnosis, gnostic,* and *gnosticism* has been sharply criticized (and with good reason). It is surely not necessary to repeat the arguments scholars such as Karen King or Michael Williams have used to make clear how problematic the old terms are.[3] Although I agree that the categories used by ancient "proto-orthodox" heresiologists and taken over by nineteenth- and twentieth-century scholars of ancient Christianity are highly problematic if we want to describe ancient realities, I think that (at least for the moment) it does not help to invent new labels such as "biblical demiurgical" (as Williams does) or to drop the term *gnostic* completely. I will thus use the usual terminology in a manner as cautious as possible and following the main lines of the "working definition" given by Roeloef van den Broek:

> It is undeniable that there existed in Antiquity a broad and variegated religious current characterized by a strong emphasis on esoteric knowledge (Gnosis) as the only means of salvation, which implied the return to one's divine origin. This religious current can best be referred as the "Gnostic movement" or "Gnostic religiosity." The great Gnostic systems of the 2nd

---

2. Pratscher, "Bedeutung," p. 150 (citing the English conclusion).

3. See, e.g., Michael A. Williams, *Rethinking 'Gnosticism': An Argument for Dismantling a Dubious Category* (Princeton: Princeton University Press, 1996); and Karen L. King, *What Is Gnosticism?* (Cambridge, Mass.: Harvard University Press, 2003); and A. Marjanen, ed., *Was There a Gnostic Religion?* Publications of the Finnish Exegetical Society 87 (Göttingen: Vandenhoeck & Ruprecht, 2005). In addition, important recent monographs have demonstrated how problematic it is to label ideas of Valentinus and his followers as "gnostic" in the usual sense: Christoph Markschies, *Valentinus Gnosticus? Untersuchungen zur valentinianischen Gnosis mit einem Kommentar zu den Fragmenten Valentins,* WUNT 65 (Tübingen: Mohr, 1992) shows that Valentinus himself should not be called "gnostic" in the usual sense; and Ismo Dunderberg, *Beyond Gnosticism: Myth, Lifestyle, and Society in the School of Valentinus* (New York: Columbia University Press, 2008); and Dunderberg, "Valentinus and His School," *Revista Catalana de Teología* 37, no. 1 (2012): 131-52, draws the same conclusion even for Valentinus's followers.

and 3rd centuries are integral parts of this broader Gnostic movement and should not be isolated from it. The main character of these systems is that their central ideas are expressed in myths, which vary from one system to another, but as a whole display strong similarities. For that reason, and to maintain the link with the Gnostic current in general, it is preferable to speak here of mythological Gnostic texts or systems.[4]

It seems wise, therefore, to work with the following distinctions when we try to classify the sources:

(1) a distinction between ancient heresiologists' perspectives and sources written and transmitted by gnostics themselves;
(2) a distinction between sources coming from more or less clearly definable groups developing a specific mythic system (like Sethians or Valentinians)[5] and sources that can be seen as coming from parts of or transmitted by what van den Broek would call the broader "gnostic movement."

In addition, we should always be aware (1) that because of a much more fragmentary state of sources every image of ancient gnostic groups and their histories will always be even more fragmentary than our images of proto-orthodox authors and groups, and (2) that gnostic groups did not *only* produce gnostic writings to develop their theologies, but also used and interpreted texts such as the Gospel of John.[6] After all, Peter plays an interesting role in the Fourth

4. R. van den Broek, "Gnosticism I: Gnostic Religion," *Dictionary of Gnosis and Western Esotericism,* ed. W. J. Hanegraaff (Leiden: Brill, 2005), 1.403-16 (esp. p. 404).

5. It would, of course, be ideal to have the chance even to describe diachronic developments within these groups. As far as I see, at least regarding the images of Peter, the extant sources do not allow us to go so far.

6. See, e.g., the material in Martin Hengel, *Die johanneische Frage: Ein Lösungsversuch. Mit einem Beitrag zur Apokalypse von Jörg Frey,* WUNT 67 (Tübingen: Mohr, 1993), pp. 37-60; A. Wucherpfenning, *Heracleon Philologus: Gnostische Johannesexegese im zweiten Jahrhundert,* WUNT 142 (Tübingen: Mohr, 2002); T. Nagel, "Die Gnostisierung der johanneischen Tradition. Das 'Geheime Evangelium nach Johannes' (Apokryphon Johannis) als gnostische Zusatzoffenbarung zum vierten Evangelium," in *Kontexte des Johannesevangeliums: Das vierte Evangelium in religions- und traditionsgeschichtlicher Perspektive,* ed. by Jörg Frey and Udo Schnelle, WUNT 175 (Tübingen: Mohr Siebeck, 2004), pp. 675-94; Charles E. Hill, *The Johannine Corpus in the Early Church* (Oxford: Oxford University, 2004), pp. 205-93; and L. R. Zelyck, *John among the Other Gospels: The Reception of the Fourth Gospel in the Extra-Canonical Gospels,* WUNT 2/347 (Tübingen: Mohr Siebeck, 2013), pp. 85-191. A similar problem is at stake with the *Acts of Peter and the Twelve Apostles,* the only copy of which comes from the library of Nag Hammadi (NHC VI 1). This (partly quite strange) writing should, however, probably

Gospel.[7] Unfortunately, there seems to be no chance to reconstruct how, for example, ancient Valentinian exegetes understood Peter's role in the Fourth Gospel (or other Christian writings that they read).[8] I will thus try to put the sources I use into the following order: I will first consider texts from two different gnostic systems, that is, Sethianism and Valentinianism;[9] then go to writings that (with more or less good reasons) can be assigned to the broader gnostic movement (texts showing no traces of a special system or cosmology); and then, finally, discuss a few examples showing the other, namely, proto-orthodox perspective on images of Peter in a few of these groups.

"Sethian" Perspectives

According to David Brakke, one should limit the use of the term *gnostic* to texts coming from so-called Sethians[10] or "classic Gnostics."[11] This would mean to look out for texts that show traces of the gnostic myth that one can

---

not be classified as gnostic. Of course, one can, as Pratscher does, well argue that already its inclusion in a codex with gnostic writings means that it had been understood as gnostic by some of its readers. Pratscher is surely right that, if we want to create an overview of gnostic perspectives on Peter, we have to admit that many gnostics also read texts as gnostic that were not Gnostic per se, the most well-known example surely being the Gospel of John. In the case of the *Apocryphon of John*, however, we have seen that a gnostic reading of a text could change the image of Peter in this text considerably. An analysis of Peter in the *Acts of Peter and the Twelve Apostles* would thus lead us to the image created by this text, but perhaps not to a gnostic perspective on Peter. Again, however, this should make us aware of the limits of our research — the perspectives of real people have always been much broader and much more differentiated than what our remaining sources can tell us.

7. For a recent full discussion of the figure of Peter in the Gospel of John see, e.g., T. Schultheiss, *Das Petrusbild im Johannesevangelium,* WUNT 2/329 (Tübingen: Mohr Siebeck, 2012).

8. For a very small exception see Heracleon's interpretation of John 4:33 mentioned below.

9. Due to space reasons I skip writings from other quite well-known and at least more or less well-documented groups like Manicheism. See Pratscher, "Bedeutung," pp. 143-44.

10. Even the use of the term *Sethian* has been controversial. It is, for example, quite clear that there never has been a group which called itself Sethians. See, e.g., Frederik Wisse, "Stalking Those Elusive Sethians," in *The Rediscovery of Gnosticism: Proceedings of the International Conference on Gnosticism at Yale, New Haven, Connecticut, March 18-21, 1978,* ed. Bentley Layton, SHR 78 (Leiden: Brill, 1981), pp. 563-78; Michael A. Williams, "Sethianism," in *A Companion to Second-Century Christian "Heretics,"* ed. A. Marjanen and P. Luomanen, VCSup 76 (Leiden: Brill, 2005), pp. 32-63 (esp. pp. 32-34); and G. P. Luttikhuizen, "Sethianer?" *ZAC* 13 (2009): 76-86.

11. See D. Brakke, *The Gnostics: Myth, Ritual, and Diversity in Early Christianity* (Cambridge, Mass.: Harvard University Press, 2010), pp. 29-51.

find in the *Apocryphon of John* (NHC II 1; III 1; IV 1; BG 2) and its parallel in Irenaeus of Lyons, *Adv. haer.* 1.29 (or closely related myths).[12] If we take this route, however, the number of relevant sources diminishes rapidly. In none of the writings that Brakke or, in a comparable way, Hans-Martin Schenke would call gnostic in the Sethian sense does Peter play a significant role.[13] But even this observation is not without value. We can turn it on its head: Perhaps the most important point regarding the writings usually classified as Sethian is that Peter *does not play any role* in them. This, however, does not necessarily mean that these texts do not have any perspective at all on Peter. While in some Sethian writings such as the *Apocalypse of Adam* (NHC V 5), *Zostrianos* (NHC VIII 1), *Melchisedek* (NHC IX 1), or others, there are no hints at all that disciples of Jesus are of any interest for the system and its believers, at least in a few cases some New Testament protagonists appear, and this is relevant for our question.

Apocryphon of John

According to the most well-known (perhaps even "classical") such writing, the *Apocryphon of John* (NHC II 1; III 1; IV 1; BG 2; see also Irenaeus of Lyons *Adv. haer.* 1.29), which is usually seen as the primary example of Sethian gnosis, John ("the brother of James, both are the sons of Zebedee") is the disciple who receives the decisive revelation. Peter does not play a role in this text. It would, however, not be wise to put it aside too quickly. As Titus Nagel has shown, at least the long version of the *Apocryphon of John* wants to be read as a "Johannine Gospel text," a kind of "secret Gospel of John," which tries to complete the Fourth Gospel's cosmology, Christology, and soteriology from a gnostic perspective.[14] In other words, the *Apocryphon of John* wants to be read and understood as a complementary text *together* with the Gospel of John. This is

---

12. H.-M. Schenke, "Das sethianische System nach den Nag-Hammadi-Handschriften," in *Der Same Seths: Hans-Martin Schenkes Kleine Schriften zu Gnosis, Koptologie und Neuem Testament,* ed. G. Schenke Robinson, G. Schenke, and U.-K. Plisch, NHMS 78 (Leiden: Brill, 2012), pp. 285-92 (esp. 286), describes the main features of this mythology. These include the inferior creator deity (Yaldabaoth), and the idea that "Sethians" are in some real sense "seed" (descendants) of Seth, portrayed as the great spiritual progenitor and archetype. See also Alastair H. B. Logan, *Gnostic Truth and Christian Heresy: A Study in the History of Gnosticism* (Edinburgh: T&T Clark, 1996).

13. See the overview in Brakke, *Gnostics,* pp. 50-51; see also Schenke, "System," pp. 285-86.

14. See Nagel, "Gnostisierung," p. 692, and also pp. 675-76.

achieved by embedding the Sethian myth into a context filled with allusions to the Fourth Gospel. Not only is the text's frame story (telling about the dispute between John and a Pharisee called Arimanias) full of parallels to Johannine texts and ideas, even John's questions on the mountain and his questions to the Savior show clear Johannine colors.[15]

It is not possible to recapitulate Nagel's observations in all detail here. If he is right, however, Peter plays a role for the group behind this text exactly because he does not play a role in the text anymore. If at least the long version of the *Apocryphon of John* wants to be understood as a "secret" complement to the Fourth Gospel that has to be read together with the Gospel of John, then perhaps the shift from a group of disciples to one disciple receiving the decisive revelation could be meaningful. In the Gospel of John several disciples play important roles — we hear of Andrew, Philip, Nathanael, Mary Magdalene, and others.[16] In addition, starting with chapter 13 Peter and the "Beloved Disciple" form a pair.[17] We find the two of them not only at the Last Supper or at the high priestly palace; it is mainly in the Gospel's postresurrection scenes of chapters 20–21 where they are presented as a pair of witnesses several times. It is quite clear that, if compared to the Beloved Disciple (at least for the Johannine community), Peter is slower, less of an example, and of secondary importance. It seems, however, that at the time the Fourth Gospel was written, Peter had already been such an important figure that the Fourth Gospel had to relate its message to him (not too negatively) if the group behind the text using partly very special traditions about Jesus and going back to the authority of the Beloved Disciple wanted to be accepted by other "mainstream" followers of Christ.[18]

---

15. For concrete examples see Nagel, "Gnostisierung," pp. 677-81, who shows that the later redaction of the text's long version goes even further in this attempt to appropriate Johannine elements.

16. Regarding their distinct roles in the Gospel of John see now the respective studies in S. A. Hunt, D. Francois Tolmie, and R. Zimmermann, eds., *Character Studies in the Fourth Gospel,* WUNT 314 (Tübingen: Mohr Siebeck, 2013).

17. Regarding the role of the "Beloved Disciple" in the Gospel of John see, e.g., Richard J. Bauckham, "The Beloved Disciple as Ideal Author," *JSNT* 49 (1993): 21-44; I. Dunderberg, "The Beloved Disciple in John: Ideal Figure in an Early Christian Controversy," in *Fair Play: Diversity and Conflicts in Early Christianity: Essays in Honour of Heikki Räisänen,* ed. I. Dunderberg, C. M. Tuckett, and K. Syreeni, NovTSup 103 (Leiden: Brill, 2002), pp. 243-69; and J. L. Resseguie, "The Beloved Disciple: An Ideal Point of View," *Character Studies in the Fourth Gospel,* ed. S. A. Hunt, D. F. Tolmie, and R. Zimmermann, WUNT 314 (Tübingen: Mohr Siebeck, 2013), pp. 537-49.

18. If we are allowed to use the idea of "mainstream Christians" at the turn of the first to the second century CE.

If we connect the *Apocryphon of John* to the Fourth Gospel, this image changes quite obviously. The *Apocryphon* identifies the Beloved Disciple (whose identity remains hidden in the Gospel) with John the Son of Zebedee and makes him the receiver of the key revelation necessary for the salvation of souls. Peter does not play a role anymore — the group behind the *Apocryphon* seems to have given up what in John still seems to have been at least a somewhat more positive relation to Peter. In other words, the *Apocryphon's* silence on Peter is a speaking silence: Peter is *not* the one who received the decisive revelation.

Gospel of Judas

A second example must be added: the *Gospel of Judas.* Even if the text's exact attribution to a special gnostic group has been disputed, it still seems the best solution to understand it as a witness of (and perhaps later stage of) Sethian gnosis.[19] Comparably to the *Apocryphon of John,* the extant *Gospel of Judas* connects a "Sethian cosmology" to a frame story that, in many of its parts, alludes to Gospel texts that came to be parts of the later New Testament canon.[20] Contrary to the *Apocryphon of John,* however, the *Gospel of Judas* does not develop any positive attitude to any of the New Testament texts; it wants to be understood as a "countergospel," that is, a gospel against others. In other words, the *Gospel of Judas* tells a story of Jesus' Last Supper, his deliverance, and his passion, but does so from a perspective completely different from what is given in the canonical Gospels. In addition, at least in several cases one gets the impression that the text even needs an audience that at least knows the "usual" story told by the Gospels. If, however, one has to know at least *a* (not necessarily written) gospel story to understand fully the *Gospel of Judas's* polemical stance, then again, that Peter plays no role in the *Gospel of Judas* does not mean that the group behind the text has no perspective on

19. See mainly John D. Turner, "The Place of the *Gospel of Judas* in Sethian Tradition," in *The Gospel of Judas in Context: Proceedings of the First International Conference on the Gospel of Judas,* ed. M. Scopello, NHMS 62 (Leiden: Brill, 2008), pp. 187-237; and (more critical) Turner, "The Pseudo-Sethianism of the *Gospel of Judas,*" *RSLR* 43 (2008): 571-604.

20. Regarding the *Gospel of Judas's* reception of New Testament Gospels see Simon Gathercole, "Matthean or Lukan Priority? The Use of the NT Gospels in the *Gospel of Judas,*" in *Judasevangelium und Codex Tchacos: Studien zur religionsgeschichtlichen Verortung einer gnostischen Schriftensammlung,* ed. Enno E. Popkes and G. Wurst, WUNT 297 (Tübingen: Mohr Siebeck, 2012), pp. 291-302; and (regarding the reception of John) Zelyck, *John,* pp. 168-74.

Peter. He, then, must be seen as part of the group of disciples, which surely represents the growing proto-orthodoxy and which is criticized sharply for their misunderstanding of Jesus as the Son of *their* God who asks for bloody sacrifices.[21] Again, one could debate about the concrete object of the *Gospel of Judas*'s polemics. Is it, as Karen King and Elaine Pagels have proposed, a polemic against proto-orthodox stances to martyrdom?[22] Or does the text criticize second-century developments in the understanding of Christian "offices" and "cults"?[23] Be that as it may, even if the *Gospel of Judas* presents Jesus' disciples — with the exception of Judas Iscariot — en bloc, it expects readers who know more about the Gospel stories than it explicitly tells. And these readers will know that Peter is not merely one disciple, but instead a very important representative of the group of disciples.

As far as I can see, the two examples mentioned already present a shift of the image Pratscher provides. At least in my eyes, the "zero" role of Peter that we find in the two texts mentioned above does not mean a neutral stance toward Peter. On the contrary, it means a (not openly expressed, but clear) negative attitude, which in the case of the *Gospel of Judas* seems even sharper than in the *Apocryphon of John*.

The *Gospel of Judas* and the *Apocryphon of John* are not the only texts where one could argue in this way; other writings, the attribution of which is much less clear, could be added. Let me mention at least one:[24] the *Sophia of Jesus Christ* (NHC III, pp. 90.14-119.17; BG 3, pp. 77.8-127.12; see also P.Oxy. 1081), a dialogue gospel with clear parallels to another writing called *Eugnostos* (NHC III 3 [short version] and NHC V 1 [long version]). This is a clearly gnostic writing, which, however, does not offer a full gnostic myth but (while mentioning only parts of it explicitly) presupposes it.[25] It is thus not absolutely

---

21. For a slightly different view see, however, N. Denzey Lewis, "Astral 'Determinism' in the *Gospel of Judas*," in her *Cosmology and Fate in Gnosticism and Graeco-Roman Antiquity: Under Pitiless Skies*, NHMS 81 (Leiden: Brill, 2013), pp. 165-80 (esp. pp. 175-79).

22. See Elaine Pagels and Karen L. King, *Reading Judas: The Gospel of Judas and the Shaping of Christianity* (New York: Viking, 2007); and Karen L. King, "Martyrdom and Its Discontents in the Tchacos Codex," in *The Codex Judas Papers: Proceedings of the International Congress on the Tchacos Codex Held at Rice University, Houston Texas, March 13-16, 2008*, ed. April D. DeConick, NHMS 71 (Leiden: Brill, 2011), pp. 23-42.

23. See the argument by Tobias Nicklas, "Die andere Seite: Das Judasevangelium und seine Polemik im Kontext altkirchlicher Diskurse," in *The Apocryphal Gospels within the Context of Early Christian Theology*, ed. Jens Schröter, BETL 260 (Leuven: Peeters, 2013), pp. 127-55.

24. One could compare the role of special disciples as part of the collective in other texts such as the *Pistis Sophia* or *1 Jeu*.

25. For further discussion see Judith Hartenstein, "Die Weisheit Jesu Christi (NHC III,4/

clear whether it can be classified Sethian in the usual sense, or has to be under-stood in another way. The text narrates a postresurrection revelation of Christ, who appears in the form of an angel of light to his twelve men and seven women disciples. After having answered thirteen questions coming from dif-ferent disciples, Jesus disappears, and the disciples start preaching the gospel.

For our inquiry, it is mainly interesting that the text does not mention Peter explicitly, whereas Philip, Matthew, Thomas, and Bartholomew from the Twelve, and Mary from among the Seven, ask the decisive questions. Of course, this observation does not immediately mean that the *Sophia of Jesus Christ* offers an anti-Petrine polemic. But the neglect of Peter can be related to the overall function of the text. Whereas Catherine Barry regards the *Sophia of Jesus Christ* as a polemical writing,[26] Judith Hartenstein argues that the text wants to connect (nongnostic) Christian and gnostic ideas. That is why it can be read both by insiders and (at least to a certain degree) Christian, nongnostic outsiders. Although it mirrors the self-conception of a Christian gnostic group, it seems clear that this group is open for a mission to outsiders.[27] With such a background it seems to make good sense for the text to have made use of a open concept of "twelve plus seven disciples," which was agreeable to many other Christians. In this system Peter can be seen as included, and we do not find anything explicitly anti-Petrine; the text, however, makes clear that other disciples are decisive for the revelation of deeper truth.

Valentinian Perspectives

Compared to Sethian sources, it is even more difficult to develop an image of Peter provided by Valentinian texts. There is no mention of Peter either in

---

BG 3)," *Antike christliche Apokryphen*, vol. 1, *Evangelien und Verwandtes*, ed. Christoph Mark-schies and Jens Schröter (Tübingen: Mohr Siebeck, 2012), pp. 1122-36 (esp. 1123-26). Regarding the text's relation to *Eugnostos*, see Judith Hartenstein, "Anmerkungen zu den vier koptischen Versionen von 'Eugnostos' und der 'Sophia Jesu Christi,'" *Coptic Studies on the Threshold of a New Millenium*, vol. 1, *Proceedings of the 7th International Congress of Coptic Studies, Leiden 27 Aug.–2 Sept. 2000*, ed. M. Immerseel and J. Van der Vliet, OLA 133 (Leuven: Peeters, 2004), pp. 749-58.

26. Catherine Barry, "Un exemple de réécriture à Nag Hammadi: La Sagesse de Jésus Christ (BG,3; NH III,4)," *Les Textes de Nag Hammadi et le problème de leur classification. Actes de colloque tenu à Quebec du 15 au 19 septembre 1993*, ed. Louis Painchaud and A. Pasquier, BCNH Section Études 3 (Québec: Université Laval, 1995), pp. 151-68 (esp. 163-68).

27. Cf. Judith Hartenstein, *Die zweite Lehre: Erscheinungen des Auferstandenen als Rahmenerzählungen frühchristlicher Dialoge*, TU 146 (Berlin: Akademie, 2000), pp. 40-41.

the fragments of Valentinus's own writings (preserved in works of Clement of Alexandria and Hippolytus of Rome)[28] or in fragments of later Valentinian authors such as Heracleon (according to Origen's *Commentary on John* plus a few fragments in Clement of Alexandria), Theodotus (see Clement of Alexandria, *Excerpts*), Ptolemaeus's *Letter to Flora,* and the Valentinian *Letter of Instruction* (both transmitted via Epiphanius's *Panarion*).

This certainly has to do with the extremely fragmentary state of sources. One cannot, for example, imagine that Heracleon wrote his *Commentary on John* without mentioning Peter at all, and if we take into account Valentinus's (and his school's) stay in second-century Rome (between the time of Hyginus, 136-140 CE, and Anicetus, 155-166 CE), it seems highly improbable that it was possible for him (and his followers) simply to ignore the figure of Peter.[29]

But even if we look into the Nag Hammadi writings usually ascribed (or seen as related) to the Valentinian movement, the situation does not fundamentally change. There is simply no explicit mention of Peter in the *Prayer of the Apostle Paul* (NHC I 1),[30] the *Gospel of Truth* (NHC I 3) in the *Letter to Reghinos* (also called *Treatise on Resurrection,* NHC I 4), the *Tripartite Tractate* (NHC I 5), the *Gospel of Philip* (NHC II 3), the *Interpretation of Knowledge* (NHC XI 1), or the *Valentinian Exposition* (NHC XI 2).[31] This is also the case with the *First Apocalypse of James,* a text that is now preserved in two slightly differing Coptic versions transmitted in two manuscripts (NHC V 3 and CT 2) and that can be understood as part of the emerging second- (or perhaps early-third-) century Christian literature on James the Just.[32]

---

28. For a full discussion of all these sources see Christoph Markschies, *Valentinus Gnosticus? Untersuchungen zur valentinianischen Gnosis mit einem Kommentar zu den Fragmenten Valentins,* WUNT 65 (Tübingen: Mohr, 1992), pp. 11-290.

29. Regarding the development, role, and situation of Valentinians in second-century Rome see Peter Lampe, *From Paul to Valentinus: Christians at Rome in the First Two Centuries* (London: Continuum, 2003), pp. 292-318.

30. The question of whether this text must be understood as Valentinian is a matter of debate. See, e.g., the very cautious judgment by H.-G. Bethge and U.-K. Plisch, "Das Gebet des Apostels Paulus (NHC I,1)," in *Nag Hammadi Deutsch,* vol. 1, *NHC I,1e–V,1,* ed. H.-M. Schenke, H.-G. Bethge, and U. U. Kaiser, GCS NF 8, Koptisch-Gnostische Schriften 2 (Berlin: de Gruyter, 2001), pp. 7-11 (esp. p. 9), who see it as "doubtless" a gnostic writing.

31. I take over the list of Valentinian sources given by Dunderberg, *Beyond Gnosticism,* pp. 7, 10.

32. This literature includes the *Proto-Gospel of James* (even if its ancient title is *Birth of Mary*), the already mentioned *Apocryphon of James* and the *Second Apocalypse of James* (NHC V 4), and also Hegesippus's fragments on James the Just. Even the date of the canonical letter of James can be discussed; there seems to be no clear sign of this text's early reception before Origen.

Interestingly, according to this writing it is James the Just (and not Peter) who receives a decisive revelation both before and after Jesus' resurrection, and dies as a martyr. At the same time the Twelve, even if they do not play an active role in the text, are not only rebuked for their unbelief (NHC V 3, pp. 29.18-25; CT 42.21-24), but can almost be identified with the evil Archons (see NHC V 3, pp. 25.24-26.1; CT 12.8-17; and, even more explicitly, NHC V 3, pp. 36.1-5; CT 22.26-23.2).[33] A context where James is seen as the single receiver of revelation makes it understandable that the text performs a shift that can be compared to what we also see in fragment 5 of the "Jewish Christian" *Gospel of the Hebrews* (preserved via Jerome, *Vir. ill.* 2.12-13): a shift from Peter as the first and decisive witness of Jesus' resurrection (see 1 Cor. 15:5) to James the Just.

Although, as is well known, the Gospel of John obtained broad interest in Valentinian writings, one should also not underestimate Valentinian interest in Pauline writings,[34] traces of which can already be found in Ptolemaeus's *Letter to Flora* (with quotes from Rom. 7:12; 1 Cor. 5:7-8; Eph. 2:15; 3:14), the *Gospel of Philip* (with many quotes from and allusions to Pauline literature), or the *Treatise on Resurrection* partly playing with 1 Corinthians 15 and other Pauline texts.[35] A look into the *Gospel of Truth* is even more revealing. In her study "Biblical Interpretation in the Gnostic *Gospel of Truth* from Nag Hammadi," Jacqueline A. Williams identifies eleven probable allusions to Pauline writings (including Romans, 1-2 Corinthians, and Colossians, plus one additional probable allusion to Hebrews) plus eight possible allusions (including Romans, 1-2 Corinthians, Ephesians, Philippians, plus three possible allusions to Hebrews),[36] whereas there is not even a single "dubious" allusion to any

---

33. For a comparable view see J. Brankaer and H.-G. Bethge, *Codex Tchacos: Texte und Analysen,* TU 161 (Berlin: de Gruyter, 2007), p. 424.

34. Regarding the understanding of Paul and his writings in gnostic, including Valentinian, exegesis see Elaine Pagels, *The Gnostic Paul: Gnostic Exegesis of the Pauline Letters* (Philadelphia: Trinity Press International, 1975).

35. For an overview see M. L. Peel, "The Treatise on the Resurrection: Introduction," *The Coptic Gnostic Library* (Leiden: Brill, 2000), 1:123-46 (esp. pp. 132-33). For a comparison of Paul's and the *Treatise's* view of resurrection, see P. Skiba, "The *Treatise on Resurrection* and 1 Corinthians 15: Gnostic and Christian Views of Resurrection," in *Directions in New Testament Methods,* ed. M. Albl, P. R. Eddy, and R. Mirkes, Marquette Studies in Theology (Milwaukee: Marquette University Press, 1993), pp. 53-61.

36. See the overview given by Jacqueline A. Williams, *Biblical Interpretation in the Gnostic Gospel of Truth from Nag Hammadi,* SBLDS 79 (Atlanta: Scholars Press, 1988), pp. 179-83. Of course, Williams's decisions can be debated in a few cases, but her general results show a clear tendency.

Petrine writing (1-2 Peter, nor even Mark).[37] The only clear positive use of a (later) canonical Petrine writing in a Valentinian text I found is in the *Gospel of Philip* 111b, wording from 1 Peter 4:8 ("Love covers over a multitude of sins," in a context alluding to the parable of the good Samaritan), perhaps better seen as a saying that could have been known independently from 1 Peter. Origen, in *Commentary on John* 13.17, could be added according to whom Heracleon used the *Kerygma Petrou* for his interpretation of John 4:22.[38]

All in all this creates a very negative image. Valentinian writings ignore Peter, ascribe traditions about Peter to other disciples, criticize the Twelve for lack of proper understanding, and show no interest in Petrine writings, while Paul and John (and partly Matthew) play an important role in the exegesis reflected in Valentinian writings. This combines well with what some ancient Christian proto-orthodox authors tell us.[39] Whereas Heracleon's exegesis of John 4:33 mentioned in Origen's *Commentary on John* 13.35 seems to criticize the disciples as thinking "carnally" (at least in this special scene), according to Tertullian (for example in *Praescr.* 23) heretical groups such as followers of Marcion and Valentinians devalued Peter and the disciples.

Other Perspectives: More Texts Discussed as Gnostic in a Broader Sense

The overall situation, however, seems to be even more complex. If we concentrate solely on sources that, more or less clearly, can be ascribed to a known gnostic system, we will lose many interesting texts from sight. Interestingly,

---

37. Taking account of the ancient tradition of Mark as Peter's *hermeneutēs* (going back to Papias of Hierapolis, according to Eusebius, *H.E.* 3.39.15), I include the Gospel of Mark as a "Petrine" writing in the broadest sense here. Of course, if one looks into the very scarce traces of a reception of Mark in the second century, it is not necessary to put too much emphasis on the fact that the *Gospel of Truth* obviously does not use Mark. The same is the case with 2 Peter.

38. Fragment 21 (John 4:22: "You worship what you do not know"): "Heracleon understands 'you' as the Jews [and] the gentiles. He quotes the *Preaching of Peter*: 'We must not worship in Greek fashion, accepting the works of matter and adoring wood and stone; nor in Jewish fashion worship the divine, since they, thinking that they alone know him, do not know him and worship angels and the months and the moon'" (R. M. Grant, trans., *Second-Century Christianity: A Collection of Fragments,* 2nd ed. [Louisville: Westminster John Knox, 2003], p. 74).

39. See also Pratscher, "Bedeutung," pp. 112-13 n. 5, who mentions Irenaeus of Lyons, *Adv. haer.* 3.12.7 as witnessing that Valentinians regarded Peter and the disciples as imperfect. Irenaeus's highly polemical statement, however, seems not to reflect a special group, but gnostics in general — and thus does not help very much in regard to our question.

many writings the exact gnostic character of which can be discussed not only were transmitted along with clearly Sethian and/or Valentinian writings but were also sometimes bound together with them in the same codices.

Our only (partly fragmentary) manuscript of the above-mentioned *Gospel of Judas* is part of a collection of texts in the so-called Codex Tchacos (hereafter CT). This collection starts with the *Epistle of Peter to Philip,* a text also found in the Nag Hammadi cache (NHC VIII 2). The exact classification of the *Epistle* itself is highly difficult. The text shows contacts with the second- to third-century *Apocryphal Acts of the Apostles.* In addition, a literary contact with the *Gospel of Mary* could be discussed.[40] On the whole, I would tend to understand it as a story about the origins of the Jesus movement, quite obviously playing with stories told (or at least motifs mentioned) in the book of Acts (plus John 1 and Matthew 28), but narrated from a different perspective.[41]

The text also includes a shortened version of a gnostic Sophia myth that shows some parallels to the *Apocryphon of John* or the *Sophia of Jesus Christ* (NHC III 4; BG 3; P.Oxy. 1081).[42] Although it would go too far to classify this text as clearly Sethian, at least it seems to have been possible in the ancient setting to read it together with some clearly Sethian texts.[43] Interestingly, both copies of this writing extant today can be found in codices where they are closely connected to texts usually labeled Sethian. The Nag Hammadi version of the *Epistle* is found in codex VIII, where it is transmitted together with only one other writing called *Zostrianos* (NHC VIII 1), which is very clearly Sethian in nature. The second version opens the well-known Codex Tchacos, where it is followed by the *First Apocalypse of James,* the *Gospel of Judas,* and a writing called *Allogenes.* Although the exact nature of the *First Apocalypse of James* is

40. For a cautious view see, e.g., Hartenstein, *Zweite Lehre,* pp. 169-70.

41. Regarding the relation of the text to Acts see M. Kaler, "The Letter of Peter to Philip and Its Message of Gnostic Revelation and Christian Unity," *VC* 63 (2009): 264-95, who, however, partly overemphasizes the Pauline character of the text. Regarding John 1 and Matthew 28, see K. Koschorke, "Eine gnostische Pfingstpredigt: Zur Auseinandersetzung zwischen gnostischem und kirchlichem Christentum am Beispiel der 'Epistula Petri ad Philippum' (NHC VIII,2)," *ZTK* 74 (1977): 323-43; and Koschorke, "Eine gnostische Paraphrase des johanneischen Prologs: Zur Interpretation von 'Epistula Petri ad Philippum' (NHC VIII,2) 136,16-137,4," *VC* 33 (1979): 383-92, mentioned also by Pratscher, "Bedeutung," p. 132 n. 81.

42. For a more differentiated analysis of Ep. Pet. Phil.'s myth see Brankaer and Bethge, *Codex Tchacos,* pp. 425-27.

43. See H.-G. Bethge and J. Brankaer, "Der Brief des Petrus an Philippus (NHC VIII,2 / CT 1)," in *Antike Christliche Apokryphen in deutscher Übersetzung,* vol. 1, *Evangelien und Verwandtes,* ed. Christoph Markschies and Jens Schröter (Tübingen: Mohr Siebeck, 2012), pp. 1195-1207 (esp. p. 1199).

unclear, the *Gospel of Judas* and *Allogenes* both seem to belong to a Sethian group of writings. Even if this does not mean that the *Epistle of Peter to Philip* was written by Sethian gnostics themselves, it was at least copied and (very probably) read together with some of their writings.

Contrary to what we found in the Sethian writings discussed above, the role of Peter in the *Epistle of Peter to Philip* is positive. According to the text in NHC VIII 2, pp. 132.10-133.8 (parallel in CT, p. 1.1-4), Peter sends a letter to his fellow apostle Philip (and the brothers who are with him). That the text starts with a pseudepigraphic letter ascribed to Peter means that Peter is understood as an authority (of the past). In the letter itself, this pseudo-Peter, who calls himself "the apostle of Jesus Christ," is understood as being in direct and constant relation to Jesus Christ, who is called "our Lord," "Savior of the World," and "our God Jesus." Because he has received orders from Jesus, Peter brings together the disciples, who need to learn where they must preach the gospel. Philip follows Peter's order (NHC VIII 2, p. 133.8-11; CT lacunose), and Peter calls together the rest of the disciples who go to the Mount of Olives (NHC VIII 2, p. 133.12-16), where they pray to the "Father of Light" (NHC VIII 2, p. 133.22; parallel CT, p. 2, 5-6) and to Christ, the "Son of Life and Immortality" (NHC VIII.2, p. 134.4-5; CT lacunose). After that, Jesus appears and answers a series of the apostles' questions.

During Jesus' epiphany we only hear about the apostles as a collective in dialogue with Jesus. If we read the text as a unified whole, Peter is surely understood as part of this group; as a single figure, however, he appears only after Jesus has disappeared again. On the disciples' way back to Jerusalem a new problem arises, the problem of "suffering": if the Lord himself has suffered, how far will the disciples have to suffer (NHC VIII 2, p. 138.13-17)?[44] The following text offers two responses, the first from Peter himself, who makes clear that the disciples have to suffer; the second one by a revelatory voice — obviously by the Lord — which confirms Peter's statements: "I have often told you: it is necessary for you to suffer."

If we look into the details we could even go further and state that the Lord confirms Peter's statement and Peter has more or less anticipated the Lord's answer. In the *Epistle of Peter to Philip*, Peter plays the role of the main author-

---

44. The question of how a text with such a certainly nondocetic Christology came to be gnostic or gnosticized has puzzled scholars. See, e.g., A. Marjanen, "A Suffering of One Who Is a Stranger to Suffering: The Crucifixion of Jesus in the Letter of Peter to Philip," in Dunderberg, Tuckett, and Syreeni, *Fair Play*, pp. 487-98, who concludes (p. 498) that the text might have been written in a situation of persecution and that this might have affected its nondocetic stance.

ity among Jesus' disciples. In NHC VIII 2, p. 139.10, a passage without extant parallel in CT, one could even discuss whether the words "his disciples" refers to Peter's or the Lord's disciples.[45] In any case, Peter has received decisive revelations (even if no special revelations to him are explicitly mentioned), he is responsible for the disciples' unity, and he speaks in accordance with the Lord. That is why the disciples should listen to his voice (NHC VIII.2, p. 139.19). Filled with the Holy Spirit, Peter gives a speech in which he interprets Jesus' cross, suffering, and resurrection. After his speech, the other apostles are filled with the Holy Spirit, and that allows them all to do miraculous healings. They separate from each other and start to preach "the Lord Jesus."

This is, in fact, an image of Peter very different from what we find in the *Gospel of Judas*. The *Epistle of Peter to Philip* takes over proto-orthodox ideas of Peter as a primary witness to the risen Lord, as a leader of the apostles, and as a decisive authority of what is developing into a "church." Does this have to do with the fact that the *Epistle* is also concerned with the burning question of suffering, which is connected to a nondocetic Christology? And has the figure of Peter been chosen in this context because his own (and many disciples') fate as a martyr/martyrs was already well known? The text, actually, does not mention anything that would point concretely in this direction.

All this is, however, only part of the picture, a necessary basis of the text's main function. In what may be compared to his Pentecost speech in Acts 2, the *Epistle's* Peter becomes the decisive interpreter of a tradition about Jesus that is not far from what we find in 1 Corinthians 15:3-5. Integrated in a writing that contains at least the main lines of a gnostic myth, he develops an idea of why Jesus and the disciples had to suffer — very probably in a context of suffering and persecution.

Of course, we can only speculate about anything further. Is the use of the figure of Peter a sign of a struggle between two different groups that claimed his authority as decisive? One gets at least the impression that the group behind this text did not understand itself only as a small elite surrounded by other Christians. Otherwise, the myth of a common revelation to the disciples and a mission done by all of them seen as a unit surely would not make sense for them.

To me, however, the most interesting point is that the *Epistle of Peter to Philip* has been transmitted in codices alongside two texts with quite different views. Whereas for *Zostrianos* Jesus and his disciples do not play any role,

---

45. See also the discussion in Pratscher, "Bedeutung," p. 134 nn. 89-90 (for further secondary literature).

we have seen how negative their function is in the *Gospel of Judas*. At least for some reader(s) or collector(s) in the ancient world, however, this obvious contradiction doesn't seem to have been a major problem.

(Gnostic) Apocalypse of Peter

Interestingly, another Petrine text in the Nag Hammadi corpus is concerned with suffering as well. In the *Apocalypse of Peter* (NHC VII 3, pp. 70.14-84.14) Peter plays an even more important role than in the *Epistle of Peter to Philip*. In many respects this text confronts the interpreter with problems. It is almost impossible to date this text with a sufficient degree of certainty (sometime in the third century CE?)[46], and one can only speculate regarding its place of origin (Syria? Egypt?). Even the text's gnostic character is a matter of debate; no traces of a Sophia myth or a description of the *Plēroma* can be found. The main elements in the text that could allow for the label gnostic are its reference to Archons, the idea of the souls' return to their origin, the impact of knowledge (= gnosis) for salvation, and finally, the text's docetism.[47]

The text connects two main parts, a long polemic obviously directed against proto-orthodox circles in the form of a revelation of the Savior (p. 72,4-81,3) and a vision of his passion that, however, is interpreted in a docetic manner (p. 81,3-82,17).[48] The story is partly told by Peter himself, a perspective that only changes in the last sentence, which speaks about him in the third-person

---

46. A. Lorenzo Molinari, "The Apocalypse of Peter and Its Dating," *Coptica — Gnostica — Manichaica: Mélanges offerts à Wolf-Peter Funk*, ed. L. Painchaud and P.-H. Poirier, BCNH, Section Études 7 (Leuven: Peeters, 2006), pp. 583-605 (esp. p. 605), however, dates the text in the time between 320 and 340 CE.

47. For a brief introduction and English translation, see James Brashler and Roger A. Bullard, "Apocalypse of Peter (VII,3)," *NHL*, pp. 372-78l; and for a German equivalent, H. Havelaar, "Die Apokalypse des Petrus (NHC VII,3)," *Nag Hammadi Deutsch*, vol. 2, *NHC V,2 XIII,1, BG 1 und 4*, ed. H.-M. Schenke, H.-G. Bethge, and U. U. Kaiser, GCS 12, Koptisch-Gnostische Schriften 3 (Berlin: de Gruyter, 2003), pp. 591-600 (esp. 592-95), who also offered the most important full study of this writing: H. Havelaar, *The Coptic Apocalypse of Peter (Nag Hammadi Codex VII,3*, TU 144 (Berlin: de Gruyter, 1999). Regarding the gnostic character of the writing see also A. Werner, "Koptisch-gnostische Apokalypse des Paulus," in *Neutestamentliche Apokryphen*, vol. 2, *Apostolisches, Apokalypsen und Verwandtes*, ed. W. Schneemelcher, 6th ed. (Tübingen: Mohr Siebeck, 1997), pp. 633-43 (esp. p. 636).

48. The term *docetic*, however, is certainly comparably as problematic as *gnostic*. For a detailed discussion see already N. Brox, "'Doketismus' — eine Problemanzeige," *ZKG* 95 (1984): 301-14. A detailed reevaluation of the underlying concepts, however, remains a *desideratum*.

singular. Perhaps even more than in the *Epistle of Peter to Philip,* Peter is understood as "the" decisive authority of this text. In p. 71,15-72,3 we read:

> But you yourself, Peter, become perfect [τέλειος] in accordance with your name,[49] along with me, the very one who chose you. For from you I have made a beginning for the remnant whom I have summoned to knowledge. Therefore be strong for the duration of the imitation of the righteousness [δικαιοσύνη] of him who originally summoned you. He summoned you to know him properly regarding the shedding (of blood) which tore him — even the sinews of his hands and his feet — and (regarding) the crowning by those of the middle region [μεσότης], and regarding the body [σῶμα] of his radiance. In the hope of service [διακονία] he was brought forth for the sake of an honorable reward. Thus he will correct you three times this night.[50]

Playing perhaps with Matthew 16:18, the passage distinguishes between two callings of Peter: The calling by the one "who originally summoned you," that is, the fleshly Jesus, who corrected Peter "three times this night," and the calling by the Savior, who chose him to make "a beginning for the remnant whom I have summoned to knowledge." As long as the "imitation" of the fleshly Jesus' "righteousness" (which is obviously seen as something negative) endures, Peter has to remain strong — because Jesus and his followers are under those of the "middle region."

The text thus describes Peter as *the* disciple chosen to become an ἀρχή ("beginning," "foundation") "for the remnant," whom the Savior has "summoned to knowledge." Peter is the one who has to be strong and to become perfect; and only he communicates appropriate knowledge of the Savior, a knowledge that is decisive for salvation. After a vision where Peter obviously learns how to see and to hear properly (p. 72,4-73,10) he receives a first revelation of a "mystery" (p. 73,16). This is given in a highly polemical monologue of the Savior directed against the alleged errors of proto-orthodox groups,[51] who are understood as "blind and deaf" and do not understand mysteries (p. 76,28),

49. The meaning of this enigmatic expression has been discussed controversially. See, e.g., Havelaar, *Coptic Apocalypse,* p. 81.

50. J. Brashler, trans., "NHC VII,3: Apocalypse of Peter. Text, Translaton, and Notes," in *The Coptic Gnostic Library: A Complete Edition of the Nag Hammadi Codices* (Leiden: Brill, 2000), 4:218-47 (esp. pp. 221-23).

51. For a more detailed discussion of the adversaries addressed by the text, see Havelaar, *Coptic Apocalypse,* pp. 193-204. I would perhaps be a bit more cautious, however, regarding the question of whether there is a chance to reconstruct any community behind this text.

and against their rulers, their beliefs, and the organization of their communities (p. 73,10-81,3). Comparable to what we find in the passion account of the *Acts of John*, the *Apocalypse of Peter* then gives an alternative interpretation of Jesus' passion; again, the motif of blindness (perhaps taken from Matthew 23) plays a role. Only Peter sees what is truly happening. The text distinguishes between a "living Jesus" (p. 81,18) who is "above the cross, glad and laughing"[52] (p. 81,16f.), and who later is identified with the "Savior" (p. 82,9.28), while the one crucified is only "his physical part, which is the substitute" (p. 81,21f.). Whereas the others are called "born blind" (p. 83,3), looking only at the substitute, the figure suffering on the cross, only Peter is the "one to whom these mysteries have been given, to know through revelation that he whom they crucified is the firstborn, and the home of demons, and the clay vessel in which they dwell, belonging to Elohim, and belonging to the cross that is under the law" (p. 82,18-26).

The last sentences mentioned are revealing. Everybody who believes in the Jesus suffering on the cross belongs to the ones born blind and to Elohim, who is obviously understood as a demonic demiurge, and thus such a person does not see the real Savior, who "stands joyfully looking at those who persecuted him." Such believers are also "divided upon themselves" (p. 82,31-33). Peter, however, has to be "strong" (p. 82,18 and 84,10), and should not fear his enemies, because the Savior will be with him (p. 84,8-9; cf. Matt. 28:20?). On the level of the story these enemies are the "priests and the people" (p. 72,5-6). It is clear, however, that the real opponents are the representatives of proto-orthodoxy, seen as dangerous enemies of the group of gnostics behind our text.

Perhaps it is now, finally, also possible to understand the mysterious sentence, "Thus he will correct you three times this night," quoted above (p. 72,2-3). It appears that this sentence builds on Peter's triple denial of Jesus told in the canonical passion accounts. Contrary to the canonical Gospels — with a probable focus on Matthew, which is perhaps the text's main partner in dialogue (or better: polemic) — this denial of *Jesus* is not understood as a sign of weakness, but a sign that Peter does not want to know the fleshly Jesus, and so can be worthy of becoming chosen as the decisive recipient of knowledge. The text thus, of course, plays with the figure of Peter and his authority, and claims him for its own group and its own ideas of knowledge. But it is not absolutely clear whether this was *only* in response to Peter functioning as an

---

52. The motif of the "laughing Saviour" occurs in different gnostic writings. Regarding its significance see C. Clivaz, "What Is the Current State of Play on Jesus' Laughter? Reading the *Gospel of Judas* in the Midst of Scholarly Excitement," in *Judasevangelium und Codex Tchacos: Studien zur religionsgeschichtlichen Verortung einer gnostischen Schriftensammlung*, ed. E. E. Popkes and G. Wurst, WUNT 297 (Tübingen: Mohr Siebeck, 2012), pp. 213-42.

authority for the "other side," or whether those who produced this text took the opportunity to reinterpret Peter's partly quite negative and weak role in the canonical passion accounts as a sign that he knew the real character of the earthly Jesus and his passion earlier, better, and deeper than the others.

Other Perspectives on Peter

Gospel of Thomas

Whereas in texts mentioned above, Peter plays a decisively positive role, others devalue his impact and make him a figure of minor importance. This is quite clearly the case for the *Gospel of Thomas* (completely preserved in NHC II 2, but see also the Greek fragments P.Oxy. 1, 654, and 655), the exact gnostic character of which is debated.[53] According to logion 1, Didymos Judas Thomas wrote down Jesus' hidden words, the meaning of which has to be found to avoid death,[54] and we only rarely read about Peter. When (in logion 12) the disciples ask Jesus who will be great over them after his departure, Jesus does not point to Peter or Thomas, but mentions "James the Just, for whose sake heaven and earth came into being."[55]

This, of course, resembles an attitude to James comparable to what we

---

53. I agree with Jens Schröter, *Erinnerung an Jesu Worte: Studien zur Rezeption der Logienüberlieferung in Markus, Q und Thomas*, WMANT 76 (Neukirchen-Vluyn: Neukirchener, 1997), who discusses "Jesusüberlieferung auf dem Weg zur Gnosis" (pp. 122, 140). For a discussion of the problem of the text's religio-historious background see E. E. Popkes, "Das Thomasevangelium als *crux interpretum*: die methodischen Ursachen einer diffusen Diskussionslage," in *Jesus in apokryphen Evangelienüberlieferungen: Beiträge zu außerkanonischen Jesusüberlieferungen aus verschiedenen Sprach- und Kulturtraditionen*, ed. J. Frey and J. Schröter, WUNT 254 (Tübingen: Mohr Siebeck, 2010), pp. 271-92 (esp. 279-91).

54. Regarding the role of the text within early Christian Thomasine literature, see M. Janßen, "'Evangelium des Zwillings.' Das *Thomasevangelium* als Thomas-Schrift," in *Das Thomasevangelium: Entstehung — Rezeption — Theologie*, ed. Jörg Frey, E. E. Popkes, and J. Schröter, BZNW 157 (Berlin: de Gruyter, 2008) pp. 222-48.

55. Translation according to U.-K. Plisch, *The Gospel of Thomas: Original Text with Commentary*, trans. Gesine Schenke Robinson (Stuttgart: Deutsche Bibelgesellschaft, 2008), p. 61. Regarding the *Gospel of Thomas*'s complex relation to Jewish-Christian writings and traditions evoked by the mention of James the Just in logion 12, see P. Luomanen, "'Let Him Who Seeks, Continue Seeking': The Relationship between the Jewish-Christian Gospels and the Gospel of Thomas," in *Thomasine Traditions in Antiquity: The Social and Cultural World of the Gospel of Thomas*, ed. J. M. Asgeirsson, April DeConick, and Risto Uro, NHMS 59 (Leiden: Brill, 2006), pp. 119-53.

found in the *First Apocalypse of James* mentioned above, and which can be seen in many other (mainly second- and post-second-century) Christian writings. In the *Gospel of Thomas,* however, this attitude is striking, as already in the next logion (13) it is again Thomas who receives the revelation of three words that he cannot reveal to the others because they would stone him. Logion 13 is also of special impact for our problem because, comparably to the scene in Mark 8:27-30 and Synoptic parallels, Jesus asks the disciples how they see him. Contrary to what we find in the Synoptics, however, he does not receive only one answer (by Peter), but three:

> Simon Peter said to him: You are like a righteous angel.
> Matthew said to him: You are like an (especially) wise philosopher.
> Thomas said to him: Teacher, my mouth [cannot] at all say to whom you are like.[56]

Titles a reader of the Synoptic Gospels would expect are completely avoided, and Thomas's statement is clearly the climax of the three. By contrast, Peter's understanding of Jesus is certainly seen as one of those not fully appropriate. This does not necessarily mean that Peter is understood as a purely negative figure. But it does show that the *Gospel of Thomas* roots its Jesus traditions more in the figure of Thomas, and also polemicizes against other traditions, including those attributed to Peter, whose understanding of Jesus (from *Gospel of Thomas*'s perspective) did not go far enough. Logion 114 goes in the same direction, with Peter demanding that Mary leave the disciples because, as a woman, she is not worthy of life. Even if Jesus' response is also in line with the text's antifeminist attitude, he rebukes Peter: If a woman "makes herself male, [she] will enter the kingdom of heaven."[57]

In short, although even the Synoptics do not paint Peter as a purely positive figure, and the Gospel of John puts him into relation with the Beloved Disciple, the *Gospel of Thomas* minimizes his role and even seems to devalue him as a figure of authority in order to place its own tradition bound to Thomas (and emphasizing the impact of James the Just) in a better light.[58]

---

56. Translation adapted from Plisch, *Thomas,* p. 63, who in the first line has a "just messenger" instead of a "righteous angel."

57. Translation Plisch, *Thomas,* p. 243. Regarding the background of this saying see, e.g., Marvin Meyer, *Secret Gospels: Essays on Thomas and the Secret Gospel of Mark* (Harrisburg, Pa.: Trinity Press International, 2003), pp. 76-95, who connects the text's image of femaleness to the idea that the "dying cosmos of the mother goddess" must be transcended (p. 92).

58. See the comparable judgment by Pratscher, "Bedeutung," p. 123.

Gospel of Mary

The situation of conflict between Peter and Mary (probably Mary Magdalene) underlying *Gospel of Thomas* in 114 resembles the (fragmentary) *Gospel of Mary* (Berlin Codex BG 1; P.Oxy. 3525 and P.Ryl. 463), where we read about Peter several times. Unlike the *Gospel of Thomas,* the *Gospel of Mary* emphasizes Mary's role — she is the bearer of decisive revelation, and she plays the role of a beloved disciple. It is a matter of debate whether Peter is seen as a totally negative figure within a group for whom traditions about Mary Magdalene were decisive, or whether the text still reflects a connecting bridge between an emerging proto-orthodoxy and a group going in gnostic directions.[59] In any case, the text mentions Peter quite characteristically as the speaker for the group of disciples asking Jesus (called "the Savior") about the "sin of the world." But the text also describes him as weeping together with the others after Jesus' departure.

In this situation, it is Mary who takes the initiative, and thus turns "their hearts to the good," after which they begin to discuss Jesus' teachings. Peter even seems to acknowledge Mary's status as being loved by "the Savior" "more than the rest of women,"[60] and asks her to tell to all the other disciples the secret revelation that she received from Jesus. Unfortunately, none of the extant witnesses of our text completely preserves her response — four pages missing in the key manuscript, BG 1! That Mary appears to reveal her hidden knowledge to the other disciples might suggest that there is still a bond of connection between the circles who may have revered Mary as a special witness and the proto-orthodox, for whom the disciples as a group were authoritative. But a passage in the Berlin Codex (BG 1, pp. 17-18) is probably decisive: after the end of her speech, Andrew and Peter question the authenticity of her revelation. Whereas Andrew openly expresses his unbelief, Peter simply calls into question the possibility that Jesus spoke "with a woman without our knowing, and not openly" (p. 17,19-20). When Mary begins to weep because she understands Peter to be presuming that she is "lying about the Savior" (p. 18,5), Levi takes her side:

---

59. For different views see, e.g., A. Graham Brock, *Mary Magdalene, the First Apostle: The Struggle for Authority,* HTS 51 (Cambridge, Mass.: Harvard University Press, 2003), pp. 81-86 (and publications cited by her); Esther A. de Boer, *The Gospel of Mary: Beyond a Gnostic and a Biblical Mary Magdalene,* JSNTSup 260 (London: T&T Clark, 2004), pp. 60-100; and the very moderate view expressed by Christopher M. Tuckett, *The Gospel of Mary,* Oxford Early Christian Gospel Texts (Oxford: Oxford University, 2007), pp. 196-201.

60. Translations by Tuckett, *Gospel of Mary,* pp. 86-103.

Peter, you have always been hot-tempered. Now I see you are arguing against the woman like the adversaries. But if the Savior made her worthy who are you then to reject her? Certainly the Savior knows her very well. That is why he loved her more than us. Rather let us be ashamed and put on the perfect man and acquire him for ourselves as he commanded us, and let us preach the gospel, not laying down any other rule or other law beyond what the Savior said (p. 18,7-21; see also comparable P.Ryl. 463, p. 22).

The following final sentence of the text differs between the Coptic BG 1 and the Greek parallel version in P.Ryl. 463. According to BG 1, "they" (probably all the disciples) go out to proclaim the gospel; but according to P.Ryl. 463 it is only Levi who departs and preaches. This difference is, of course, not without significance. Whereas in the Coptic version the reader is left with the impression that, finally, unity wins over conflict, in the Greek version this is definitely not the case.

Be that as it may, Peter's role in the *Gospel of Mary* is certainly not a positive one. He is neither Jesus' beloved disciple, nor does he understand and acknowledge that this role was reserved for Mary, and so he does not accept her witness about special revelations received by the Savior. At the same time, Mary is presented as being active in strengthening and teaching the desperately weeping disciples in a situation of need. She is the one who gives what at least Andrew and Peter do not want to accept — partly because she is a woman. Does this at least partly mirror the perspective of a group of Christ followers believing in special revelations to Mary Magdalene, which they would like to share with members of a proto-orthodoxy following the lead of Peter (and Andrew)? If yes, then the figure of Levi (at least according to BG 1) seems to reflect the hope that there still could be a bridge to unite both groups to preach the gospel.

Even with the diversity of texts reviewed, the picture emerging is by no means complete. One could, for example, add the witness of the *Epistle of James* (NHC I 2), where we read about a special revelation to James *and* Peter. However, this text makes it absolutely clear that James is the decisive figure. Or consider the witness of the *Pistis Sophia*, criticizing but not neglecting Peter, and also showing redactional tendencies that point to an increasing anti-Petrine stance between its older book 4 and the younger books 1-3.[61] It is, however, perhaps better to look into a different group of sources before coming to a conclusion.

---

61. For more details on the images of Peter in this text, see Pratscher, "Bedeutung," pp. 113-18, 126-28.

Gnostic Perspectives in Patristic Sources

The situation does not change very much when we leave the Nag Hammadi texts and look for some additional information in ancient heresiologists' perspectives on what gnostics thought about Peter. Of course, we have to be even more cautious with these polemical sources than with the writings thought to come from gnostics. Although Pratscher has banned these texts to a very long footnote,[62] I would like to have at least a look into a few of them.

Irenaeus

Although Irenaeus of Lyons (*Adv. haer.* 1.24.1) establishes a link between Basilides and Simon Magus (the arch-heretic already mentioned in Acts 8:9-24), according to Clement of Alexandria (*Strom.* 7.106.4), Basilides (founder of the Basilidians)[63] claimed that his teacher Glaukias (otherwise unknown) had been Peter's interpreter *(hermēneus)*. Short pieces of information given by Clement (*Strom.* 7.108.1) and Hippolytus (*Haer.* 7.20.1) can be added, according to which the Basilidians also claimed that their teachings went back to the apostle Matthew, who had received secret teachings from Jesus himself.[64] This makes it quite plausible that the Basilidians tried to root their own teachings in apostolic tradition and, at the same time, claimed to be in the possession of secret truths. In this case, the story about Glaukias's relation to Peter could even have been proffered as a counterstory to the well-known tradition about Mark as Peter's interpreter mentioned by Papias of Hierapolis (quoted by Eusebius, *H.E.*, 3.39). Moreover, if one takes into account how Christian tradition has developed Peter and Simon Magus into deadly enemies,[65] then even Irenaeus's story could make sense.

---

62. Pratscher, "Bedeutung," pp. 112-13 n. 5. The following examples are also quoted in Pratscher's note; I have only chosen some of them, however.

63. For more information see Birger A. Pearson, "Basilides the Gnostic," in Marjanen and Luomanen, *A Companion,* pp. 1-31; and, even more important, W. A. Löhr, *Basilides und seine Schule: Eine Studie zur Theologie und Kirchengeschichte des 2. Jahrhunderts,* WUNT 83 (Tübingen: Mohr Siebeck, 1996).

64. See Pearson, "Basilides," p. 3.

65. Regarding the history of the figure see A. Ferreiro, *Simon Magus in Patristic, Medieval and Early Modern Traditions,* Studies in the History of Christian Traditions 125 (Leiden: Brill, 2005).

Further Patristic Sources

A few more sources deserve to be mentioned, the most interesting of which is perhaps a passage in Irenaeus (*Adv. haer.* 1.30.13, a part of Irenaeus's longer treatment of Ophites and Sethians, in 1.30.1-14). According to Irenaeus, Sethians and Ophites offered an interpretation of Jesus' life and passion very different from what we read in the New Testament Gospels. They distinguished very clearly between the man Jesus and heavenly Christ, who at a certain point in Jesus' life descended on him. Only from this point was it that Jesus began to work miracles. These miracles, however, made the evil powers and Jesus' earthly father angry at him, so that he was crucified, while Christ (together with Sophia) departed from him into the incorruptible Aeon. Christ, however, did not forget Jesus, and sent a heavenly power into him, which made him rise from the dead "in the body, which they call both animal and spiritual." This teaching, according to Irenaeus, is connected to a polemic against Jesus' disciples that most of them misunderstood: that Jesus without Christ had no miraculous powers and, more important, that they thought Jesus was risen in a body of this world and did not understand who had done this to him. Interestingly, this polemic is connected to a quotation of Paul (1 Cor. 15:50); the disciples did not know that "flesh and blood do not attain to the kingdom of God." Again, Peter is not explicitly mentioned. But if we consider that in many Christian circles he seems to have been well known as the primary, or at least a crucial, witness of Jesus' resurrection, then this argument must at least implicitly be directed against him. This must be even more the case if the argument was originally accompanied by a conscious quotation of 1 Corinthians 15:50, which is a later part of the same text, which mentioned Kephas, that is, Peter, as the first witness of Jesus' resurrection (1 Cor. 15:5).

Conclusion

My review of gnostic images of Peter is far from being complete, and many more texts, such as the passion account given in the apocryphal *Acts of John*, or the *Kerygmata Petrou* (one of the sources of the later pseudo-Clementines),[66] could be discussed. I have also totally neglected the Manicheans, who used the apocryphal *Gospel of Peter*.[67] It is, however, not only the limits of space

---

66. See also Pratscher, "Bedeutung," pp. 128-30.

67. See, e.g., M. Tardieu, "Le procès de Jésus vu par les Manichéens," *Apocrypha* 8 (1997): 9-23.

that prevent us from painting a full picture. As I mentioned more than once, this is also due to the character of the sources that we have and, even more, the many important questions about gnostic use of texts such as the Gospel of John that cannot be addressed here. We came across aspects of this problem when we noted the relation of the *Apocryphon of John* and the Fourth Gospel. One could also note that a nongnostic writing such as the *Acts of Peter and the Twelve Apostles* was transmitted within the Nag Hammadi library (NHC VI 1), and the transmission of the Coptic *Acts of Peter* in BG 4 alongside the allegedly anti-Petrine *Gospel of Mary*.[68]

In addition, we must always keep in mind that there must have been many sources lost, and so groups (or viewpoints) to which our only access is via a few polemical remarks by ancient proto-orthodox heresiologists. We have seen that (some of) the Basilidians, perhaps, claimed Petrine authority, but we have only very few short notices that can help us to discuss the matter. In many cases this lack of sources makes it much more difficult to contextualize their ideas in more or less concrete historical settings. A few lines, however, are relatively clear.

Even if the writings usually ascribed to Sethian groups and those labeled Valentinian do not mention Peter explicitly, we could, at least in a few cases, argue that this reveals a negative attitude toward him (including an attempt to minimize his role). Our review of Sethian and of Valentinian material showed an almost unanimously negative (although not sharply polemical) stance against Peter and Petrine traditions and writings.

This negative view of Peter changes, however, when we consider texts usually ascribed to what is called the "broader gnostic movement." Here, we found two clear cases of a clear pro-Petrine attitude. Interestingly, in both the *Epistle of Peter to Philip* and the *Apocalypse of Peter* from Nag Hammadi this positive view of Peter is connected with an interest in Jesus' passion. Although, according to both texts, Peter is an authoritative figure and also a mediator of secret truths, these truths are, to a high degree, contrary to each other. Whereas the *Epistle of Peter to Philip* (although in some aspects seemingly near to Sethian thought) develops a nondocetic Christology, in the *Apocalypse of Peter* we meet a Savior laughing about the body that was crucified.

On the whole the texts discussed reflect three different views.

1. In several writings we found a more or less open, partly explicit, partly implicit polemic against Peter. These writings note that Peter is an authority;

---

68. For more information see H.-M. Schenke, "Die Tat des Petrus (BG 4)," in Schenke, Bethge, and Kaiser, *NHC V,2 — XIII,1, BG 1 und 4,* pp. 845-53 (esp. pp. 846-50).

but he is the authority of the "others." Perhaps the sharpest example is the *Gospel of Judas* with its polemics against the disciples' total lack of understanding, which partly corresponds to what we found in Irenaeus's description of Ophites and Sethians. Other texts were less sharply negative, but still diminished Peter's authority implicitly by not mentioning him where he should be mentioned *(Apocryphon of John),* or by relating him to other recipients of true revelation *(Epistle of James,* NHC I 2).

2. Comparable to these texts, other writings also more or less try to put Peter in relation to other apostolic authorities, whose secret revelations are of greater relevance. This can happen in a sharper manner (as in *Pistis Sophia*) or in a less sharp way, in some case *(Gospel of Mary)* perhaps even reflecting an attempt to build bridges between different Christian communities.

3. Finally, we found writings claiming Peter as "their" authority. According to these writings, such as the *Epistle of Peter to Philip* or the Nag Hammadi *Apocalypse of Peter,* Peter remains the great authority. In these texts, however, he belongs to the "in-group" behind the text, and not to the proto-orthodox opponents. In both of these texts, canonical images and roles of Peter are developed in a way that he becomes the true interpreter of gnosis. Whereas in the *Epistle of Peter to Philip* perhaps Peter's role in Acts is decisive, the Coptic *Apocalypse of Peter* plays with canonical traditions of Jesus' passion (perhaps mainly those in the Gospel of Matthew) and Peter's somewhat problematic role therein, which from a gnostic counterperspective, however, can be radically reinterpreted.

What, in addition, strikes me very much is that, obviously, texts with very different attitudes could be put alongside one another and read together. The best example is surely the combination of the *Gospel of Judas* — perhaps the text most hostile to Jesus' disciples representing "orthodoxy" — and the *Epistle of Peter to Philip,* copies of both found in Codex Tchacos. It seems that the compiler of this codex was not mainly interested in different and partly contradicting images of Peter, but was led by questions different from ours. Is it possible that some of our reconstructions of ancient groups and readers behind ancient texts and their polemics against each other should sometimes be shaped a bit more strongly by what the combinations of different writings in ancient manuscripts tell us? This would, however, be another exciting task, the fulfillment of which would go far beyond the limits of this essay.

CHAPTER 16

Peter in Noncanonical Traditions

Paul Foster

Introduction

There have been numerous studies focusing on traditions relating to Peter in the canonical Gospels and other New Testament writings.[1] In contrast to the approach that is characterized by close analysis of biblical traditions, others have attempted to gain a firmer traction on the "historical Peter" by integrating archaeological evidence, or traditions preserved among proto-orthodox writers.[2] Theological interest in Peter has continued unabated, with some viewing a correct understanding of Peter and his apostolic role as a basis for a deeper ecumenical dialogue among the main branches of the Christian church.[3] More recently, there have been attempts to draw together the analysis of textual traditions and historical or theological concerns through the use of "social memory."[4] Although the link between memory and "history" is not unproblematic,

---

1. One of the most influential of these studies is Raymond E. Brown, Karl P. Donfried, and John Reumann, eds., *Peter in the New Testament* (Minneapolis: Augsburg, 1973).

2. One of the significant representatives of this approach is Oscar Cullmann, *Peter: Disciple, Apostle, and Martyr: A Historical and Theological Essay,* 2nd ed. (Philadelphia: Westminster, 1962).

3. Hengel sees Peter's role as forming an apostolic foundation for the church in its totality, and hence sees Peter as the figure around whom the various denominations can find rapprochement and thus reunify. See Martin Hengel, *Der unterschätzte Petrus. Zwei Studien* (Tübingen: Mohr Siebeck, 2006); English trans., *Saint Peter: The Underestimated Apostle* (Grand Rapids: Eerdmans, 2010), see esp. p. 102.

4. Markus Bockmuehl, *The Remembered Peter,* WUNT 1/262 (Tübingen: Mohr Siebeck,

nonetheless those studies attest the continuing interest in the figure of Peter. Furthermore, in some circles there is a desire to co-opt this reconstructed Peter as a figure with ongoing utility for contemporary ecclesial debates.

Such appropriations of Peter are not new. It appears that this process was well underway in the New Testament itself. Mark employs the misunderstanding of Peter and the other disciples as the foil by which he advances his Christology of the cross and suffering. Matthew recasts Markan traditions to place the figure of Peter at the center of his understanding of the *ekklesia* as the people of God, over and against those who continue their attendance of synagogues. Luke, in his second volume, presents Peter at the Jerusalem Council as the voice of moderation and mediation. The Petrine voice is also employed as a basis of unity, where the eponymous author of 2 Peter commends the Pauline epistles to his readers (2 Pet. 3:15). Despite all this unrelenting work on Peter, there is one body of literature that has been relatively neglected. In his discussion of Peter, under the heading "The Apocryphal Writings," Karl Donfried first notes, "This subject is one of several important areas which go beyond the scope of this essay."[5] He then continues by fleetingly mentioning some of the texts from the Nag Hammadi corpus, including briefly the *Gospel of Thomas*. Not only is this miscellany of writings to some degree unrepresentative of the portrayals of Peter in the noncanonical writings, but also the overly simplistic classification of these texts as either pro- or anti-Petrine reduces the varied perspectives they contain to a single, and at time unrepresentative issue or theological concern.[6]

In place of either comments about Peter in a single noncanonical text, or a focus on texts that simply bear Peter's name,[7] a different approach will be adopted here. Following the traditional arrangement of texts in collections of the New Testament Apocrypha, this discussion will consider in turn the representations of Peter in noncanonical gospels, acts, apocalypses, and epistles.[8]

2010); Bockmuehl, *Simon Peter in Scripture and Memory: The New Testament Apostle in the Early Church* (Grand Rapids: Baker Academic, 2012).

5. Karl P. Donfried, "Peter," *ABD* 5:251-63, here p. 263.

6. Donfried ("Peter," p. 263) concludes his brief survey of certain Nag Hammadi texts by stating that "since both the gnostic anti- and pro-Petrine tendencies present a view of Peter reconstructed through gnostic eyes, both tendencies would be rejected by such NT writings as 2 Peter." It is questionable, however, whether writings such as 2 Peter are in fact responding to gnostic tendencies, or whether such diverse views concerning Peter predate emergent Christian "gnosticism."

7. E.g., F. Lapham, *Peter: The Myth, the Man and the Writings: A Study of Early Petrine Text and Tradition*, JSNTSup 239 (London: Sheffield Academic, 2003).

8. Key examples of such compendia of texts include M. R. James, *The Apocryphal New Testament* (Oxford: Clarendon, 1924); Eduard Hennecke and Wilhelm Schneemelcher, eds.,

Although even this arrangement is an artificial construct, and at times the classification of a text into one or another of these groupings can be questioned, the compendious nature of such reference works means that the majority of early Christian noncanonical writings are covered by these categories. Even though these groupings are a modern construct, this taxonomy not only is a convenient system but also helpfully reflects some of the broad genres encompassed in early noncanonical writings. This study, however, will not be constrained by focusing solely on the texts contained in the major compendia of the New Testament Apocrypha. Rather, it will also make reference to other, later noncanonical writings where valuable insights can be found, or further reinforced.

The Noncanonical Gospels

Without doubt, the category of noncanonical gospels has occasioned the most interest, both in scholarly literature and at a more popular level. While some of the texts commonly listed in this category were preserved in usage through scribal copying and transmission,[9] the majority have become known only more recently, through various manuscript discoveries from the 1880s onward. The two earliest texts to have been rediscovered in the modern period, the Fayûm Fragment (P.Vindob. G. 2325) and the *Gospel of Peter* (P.Cair. 10759), are of interest for this present study because they both contain references to Peter.[10] With the passage of time, a greater range of noncanonical gospel texts was rediscovered. Though not all of these include references to Peter, a significant selection do. Such texts offer rich and multifaceted portrayals of the apostle. Moreover, it is often possible at times to discern the characterization of Peter being deployed for larger theological purposes.

Neutestamentliche Apokryphen in deutscher Übersetzung, 2 vols., 5th ed. (Tübingen: J. C. B. Mohr [Paul Siebeck], 1987-1989 [6th ed. is a corrected reprint of the 5th ed. [1990]), Eng. trans. Robert McL. Wilson, *New Testament Apocrypha* (Louisville: Westminster John Knox, 1991-1992); J. K. Elliott, *The Apocryphal New Testament* (Oxford: Clarendon, 1993); Christoph Markschies and Jens Schröter, eds., *Antike christliche Apokryphen in deutscher Übersetzung* (Tübingen: Mohr Siebeck, 2012).

9. Prime examples in this category are the so-called *Protevangelium of James* and the *Infancy Gospel of Thomas,* neither of which refers to the figure of Peter. This is unsurprising since the events they depict occur in a narrative time prior to the call of Peter.

10. The text known as the Fay(y)ûm Fragment (P.Vindob. 2325) was first published by G. Bickell in 1885, after it was found in the papyrus collection of Archduke Rainer in Vienna. The next noncanonical gospel to come to light was the *Gospel of Peter* discovered at Akhmîm in Upper Egypt during the winter season dig of 1886/1887, with the *editio princeps* published in 1892.

The Fayûm Fragment (P.Vindob. G. 2325)

Although included in all major collections of noncanonical gospels, and potentially having the distinction of being the first of the newly discovered apocryphal gospel texts, its inclusion raises some fundamental questions about the categorization of "noncanonical gospels." At most the surviving fragment contains seven lines of text, and although the tops of the three letters on line seven are partially visible they are all uncertain. The text contains a version of the cock-crow story, with parallels found in Matthew 26:30-31, 33-34, and Mark 14:26-27, 29-30. Understandably, the fragmentary state of this text has occasioned questions about what it may have been originally as to extent and use. Is it part of a larger independent noncanonical gospel (the most popular suggestion being that it is an otherwise unattested fragment of the *Gospel of Peter*[11]), or is it an excerpt or textual variant of either the Matthean or Markan text, or a type of harmonistic account, or is it a pre-Synoptic tradition standing behind the Markan text?[12]

Regardless of the correctness of any of these theories, for this discussion the important feature is the reference to Peter as a named character in the Fayûm Fragment. After Jesus' declaration that the apostles will be "scandalized," and the citation of the Septuagint version of Zechariah 13:7 (in harmony with Mark 14:27: "I will strike the shepherd and the sheep will be dispersed"; but cf. the wording of the Septuagint text: "strike the shepherds and the sheep shall be scattered"),[13] Peter responds. At this point, however, the text becomes even more fragmentary.

---

11. The connection with the *Gospel of Peter* was first proposed by G. Bickell, *Papyrus Erzherzog Rainer: Führer durch die Ausstellung mit 20 Tafeln und 90 Textbilderung* (Vienna, 1895), but has been most recently championed by Dieter Lührmann in several publications; see *Fragmente apokryph gewordener Evangelien* (Marburg: Elwart, 2000), pp. 73-74, 80-81. This view has been challenged independently by Thomas J. Kraus, "*P.Vindob.G* 2325: The So-called Fayûm Gospel — Re-Edition and Some Critical Conclusions," in Thomas J. Kraus, *Ad fontes: Manuscripts and Their Significance for Studying Early Christianity*, TENTS 3 (Leiden: Brill, 2007), pp. 69-94; and Paul Foster, *The Gospel of Peter: Introduction, Critical Edition and Commentary*, TENTS 3 (Leiden: Brill, 2010), pp. 80-82.

12. For a discussion of these possibilities see Thomas J. Kraus, "*P.Vindob.G* 2325: The Fayûm Fragment," in *Gospel Fragments*, ed. Thomas J. Kraus, M. J. Kruger, and T. Nicklas, OECGT (Oxford: Oxford University Press, 2009), pp. 219-227, here pp. 225-26.

13. See Thomas J. Kraus, "The Fayum Gospel," in *The Non-Canonical Gospels*, ed. Paul Foster (London: T&T Clark, 2008), pp. 150-56, here p. 153.

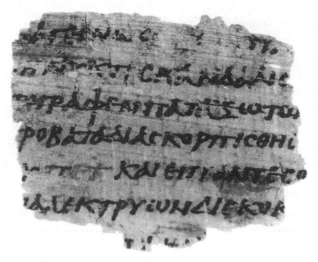

The Fayûm Fragment

Starting in the fourth line:

ει-]

[ποντος το]υ πετ(ρου)· και ει παντες, ο[υκ εγω. . . .]
[. . . Ιη(σους)· πρι]ν αλεκτρυων δις κοκ[κυσει τρις]
[. . . με α]παρν[ηση.]

Two features stand out immediately in relation to the name Peter in the fragment. First, the name Peter occurs in suspended form (omitting the fourth to sixth letters); and second, the abbreviated form πετ is written in red ink, with red dots written above the π and the τ of the πετ. Though the extant text itself is too brief to permit one to draw any conclusions or theories concerning whether the representation of Peter is significantly different from the Synoptic parallels, the paratextual features invite comment. Typically, in New Testament manuscripts the name of Peter is not abbreviated. Rather, the so-called *nomina sacra* are the abbreviated terms.[14] The abbreviation of the name Peter is formed differently from the typical forms of *nomina sacra*. Although contracted forms (typically first and last letter) are far more common in general than suspended forms, both forms do occur. However, suspended forms tend to occur only to abbreviate the name Jesus, and are found in earlier manuscripts. Thus the

14. Larry W. Hurtado, "The Origin of the *Nomina Sacra:* A Proposal," *JBL* 117 (1998): 655-73.

suspended form of the name Peter is highly unusual. Furthermore, *nomina sacra* are regularly written with a supralinear stroke above the abbreviated form, which is not the case here. The use of red ink is also unusual, but not without examples elsewhere.[15] While it is not possible to determine the precise significance of the abbreviation and the use of red ink, it is reasonable to infer that the author considered the name of Peter worthy of being highlighted.

The Gospel of Peter

One would perhaps expect a gospel text that bore the name of Peter to be one of the richest sources for studying the portrayal of the apostle in noncanonical sources. Unfortunately, that is not the case. Perhaps Joseph Verheyden has made the best attempt to understand something of Peter's literary role in the *Gospel of Peter.* He suggests that initially "turning Peter into the narrator of the story may seem like a revolutionary move."[16] However, as he points out, this is not as innovative as one might think. The Petrine voice is used to narrate a number of other texts as well, perhaps the canonical Petrine epistles, the earliest examples of this phenomenon. However, in the extant portion of the *Gospel of Peter* (the first text contained in the Akhmîm codex), the first-person voice of the narrator is heard only twice, and it is not until the final verse of the surviving portion of the manuscript that it becomes explicit that "Simon Peter" is the narrator.

The first occasion where the first-person voice is employed is when it is used to describe the clandestine hiding of the disciples as part of the immediate aftermath of the crucifixion. The narrator's voice is introduced in the following manner:

15. P.Oxy. 840 is another example of a noncanonical gospel text using red ink at places, although for different reasons. It uses red ink in four ways. Red circles are used to highlight punctuation marks; red outlines are placed over the black supralinear strokes in *nomina sacra,* but the letters themselves are not written in red; enlarged black letters are reinked in red; and red outlines are given to accents and breathing marks. For a fuller discussion see Michael J. Kruger, *The Gospel of the Savior: An Analysis of P.Oxy. 840 and Its Place in the Gospel Traditions of Early Christianity* (Leiden: Brill, 2005), pp. 48-49. Primarily, color seems to function as an aid to the reader to highlight text that would need to be read differently from what was written, or to draw attention to a reading mark such as an accent, breathing, or section break.

16. Joseph Verheyden, "Some Reflections on Determining the Purpose of 'Gospel of Peter,'" in *Das Petrusevangelium als Teil spätantiker Literatur,* ed. Tobias Nicklas and Thomas J. Kraus, TU 158 (Berlin: de Gruyter, 2007), pp. 282-99, here p. 283.

ἐγὼ δὲ μετὰ τῶ(ν) ἑταίρων μου ἐλπούμην καὶ τετρωμένοι κατὰ διάνοιαν ἐκρυβόμεθα.

But I, with my companions, was grieved, and being wounded in mind we hid. (*Gos. Pet.* 7.26a)

The first-person narrative continues throughout *Gospel of Peter* 7.26-27. However, because Peter is not explicitly named, there is little, if anything, that can be gleaned specifically concerning the way the text might seek to characterize him. Instead, it provides an expanded reflection on the state of mind of the disciples as a group.[17]

The second and only other occasion when the text breaks into first-person narrative is when the text mentions "we the twelve disciples of the Lord" (*Gos. Pet.* 14.59), followed in the next verse by the sole occasion when Peter is explicitly identified in the text.

ἐγὼ δὲ Σίμων Πέτρος καὶ Ἀνδρέας ὁ ἀδελφός μου λαβόντες ἡμῶν τὰ λίνα ἀπήλθαμεν εἰς τὴν θάλασσαν, καὶ ἦν σὺν ἡμῖν Λευείς ὁ τοῦ Ἀλφαίου ὃν κυ̅.

But I, Simon Peter, and Andrew my brother, taking our nets went to the sea, and there was with us Levi the brother of Alphaeus, whom the Lord . . . (*Gos. Pet.* 14.60).

Here, a number of the disciples are mentioned by name. However, the focus falls more heavily on Peter since he is named first, and is also the narrator of this section of the text. The practice of placing Peter's name first in lists or contexts where other disciples are also named is common in early Christian writings, and in all likelihood is derived from the canonical Gospels (e.g., Matt. 4:18; 10:2 // Mark 3:16 // Luke 6:14; John 21:2). While this partially preserved introduction is the only fragment of the final scene in the extant portion of the *Gospel of Peter,* it does appear "that the narrative is about to offer a reworked resurrection appearance of Jesus to the disciples which may well parallel that known from Jn 21.1-23."[18] However, without the details of what follows, it is impossible to know exactly how the author of the *Gospel of Peter* recasts the figure of Peter in this scene. Notwithstanding this serious limitation, two things may be gleaned from this material. First, Peter is given the narrator's voice (at least in this scene), and

17. Foster, *Gospel of Peter,* pp. 354-57.
18. Foster, *Gospel of Peter,* p. 511.

second, he supplies the background information that explains the presence of the disciples beside the sea. In the Fourth Gospel, the scene change from the disciples in a room with Jesus in Jerusalem (John 20:26-29) to the setting beside the Sea of Tiberias (John 21:1) is rather abrupt and without explanation. So, the author of the *Gospel of Peter* appears here to be pursuing one of the features attested elsewhere in the noncanonical text through his rewriting of the story.[19] That feature is resolving inconsistencies in the canonical narrative by filling gaps with additional background information, or through offering "a stylistically more developed text with greater points of narrative tension."[20] Hence, the author here appears to offer an explanation for the change of location from Jerusalem with the description of the disciples quitting the city (*Gos. Pet.* 14.59), and their relocation beside the sea (*Gos. Pet.* 14.60).

These are the chief insights that the *Gospel of Peter* offers concerning its eponymous narrator. What can be gleaned from the text concerning Peter is slight, and suggests that there is no basis for seeing a radical recharacterization of Peter in this gospel text.

The Gospel of Thomas

As with the *Gospel of Peter,* there are two references to Peter in the *Gospel of Thomas.* This, however, is where the similarity ceases. Not only are the references more explicit, but also they are deployed not in a narrative account but in a collection of loosely related sayings.

The first reference to Peter occurs in one of the longest logia in the *Gospel of Thomas,* which appears with a basic narrative framework. Although the numbering is indeed a modern invention, the repeated introductory formula "Jesus said" tends to delineate the short units in *Thomas.* Admittedly, in saying 13, where the first reference to Peter is found, the "Jesus said" formula occurs twice. However, this material is best taken as a single unit because of the

---

19. Henderson characterizes the *Gospel of Peter* as "rewritten gospel" and as thus following the wider phenomenon of the rewritten Bible. Although the generic parallels between rewritten biblical texts and the *Gospel of Peter* should perhaps not be pressed, there is no doubt that in some sense the *Gospel of Peter* is rewriting earlier traditions. See Timothy P. Henderson, *The Gospel of Peter and Early Christian Apologetics,* WUNT 2/301 (Tubingen: Mohr Siebeck, 2011), pp. 32-43.

20. Paul Foster, "Passion Traditions in the *Gospel of Peter,*" in *Gelitten Gestorben Auferstanden: Passions- und Ostertraditionen im antiken Christentum,* ed. Tobias Nicklas, A. Merkt, and J. Verheyden, WUNT 2/273 (Tubingen: Mohr Siebeck, 2010), pp. 47-68, here p. 67.

connection between these two parts, which is achieved both thematically and through the dialogue between Jesus and Thomas. In fact, the second "Jesus said" is part of the dialogue, and is not the introduction to a new unit. The saying reports the following exchange involving Jesus, Simon Peter, Matthew, and Thomas:

> Jesus said to his disciples, "Compare me to someone and tell me whom I am like."
>
> Simon Peter said to him, "You are like a righteous angel."
>
> Matthew said to him, "You are like a wise philosopher."
>
> Thomas said to him, "Master, my mouth is wholly incapable of saying whom you are like."
>
> Jesus said, "I am not your master. Because you have drunk, you have become intoxicated from the bubbling spring which I have measured out."
>
> And he took him and withdrew and told him three things. When Thomas returned to his companions, they asked him, "What did Jesus say to you?"
>
> Thomas said to them, "If I tell you one of the things which he told me, you will pick up stones and throw them at me; a fire will come out of the stones and burn you up." (*Gos. Thom.* 13)

What is presented here is reminiscent of the Caesarea Philippi scene (Matt. 16:13-17 // Mark 8:27-29 // Luke 9:18-20). Yet the purpose appears to be to correct or even to subvert the christological perspectives offered by other disciples.[21] For the purpose of this study, the interesting aspect is what is attributed to Simon Peter, who is the first listed disciple, the description of Jesus as being "like a righteous angel." Unlike the Synoptic accounts, where other unnamed characters offer inadequate answers before Peter offers the correct understanding, here it is Peter who speaks first and "delivers the weakest characterization of Jesus."[22] This displacement of Peter as the disciple with the correct insight

21. F. F. Bruce suggests, "Here the answers are attempts to depict Jesus as the Gnostic Revealer. Those who have imbibed the *gnosis* which he imparts (the 'bubbling spring' which he has spread abroad) are not his servants but his friends [cf. John 15:14], and therefore 'Master' is an unsuitable title for them to give him." F. F. Bruce, *Jesus and Christian Origins Outside the New Testament* (Grand Rapids: Eerdmans, 1974), pp. 118-19. This may be part of what the author of the *Gospel of Thomas* seeks to communicate, but there is also a signal desire to promote Thomas's role over that of the other disciples.

22. U.-K. Plisch, *The Gospel of Thomas: Original Text with Commentary* (Stuttgart: Deutsche Bibelgesellschaft, 2008), p. 64.

appears to be a not too subtle attempt to assert the superiority of Thomas, and of those who adhere to the teachings contained in this gospel.

The second saying that mentions Peter is the infamous final logion in the *Gospel of Thomas:*

> Simon Peter said to them, "Mary should leave us, for females are not worthy of life." Jesus said, "See, I am going to attract her to make her male so that she too might become a living spirit that resembles you males. For every female (element) that makes itself male will enter the kingdom of heaven." (*Gos. Thom.* 114)

This tension between Peter and Mary (presumably Magdalene) occurs elsewhere in the noncanonical gospel traditions.[23] Here Peter is characterized as launching a direct attack on Mary, stating that she is unworthy of life. Some have seen Peter as deployed here as a cipher for the emerging orthodox church, with its patriarchal power structures that were exclusionary of women. However, as Richard Valantasis comments, "Such a symbolic reading need not provide the starting point."[24] Hence, taking "Peter" here as the figure Peter, and not as a cipher, one sees that he is characterized as an antagonistic figure who both denigrates Mary specifically and women more generally. It is not possible to decide with confidence whether what stands behind this outburst are differences in institutional policies in regard to gender roles in early Christian groups, or a reflection of a memory of personal jealousy between Peter and Mary. Regardless of what might be the "backstory," Jesus' reply contains an implied rebuttal of Peter's proposition, as well as an explicit affirmation of Mary. However, Jesus' positive statement has been seen by some as entailing a partial confirmation of Peter's point of view by stating that it is only if females become male that they will enter the kingdom. Such a reading is too crude, however, and does not reflect the likely wider soteriological background to this text. In Valentinian cosmology, the individual experiences salvation through the reunification of the feminine soul with her masculine heavenly counterpart. This perspective is found, for instance, in the *First Apocalypse of James,* where the text states that "the perishable has gone up to the imperishable and the female element has attained to this male element" (NHC V 3, p. 41). Salvation in this scheme is mystical, and entails the reunification of the soul and its return to the one who is the highest power. While not articulated with the

---

23. See the *Gospel of Mary* (BG 8502 17,7-18,15).
24. Richard Valantasis, *The Gospel of Thomas* (London: Routledge, 1997), p. 194.

same level of cosmological sophistication, the *Gospel of Thomas* might reflect an embryonic stage in a type of belief system that shares similar soteriological underpinnings. For others, however, the statement reflects a stage when an encratite perspective was becoming dominant in a Thomasine community, with the refashioning of gender for women stressing "particularly celibacy and their refusal to bear children."[25] Regardless of which specific interpretation is correct, both the references to Peter in the *Gospel of Thomas* present him as a type of antihero, against whose views correct perspectives can be articulated.

The Gospel of Mary

The figure of Peter is more prominent in the *Gospel of Mary*, with him being named explicitly on seven occasions. Given that the first part of the extant text (BG 8502) commences in the middle of a dialogue, it seems likely that the two figures engaged in discussion may have been mentioned by name previously. These two characters are "the Savior" and Peter. However, it is also possible that the Savior is responding to a sequence of questions coming from different disciples in turn. Apart from "the Savior" (twelve times) and Peter (seven times), other named figures in the extant portion of the text include Mary (eight times), Andrew (once), and Levi (once). After the initial reference to Peter, where he is in dialogue with the Savior, the other six references to him occur in contexts where he is in dialogue with or in discussion about Mary.

The first reference to Peter occurs after the Savior answers the question, "Will matter then be utterly destroyed or not?" from an interlocutor who cannot be identified because of the fragmentary state of the text. After answering that question, Peter seems to bring a series of theological or cosmological questions to an end with the following comment and question:

> Peter said to him, "Since you have explained everything to us, tell us this too. What is the sin of the world?" (BG 8502, p. 7.10-12)[26]

Here, Peter functions as a literary foil. His question allows the Savior to correct this misperception concerning sin, by declaring, "There is no sin" (BG 8502,

---

25. April D. DeConick, *The Original Gospel of Thomas in Translation: With a Commentary and New English Translation of the Complete Gospel*, LNTS 287 (London: T&T Clark, 2006), p. 297.

26. Here and throughout this section the translation is taken from Christopher M. Tuckett, *The Gospel of Mary*, OECGT (Oxford: Oxford University Press, 2007), p. 87.

p. 7.13). Although some have detected a very direct polemic against proto-orthodox views,[27] it is equally possible that the text is structured in such a way as to allow the author to articulate his own views in the common style of a dialogue (compare the Socratic dialogues), without any specific attempt to correct or counter an alternative theology.[28] Here then, Peter's role is limited. He may simply be portrayed as a dialogue partner, articulating an incorrect view that requires correction by the Savior.

The second scene in which Peter appears occurs where he appears to affirm Mary's special status as a privileged recipient of revelatory knowledge.

> Peter said to Mary, "Sister, we know that the Savior loved you more than the rest of women. Tell us the words of the Savior which you remember, which you know but we do not, and which we have not heard." (BG 8502, p. 10.1-6)

The familial language expressed in the address "sister" is an acknowledgment of Mary's role as a disciple and fellow believer.[29] However, gender identity is significant in the way Peter identifies Mary both as "sister" and as having a special relation with the Savior in comparison with "women." Peter's purpose in acknowledging Mary's special relationship with the Savior is to persuade her to disclose teaching to which Peter and his companions did not have access. Mary responds to the invitation and provides lengthy esoteric teaching, which presumably spanned several manuscript pages, including the four pages missing from the text. Once again, Peter functions as a foil, and his role is to allow Mary space to speak. His own views are not articulated to any great extent, and consequently, as Christopher Tuckett notes, "at one level, Peter simply functions as a minor character, simply speaking to lead the narrative on to the next part."[30]

At the conclusion of Mary's extended teaching, the three named disciples respond in different ways. Andrew's reaction is one of blanket rejection: "I myself do not believe that the Savior said this. For these teachings seem to be (giving) strange ideas" (BG 8502, p. 17.13-15). Peter provides a lengthier answer, which although negative in orientation is perhaps slightly softened in comparison with Andrew's response, because it is framed as a series of questions.

27. Karen L. King, *The Gospel of Mary of Magdala: Jesus and the First Woman Apostle* (Santa Rosa: Polebridge, 2003), p. 127.

28. Tuckett, *Gospel of Mary,* p. 141.

29. Esther A. de Boer, *The Gospel of Mary: Beyond a Gnostic and a Biblical Mary Magdalene,* JSNTSup 260 (London: T&T Clark, 2004), p. 61.

30. Tuckett, *Gospel of Mary,* p. 169.

Peter answered and spoke about the same things. He asked them about the Savior: "He did not speak with a woman without our knowing, and not openly, did he? Shall we turn around and all listen to her? Did he prefer her to us?" (BG 8502, p. 17.16-22)

As is the case with *Gospel of Thomas* 114, here Peter speaks against Mary and employs misogynistic rhetoric. Esther de Boer views Peter's rhetoric as shaped by gender issues, yet at a deeper level sees it as flawed and contradictory. Initially, he acknowledges her status as a fellow disciple, and thus calls on her to disclose her revelatory knowledge. However, for Peter here, Mary "is a woman and as a woman she is a threat and inferior to men. As a woman the Savior cannot have spoken to her alone; as a woman he and the others cannot listen to her; as a woman the Savior cannot have placed her above men."[31] In the end it is the text that passes its own assessment of Peter's reaction through words placed on the lips of Levi. Before Levi intercedes on her behalf, Mary is so stung by Peter's response that she weeps (no reference is made to Andrew's even more damning attack). Mary affirms the validity of her revelatory knowledge of the Savior. Then Levi leaps to her defense.

Levi answered and said to Peter: "Peter, you have always been hot-tempered. Now I see you arguing against the woman like the adversaries. But if the Savior made her worthy, who are you then to reject her? Certainly the Savior knows her very well. That is why he loved her more than us." (BG 8502, p. 17.16-22).[32]

Tuckett cautions against stereotyping the issues behind this text exclusively along gender lines. According to him, any interpretation that offers a gender-based explanation must also account for the role of Levi alongside Mary.[33] Also, if the date for the text is relatively early, perhaps in the second quarter of the second century, then it is probably anachronistic to cast the tensions in terms of full-fledged polarities between "orthodox" and "gnostic" Christianities. However, given the critique of Peter against the legitimacy of Mary's revelatory teaching, the text might reflect the initial stages of tension between

---

31. De Boer, *Gospel of Mary*, p. 62.

32. Here the translation follows the Coptic text. The incident is also recorded in P.Rhy. 463. Tuckett notes that "there are differences between Coptic and Greek versions, and it is almost impossible to determine with any certainty which version offers the more original form of the text" (*Gospel of Mary*, p. 194).

33. Tuckett, *Gospel of Mary*, p. 196.

emergent mainstream Christianity and groups that adhered to a more esoteric form of Christian teaching. On this view, the *Gospel of Mary* is written from the perspective of those who defend esoteric revelatory teaching as authentic, and the text presents Mary as an emblematic character who defends such an interpretation. Equally, Peter is cast as the figure who stands in opposition to esoteric teaching. This characterization may in fact reveal that Peter had been claimed as a foundational figure for emergent mainstream Christianity by the time the text was written.

Jewish-Christian Gospels

The Jewish Christian are treated here collectively, not simply as a matter of convenience, but because of the difficulty of identifying the number of discrete texts that fall into this category, and the problem of determining which cited traditions belong to those texts.[34] The *Gospel of the Ebionites* is the modern title given to those gospel fragments preserved in Epiphanius's *Panarion* under the section where he discusses the Ebionites. Epiphanius, however, designates the text differently, noting that "the Ebionites accept the Gospel according to Matthew (30.3.7), but refer to it as the *Gospel according to the Hebrews* (30.3.7), as Matthew (30.13.2-3), and as τὸ Ἐβραϊκόν, the Hebrew Gospel (30.13.2-3)."[35]

> In the Gospel they have, called according to Matthew, but not wholly complete, but falsified and mutilated (they call it the Hebrew *Gospel*), it is contained that "There was a certain man named Jesus, and he was about thirty years old, who chose us. And coming unto Capernaum he entered into the house of Simon who was surnamed Peter, and opened his mouth and said: 'As I passed by the lake of Tiberias, I chose John and James the sons of Zebedee, and Simon and Andrew and <Philip and Bartholomew, James *the son* of Alphaeus and Thomas> Thaddaeus and Simon the Zealot and Judas the Iscariot: and you, Matthew, as you sat for receipt of tax I called, and you followed me. You therefore I desire to be twelve apostles for a testimony to Israel.'" (*Panarion* 30.13.2-3)

34. See Andrew Gregory, "Help or Hindrance: Does the Modern Category of 'Jewish-Christian Gospel' Distort Our Understanding of the Texts to which It Refers?" *JSNT* 28 (2006): 387-413.

35. Gregory, "Help or Hindrance," p. 394.

In this apparently variant form of Matthew's Gospel (although presumably the detail about Jesus being thirty is drawn from Luke 3:23) the disciple list deviates from the typical pattern. Although the setting is in Peter's house, in the actual listing of the Twelve Peter is mentioned in third place, but named solely as Simon. This differs from the first Gospel, where the evangelist states, "The names of the twelve apostles are these: the first Simon, who is called Peter . . ." (Matt. 10:2). The source cited by Epiphanius appears to conflate an incident in the house of Simon (Matt. 8:14 // Mark 1:29 // Luke 4:38) with the disciple lists (Matt. 10:2-4 // Mark 3:16-19 // Luke 6:14-16). In none of these lists are John and James placed before Peter, and in all of them James is named prior to John. Furthermore, the source behind the *Panarion* is unique in placing Matthew after Judas Iscariot, with a direct address to Matthew. Moreover, whereas Matthew's Gospel simply states that Simon was the one "who was called Peter," in the *Panarion* "Peter" is taken to be a "surname" rather than a new given name. It is possible to speculate concerning the displacement of Peter from first position, but ultimately the motivation is not transparent. It is more obvious that the author wished to stress the role of Matthew at the end of the list.

The *Gospel of the Nazoreans* is known primarily from citations contained in the writings of Jerome, who refers to a "gospel that the Nazoreans read."[36] As Andrew Gregory notes (and as is reinforced by modern compendia of Jewish-Christian gospels), "There may also be fragments of the gospel in a Latin translation of Origen and in the *Theophania* of Eusebius of Caesarea."[37] Among the references to Peter in this body of tradition is the conflation of the two forms of the double-tradition instruction concerning forgiveness of a repentant brother (Matt. 18:15, 21-22 // Luke 17:3-4).

> He says, "If your brother has sinned by a word, and repented, receive him seven times a day." Simon, his disciple, said to him, "Seven times a day?" The Lord answered, "Yes, I tell you, as much as seventy times seven times! For in the prophets also, after they were anointed by the Holy Spirit, a word of sin [sinful speech?] was found." (Jerome, *Against Pelagius*, 3.2)

---

36. Jerome provides multiple descriptions of this text but attributes its use to the Nazoreans. "In the Gospel according to the Hebrews, which is written in the Chaldee and Syrian language, but in Hebrew characters, and is used by the Nazarenes to this day (I mean the Gospel according to the Apostles, or, as is generally maintained, the Gospel according to Matthew, a copy of which is in the library at Cæsarea)" (Jerome, *Against Pelagius* 3.2).

37. Gregory, "Help or Hindrance," p. 402.

The opening statement from Jesus finds its closest parallel in Luke 17:3-4, whereas the ensuing question from Peter is found only in the Matthean form of the tradition (Matt. 18:21). Not only has Matthew reshaped the tradition as a dialogue between Jesus and Peter, but "within the dialogue Matthew further radicalizes the saying by introducing 'seventy times seven.'"[38] This pastiche of gospel traditions adds little to the characterization of Peter, apart from calling him Simon rather than maintaining the Matthean use of the name Peter. The tradition appears to have harmonistic features, but does not develop the characterization of Peter.

In a more generalized reference in his *Commentary on Matthew*, Jerome mentions that "the Jewish Gospel has: And he denied, and he swore, and he cursed" (Jerome, *Commentary on Matthew* 26.74). Here, Jerome's point is to illustrate a variation in the textual form. There is little additional information concerning Peter.

Origen also highlights a difference from Matthew in a document he describes as "the so-called Hebrew Gospel" relating to the saying concerning a camel passing through the eye of the needle. This tradition has been attributed either to a *Gospel of the Hebrews,* or, more often, to the *Gospel of the Nazoreans.*[39] In his comments on this passage, Origen cites the so-called Hebrew gospel as reading:

> And he turned and said to Simon, his disciple, who was sitting by him: Simon, son of Jona, it is easier for a camel to go through the eye of a needle than for a rich man to enter into the kingdom of heaven. (Origen, *Commentary on Matthew* 15.14, on Matthew 19:16-30, in the Latin rendering)

In this form of the tradition Peter is introduced earlier in the narrative. In Matthew 19:23 Jesus addresses the saying to his disciples as a group. Peter is introduced only at a secondary stage with the comment, "Behold we have left everything and followed you; what then will there be for us?" (Matt. 19:27). Moreover, the form Origen cites uses the name "Simon, son of Jona," appearing to introduce Johannine nomenclature for Peter into an otherwise Matthean tradition. Such relatively minor alterations say less about Peter and more about the fluidity in the transmission of gospel sayings.

---

38. Harry T. Fleddermann, *Q — A Reconstruction and Commentary* (Leuven: Peeters, 2005), p. 801.

39. See Philip Vielhauer and Georg Strecker, "Jewish-Christian Gospels," in Hennecke and Schneemelcher, *Neutestamentliche Apokryphen*, p. 161 (frag. 16); Jörg Frey, "B. V.1.4 Die Fragmente des Nazoräerevangeliums," in Markschies and Schröter, *Antike christliche Apokryphen*, pp. 642-43, 653 (frag. 10).

Unsurprisingly, as a whole, the Jewish-Christian gospels, as preserved in a few patristic citations, add very little to the characterization of Peter. This may well be due to the fact that all that survives is a selection of excerpts rather than a continuous text of any of these gospels.

Apocryphal Acts

As a group, the so-called apocryphal acts of apostles texts (AAA) tend to be significantly longer than the surviving fragments, or even complete texts, of the various noncanonical gospels. Scholars typically give prominence to five such writings as being the early representatives of this genre. These five texts are the *Acts of Paul,* the *Acts of Peter,* the *Acts of John,* the *Acts of Andrew,* and the *Acts of Thomas.* Although opinion concerning the relative dating of these texts is disputed, most would date them between the middle of the second century and the middle of the third century. Perhaps the one point where a broad consensus has emerged is in seeing the *Acts of Thomas* as the latest of these texts, with a date sometime in the first half of the third century. There are also a number of later apocryphal acts of apostles texts dating from the third century down into the early medieval period. A number of challenges confront scholars working on these texts. In cases where a single manuscript of one of the early or later apocryphal acts exists, the text is often lacunose. By contrast, in cases where there are multiple manuscript witnesses, the text forms are often disparate and reflect an ongoing process of modification and rewriting of these traditions.

The approach here will be primarily to work with standard scholarly editions of these texts, in order to consider the way in which Peter is depicted. In some of these texts, such as the eponymous *Acts of Peter,* where the apostle is mentioned on more than one hundred occasions, the volume of references is so large that a certain degree of selectivity is essential. In several of the other texts, Peter is named only on a handful of occasions. These texts will be discussed in the order of one significant proposal concerning their relative chronological sequence.[40] Jan Bremmer's suggested dates for the five major acts are *Acts of Andrew,* 150 CE, perhaps in Alexandria; *Acts of Peter,* 180-190 CE, perhaps in Rome; *Acts of Paul,* 185-195 CE, perhaps in Asia Minor; *Acts of John,* 200-250 CE, perhaps in eastern Syria; and *Acts of Thomas,* 200-250

---

40. Jan N. Bremmer, ed., *The Apocryphal Acts of Thomas* (Leuven: Peters, 2001), pp. 152-53.

CE, perhaps in eastern Syria. This scheme is followed here for convenience, while noting that the dating issues are extremely complex, and judgments are frequently based on inferences from internal factors rather than any solid external indicators.

Acts of Andrew

The text of the *Acts of Andrew* has not survived in its complete early Greek form. However, a number of fragmentary texts survive in Coptic, Armenian, and Greek, and most significantly the sixth-century Latin epitome of Gregory of Tours. The latter permits an overall understanding of the shape and contents of the text. As J.-M. Prieur observes, "[Gregory's] Latin summary of this book preserves the basic features of the narrative framework, and for this reason it is priceless."[41] Having this epitome thus means that the surviving fragments can be placed in the correct order, as well as allowing for an appreciation of the gaps that now exist between the extant fragments.

The only surviving reference to Peter in this text occurs in a visionary experience, set atop a mountain. Although there are resonances with the transfiguration account, this is not a retelling of that incident. Peter is named four times, but in many ways his role is incidental.

> And lo, there stood by me my beloved brethren the apostles Peter and John; and John reached his hand to Peter and raised him to the top of the mountain, and turned to me and asked me to go up after Peter, saying: "Andrew, you are to drink Peter's cup." (*Acts of Andrew* 20)

The purpose of the reference to Peter is to communicate that Andrew will also partake of the "cup" of martyrdom as Peter had. If the *Acts of Andrew* predates the *Acts of Peter*, then traditions concerning Peter's martyrdom may had been circulating prior to the latter text. Perhaps this is due to early knowledge of Peter's martyrdom as suggested by the final chapter of John's Gospel (John 21:18). Here, however, the text seeks to foreshadow the martyrdom of Andrew, which will be depicted later in the text, by linking it with the presumably better-known martyrdom account of Peter. The text also utilizes the familiar element of a central trio of apostles. Although here James is displaced (cf. Mark 9:2) to make room for Andrew.

---

41. J.-M. Prieur, "Andrew, Acts of," *ABD* 1:244-47, here p. 245.

Acts of Peter

The literary remains of the *Acts of Peter* are more extensive than those of the *Acts of Andrew*. Again, however, the extant portion of the text is lacunose, with perhaps only two-thirds surviving (based on the *Stichometry of Nicephorus*, the ninth-century patriarch of Constantinople, which states that the text was 2,750 lines in length). The largest surviving fragment is found in the Latin Codex Vercellenis 158 (sixth to seventh century).[42] The text contains numerous noncanonical traditions relating to Peter. There is a special focus on Peter's opposition to Simon Magus, which climaxes with a miracle contest between the two in Rome. The text also contains an account of Peter's martyrdom. Given that this martyrdom account survives separately "as the *Martyrdom of Peter* in three Greek manuscripts and in Coptic (fragmentary), Syriac, Ethiopic, Arabic, Armenian, and Slavonic versions,"[43] this section of the text may have had a earlier circulation prior to its incorporation into the *Acts of Peter*.

In the *Acts of Peter* the text never addresses Peter as "Simon" or "Simon Peter." The reason for this is obvious. The name Simon is reserved for the villain of the text, Simon Magus. The opening chapters of the version of the *Acts of Peter* contained in Codex Vercellenis 158 contain no reference to Peter. Consequently it has been questioned whether the first three chapters actually formed part of the earliest text of the *Acts of Peter*. Chapters four and five introduce the main protagonists, Simon Magus and Peter, in that order. Peter is shown to be the recipient of divine visions, and according to the text, as the recipient of revelation he travels to Rome in the foreknowledge that his task is to confront Simon Magus.

> Peter then, admonished by the vision, related it unto the brethren without delay, saying: It is necessary for me to go up unto Rome to fight with the enemy and adversary of the Lord and of our brethren. (*Acts of Peter* 5)

Although the confrontation is delayed in the narrative, this sets up the key tension that drives the story line forward. The conflict with Simon Magus occupies sections 12-18, 23-32. In this material Peter is portrayed as the defender of the true teachings of Christ in the face of the deviant ideas promulgated by

---

42. It is also suggested that the text was composed in Asia Minor rather than in Rome, where the text is set. R. F. Stoops, "Peter, Acts of," *ABD* 5:244-47, here p. 267.

43. Stoops, "Peter, Acts of," p. 267.

Simon. The protracted stages in the miracle confrontation come to a climax with Simon promising a final conclusive miracle:

> For tomorrow I shall forsake you, you godless and impious ones, and fly up unto God whose Power I am, though I am become weak. Whereas, you have fallen, I stand. I shall ascend to my Father and say to him, "I am also your son who stands. They have desired to pull me down, but I consented not with them, but returned back to myself." (*Acts of Peter* 31[2])

Simon does not disappoint the assembled inhabitants of Rome, who on the next day see him flying over the temples and hills of the city. At this point the narrative notes the presence of "believers" who look to Peter in a plaintive desire for a response. Neither does Peter disappoint.

> And beholding the incredible spectacle Peter cried to the Lord Jesus Christ, "If you allow him to do what he has undertaken, all who believe in you will be overthrown, and the signs and wonders which you have shown to them through me will not be believed. Make haste, O Lord, show your grace and let him fall from the height and be disabled but let him not die; but let him be brought to nothing, and break his leg in three places. And he fell from the height and broke his leg in three places." And they cast stones at him and went away home having faith in Peter. (*Acts of Peter* 32[3])

The outcome of the story is no less gory. Simon undergoes corrective surgery on his leg, but dies during the operation. Although Simon's miracle is undoubtedly more spectacular, it is Peter who bests the arch-heretic, and according to the story line preserves the true faith. From here the narrative quickly moves to its close, with one of the most famous noncanonical stories concerning Peter — the account of his martyrdom.

The so-called *Martyrdom of Peter* circulated independently of the *Acts of Peter*, but there are reasons for understanding the form in the *Acts of Peter* as being the earliest form preserved.[44] It contains perhaps what are the best known of the apocryphal traditions surrounding Peter. The two most familiar are the *Quo vadis* story, and the depiction of Peter being crucified upside down. It is difficult to tell whether these legendary events found their origin in the *Acts of Peter* or were preexisting elements incorporated into this text.

---

44. The form of the martyrdom story was both incorporated into and expanded to form other later texts. See Stoops, "Peter, Acts of," p. 268.

Given the increased frequency of martyrdom accounts from the second half of the second century onward, it may be the case that the earliest form of the *Acts of Peter* was in fact the origin of these two stories.[45]

The *Quo vadis* story portrays Peter as a special figure whose safety is a concern to believers in Rome, and one who is worthy to receive a visionary encounter with the risen Christ. After being encouraged to quit Rome to preserve his life, Peter responds that believers should not behave like deserters. This statement may have both a pastoral and corrective function for those who faced the possibility of martyrdom. This might be particularly relevant, especially if the account was written in Asia Minor as is often proposed. Perhaps originally in a milieu where there were early outbreaks of persecution, the text counsels against fleeing from martyrdom. Peter, however, is persuaded by fellow believers that he can continue serving the Lord if he leaves the city; and upon reflection he acquiesces to this advice. Whether this vacillation is picking up portrayals of Peter in the canonical Gospels (such as his denial of Jesus) is hard to tell. There are no direct literary parallels, and even the conceptual affinities are only slight. So it may be best to think of these details as forming an independent narrative device. The *Acts of Peter* reports that, after departing through "the gate," Peter sees Jesus entering into Rome, whereupon the following dialogue ensues:

> And when he saw him, he said, "Lord, where are you going?" And the Lord said to him, "I go to Rome to be crucified." And Peter said to him, "Lord, are you being crucified again?" He said to him, "Yes, Peter, I am being crucified again." And Peter came to himself, having seen the Lord ascending into heaven. Then he returned to Rome, rejoicing, and glorifying the Lord, because he said, "I am being crucified," which was about to happen to Peter. (*Acts of Peter* 35[6])

In this manner, the narrative casts Peter as an exemplary martyr going willingly and in full knowledge of the fate that was about to befall him.

This, therefore, is the key text that instantiates traditions about the mar-

---

45. Frend describes the period of 165-180 as "the years of crisis" for the church in terms of growing aggression both intellectual and physical in nature. The joint reigns of Marcus Aurelius and Lucius Verus were remembered as a time when "very great persecution again disturbed Asia" (*H.E.* iv.15.1). Further, Frend notes that such persecutions "continued until the end of Marcus Aurelius' reign with their main impact in 164-168 and 176-178, and they had the full weight of public opinion behind them": W. H. C. Frend, *Martyrdom and Persecution in the Early Church* (Oxford: Blackwell, 1965), p. 268.

tyrdom of Peter in Rome. It also contains the legend of Peter's inverted crucifixion (*Acts of Peter* 37[8]). However, since the accompanying explanation of the inverted crucifixion is so heavily infused with a mythical protology, which explains how one is born with the head facing down to the earth, it may be supposed that the form of death described was created in order to legitimate the theology of cosmic origins that follows in the text. Though there is a tendency to read John 21:18-19 as a description of Peter's crucifixion, this view of the verses more likely involves reading later noncanonical traditions back into the Johannine account.[46] Hence, at times the description of Peter's martyrdom in the *Acts of Peter* is invoked almost as proof of such an interpretation of John 21:18-19.[47] However, the stretching out of hands (presumably to be bound) and being led by another (v. 18) simply describe an involuntary death, not a precise mode of execution.[48]

This text of the *Acts of Peter* focuses on the figure of Peter, yet it makes only a few extended connections with canonical traditions. Such links function as starting points or hooks on which the author can hang a creative and new narrative. The *Acts of Peter* has two main purposes. First, it serves to co-opt Peter as a defender of mainstream Christianity against certain alternative forms that are seen as deviant by the author. To this end, Simon Magus becomes the focal point for vividly instructing believers that they must maintain their commitment to apostolic-based Christianity. In this text, the Magus is a stereotypical representation of all heretical influences, as judged by the intended readers of this work. Second, the text strongly promotes a martyrological fervor, with Peter presented as the key example of the martyr's faith and resilience. In these ways, the portrayal of Peter is radically reshaped to serve contemporary needs rather than accuracy or historical connections.

---

46. E.g., G. R. Beasley-Murray, *John*, WBC 36 (Waco: Word, 1987), p. 408. Perhaps the earliest extant example of this type of interpretation is found in Tertullian *Scorpiace* 15 (PL 2:151B): "another fastened Peter with a belt when he was bound to the cross."

47. After referring to the *Acts of Peter*, Lincoln states, "The consistency about the basic tradition of crucifixion in Rome makes it likely that the readers of John 21 would also have understood Peter's martyrdom to have also taken place in that city during the Neronian persecutions": Andrew T. Lincoln, *The Gospel according to John*, BNTC (London: Continuum, 2005), p. 519.

48. This is perhaps most clearly observed by Rudolf Bultmann, who states that the phrase "you will stretch out your hands" (John 21:18), "is neither to be related to crucifixion . . . nor does it relate to a criminal." Rudolf Bultmann, *The Gospel of John: A Commentary* (Oxford: Blackwell, 1971), p. 713 n. 7.

Acts of Paul

Perhaps the best known of the major apocryphal acts, the *Acts of Paul* was also the longest according to the *Stichometry of Nicephorus,* 3,600 lines, of which approximately 2,600 survive.[49] Although various Greek fragments exist, the most extensively preserved text is in "the fifth-sixth century Heidelberg manuscript (P.Heid.) [which] contains extensive remains of the whole of the Acts of Paul."[50]

It is not entirely certain, however, whether the *Acts of Paul* mentions Peter. J. K. Elliott presents only a brief portion of text set in Tyre,[51] although he notes that M. R. James adds certain fragments found in C. Schmidt's reconstruction.[52] According to his presentation of the fragments, James postulates that Paul has arrived in Jerusalem and met with Peter there.[53] The fragmentary text reads:

> through Paul. But . . . was troubled because of the questioning (examination) that (was come) upon Peter . . . and he cried out, saying: Verily, God is one, and there is no God beside him: one also is Jesus Christ his Son, whom we . . . this, whom you preach, did we crucify, whom . . . expect in great glory, but you say that he is God and Judge of the living and the dead, the King of the ages, for the . . . in the form of man.

Given the state of this fragment and the speculative nature of its placement by James in relation to Schmidt's reconstruction, it is uncertain whether the figure of Peter actually appeared in the *Acts of Paul.* If he did, then the fragmentary nature of this depiction of the incidents allows one to say very little beyond the fact that Peter is presented as a well-known figure, who had been subject to some kind of cross-examination. In short, apart from attesting the wide circulation of traditions pertaining to Peter, this fragment offers little insight into the specific details of his characterization.

---

49. Nicephorus was patriarch of Constantinople from April 12, 806 until March 13, 815.

50. The Coptic text was restored by piecing together about two thousand fragments from the badly mutilated P.Heid. See Elliott, *Apocryphal New Testament,* p. 352.

51. Elliott, *Apocryphal New Testament,* p. 376.

52. C. Schmidt, *Acta Pauli aus der Heidelberger Kopischen Papyrushandschrift Nr 1* (Leipzig, 1905; repr., Hildesheim: Gerstenberg, 1965), *Tafelband,* with German trans. (Leipzig, 1904; repr., Hildesheim: Gerstenberg, 1965).

53. James, *Apocryphal New Testament,* p. 287.

Acts of John

Peter is depicted on three occasions in the reconstructed text of the *Acts of John*.[54] The first reference is a "historical flashback" to a scene known in the canonical Gospels. A lady named Drusiana relates to the assembled company her vision of a polymorphic appearance of the Lord "in the likeness of John, and in that of a youth" (*Acts of John* 87).[55] In support of Drusiana, and in order to defend the normalcy of her vision, John recounts the call of the four apostles beside the Sea of Galilee when, according to this version of the story, Jesus appears to James and John in different guises.

> For when he had chosen Peter and Andrew, who were brothers, he came to me, and James my brother, saying: I have need of you, come unto me. And my brother hearing that, said: John, what would this child have that is upon the seashore and called us? And I said: What child? And he said to me again: The one that is beckoning to us. And I answered: Because of our long watch we have kept at sea, you do not see correctly, my brother James; do you not see the man that stands there, comely and fair and of a cheerful countenance? But he said to me: Him I see not, brother; but let us go forth and we shall see what he would have. (*Acts of John* 88)

In this context, Peter and Andrew simply are introduced to point to a familiar scene in the canonical Gospel story line. The character of Peter is neither developed nor explained in this context.

There is slightly greater development in the character of Peter in the second, related scene that depicts him. The transfiguration story is also described with the accent on the multiple transformed appearance of the Lord. John describes the mountain experience introducing the incident as the time when the Lord "had taken with him me and James and Peter to the mountain" (*Acts of John* 90). As in the previous example, here also Peter is named to refer to a well-known Gospel story. However, in the next section a further detail is pro-

---

54. The composite text is reconstructed from fragments preserved in different manuscripts. The reconstructed form may bring together stories from different sources with differing theological perspectives. A Valentinian influence appears to pervade the outlook of chapters 94-102, 109, but is not present in other sections such as the immediately preceding chapters 87-93. See E. Junod and J.-D. Kaestli, eds., *Acta Iohannis*, vol. 1, *Praefatio — Textus*, vol. 2, *Textus alii — Commentarius — Indices*, CCSA 1-2 (Turnhout: Brepols, 1983).

55. For a discussion of polymorphic appearances in this text see Paul Foster, "Polymorphic Christology: Its Origins and Development in Early Christianity," *JTS* 58 (2007): 66-99.

vided that reveals a character trait common to Peter and James, but not part of the canonical transfiguration story. According to the narrative, Peter and James become annoyed with their fellow apostle John because he did not permit the Lord to have solitude, but spoke with him privately on the mountain.

> But Peter and James were angry because I spoke with the Lord, and they beckoned to me that I should come to them and leave the Lord alone. And I went, and they both said to me: He (the old man) that was speaking with the Lord upon the top of the mount, who was he? For we heard both of them speaking. And I, having in mind his great grace, and his unity which hath many faces, and his wisdom which without ceasing looks upon us, said: That you shall learn if you inquire of him. (*Acts of John* 91)

There appears to be more going on here than simply a concern over the Lord having his solitude interrupted. John is portrayed as enjoying a greater level of perception concerning the nature of the Lord than either Peter or James. It is not the case that those two apostles are passive dullards, however. Instead, they actively attempt to hinder John from gaining deeper insight by beckoning him away from the Lord. Although not greatly developed, here again, Peter is portrayed as a figure of constraint, or control by those promoting a form of Christianity that was not part of the emergent mainstream strand of the religion.[56]

Acts of Thomas

The *Acts of Thomas* is the only complete AAA text among the five early major acts, being preserved in Syriac, which is now commonly understood as the original language of this text.[57] References to Peter are only slightly more numerous in the *Acts of Thomas* than in the *Acts of Paul*. The first reference to Peter occurs in the opening sentence of the text, with him being named at the head of a list of eleven apostles. (This is a post-Pentecost list, with Judas Iscariot

56. Some Greek manuscripts contain a further reference to Peter in the description of events after the death and interment of John: "On the next day we dug in the place, and we did not find him, but only his sandals. And the earth was springing up like a well, and after that we remembered what was spoken by the Lord to Peter."

57. The most convenient English translation is A. F. J. Klijn, *The Acts of Thomas: Introduction, Text, and Commentary,* 2nd rev. ed., NovTSup 108 (Leiden: Brill, 2003). The standard edition of the Syriac text remains that of William Wright, *Apocryphal Acts of the Apostles* (1871; repr., Amsterdam: Olms, 1968).

absent because of his death.) The text opens "And when all the apostles had been for a time in Jerusalem, — Simon Cephas and Andrew . . , they divided the countries among them . . ." (*Acts of Thomas* 1).[58] Apart from naming Peter as "Simon Cephas" the text shows little interest in him. Only the assignment of India to Judas Thomas is mentioned. Readers are not informed of the allocation of lands to other apostles. The author's focus is not on Peter or any other of the apostles at this point; they are used as a device to connect the ensuing ministry of Thomas with the canonical Acts, and to legitimize that activity by having it under the purview and shared responsibility of the Eleven collectively.

The second reference to Peter is tangential to the main point being made. Commending the virtue of humility, the *Acts of Thomas* gives the following as an illustration.

> And humility is a mighty power, for our Lord said to Simon the Apostle: "Return your sword back (to its sheath); if I am willing to ask strength of my father, he will give me more than twelve legions of angels." (*Acts of Thomas* 86)

The form of the citation stands closer to Syriac tradition of the canonical version of this incident (John 18:11; cf. Matt. 26:52).[59] More significant for the purpose of our discussion is that Peter is not designated by that name, but is called Simon. Like the previous reference to him as "Simon Cephas," this may be avoidance of a Greek name in preference for one that would have been more familiar to Syriac readers. However, apart from these two incidental references to Peter, the *Acts of Thomas* shows no interest in the figure of Peter, and concentrates the story on Thomas, after whom the text is named.

Acts of Philip

Among the later AAA texts, the *Acts of Philip* is one of the longest accounts, especially in the form recently discovered at the Xenophontos monastery in Greece. The critical edition of the text ascribes a minor role to Peter in a few scenes in this lengthy text.[60]

---

58. F. C. Burkitt notes that "the list of Apostles at the beginning of the Acts of Thomas tallies exactly with that of S (*scil.* Syr s) in Matt. X 2-4, but with no other authority." F. C. Burkitt, *Evangelium Da-Mepharresche* (Cambridge, 1904), 2:104.

59. Klijn, *Acts of Thomas*, p. 174.

60. See François Bovon, Bertrand Bouvier, and Frédéric Amsler, eds., *Acta Philippi*, vol. 1

The first series of references to Peter occurs at the beginning of the third act, when Philip arrives in the region of Parthia. Philip addresses Peter and others in a highly reverential fashion. In this way the text appears to derive a status for Philip through the authorization that is given to him by Peter and also later John as well. The opening of the third act relates the encounter in the following fashion:

> When Philip, the apostle of Christ, arrived in the realm of Parthia, suddenly he encountered in a certain city Peter, the apostle of Christ, along with the other disciples with him as well as some women, who were imitating the male faith. Philip said to Peter and those with him: "I beg you, inspired ones, I beg you who have received the crown of Christ in the apostolic order, strengthen me also, so that when I depart I might preach the gospel and be numbered among you in your glory in the heavens and in the zeal, delight, mortification of the flesh, and courageous heart of those who are humble in continence." (*Acts of Philip* 3.1)

The request results in the apostolic company engaging in prayer on behalf of Philip. As the narrative unfolds, Philip describes his ministry in Athens (*Acts of Philip* 2), and requests prayer from both John and Peter in order that, in his own words, "I too might perfect my apostleship just as the Lord has entrusted it to me" (*Acts of Philip* 3.3). Here, Peter is portrayed positively as a source of authority, and his endorsement of Philip reveals a solidarity of purpose between the apostles.

The next reference to Peter may reflect an awareness of a tradition also found in the *Acts of Thomas* concerning the apostles being apportioned a specific geographical area for their ministry. Whereas in the *Acts of Thomas* only Thomas's geographical region is explicitly described, in the *Acts of Philip* there is a fuller list matching apostles with regions. This, however, is a narratival device that both allows for a description of Philip's disappointment over his allotted area, and, in line with the picaresque nature of this text, allows the narrative to progress to its next episodic location. Unsurprisingly, Peter is allocated the city of Rome, which according to tradition was the place of his martyrdom.

Textus, CCSA 11 (Turnhout: Brepols, 1999); and F. Amsler, ed., *Acta Philippi,* vol. 2, *Commentarius — Indices,* CCSA 12 (Turnhout: Brepols, 1999). For a recent English translation see François Bovon and C. R. Matthews, *The Acts of Philip: A New Translation* (Waco: Baylor University Press, 2012).

> When the Savior divided the apostles according to city and region so that each one of them might proceed to the place that had been appointed to them by lot, just as they were assigned, the lot came first to Peter to depart for Rome. (*Acts of Philip* 8.1)

Here the *Acts of Philip* weaves into its narrative a well-known and strongly attested tradition concerning Peter. The text relates the travels and activities of Philip, but it achieves this not by ignoring or denigrating other apostolic figures such as Peter but by portraying Philip's activities as consonant with theirs. In this way Philip gains legitimation by acting in the same way as the other apostles and with their explicit support.

The second reference to Peter in the eighth act is fascinating because of what it reveals about the textual knowledge of the author of the *Acts of Philip*, and perhaps also concerning the canonical status of the Petrine epistles. Philip continues bemoaning the fact that he had been apportioned "the land of the Greeks," since he fears they will reject his message and he will return evil for evil. The Savior tells Philip that this is a great opportunity for him and a potential blessing to resist returning evil. The Savior also recalls the time of the Watchers, and the forgiveness that was extended to the pairs of animals that entered the ark. The text states,

> This is also why your brother Peter remembered what had been done by Noah on the day of the punishment of the sinners and said to me: "Do you wish me to forgive my brother up to seven times, in the same way that Noah forgave?" And I answered him: "I do not wish you to act according to Noah's model alone, but you are to forgive seventy times seven." Now then, Philip, do not be faint-hearted about doing good to those who do evil to you. (*Acts of Philip* 8.12)

Although the inquiry concerning how many times one should forgive a brother takes up Peter's question in Matthew 18:21, the comment about Noah does not come from that context. However, the reference to Peter remembering Noah appears to recall at least one text from the Petrine epistles, most likely 2 Peter 2:4-5, with its dual reference to the angels who sinned and the depiction of Noah as a preacher of righteousness.[61] Alternatively, the text might be recalling

---

61. As Richard J. Bauckham observes, "The story of the Watchers was closely connected with the flood (in *1 Enoch* the flood comes as a consequence of the activity of the Watchers and their sons), and this connection is found in other examples of the traditional paraenetic

1 Peter 3:19-20 with its description of Christ's proclamation to the spirits in prison who were disobedient in the days of Noah.[62] Or the reference in *Acts of Philip* could be to a pastiche of these Petrine traditions. In any case, the reference to Peter here functions to promote a forgiving attitude. The ability of the author to readily make these literary links to the Petrine epistles probably reflects the later date of the text, and the positive and unproblematic portrayal of Peter suggests that the text was written broadly within the parameters of mainstream Christianity.

The final tradition relating to Peter in the *Acts of Philip* also reflects a tradition known from other writings. Discussing the temptation of lustful thoughts in relation to women, the *Acts of Philip* uses Peter as an example of overcoming such a disposition (although the answer to his prayer is extremely distasteful to modern sensibilities).

> For this reason our brother Peter fled from every place in which a woman was present. But he was still in danger of falling into scandal over his own daughter, and he prayed to the Lord, and she was paralyzed on her side so that she might not be deceived. (*Acts of Philip* 15.36)

Although not part of the extensive Codex Vercellenis text of the *Acts of Peter*, this compressed version of the story of Peter's paralyzed daughter provides a different reason for her affliction than that contained in the *Acts of Peter* fragment contained in Codex Berol. 8502.4. In the *Acts of Philip* Peter's daughter is a paralytic in order that Peter may be kept from "falling into scandal over his own daughter." Given the foregoing discussion in the *Acts of Philip*, this would appear to be a case of one who "gazes at a woman and desires her in his heart" (*Acts of Philip* 15.36). However, if readers are assumed to be familiar with the tradition in the *Acts of Peter* (Berol. 8502.4), then this may relate to others being tempted by Peter's daughter and her potential loss of sexual purity is viewed as possible cause of scandal for Peter.

---

schema which this passage follows (3 Macc 2:4; *T. Napht.* 3:5)." Richard J. Bauckham, *Jude, 2 Peter*, WBC 50 (Waco: Word, 1983), p. 249.

62. In relation to the tradition in 1 Peter, John H. Elliott notes that during the Second Temple period there was an intense focus on the angelic rebellion and the salvation of Noah and his family. He states, however, "that this Petrine text as a whole (vv. 19-22) has no complete parallel in either Israelite or contemporary Christian sources and represents an *original contribution* of the Petrine author." John H. Elliott, *1 Peter*, AB 37B (New York: Doubleday, 2000), p. 656.

Peter said unto them: As the Lord lives this is good for her and for me [his daughter's paralysis]. For on the day when she was born to me I saw a vision, and the Lord said unto me: "Peter, this day is a great temptation born unto thee, for this daughter will bring hurt unto many souls if her body continue whole." . . . Now when the girl was ten years old, a stumbling block was prepared for many by reason of her. And a very rich man, Ptolemy by name, when he saw the girl with her mother bathing, sent for her to take her to wife; but her mother consented not. And he sent often for her, since he could not wait. . . . Ptolemy brought the girl and laid her down before the door of the house and departed. But when I perceived it, I and her mother, we went down and found the maiden, that one whole side of her body from her toes even to her head was palsied and withered: and we bore her away, praising the Lord which had preserved his handmaid from defilement and shame and (corruption?). This is the cause of the matter, why the maiden remains so to this day. (*Acts of Peter*, Berol. 8502.4)

Again, by the time the *Acts of Philip* is composed there are rich and varied Petrine traditions available to the author. He employs these with great dexterity, although his main character is not Peter. This suggests that such traditions were possibly in wide circulation.

Acts of Peter and the Twelve Apostles

This text is the only tractate that fits the genre of acts literature among the Nag Hammadi corpus. D. M. Parrott and Robert McL. Wilson divide the text into four sections.[63] The first (1.1–2.10) sets the scene and introduces Peter as the first-person narrator.[64] In the second section (2.10–5.18) Peter meets a pearl merchant eventually named as Lithargoel. In the third section (5.19–8.11) Peter and his friends travel to Lithargoel's city. In the final section (8.11–12.19) Lithargoel appears as a physician, but confirms his identity as "Jesus Christ, the Son of the living God" (9.11-12).

The beginning of the text is broken, but opens with a group of disciples making a ship voyage. Upon arrival at a small city Peter speaks on behalf of the group and enquires about the name of the place. He is given a meta-

---

63. D. M. Parrott and R. McL. Wilson, "The Acts of Peter and the Twelve Apostles (VI,1)," in *The Nag Hammadi Library*, ed. James M. Robinson (Leiden: Brill, 1996), p. 287.
64. Parrott and Wilson, "Acts of Peter and the Twelve Apostles," p. 287.

phorical answer by the residents: "The name of this city is Habitation, that is, Foundation [. . .] endurance" (2.2-4). The chief point here in relation to Peter is that he is presented as the spokesperson for the group, implying some kind of authority or leadership role. The first-person narrative continues with Peter describing his role in seeking lodgings for the group. Upon meeting a stranger who Peter believes may be able to help him find lodgings, Peter addresses him as "my brother and my friend" (2.35). The stranger then commends this form of address, and declares himself to be a fellow stranger. He then immediately breaks off the conversation ostensibly to sell pearls, crying out "pearls, pearls." However, when the rich gather he refuses to reveal anything to them. Peter disappears from the narrative at this juncture, and is mentioned again only after the man offers beggars the opportunity to receive something of value at no cost. Here the story may be playing off the parable of the pearl (Matt. 13:45-46); however, if that is the case the brief parable has grown into a full-fledged narrative. Throughout the narrative Peter functions as a dialogue partner who permits Lithargoel to disclose whatever information he chooses.

After Lithargoel is disclosed to Peter as being Jesus Christ, the disciples are commanded to return to the city called Habitation, where they are to endure the hardships of faith, and to provide for the poor. In response to this command,

> Peter answered and said to him, "Lord, you have taught us to forsake the world and everything in it. We have renounced them for your sake. What we are concerned about (now) is the food for a single day. Where will we be able to find the needs that you ask us to provide for the poor?"
>
> The Lord answered and said, "O Peter, it was necessary that you understand the parable that I told you! Do you not understand that my name, which you teach, surpasses all riches, and the wisdom of God surpasses gold, and silver and precious stone(s)?" (10.14-30)

Although the text may reflect encratite tendencies in the prohibition of eating meat, it is not otherwise ascetic, nor does it promote any highly developed cosmology.[65] Rather, Peter and the apostles are presented as examples of world-denying faith, and their evangelistic commitment and unwavering commitment to the message of Jesus likely were intended to make this an exemplary text for readers.[66] Peter is portrayed as an example of apostolic

---

65. Parrott and Wilson, "Acts of Peter and the Twelve Apostles," p. 289.

66. It has been noted that codex VI in the NHC is not itself "gnostic" but a miscellany of spiritual writings. Parrott and Wilson, "Acts of Peter and the Twelve Apostles," p. 289.

faith, as understood by the author of this text. There are very few links with his role in the canonical traditions beyond that of him being a representative spokesperson for the disciples.

Noncanonical Epistles and Apocalypses

The decision to treat apocryphal letters and apocalypses together here is not simply a matter of convenience. Nor does it reflect simply the fact that non-canonical epistles do not occur with great frequency.[67] Rather, in the main noncanonical letter where Peter is mentioned, the *Epistula Apostolorum*, although the text commences in epistolary form its genre soon changes to that of an apocalypse. So while in general the generic distinction between epistles and apocalypses is a meaningful one for the corpus of noncanonical literature as a whole, that distinction is less pertinent when tracing the figure of Peter within that corpus.

Epistula Apostolorum

The text known as the *Epistula Apostolorum* purports to be a letter of Jesus Christ revealed to the council of the apostles (presumably the Jerusalem Council of Acts 15). It is stated in the text that the letter "was written because of the false apostles Simon and Cerinthus, that no one should follow them" (*Ep. Apos.* 1). The purported apostolic authors list their names at the beginning of the second section.

> John, Thomas, Peter, Andrew, James, Philip, Bartholomew, Matthew, Nathanael, Judas Zelotes, and Cephas, write unto the churches of the east and the west, of the north and the south, the declaring and imparting unto you that which concerns our Lord Jesus Christ: we do write according as we have seen and heard and touched him, after that he was risen from the dead: and how that he revealed unto us things mighty and wonderful and true. (*Ep. Apos.* 2)

---

67. Elliott comments on the relatively low use of the epistolary genre in noncanonical texts: "This form was not generally used: writers preferred narrative or an apocalypse for their material as a whole." Elliott, *Apocryphal New Testament*, p. 537.

What is striking here is that among the eleven names listed Peter is mentioned in third place (not in the typical first place) and Cephas is listed in eleventh place as though he were a distinct figure from Peter in the mind of the author of this text. Given the author's knowledge of false apostles of various gospel stories (see esp. *Ep. Apos.* 5), it beggars belief that the author seems unaware that Peter and Cephas were one and the same person. Yet that appears to be the most straightforward explanation of the text as it has been preserved.

Peter appears again later in one of the historical reminiscences, when the text recalls the resurrection events. In a creative retelling of the visits to the tomb, the text recounts the appearance of the risen Lord to the women, and his instruction to go and tell the apostles that he is alive. The disciples disbelieve the women, so the women return to the tomb and tell the Lord of their unsuccessful attempt to convince the disciples of his resurrection. At this point Jesus proposes they should all go to the disciples together. On arriving, he twice addresses Peter directly.

> Come, do not be afraid. I am your master, whom you Peter denied three times; and now do you deny again? . . . But that you may know that it is I, put thy finger, Peter, into the print of the nail-prints of my hands, and you, Thomas, put your finger into the spear-wound of my side; but you, Andrew, look at my feet and see if they do not touch the ground. (*Ep. Apos.* 11)

Though Peter is not the only named apostle in this passage, he is the chief representative of the disciples' unbelief. Again, the text freely modifies the canonical tradition. Whereas in John's Gospel Thomas alone is invited to assuage his unbelief through a tactile inspection of Jesus' wounds (John 20:27),[68] here that option is first given to Peter.

Hence in the *Epistula Apostolorum* Peter traditions are creatively recast for the author's own narratival purposes. More strikingly, either due to a simple slip or because of ignorance, the author presents Peter and Cephas as separate people. This may attest the relative unimportance of Peter for the author, who wished to evoke the collective authority of the apostles, rather than understanding Peter to possess some representative primacy.

---

68. The *Epistula Apostolorum* collapses the temporal gap between Jesus' first appearance to the disciples without Thomas in which he shows his wounds (John 20:19-20), and his subsequent appearance to Thomas with the direct invitation to Thomas to touch the wounds (John 20:27). As Bultmann notes, the evangelist's mention of the wounds in John 20:20 is a forward-looking "allusion to the Thomas narrative that follows." Bultmann, *Gospel of John*, p. 691.

Apocalypse(s) of Peter

There are three texts that bear the name "*Apocalypse* (or *Revelation*) *of Peter.* Two of these are related recensions of the same text, a shorter Greek form (discovered at Akhmîm in 1886-87), as well as a longer Ethiopic form."[69] However, the third text bearing the same name, a Nag Hammadi tractate (NHC VII 3), is unrelated.

The Greek fragment bears no title, and nowhere internal to the text does it name Peter as the implied author. Notwithstanding this, it was quickly identified as a fragment of the previously nonextant *Apocalypse of Peter.* The positive reasons for this were twofold. First, the text is attributed to one of the "twelve disciples" (*Apoc. Pet.* 2), and the putative author is the spokesperson for the disciples. Second, there are passages in the text that agree with a patristic citation of the *Apocalypse of Peter.*[70] So, although the Akhmîm text is almost certainly a fragment of the *Apocalypse of Peter,* it offers little insight into the representation of Peter in noncanonical literature beyond the fact that he acts as spokesperson for the Twelve, and he becomes a type of an apocalyptic seer to whom revelatory knowledge is disclosed.[71]

By contrast, the longer Ethiopic text names Peter on several occasions. In the opening semititular line of the Ethiopic version, the work is described as relating "the second coming of Christ and resurrection of the dead which Christ revealed through Peter to those who died for their sins, because they did not keep the commandments of God, their creator" (Ethiopic *Apoc. Peter* 1).

Here Peter is cast in the role of an apocalyptic seer, after the model of the portrayals of such figures in early Jewish apocalypses (see *1 Enoch* 1; *2 Enoch* 1). This role as a figure mediating divine insight becomes explicit when Jesus exhorts his disciples to "learn a parable from the fig tree," and the text presents

69. The relationship between the surviving Ethiopic and Greek forms of the text is complex, and not yet fully resolved. The differences between the two forms reflect the fluidity in the process of textual transmission. However, both of the surviving forms are likely developments of a base text. The text is significant because it is viewed as the "earliest extant Christian document that describes Heaven and Hell." Elliott, *Apocryphal New Testament,* p. 595. Moreover, although it is often linked with the Bar Kokhba revolt (see Bauckham 1983, pp. 269-87; and Bauckham, "The *Apocalypse of Peter:* A Jewish Christian Apocalypse from the Time of Bar Kokhba," *Apocrypha* 5 (1994): 7-111, that association is not certain.

70. Clement, *Eclogae Propheticae,* 41, 48-49. See J. A. Robinson and M. R. James, *The Gospel According to Peter, and the Revelation of Peter* (Cambridge: Cray and Sons, 1892), p. 80.

71. On the role of Peter as an apocalyptic seer especially in Matthew's Gospel see John R. Markley, *Peter — Apocalyptic Seer,* WUNT 2/348 (Tubingen: Mohr Siebeck, 2013).

the following response: "And I, Peter, answered and said to him, 'Interpret the fig tree to me: how can we understand it?'" (Ethiopic *Apoc. Pet.* 2). The interpretation of the fig tree leads into Peter being given a vision of the souls of all humanity in God's right hand. Peter asks some deep metaphysical questions concerning the sinners whose fate is eternal damnation.

> Lord, allow me to speak your word concerning the sinners, "It were better for them if they had not been created." And the Savior answered and said to me: "Peter, why do you say that not to have been created were better for them? You resist God. You would not have more compassion than he for his image: for he has created them and brought them forth out of not being. Now because you have seen the lamentation that shall come upon the sinners in the last days, therefore your heart is troubled; but I will show you their works, whereby they have sinned against the Most High." (Ethiopic *Apoc. Pet.* 2)

This passage is key to the apocalyptic narrative that follows since it leads into the graphic description of torments that await those to "be punished eternally" (Ethiopic *Apoc. Pet.* 6).[72] As with seer figures in other apocalypses, Peter functions here both as a known figure and as a narratival device that allows the author of the apocalypse to disclose his own literary vision of the final judgment. Though the fig tree incident is dependent on the Synoptic tradition, it is not the content of that tradition that is important for the author of the Ethiopic *Apocalypse of Peter*. Rather, the reference to the fig tree is used to create a link with a known tradition in order to legitimize the new revelation that this text is depicting. At the end of the ensuing vivid description of hell, Peter is charged to spread the gospel since the Lord states, "My words shall be the source of hope and of life, and suddenly shall the world be ravished" (Ethiopic *Apoc. Pet.* 14). The following vision of paradise is set during a mountaintop scene, which appears to be based on the transfiguration story. This identification is made on the basis of the appearance of two men with radiant bodies and shining clothes, who are identified as Moses and Elijah. Again the *Apocalypse of Peter* links its own visionary teaching with canonical stories. The transfiguration appears to have been a particularly suitable text to redeploy, not only because of its own visionary content, but also because the command to silence and

---

72. While there is significant overlap between the extant portion of the Greek text and the Ethiopic, the ordering of the material is different. In the Greek text the vision of paradise precedes that of hell, whereas in the Ethiopic the order is different.

secrecy in the Synoptic tradition invited later authors to "reveal" more of that previously undisclosed knowledge.[73]

The Nag Hammadi *Apocalypse of Peter* is of a different character from both the Greek and Ethiopic versions of the text discussed above. The text assumes a pleromic cosmology, with the lower earthly realm being hostile to those who possess immortal souls. By contrast, the immortal soul receives its power in the form of an intellectual spirit. However, because such souls have been displaced, through the process of joining with one of those who misled them (*Apoc. Pet.,* NHC VII 3, pp. 77-78), they now exist in the lower physical realm, and are entrapped until the parousia of the Lord.

Within this text Peter once again functions as an apocalyptic seer, although the content of the teaching he receives is markedly different from the other text bearing the same name. In the Nag Hammadi text it is the Savior who initiates communication with Peter.

> As the Savior was sitting in the temple . . . he said to me, "Peter, blessed are those above belonging to the Father, who revealed life to those who are from the life, through me. . . . But you yourself, Peter, become perfect in accordance with your name with myself, the one who chose you, because from you I have established a base for the remnant whom I have summoned to knowledge." (*Apoc. Pet.* 70.14-20)

Peter is commanded to become perfect, and he himself is appointed as "a base for the remnant." Here then, Peter takes a position of priority, but it is not associated with his preeminence among the Twelve.

One interesting section involving Peter in this text is a scene that partially parallels the *Acts of John* 97.7-10. In the latter text it is John who is the central protagonist, whereas in the *Apocalypse of Peter* it is Peter who becomes Jesus' dialogue partner. Observing the crucifixion, Peter encounters three Jesus-like figures. Peter says,

> I saw him [i.e., Jesus] seemingly being seized by them. And I said, "What do I see, O Lord, that it is you yourself whom they take, and that you are grasping me? Or who is this one, glad and laughing on the tree? And is it

73. Adela Yarbro Collins also notes how the transfiguration account employs the command to silence as "an anticipation and preview of the resurrected state of Jesus." Adela Yarbro Collins, *Mark*, Hermenia (Minneapolis: Fortress, 2007), p. 429. The eschatological features of both the transfiguration and resurrection may suggest another reason why the story evoked helpful resonances in the context of an apocalyptic text.

another one whose feet and hands they are striking?" The Savior said to me, "He whom you saw on the tree, glad and laughing is the living Jesus. But the one into whose hands and feet they drive nails is his fleshly part, which is the substitute being put to shame, the one who came into being in his likeness. But look at him and look at me." (*Apoc. Pet.* 81.4-24)

In this context Peter becomes a vehicle for promoting the text's christological understanding of Jesus as a docetic redeemer figure.[74] Furthermore, the author joins "one of the core beliefs of docetism, namely that the divine Christ did not suffer, with a polymorphic christology which enable Jesus to be both the laughing figure on the cross and simultaneously engaging in discussion with Peter about what is being observed."[75]

Perhaps most strikingly in this text Peter is portrayed as a figure of resistance against ecclesial authorities. Thus the Savior describes to Peter the false leadership from such figures, and Peter's own role in confronting them.

And there shall be others of those who are outside our number who name themselves bishop and also deacons, as if they have received their authority from God. They bend themselves under the judgment of the leaders. Those people are dry canals. . . . Come, therefore, let us go on with the completion of the will of the incorruptible Father. For behold, those who will bring them judgment are coming, and they will put them to shame. But me they cannot touch. And you, O Peter, shall stand in their midst. Do not be afraid because of your cowardice. Their minds shall be closed, for the invisible one has opposed them. (*Apoc. Pet.* 79.22-30; 80.23–81.3)

This is a reinvention of Peter as a figure who supports the theology and the ecclesial opposition enshrined in the Nag Hammadi text.

The Letter of Peter to Philip

This letter is another example of a text that, despite its title, does not fit solely into the epistolary genre, but is more squarely apocalyptic. As Marvin Meyer observes, the *Letter of Peter to Philip* can perhaps be seen as a gnostic dialogue,

74. J. Brashler and R. A. Bullard, "Apocalypse of Peter (VII,3)," in *The Nag Hammadi Library*, ed. James M. Robinson (Leiden: Brill, 1996), p. 372.
75. Foster, "Polymorphic Christology," pp. 66-99.

although "it is less true a dialogue than a revelatory discourse of Christ in answer to questions raised by the apostles."[76] This text is also found among the Nag Hammadi corpus (NHC VIII 2), and is part of the wider epistolary literature among the so-called gnostics.[77]

The text opens with the titular superscript, "the letter of Peter which he sent to Philip." The author follows this title with a note of self-designation, "Peter, the apostle of Jesus Christ." The letter does not seek to delegitimate Peter's apostolic status; instead it appears to claim, or co-opt, such a status in order to provide an authority base for its own teachings. The letter becomes a vehicle to promote the cosmological understanding it presents. This is achieved through the collective question of the apostles: "Lord, we would like to know the deficiency of the aeons and their pleroma; and how are we detained in this dwelling place?" (NHC VIII 2, p. 134.20-24). Peter is portrayed as the leader of the apostolic band, and he is able to call together a meeting of the other apostles for the purpose of commissioning and instructing Philip. The gathering takes place on the Mount of Olives, where Christ appears in an epiphanic vision of great light, and is described as "an illuminator in the darkness." The bulk of the text then comprises a revelatory speech of Christ. Peter only comes to the fore at the end of this utterance. An unnamed apostle asks, "If he our Lord suffered, how much more must we?" It is Peter who provides the answer: "He suffered on our behalf, and it is necessary for us to suffer because of our smallness." (p. 138.18-20).

After the events on the Mount of Olives, the apostles return to Jerusalem, where they give instruction concerning salvation to the multitudes in the Jerusalem temple. The setting appears to be intended to evoke recollection of similar traditions in Acts (see Acts 3:1–4:37). Such a link with canonical tradition is probably an intentional device employed to give an air of historicity to this text. Peter then addresses his fellow disciples, and by implication the readers of this letter, with the rhetorical question, "Did our Lord Jesus, when he was in the body show us everything?" (p. 139.11-12). This question presents Peter as a staunch defender of the sort of postresurrection revelatory teaching that is common among various texts in the Nag Hammadi corpus. Interestingly, the same issue is at stake in the *Gospel of Mary*. However, in that text it is Peter who stands in opposition to Mary Magdalene's defense of revelatory teaching

---

76. Marvin W. Meyer, "The Letter of Peter to Philip (VIII,2)," in Robinson, *Nag Hammadi Library*, p. 433.

77. Other examples include Ptolemy's *Letter to Flora*, and Valentinus's letters. See Meyer, "Letter of Peter to Philip," p. 431.

(see BG 8502, p. 17.13-22). Here, in marked contrast, Peter is cast as the true supporter of further revelatory teaching. This is a notable development, and it calls on readers of the *Letter of Peter to Philip* to remember Peter, not as an antagonist and representative of the branch of Christianity that opposes the stance of the text, but rather as both the leader of the apostolic band and the one who legitimates the type of teaching that this epistolary text promotes. This is perhaps a more sophisticated strategy than that adopted in the *Gospel of Mary*, in that it acknowledges the centrality of Peter; but, instead of condemning him as a dull-witted representative of mainstream Christianity, the text co-opts him as being the key promoter of the views taught within it.

Conclusions

As we have seen, the figure of Peter is to be found in numerous noncanonical New Testament texts, which cover a range of genres, including gospels, acts, apocalypses, and epistles. The range of representations of the Petrine character is striking for its diversity. In some texts Peter is a figure of peripheral interest; in others he is the central heroic character. Various texts cast him as the chief opponent of postresurrection teaching, whereas in others he teaches the validity of such revelatory teaching. At times, certain texts link their own narratives to events in the canonical tradition. However, this is usually done as a strategy for legitimizing the contents or teaching of the dependent text.

Two key features stand out as repeated elements in various noncanonical texts: Peter was the leader or spokesperson of the Twelve, and he was present during the revelatory events of the transfiguration. In particular, the latter is frequently referenced, not because of the intrinsic historical value of that tradition, but because it is richly suggestive of the role of revelatory visions and apocalyptic teaching. Therefore, the Peter of the noncanonical traditions is not a figure that emerges from "memory [that] embodies the archetype of an apostolic ministry that serves the entire church."[78] Instead, the representation of Peter is both diverse and highly contested. The traditions that are found in noncanonical texts are largely literary reinventions of Peter. The various ways Peter is represented function to support the perspectives of the texts in which they are found. Thus these vastly differing representations reflect the theological concerns of the authors of the texts that have been surveyed rather than stemming from historically reliable traditions concerning Peter. Given

---

78. Bockmuehl, *Simon Peter in Scripture and Memory*, p. 183.

this diversity in a large selection of noncanonical texts, one may be pressed to consider whether traditions in canonical texts and the writings of mainstream patristic authors are any less likely to be prone to the same forces of reinvention, which serve the legitimation of theological positions. However, that is a question for another discussion.[79]

Actually, it appears that various factions in the Christian movement of the second and third centuries (and beyond) continued to contest the role of Peter. The fundamental tradition that remained fairly stable was Peter's traditional role as leader and spokesperson for the foundational band of apostles. As such, both by recasting Peter and by ascribing to him the varied theological positions advocated within the texts described here, those authors sought to provide foundational authority for their own perspectives. On occasion, however, it appears that Peter was already so heavily associated with opposing positions that the only strategy left available to certain authors of noncanonical texts was to represent him as antihero. That is especially the case in the two texts that narrate descriptions of Peter's interactions with Mary Magdalene. In the *Gospel of Thomas* the portrayal of Peter is, at best, ambivalent. He questions the legitimacy of Mary's discipleship. The Jesus of the *Gospel of Thomas* quashes this attempted denigration of Mary.[80] Although the polemic is stronger in the *Gospel of Mary*, in some ways the resolution is weaker. That is because "in the *Gospel of Mary* it is Levi who levels the conflict between Peter and Mary, in the *Gos. Thom.* 114 it is Jesus."[81]

Perhaps the greatest demonstration of the flexibility and creativity to be found in representations of Peter involves the way his attitude is portrayed in relation to postresurrection revelatory teaching in different texts. In the *Gospel of Mary* Peter stands in opposition to Mary's claim to have received new and authentic teaching from the risen Christ. By contrast, in the *Letter of Peter to Philip* it is Peter who transmits such postresurrection teaching and also advocates its legitimacy.

Concerns of second- and third-century mainstream Christianity are also projected onto the portrayal of Peter. The heresiological perspectives of the period are reflected in the *Acts of Peter*. In this text, creative imagination rather than historical tradition greatly develops the embryonic canonical story

---

79. The diversity and inventiveness of the noncanonical traditions concerning Peter appear to challenge Markus Bockmuehl's contention that such traditions were living memories that result in a reflection that "contributes materially to genuine historical questions." Bockmuehl, *Remembered Peter*, p. 16.

80. See the discussion in Plisch, *Gospel of Thomas*, pp. 245-46.

81. Plisch, *Gospel of Thomas*, p. 245.

involving Simon Magus and Peter (Acts 8:14-24). In the *Acts of Peter* these two figures are portrayed as being involved in a protracted miracle contest. This extended narrative addresses wider second-century concerns rather than drawing on reliable oral traditions or social memories of events from the first century. Therefore, the *Acts of Peter* shares the wider depiction of Simon Magus with patristic writers such as Justin and Irenaeus, and also with other noncanonical texts such as the *Acts of Peter and Paul* and the pseudo-Clementines.[82] Similarly, the account of the martyrdom of Peter in the form contained in the *Acts of Peter* also serves as a vehicle for early Christian ideology concerning the efficacy and spiritual power of martyrdom.

The figure of Peter is varied and versatile in noncanonical New Testament writings. There are very few fixed elements, and although at times connections with canonical traditions are present, the various characterizations of Peter represent considerable flexibility and freedom. Peter can be utilized as an emblematic figure, and pressed into the service of various theological agendas. At times he is represented as antihero, whose perspectives need to be negated. However, overall he is represented positively. Yet, apart from his priority among the apostles and his presence at the transfiguration, little is seen as central or essential. So who is the Peter of the noncanonical texts? Probably the simple answer is whoever the authors wanted, or needed him to be.

---

82. Pseudo-Clementine *Homilies* 2.23; *Recognitions* 2.11.

CHAPTER 17

When Did Peter Become Bishop of Antioch?

Paul Parvis

When I first proposed this title at a meeting of the CSCO committee organizing the Edinburgh conference on Peter, one of my New Testament colleagues thundered, "Never!" In one sense that is obviously true, but in another sense the answer is as anachronistic as the question itself would be if I were actually asking when as a matter of historical fact was Peter installed on the episcopal throne of Antioch.

Instead, what I want to do is to look, briefly and selectively, at the stages in which, and the mechanisms by which, meaning came to be pumped into that otherwise anachronistic question. And I am doing so in the hope that our quest will reveal not only something about the Petrine historiographical tradition but also about the changing nature of the perception — and therefore the reality — of the episcopal office in late antiquity.

Origen

We will begin, not in late antiquity, but in 1952, when Oscar Cullmann published his influential but seriously misguided *Peter: Disciple — Apostle — Martyr.*[1]

Cullmann there claims that while "the tradition of the episcopate at Antioch is exceedingly hard to defend on historical grounds . . . it must never-

---

1. Oscar Cullmann, *Peter: Disciple — Apostle — Martyr,* trans. Floyd V. Filson (London: SCM, 1953 [German 1952]).

theless be emphasized that this tradition is much older and better attested than is that of the Roman episcopate" (p. 231). The reason for his assertion is, of course, that the Antiochene tradition provides a stick with which to beat Romanist pretensions. We shall see that this is far from being the first time that competing theological claims have muddied the waters of Peter's ecclesiastical career — perhaps just as well, since without that turbidity there would be virtually nothing to see.

Cullmann's first exhibit — and the point at which all discussions of an Antiochene episcopate must perforce begin — is Origen's sixth homily on Luke, where we are told,

> Unde eleganter in cuiusdam martyris epistola scriptum repperi, Ignatium dico, episcopum Antiochiae post Petrum secundum, qui in persecutione Romae pugnavit ad bestias [which is followed by a citation of Ignatius (*Ephesians* 19)].[2]

According to Cullmann, this is evidence for "the tradition that Peter founded the church at Antioch" (p. 52). In another influential — indeed, perhaps great — though equally perverse book, *Orthodoxy and Heresy in Earliest Christianity,* Walter Bauer asserts that this text provides "the first clear witness for Peter in his office as Antiochene bishop."[3] In other words, Bauer, like Cullmann, takes "the second bishop, after Peter" to mean that Peter was the first and Ignatius the second.[4] That is obviously not the only interpretation of which that phrase is patient. It might be worth noting that we are dealing here with Jerome's translation — done, according to J. N. D. Kelly, "probably in 389/90."[5]

There happens, however, to be a Greek fragment, from the Nicetas catena on Luke. But neither the Greek nor the Latin is untroubled by manuscript variants. For the Greek, Bauer uses here De la Rue's edition of 1740.[6] Pending a

2. Origen, *Die Homilien zu Lukas,* ed. Max Rauer, Origenes Werke 9, GCS 19 (35) (Berlin: Akademie, 1959), p. 34, 23-35, 1. "And so I have found written elegantly in a letter of a certain martyr — I mean Ignatius, bishop of Antioch — the second — after Peter, who fought with the beasts in the persecution in Rome."

3. Walter Bauer, *Orthodoxy and Heresy in Earliest Christianity,* trans. Philadelphia Seminar on Christian Origins, ed. Robert A. Kraft and Gerhard Krodel (London: SCM, 1972 [German 1934]), p. 117.

4. See Bauer, *Orthodoxy,* p. 118, where the passage is cited for "the succession Peter — Ignatius."

5. J. N. D. Kelly, *Jerome: His Life, Writings, and Controversies* (London: Duckworth, 1975), p. 143.

6. Rauer, *Die Homilien,* p. 34, 24-26.

full edition of the Luke catenae (to match, for example, Françoise Petit's splendid work on the Genesis catenae) we must proceed by dead reckoning (so to speak). But it is worth at least noting that the Nicetas word order, τὸν μετὰ τὸν μακάριον Πέτρον τῆς Ἀντιοχείας δεύτερον ἐπίσκοπον, is rather more favorable to an alternative interpretation: Origen means, not "the second bishop, after Peter," but "after Peter — the second bishop" — that is, the reference is to Peter, then an unnamed other who served as bishop, and then Ignatius.

Eusebius

The second set of texts we must look at comes from Eusebius. In the *Chronicon,* in Jerome's expanded, revised, and sexed-up translation, Peter "founded" *(fundasset)* the Antiochene church and is then (in year two of the emperor Claudius) "sent to Rome where he continues as bishop *[episcopus]* of that city, preaching the Gospel, for twenty-five years."[7]

But even in reference to Rome, "bishop" is Jerome's word, not Eusebius's. The early-ninth-century *Chronography* of George Syncellus, in an entry derived from the *Chronicon,* simply says προέστη, "presided over," and the Armenian version of Eusebius says that Peter was for twenty years — not twenty-five — *arajnoṛd* of the Roman church (Abraham 2055/Caius 5).[8] Now *arajnoṛd* is quite an elastic word — it basically means "head honcho," or "big cheese." It can mean "author," "captain," "chief," "guide," "director," "guardian," "principal," "overseer," and the like. Ecclesiastically, it can mean things like "prelate," "provost," "superior." But it is not a technical word for bishop.[9] So Syncellus's προέστη, or perhaps a participial προεστώς, would do quite nicely. Elsewhere in the Armenian version of the chronicle, in relating the successions in Rome, Antioch, Alexandria, and Jerusalem, the word for "bishop" is simply "bishop" — *episcopos* transliterated into Armenian.

In the list, two years later (Claudius's fourth year as emperor), we have "Primus Antiochiae episcopus ordinatur Euodius" (p. 179, line 14 Helm), and

---

7. Eusebius of Caesarea, *Die Chronik des Hieronymus,* Eusebius Werke 7, GCS 47, ed. Rudolf Helm, 3rd ed. (Berlin: Akademie, 1984), p. 179, 7.

8. Syncellus 331d = Helm, *Die Chronik des Hieronymus,* p. 401. Armenian text of Eusebius in *Eusebii Pamphili Caesariensis episcopi chronicon bipartitum,* ed. Aucher (Venice, 1818), 2:268, dated by years from Abraham and the year of the Emperor Caius (Caligula).

9. These gloss definitions are taken from Matthias Bedrossian, *New Dictionary Armenian-English* (Venice, 1875-1879, reprinted Beirut: Libraire du Liban, n.d.), p. 39b.

the bishops are numbered regularly thereafter: Ignatius the "second bishop" (p. 186, line 16 Helm), Heron the "third" (p. 194, line 24), and so on.[10]

Eusebius's *Historia ecclesiastica* is almost innocent of any connection at all between Peter and Antioch. In recounting the Simon Magus story (*H.E.* 2.13-15), Eusebius has the Magus flee, "undertaking a very long and very troublesome journey from East to West" (3.14.4), and Peter then following him to Rome (3.14.6). In contrast with, for example, the (Vercelli) *Acts of Peter,* there is no mention of Antioch anywhere in the tale.

In 3.1 there is an echo of a *sortes apostolorum* ("departure of the apostles") narrative recounting the regions of the earth allotted to various apostles.[11] We are told of Thomas, Andrew, John, Peter, and Paul. Of Peter we learn,

> And Peter seems to have preached to Jews of the Diaspora in Pontus and Galatia and Bithynia and Cappadocia and Asia. And in the end when he was in Rome he was crucified head downwards, which was the way he had himself asked to suffer. (*H.E.* 3.1.2)

"These things," Eusebius adds, "were said word for word by Origen in the third book of his commentaries on Genesis" (3.1.3). Harnack argued that "these things" (ταῦτα) covered only the Peter and Paul materials in 3.1.2 and 1.3; Junod argued that the ταῦτα covered all five apostles.[12] For our purposes it does not much matter (though I myself find Junod's argument cogent). The point here is that there is no mention of Antioch. All we have (as Junod argues) is a geographical list drawn from 1 Peter 1:1, followed by a Roman tale derived, presumably, from the *Acts of Peter.*[13] The only time Peter is actually connected with Antioch in the whole of the *Historia ecclesiastica* is in what is virtually a throwaway remark in a list of illustrious churchmen in the time of Trajan — a list that includes Ignatius, "who was the second to be allotted the episcopacy

---

10. In Rome, while, in Jerome's version, "Post Petrum primus Romanam ecclesiam tenuit Linus" (Nero 14 = Helm, *Die Chronik des Hieronymus,* p. 185, 21-22), Anencletus is *secundus episcopus* simpliciter (Titus 2 = Helm, *Die Chronik des Hieronymus,* p. 189, 17-18); Clement, *tertius Romanae ecclesiae episcopus* (Domitian 12 = Helm, *Die Chronik des Hieronymus,* p. 191, 19-20), and so on.

11. I borrow the phrase from Scott Fitzgerald Johnson, "Apostolic Geography: The Origins and Continuity of a Hagiographic Habit," *DOP* 64 (2010): 5-25, here 17.

12. Adolf von Harnack, *Der kirchengeschichtliche Ertrag des exegetischen Arbeiten des Origenes,* TU 42.1 (Leipzig: Hinrichs, 1918), pp. 14-15.

13. Eric Junod, "Origène, Eusèbe et la tradition sur la répartition des champs de mission des apôtres (Eusèbe, Histoire ecclésiastique, III, 1, 1-3)," in *Les actes apocryphes des apôtres, Christianisme et monde païen,* ed. François Bovon et al. (Geneva: Labor et Fides, 1981), pp. 233-48.

of the succession of Peter in Antioch" (τῆς κατὰ Ἀντιόχειαν Πέτρου διαδοχῆς δεύτερος τὴν ἐπισκοπὴν κεκληρωμένος, 3.36.3).

Bauer — in keeping with his interpretation of Origen's *Homily on Luke* — naturally and perversely takes this to mean that Peter was the first bishop and Ignatius the second. That entails the conclusion that Eusebius is here contradicting what he has said earlier in the same book (at 3.22), where, in a ragbag note on bishops of various sees, he says that "of those in Antioch, Evodius was appointed the first" and Ignatius the "second." The dissonance is no problem for Bauer, who says blandly, "Each passage in itself seems to me unequivocal, and a collector such as Eusebius gives us the very least reason for forcibly harmonizing contradictory statements."[14]

For that matter, Eusebius is equally wary of calling Peter "bishop" of Rome. In *Historia ecclesiastica* 3.2 we are told, "Of the church of the Romans, after the martyrdom of Paul and Peter, Linus is the first to be allotted the episcopacy [ἐπισκοπὴν]," while in 3.4.8 he is the "first after Peter to be allotted the episcopacy." In 3.21, Clement "led" [ἡγεῖτο] the Romans and "was the third in order of those who bishoped there after Paul and Peter. And Linus was the first and after him Anencletus" (τρίτον καὶ αὐτὸς ἐπέχων τῶν τῇδε μετὰ Παῦλόν τε καὶ Πέτρον ἐπισκοπευσάντων βαθμόν. Λίνος δὲ ὁ πρῶτος ἦν καὶ μετ' αὐτὸν Ἀνέγκλητος). And finally, in 4.1, Alexander received the episcopacy, "holding down the fifth succession from Peter and Paul" (πέμπτην ἀπὸ Πέτρου καὶ Παύλου κατάγων διαδοχήν). So the norm is to trace the descent from Paul and Peter (or, less commonly, Peter and Paul). That and a passage such as 3.4.9, which speaks of Clement becoming "third bishop of the Romans" (*simpliciter*) — not third bishop after Peter/Paul — simply rules out any Baueresque reading.

I do not wish to belabor the point, but there are two things worth noting here. First, it is still true for Eusebius that apostles institute bishops — they are not themselves bishops. And second, the connection between Peter and Antioch is tenuous in the extreme.

From Eusebius to Jerome and Beyond

Toward the end of the fourth century the position is changing. In the slightly mad compilation of the *Apostolic Constitutions,* which we might, with their editor Marcel Metzger, date to the 360s or so, there is a list (a long list) of bishops of various sees whom "we" apostles have ordained.

---

14. Bauer, *Orthodoxy,* p. 118.

And concerning the bishops ordained by us in our lifetime, we make known to you that they are these. . . . And of Antioch, Evodius by me, Peter, and Ignatius by Paul. . . . And of the church of the Romans, the first, Linus, son of Claudia, was ordained by Paul, and after the death of Linus, Clement was ordained second by me, Peter. (*Ap. Con.* 7.46)

And so on — and on — and on. So, Peter and Paul now do turn and turn about, rather than jointly kicking off an episcopal succession; but Peter is still not bishop of Antioch.

In a homily of his Antiochene period, John Chrysostom sings the praises of Ignatius. The fifth "garland" he weaves in his honor is to praise Ignatius as the successor of Peter — Evodius here getting the cold shoulder! After Peter had spent "much time" in Antioch, Ignatius "succeeded to the rule" (διαδέξασθαι τὴν ἀρχήν). The analogy is with a "great stone" removed "from the foundations" of a building, which must be replaced by a new, counterpoising stone if the whole building is not to be shaken. "Now thus, when Peter was about to leave here, the grace of the spirit introduced in his place another teacher as a counterpoise to Peter" (ἕτερον ἀντίρροπον Πέτρου διδάσκαλον) (*In sanctum Ignatium martyrem*, PG 50:591).

I have no wish to enter into the near-impenetrable thicket of the redaction history of the pseudo-Clementines, but I will flag up the fact that Rufinus's version of the *Recognitions* ends with Peter being given a basilica church by a rich Antiochene convert named Theophilus, a church in which a "chair" *(cathedra)* is set up for him. But what he does from the chair is teach, and he is not called a bishop (*Rec.* 10.71-72).

We are getting close, but Peter is not yet a bishop in Antioch. He had, however, already been invested with the purple in Rome. In the so-called Liberian Catalogue, for example (included within the materials assembled by the chronographer of 354), Peter is emphatically the first bishop of Rome.

Imperante Tiberio Caesare passus est dominus noster Jesus Christus duobus Geminis cons. VIII Kal. Apr., et post ascensum eius beatissimus Petrus episcopatum suscepit.[15]

15. Text from Adolf Harnack, *Geschichte der altchristlichen Literatur bis Eusebius,* Part 2, *Die Chronologie* (Leipzig: Hinrichs, 1897), 1:144. "Our Lord Jesus Christ suffered under the emperor Tiberius Caesar in the consulship of the two Gemini on the eighth day before the Kalends of April, and after his ascension the most blessed Peter received the episcopacy. . . ."

And the list then continues triumphantly with the names, dates, and lengths of reign of the bishops from Peter to Liberius. But what about Antioch?

We have already looked at Jerome's translation of Origen's *Homilies on Luke.* A couple of years earlier (probably in 387/388) Jerome had commented on Paul's letter to the Galatians.[16] In the course of the commentary he becomes embroiled in a fairly labored refutation of Clement of Alexandria's suggestion that the "Cephas" whom Paul "resisted face to face" (Gal. 2:11) was not Cephas/Peter the apostle, but someone else (one of the Seventy) of the same name. The last of his arguments is that Luke's silence about the incident in Acts is no obstacle, since he also omitted the relevant and salient fact that Peter was the first bishop of Antioch.

Denique primum episcopum Antiochenae ecclesiae Petrum fuisse accepimus, Romam exinde translatum, quod Lucas penitus omisit.[17]

A couple of years after the *Homilies on Luke,* Jerome produced his catalog of notable ecclesiastics and writers, *De viris illustribus,* beginning with Peter and ending with himself.[18] Much of the entry on Peter (like most of the early entries) relies heavily and tacitly on Eusebius, but Jerome does say,

Simon Petrus . . . post episcopatum Antiochensis ecclesiae et praedicationem dispersionis eorum qui de circumcisione crediderant, in Ponto, Galatia, Cappadocia, Asia et Bithynia, secundo Claudii anno, ad expugnandum Simonem magum, Romam pergit ibique viginti quinque annis cathedram sacerdotalem tenuit usque ad ultimum annum Neronis, id est, quartum decimum.[19]

So we now have a twenty-five-year episcopate in Rome and before that — and explicitly — an episcopate in Antioch. So to find out exactly when he became bishop of Antioch, all we now have to know is when Peter was mar-

---

16. Kelly, *Jerome,* p. 145.

17. Jerome, *Commentarii in Epistulam Pauli Apostoli ad Galatas,* ed. Giacomo Raspanti, CCSL 77A (Turnhout: Brepols, 2006). "Finally, we have received that Peter was the first bishop of Antioch and translated from there to Rome — something that Luke completely omitted."

18. According to Kelly, "There is general agreement" the *De viris illustribus* belongs "somewhere between 19 January 392 and 18 January 393, probably towards the close of the span," though others have argued for "the second half of 393" (*Jerome,* p. 174).

19. Jerome, *De viris illustribus,* ed. E. C. Richardson, TU 14.1 (Leipzig: Hinrichs, 1896), p. 6, lines 21-29.

tyred — presumably in 64 — and how long his episcopate in Antioch lasted. Gregory the Great (*Epp.* vii.37), like the *Liber Pontificalis,* says seven years; Nicephorus, eleven.

We might note how neatly all this fits into Jerome's program of self-aggrandizement. He had left Rome in some disarray after the death of Damasus and by 386 was settled in Bethlehem. In the great burst of literary and scholarly activity that followed he was busy positioning himself as the learned and industrious importer of Greek ecclesiastical culture to the Latin West — a Latin West that had shown itself to be insufficiently appreciative of his gifts and of his person. In those circumstances it suited the translator of Origen quite well to be able to speak of Peter as bishop of Antioch, translated thence to Rome.

Does that mean it was Jerome who made Peter bishop of Antioch? Not really, although his role in disseminating the myth — at least in the West — was not negligible. In his Galatians commentary, Jerome said either "we have received" *(accepimus)* or "we do receive" *(accipimus)* that Peter was bishop there. The former presumably means "we have received (from tradition)," and the latter, "we accept (as one claim among others?)." Giacomo Raspanti (the editor of the magnificent critical edition in CCSL) reads *accepimus,* although the evidence is fairly neatly balanced between the two families into which he divides the ample manuscript tradition.[20]

In any event, Peter's grip on the see of Antioch was never as secure in the East as in the West. Malalas, seemingly, and the *Chronicon Paschale,* certainly, for example, accept the tradition, the former adding helpfully that Peter not only taught in Antioch but also "enthroned himself" there.[21] On the other hand, the industrious twelfth-century chronicler Michael the Syrian makes Evodius the first bishop, with no place at all for Peter.[22]

Who? Why? When?

Two interrelated questions suggest themselves: *cui bonum?* and why? Harnack attributes the growth of the legend of Peter in Antioch essentially to me-too-

20. Jerome, *Commentarii.*

21. Malalas 248, lines 8-22; *Chronicon Paschale* 421, lines 5-8 (Bonn). See the references collected in "Excursus 3, Peter in Antioch," in *A History of Antioch in Syria, from Seleucus to the Arab Conquest,* ed. Glanville Downey (Princeton: Princeton University Press, 1961), pp. 583-86.

22. Michael the Syrian 6.2, in *Chronique de Michel le Syrien, Patriarche Jacobite d'Antioche,* ed. and trans. J. B. Chabot (Paris: Leroux, 1899), 1:163-64.

ism — "oriental" imitations of the legends that Rome was unable to control.[23] Bauer (as typically for him) interprets it as a sort of covert operation in a Roman power play.[24] In a sense, both theories are true (all shall win and all shall have prizes). But in another sense both accounts are, I think, simplistic.

What had been going on in the sixty-odd years between the last edition of the *Historia ecclesiastica* and Jerome's lucubrations? One factor is simply pious curiosity. There was a continuing — indeed, perhaps increasing — desire to know more about the apostles and the apostolic age. And so, through the operation of a sort of ineluctable law of supply and demand, more, of course, came to be "known." One fairly innocent example of that is provided by Rufinus in his Latin translation (or recension) of *Historia ecclesiastica* 3.1. He cannot resist the temptation to expand the modest list provided by Eusebius of mission fields allotted to various apostles by adding Matthew (who gets Ethiopia) and Bartholomew (who gets farther India).[25]

A second factor is a changing understanding of the episcopal office. In later antiquity we are moving toward a more jurisdictional and juridical model. It is a transition perhaps not completed until the time of Leo, but one already in train. While for someone like Irenaeus, the bishops teach what the apostles taught, in later centuries it was becoming increasingly true that the bishops are what the apostles were.

But one, quite simple answer to what had been going on is the Arian controversy. And one of the things it brought in its wake was an increasing awareness that East is East and West is West. We can, for example, think of the tart correspondence between Julius of Rome and the bishops who assembled for the great Dedication Council held in Antioch at the very beginning of 341. Their reply to an initial letter from Julius is not extant, but its contents can be reconstructed from Julius's reply to that letter and from accounts in Athanasius and Sozomen.[26] The Easterners profess in the letter that they honor "the church of the Romans as having been from the beginning the school of the apostles and the metropolis of piety [ἀποστόλων φροντιστήριον καὶ εὐσεβείας μητρόπολιν], even if the interpreters of doctrine [οἱ τοῦ δόγματος εἰσηγηταί] had come to it from the East" (Sozomen, *H.E.* 3.8.5). The apostles in question

---

23. Harnack, *Geschichte der altchristlichen Literatur bis Eusebius,* Part 2, 1:707.

24. Bauer, *Orthodoxy,* p. 117.

25. Eusebius of Caesarea, *Die Kirchengeschichte,* ed. Eduard Schwartz and Theodor Mommsen, Eusebius Werke 2, GCS n.f. 6.1 (Berlin: Akademie, 1999; Leipzig: Hinrichs, 1903-1909), p. 189, lines 4-5.

26. I owe these references to Sara Parvis, *Marcellus of Ancyra and the Lost Years of the Arian Controversy, 325-345* (Oxford: Oxford University Press, 2006), pp. 165-67.

are obviously Peter and Paul, and the East had them first. It is their teaching function that is stressed, and that, by implication, began in the East as well.

So when did Peter become bishop of Antioch? A number of the threads we have been following lead to Jerome, and it is only then that the legend really crystallizes. But it is a pity that we do not have full *acta* for the great synod that met under Constantius's auspices to mark the dedication on January 6, 341, of his shiny new church (the church of Holy Concord) in, of all places, Antioch. It would have suited the bishops of the council quite well indeed if Peter had in fact been bishop of Antioch before he ever went to Rome.

CHAPTER 18

Traces of Peter Veneration in Roman Archaeology

Peter Lampe

"I can point to the *tropaia* [the victory monuments] of the apostles. You may go to the Vatican or to the road to Ostia."

This famous quote by the Roman anti-Montanist Gaius (in Eusebius, *H.E.* 2.25.7) from about 200 CE is often used to approach the question of whether the historical Peter was ever in Rome and suffered his martyrdom (John 21:18-19; 2 Pet. 1:14) there under Nero, as *1 Clement* 5.4; 6.1-2[1] already at the end of the first century CE appears to hold.[2] This study will ignore this lively debate and exclusively focus on another topic: What was the Roman Christians' Peter story as reflected in archaeological and iconographic documents? Which aspects were important for them, especially in funerary contexts, where the existential question of death and life was posed and most archaeological and iconographic vestiges of this kind are preserved?

---

1. *Poly plēthos* in *1 Clem.* 6.1 parallels *multitudo ingens* in Tacitus, *Ann.* 15.44.
2. See further Ignatius, *Rom.* 4.3.

The Vatican Excavation Site[3]

Starting backward with the latest Peter references before the construction of St. Peter's Basilica, Constantine's (or Constantius II's)[4] architects, together with the advising local Christians, were convinced that a small and modest edicula, leaning against a Red Wall and standing above a grave-covering slab, was the apostle Peter's burial site, because they planned to integrate it into the very apse of their basilica of St. Peter. They prepared to make the effort of building extensive earthworks and erecting large substructures because, given the location of the edicula, the basilica had to be built on an unfavorable incline. In order to obtain a level building plot, they had to remove one portion of the slope and fill in the other. In addition, they had to close down a neighboring necropolis with mausoleums. Their cost-benefit calculation presupposes a significant veneration for the apostle Peter at that time. For *them*, there was no doubt where Peter was buried.

When they started working, they created a loculus in Wall g beside the edicula and inserted the bones of a male individual into it.[5] Before doing this, they had taken these skeletal relics from (presumably) the grave underneath the edicula and had wrapped them in a red cloth with gold threads. The earth remaining on the bones matches the soil from underneath the edicula and Red Wall area.[6]

---

3. For the following, see, e.g., P. Lampe, *From Paul to Valentinus: Christians at Rome in the First Two Centuries*, 6th ed. (Minneapolis: Fortress, 2010), pp. 104-16; P. Testini, *Archeologia Cristiana: Nozioni Generali dalle Origini alla Fine del Secolo VI, Propedeutica, Topografia Cimiteriale, Epigrafia, Edifici di Culto*, 2nd ed. (Bari: Edipuglia, 1980), pp. 163 86.

4. 337-361 CE. At least the apse mosaic at St. Peter's was ordered by Constantius: e.g., R. Krautheimer, "A Note on the Inscription in the Apse of Old St. Peter's," *DOP* 41 (1987): 317-20; N. Henck, "Constantius ho Philoktistes?" *DOP* 55 (2001): 279-304, here pp. 283-84.

5. The bone fragments are from almost all body areas, including the head, which excludes an often-suspected transfer of the head to the Lateran. The bones that the twentieth-century excavators found underneath the edicula were not from one individual, which is not surprising, given that they most likely were not in situ but stray finds.

6. The few animal bones found together with the human skeletal remains in the Wall g loculus most probably were also taken from the grave underneath the edicula. The Vatican slopes had been used as animal pastures before graves were built; fragments of animal bones were part of the soil, as also the soil of the funerary precinct P shows, in which the edicula grave was located. After having taken the relics from the grave, the architects covered it with a heavy slab. A legitimate reason for violating a tomb by removing bones was risk of water damage, which Damasus attests for Vatican graves. For all relevant details, see E. Dassmann, reviewing M. Guarducci's and Kirschbaum's work in this respect (in E. Kirschbaum, *Die Gräber der Apostelfürsten: St. Peter und St. Paul in Rom*, 3rd ed. [Frankfurt: Sozietäts-Verlag, 1974], pp. 223-48). Guarducci pieced

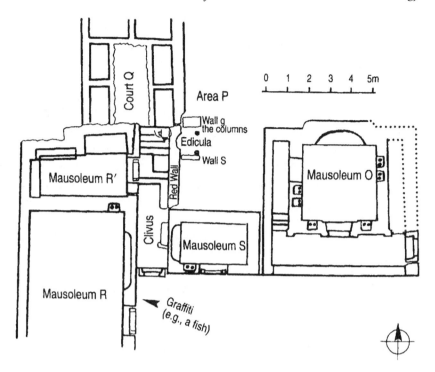

Fig. 1: Burial area P and its immediate surroundings on the Vatican hill

Subsequently, the architects drew a 2.6 meter (north-south) by about 1.5 meter (east-west) rectangle around the edicula, Wall g, and part of the Red Wall in order to encapsulate this complex into a marble-lined "box" of at least 2.6 meters in height. A larger almost 7-by-7-meter square was marked by magnificent ancient white marble columns and barriers between them, decorating and protecting the marble shrine. A baldachin resting on the columns spans above it.[7] Considering these activities, there is no doubt that the fourth-century architects were of the opinion that the skeletal remains in the Wall g loculus were St. Peter's.

---

the here-reported archaeological, geological, and paleoanthropological details into a theory, according to which these bones of a single man were indeed the authentic Peter relics — which, however, remains nothing but a possibility. Even if the bones of the loculus were taken from the grave underneath the edicula, which is most likely but not certain, nothing can "prove" that the edicula grave indeed was Peter's grave from Neronian times.

7. For a detailed description of the Constantine shrine, see Kirschbaum, *Gräber*, pp. 50-59, with figs. 6-7, 9, and table 10.

In the preceding *third* century, the edicula was partially clad in marble, and the flooring around it (i.e., the floor of the little open-air graveyard "P") was leveled and decorated with mosaics. In the same century, a few Christians also began to bury their beloved ones in the magnificent mausoleums of the necropolis immediately to the east of the venerated apostle grave. Exclusively pagan well-to-do families had built and used these mausoleums in the second century. This changed in the course of the third century. The small mausoleum M of the *Iulii*, for instance, depicts both pagan and Christian motifs. The latter include Jonah being thrown overboard and Christ posing as Sol Invictus in a carriage drawn by horses. Whether the scene of a man fishing alludes to Peter and a Good Shepherd, originally a pagan motif, hints at Christ (John 10:11) or even Peter (John 21) remains elusive. Christians were still shy about displaying their faith openly. Another Christian trace in these mausoleums, this time directly referring to Peter, is preserved in the magnificent once-pagan mausoleum H of the Valerii, just 20 meters from the venerated Petrine tomb. It is an epigraph[8] from around 300 CE, in any case from the time before the Constantine basilica was built:

PETRVS ROGA (Tau-Rho ligature or *ankh* symbol) X (ih)S
PRO SANC(tis)
HOM(ini)B(vs)
CHRE[sic]STIAN(is ad)
CO(r)PVS (t)VVM SEP(vltis)

Peter, pray to Christ Jesus
for the holy Christian people
who are buried at your body.

Although the details of the reading are much debated, because the letters drawn in red lead color and done over with black carbon paint have almost faded away, the basic theological idea is apparent: Peter praying to Christ is conceived as intercessor for the Christians resting close to his remains. The same concept also inspires the numerous contemporaneous graffiti under S. Sebastiano (below).

In the middle or first half of the third century, the edicula area needed to be stabilized by a wall. On this so-called Wall g, visitors scribbled a plethora

---

8. See the edition by M. Guarducci, *Cristo e San Pietro in un documento precostantiniano della Necropoli Vaticana* (Rome: "L'Erma" di Bretschneider, 1953). Despite all disputes about the graffito, "Petrus roga" is clearly readable, showing the concept of Peter as intercessor.

of graffiti from (at the latest) the end of the third century onward. Visits here ceased when the graffiti wall was encapsulated by Constantine's basilica. The graffiti are so numerous that a web of lines confuses the observer, showing how frequently the place was visited. Usually the visitors wrote their own names or a name of a deceased beloved one, adding a wish for salvation. Many used a common cryptographic system,[9] also known from other pagan and Christian places in and outside of Rome, showing a taste for the mysterious and for the craftily concealed, which also permeated the rhetoric of imperial times,[10] and, of course, the mystery religions. Thus secrecy during the Diocletian persecution was not the only motivation — if it was a reason at all — for the Christian cryptography.

Differently from the more or less contemporaneous graffiti under S. Sebastiano, where the invoking PETRE is often used, Peter's name here is usually abbreviated as PE or PET, with PE frequently being merged into one ligature resembling a key.[11] The difference between the frequent PETRE invocations

9. For this, see M. Guarducci, *La Tomba di Pietro: Notizie antiche e nuove scoperte* (Rome: Editrice Studium, 1959), pp. 87-139. Often her interpretations, however, are difficult to prove — which is the methodological dilemma with cryptograms.

10. See P. Lampe, "Theological Wisdom and the 'Word About the Cross': The Rhetorical Scheme in I Corinthians 1-4," *Interpretation* 44 (1990): 117-31.

11. For the name of Peter abbreviated as P, PE (often as ligature), or PET on Wall g, see Guarducci, *I Graffiti sotto la Confessione di San Pietro in Vaticano* (Vatican City: Libreria Editrice Vaticana, 1958), 1:411-78. If Guarducci is right in interpreting the single letters PE as Peter's name, then Peter is mentioned on numerous objects from the fourth and fifth centuries in the city of Rome, showing his popularity: not only funerary epigraphs (usually beside a Christ symbol), but also rings, public inscriptions (e.g., commemorating some construction work at the Coliseum), mosaics, game boards, domestic objects and Roman medals. PE, merged into one letter and then being a representation of a key, often thus becomes a symbol for good luck, like a charm. There does not seem to be a viable alternative to the Peter reading. If on epitaphs (such as in the Cyriaca Catacomb, figs. 32-33 in Guarducci, *Tomba*, pp. 102-3) this key symbol beside a Christ symbol meant PETE instead of Peter, in the sense of "pray, Christ (for the deceased buried here, as their heavenly intercessor)," then fig. 32 (Guarducci, *Tomba*, pp. 102-3) in which both the key symbol and the Christogram are decorated underneath by their own palm twig, the symbol of martyrdom, would be inexplicable. The Peter interpretation, therefore, seems more viable even on epitaphs, not just on rings and game boards. G. F. Snyder, *Ante Pacem: Archaeological Evidence of Church Life Before Constantine*, 2nd ed. (Macon, Ga.: Mercer University Press, 2003), pp. 259-63, categorically denies that a Peter veneration or a "cult" was expressed on Wall g. He does not even try to explain (1) the P, PE, and PET letters or (2) the fact that Christians commemorated their beloved ones on Wall g (see the examples below) exactly at the site of a tomb that at that time people identified as Peter's; such commemorations were only done at places of cultic reverence (see below, n. 23). (3) Furthermore, the very existence of the graffiti witnesses a frequent pilgrimage to the tomb, which implies

under S. Sebastiano and the Peter abbreviations on Wall g could suggest different groups venerating at both places, both of whom developed their own styles.[12] On Wall g (and elsewhere in the catacombs, see note 11), PE is often closely connected with the Christ symbol, which underlines a close bond between the two, the one being the representative of the other after having received the keys (Matt. 16:18-20; for this, see further below).

In one of these graffiti, introduced by *a(d) Pet(rum)*, "near Peter," that is, at the site of his tomb, a writer commemorates a *Leonia*, for whom he or she wishes life "among the living," *i(n) vi(vis) v(i)v(as) tu*, with a Chi-Rho Christogram showing the basis of such hope.[13] Other letters were inserted into this composition, among them the four letters NICA, expressing hope that Leonia will have eternal victory. Furthermore, the L of Leonia is a ligature of an L and the PE key symbol.

Margherita Guarducci invested a great deal of work into deciphering the graffiti, sometimes stretching the imagination too far. The graffito commemorating Verus, Bonifatia, Venerosa, and Vea[14] shows a Christogram flanked by the letters A and P, which she interprets as "ad Petrum." But this could just mean "life" and "peace" *(pax)*. She herself at other places interprets a singular letter A as "life." In Revelation 22:13, the returning Christ is styled Alpha and Omega, as the all-encompassing *arche* and *telos*. As "beginning," Guarducci argues, he represents a new beginning and life. Alternatively, however, it would be easier to interpret the A as *anastasis,* with Greek — besides Latin — still being well known in Roman Christianity at that time.[15]

More convincing is Guarducci's suggestion that the second Christogram above the name of Venerosa in the same graffito includes an allusion to the close union of Christ and Peter, with the Rho of the Christogram also func-

---

veneration. (4) Snyder is also unimpressed by the "Petrus roga" in the Valerii mausoleum, which implies a heavenly intercessor role. Snyder's Protestantism seems to have caused a bias, and his general denigration of Guarducci's work — as a search for "Catholic piety" on Wall g and as a "labor of love" of "little scientific" value (p. 263) — is undeserved. Although many of her readings need to be seen critically, this does not denigrate all of them.

12. In addition, the S. Sebastiano graffiti do not display any Christogram, contrary to the Vatican graffiti. This latter difference, however, could be due to the fact that the S. Sebastiano site was shut down at a time when the Vatican Wall g was still being scribbled on.

13. See Guarducci, *Tomba,* p. 109, with plates iv and ix.

14. In Guarducci, *Tomba,* pp. 113-15, with plates vi-vii, xi.

15. Although in the middle of the third century Latin became predominant in Roman Christianity, Greek was still known, with the inscriptions on the tombs of the Roman bishops still being in Greek in the third century. Not until the fourth century was Greek compulsorily abolished as the worship language (Lampe, *From Paul to Valentinus,* pp. 143-44).

tioning as P, augmented by an E.[16] The also-extant A in this conglomerate means "life/resurrection." To make things even more complicated, the name MARIA is etched across all of this by a second hand (see the different R letters), illustrating how crowded the graffiti are.

Another graffito reads VV I A (*vivas* or *vivatis in the alpha*, that is, in Christ, or alternatively "in the resurrection"). A later hand combined this and another graffito by adding: I VIA SPECI (*in via speci*, with *speci* being a nonclassical genitive of *specus*). The new text then conveys: "Victor (and) Gaudentia, may you, (being) on the way to the crypt (of Peter), live in the alpha." Apparently in the early fourth century this couple was buried somewhere in the Vatican necropolis, which one passed when visiting the Petrine tomb. The proximity of their tombs to Peter's grave seemed important enough to be mentioned — as an assurance that salvation and life in Christ will indeed materialize. Peter again seems to have been perceived as an effective heavenly intercessor here.

A Greek graffito on the famous Red Wall behind the edicula reads,

ΠΕΤΡ. . .
ΕΝ Ι

Peter is in here (ΕΝΙCΤΙ=ΕΝΕCΤΙ) or, e.g.,
Peter in peace (ΕΝ ΙΡΗΝΗ=ΕΙΡΗΝΗ),[17]

suggesting that Peter's remains were buried at the edicula site. The graffito predates Wall g as it was positioned where Wall g met the Red Wall.[18] It dates from between the construction of the Red Wall (around 160-180 CE)[19] and the

16. In Guarducci, *Tomba,* p. 115, with plates vi-vii, xi. Similarly, in a Christian seal of the S. Agnese Catacomb, for example, the Rho of the Christogram at the same time serves as P in the word SPES (fig. 202 in Guarducci, *I graffiti,* 1:396).

17. Guarducci's argument that nothing is missing after ΕΝΙ, because ΠΕΤΡ[ΟC] in the line above, with its second part curving down, does not leave any room for other letters following ΕΝΙ, does not hold. The "curving down" does not exist (see Dassmann, in Kirschbaum, *Gräber,* pp. 243-44, with fig. 56).

18. Guarducci dates the graffito to Constantinian times (contemporaneous to the above-mentioned loculus in Wall g). But this does not hold, as a second graffito from this location of the Red Wall also shows: it predates the loculus, because it was damaged by its construction (see Dassmann, in Kirschbaum, *Gräber,* pp. 243-44). Also, the Greek writing of both graffiti does not really fit the fourth century (see n. 15 above), especially in the context of all the Latin graffiti on Wall g, which Guarducci considers *older* than the *Petros eni* graffito. The opposite is the case. G. F. Snyder, *Ante Pacem,* p. 259, erroneously locates the graffito on Wall g.

19. Five tiles, covering the drainage of the Clivus, which was constructed together with

erection of Wall g (first half or middle of the third century). This means that Gaius of Rome, around 200 CE, wrote his testimony exactly within the time span in which this graffito was scratched into the red plaster. Thus there can hardly be any doubt which *tropaion* Gaius had in mind on the Vatican Hill, which means that the Constantinian architects based their construction plans on an old tradition that goes back to at least 200 CE. Alternatively, if the Gaius *tropaion* and the edicula grave had *not* been identical, two different monuments on the Vatican would have been venerated as Petrine tombs during the third century. We hear nothing of such a competition.

Even more can be said: If the excavated edicula site is identical with the *tropaion* Gaius had in mind, then *Christians* must have built the small edicula monument around 160-180 CE[20] to decorate the grave underneath. Otherwise pagans would have built it and Christians in the short time span before around 200 CE would have picked a recent pagan monument on the Vatican and arbitrarily converted it into a memorial to Peter — which seems more than unlikely.

The *Petros eni* inscription is located to the right of the edicula niche. In the published transcriptions of the epigraph a little detail was omitted: an oval above the first leg of the *Nyn* does not appear to be simply an irregularity of the plaster. The oval makes the first two legs of the *Nyn* look like the Egyptian *ankh*, the key of life (see fig. 2). If this meaning was intended, then this symbol might allude to Peter's key, thus inspiring the numerous later fusions of the Latin letters P and E into the key-shaped ligatures on Wall g in the immediate proximity of the *Petros eni* graffito.

Does the possible key-of-life symbolism have anything to do with another contemporaneous development? Around 200 CE (P66) as well as later in the third century (P75 and P45), copyists of New Testament papyri manuscripts (P66, 75, and 45) often wrote the word CTAYPOC and its derivates in an abbreviated form by omitting the diphthong AY and merging the Tau and Rho into one symbol. The result almost looks like an *ankh*, although the "eye" of the Rho is not centered above the Tau as in the *ankh* or in the Vatican graffito.

---

the Red Wall, date from 147-161 CE. Even if they were reused from somewhere else, the Red Wall would hardly date from later than 160-180 CE.

20. The edicula with its two niches in the Red Wall, which clearly were *not* later alterations to this wall, was built simultaneously with the Red Wall. For this dating and the inconveniences that the pagan builders of the Red Wall created for the people who claimed the simple Petrine grave for themselves, see Lampe, *From Paul to Valentinus*, pp. 105-8, incl. n. 7.

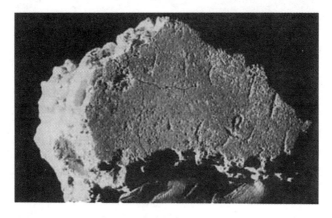

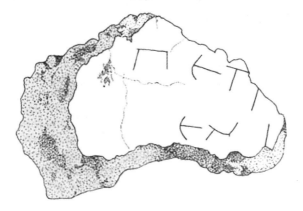

Fig. 2: *Petros eni* graffito

Nevertheless, the resemblance to the *ankh* hardly would have escaped the attention of the papyrus readers, who then would have concluded: in Christ's cross, the key to life can be found.[21] As the papyri copyists used the abbre-

21. For a photograph taken from P75, see L. W. Hurtado, *The Earliest Christian Artifacts: Manuscripts and Christian Origins* (Grand Rapids: Eerdmans, 2006), p. 237. For the *ankh* not only in the Armant inscription (fourth century or later) but also in other early Christian manuscripts since the fourth century, especially several Nag Hammadi texts, see Hurtado, *Earliest Christian Artifacts,* pp. 139-46. Hurtado rightly points out that the three papyri predate these Christian *ankh* usages. But, as we see now, they do not necessarily predate the Vatican graffito. This invites us to ask why copyists decided to abbreviate the word CTAYPOC in exactly the way they did — and not, e.g., as CTPC. Their abbreviation not only looked like a stick figure

viation independently from one another, one can reasonably assume that its invention dates back to the second century.[22]

While the Tau-Rho ligature's meaning is attached to the concept of the cross and its theological implications, the *ankh* in the Vatican Peter graffito seems to be unrelated. It rather appears to allude to the Petrine key, which opens access to heaven and life (Matt. 16:19). At the same archaeological site, the later Latin equivalent on Wall g, that is, the key symbol created by the ligature of P and E, also conveys this idea.

Moving to the *second* century, behind the Red Wall on the eastern external wall of the mausoleum R, just a few steps away from the Petrine tomb, someone scribbled in Greek: "L. Paccius Eutychos remembered Glykon." Usually such commemorating graffiti *(tituli memoriales)* were placed at important locations of cultic reverence or places of natural beauty.[23] Apparently, Eutychos — most probably a freedman of the gens Paccia — considered the Petrine tomb important enough to remember Glykon here, one of his friends or family. He must have been Christian because, for a pagan, this place would not have been of special cultic reverence or natural beauty. It is easy to imagine that Eutychos remembered Glykon by praying for him. Nearby, on the same wall, someone also drew an image of a fish. Guarducci[24] reasonably argues that these graffiti were scribbled *before* the Red Wall (built around 160 CE–180 CE) blocked access to the Petrine tomb from the south and from the alley of the necropolis. If Eutychos had wanted to visit the Petrine tomb *after* the construction of the Red Wall, he would not have passed by the mausoleum R. The latter was built between about 130 and 150 CE. Thus, already around the middle of the second century, people like Eutychos seemed to have visited and venerated the Petrine tomb. Since the edicula was built simultaneously with the Red Wall, Eutychos only saw a simple grave in the ground that Roman Christians believed to be Peter's.

---

hanging on a Tau cross but also like the *ankh,* which might have made this abbreviation even more attractive than other options.

22. Parallel to the papyrological Tau-Rho ligature, the plain letter Tau (T) was used as a symbol of the cross. Its first Roman archaeological evidence dates from around 200 CE; it was combined with a fish *acrostichon* (dating from about 200 CE if not earlier) under S. Sebastiano; see Lampe, *From Paul to Valentinus,* drawing and explanation, pp. v, 29. For the Tau cross in literary sources, see Tertullian, *Adversus Marcionem* 3.22 from 207 CE. In addition, *Barnabas* 9.7-9; Justin, *1 Apol.* 55; Minucius Felix, *Oct.* 29.

23. *CIG* 2872, for instance, or at the Didyma Apollo sanctuary, e.g., no. 539 in Th. Wiegand and A. Rehm, *Didyma, II: Die Inschriften* (Berlin: Mann, 1958).

24. M. Guarducci, *Tomba,* pp. 129-43.

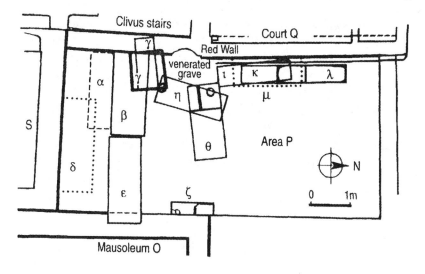

Fig. 3: Graves of burial area P

Veneration of this grave around the middle of the second century is also confirmed by another observation. Some people of the second and third centuries placed their graves close to the alleged Petrine one, but carefully avoided putting them on top of it or creating an overlap with it, while at the same time they did not care if their graves partly superimposed themselves on others. Apparently, these people, the owners of graves η, β, κ, and λ, treated the Petrine tomb differently from the other graves.

The second-century tombs that are immediately adjacent to the Petrine one and predate the Red Wall and edicula are graves γ, ι, θ, and η, with η being placed close to the Petrine grave without overlapping it but partly superimposing itself on γ and θ, so that a crowded cluster was created. It is thus plausible that η is Christian (whereas no viable clue is given for γ, ι, or θ).[25] So, already around the middle of the second century the family of η seemed convinced that

25. The axes of γ and θ are parallel to the axis of the Petrine grave, and ι lies almost at a right angle to that. Also pagan neighbors could have planned it this way. That γ had an altar-like brick top with a libation pipe running through, however, does not exclude Christianity. Still in the time of Augustine, Christians at gravesites held meals to the memory of the deceased, meals that looked "exactly like pagan superstition." The Christians brought wine with them. If several memorials were honored, each with a drink, the whole affair could end up a tipsy procession (*Conf.* 6.2). For further evidence for Christian libations in the third and fourth centuries, see Lampe, *From Paul to Valentinus*, pp. 112-13.

the Petrine tomb was a special tomb, with burial close to it desirable.[26] Graves β, κ, and λ, postdating the Red Wall, crowded the cluster even more[27] either during the third century, when we also find Christian burials in the necropolis mausoleums (see above), or at the earliest at the end of the second century.[28]

With grave η, the fish graffito, and the Eutychos epigraph, we have the first archaeological clues that some people around the middle of the second century were convinced that the simple earth tomb, above which later the edicula and the Constantine basilica would be erected, was a special grave to be venerated. Before that time, there is no chance to trace the history of this grave. A DNA analysis and radiometric dating of the skeletal remains from the loculus in Wall g might reveal further clues.

The Peter and Paul Memoria under S. Sebastiano at the Via Appia

Under the basilica of S. Sebastiano, a small paved courtyard was excavated — with three adjacent loggias, that is, roofed open rooms at the west, north, and east sides. Frescoes of flowers, birds, and animals decorate the site, and a stone bench runs along the walls — an ideal, albeit modest, place for funerary banquets. However, no gravesites could be found — only a niche to the northwest, which might have contained at least some relics of one or more deceased to justify such *refrigeria*. Funerary banquets were indeed held here, as graffiti reveal. A close-by natural spring in a rock-cut chamber, reached by steps, provided water for such rituals.

The three hundred or so graffiti covering the walls show that the complex was built for a cult of the two apostle martyrs Peter and Paul. Their memory was cultivated here from the late 250s CE onward. The facility was built after an abandoned pit of tuff had been filled in around the middle of the third century. Earlier, *in* this pit — today *under* the site of the apostle cult — a graveyard with loculi and three pagan mausoleums had existed from the middle of the *second* century to the 240s CE.[29] This cemetery had been abandoned and the pit filled in so that the new complex could be built on top of it. The new cultic

---

26. Grave η was simple, but covered with a marble lid visible on the surface. Underneath this slab, a stone-mortar mixture was laid out. Simple brick tiles protected the corpse on the sides and above.

27. β was partly put on top of γ, κ partly on top of ι, and λ partly on top of κ and ι.

28. For the chronology of these seven graves, see Lampe, *From Paul to Valentinus*, pp. 109-14.

29. See, e.g., Lampe, *From Paul to Valentinus*, pp. 28-31 (with further literature).

structure was used for approximately sixty to seventy years until about 325 CE, when the basilica of S. Sebastiano, called the *Basilica Apostolorum,* was built above. The *memoria* site then was given up.[30]

The graffiti of this complex are pre-Constantinian, not displaying a single Christogram. One graffito writer reports that a funerary banquet in honor of the two apostles was held here probably in the year 260 CE.[31] In the graffiti, Christians invoke the two apostles for salvation. For example: *Paule ed Petre petite pro Victore:* "Paul and Peter, pray for Victor" or "pray for Rufus." "Peter and Paul, remember Antonius Bassus." In order to boost the effect of their invocations, the Christians accompanied them with banquets: "Near Paul and Peter I made a *refrigerium,*" "To Peter and Paul I, Tomius Celius, made a *refrigerium,*" and so on.[32]

The path to the concept of the martyrs Peter and Paul being heavenly intercessors between the believers and God — just like Christ, who because of his sacrifice officiates as intercessor in Hebrews (7:25: "He always lives to intercede for them") — had already been paved by *1 Clement,* claiming that after their martyrdom they already "went" to a "place of glory," to a "holy place" (*1 Clem.* 5.4, 7; cf. John 14:2; also Tertullian believed that martyrs such as Perpetua and her companions were immediately removed to paradise at their death: *Anima* 55; *De resurrectione* 43). The Greco-Roman idea behind this is that deceased Christians, respectively their souls, immediately after death are taken up to God, as not only Luke 23:43 but also the early Christian sarcophagus of Prosenes from 217 proclaims ("receptus ad Deum": *ICUR* 6.17246), followed by numerous other inscriptions dating from the late third to the fifth centuries.[33] Correspondingly, the depictions of *orantes* at gravesites imply that the deceased believers are immediately with God after death.[34] This also holds

---

30. See Kirschbaum, *Gräber,* p. 159. Most researchers argue for a Constantinian date of the basilica; see, e.g., U. Leipziger, *Die römischen Basiliken mit Umgang* (Ph.D. Diss., University of Erlangen-Nürnberg, 2006), p. 46.

31. Thus the dating of R. Marichal on the basis of consular dates, "La date des Graffiti de la Basilique de Saint Sébastien à Rome," *La Nouvelle Clio* 5 (1953): 119-20, here p. 119, which, however, was contested by M. Guarducci, "Due presunte date consolari a S. Sebastiano," *Rendiconti della Pontificia Accademia di Archeologia* 28 (1955/1956): 190-95.

32. For the graffiti supplications, see A. Binsfeld, *Vivas in Deo: Die Graffiti der Frühchristlichen Kirchenanlage in Trier.* Kataloge und Schriften des Bischöflichen Dom- und Diözesanmuseums Trier VII: Die Trierer Domgrabung, vol. 5 (Trier: Dommuseum, 2006).

33. A list can be found in J. Dresken-Weiland, *Bild, Grab und Wort: Untersuchungen zu Jenseitsvorstellungen von Christen des 3. und 4. Jahrhunderts* (Regensburg: Schnell & Steiner, 2010), p. 64 n. 133.

34. See Dresken-Weiland, *Bild,* pp. 63-68. The *orans* usually represents the soul. Differ-

for the two apostles. But there is more to them, as *they* are now conceived as being able to intercede before God as heavenly mediators because of their martyrdom just like Christ.[35] Below we will see a similar juxtaposition of Christ's and Peter's and Paul's passions in the reliefs of the Iunius Bassius sarcophagus from the year 359. Here, at S. Sebastiano, some two to three generations earlier, in the aftermath of the Decian and Valerian persecutions, we witness the unfolding of a cult for interceding apostle saints distinguished by their blood offering — a cult that paved the way for the cults of other martyr saints.

How could the Via Appia cult for both apostles originate, given that by the middle of the third century, when the S. Sebastiano apostle *memoria* was established, each of the two apostles already had his own locus of veneration at the Vatican and at the Via Ostiensis, respectively, and that these other two cults continued[36] despite the new one at the Via Appia?

The Via Appia cult began in the year 258 CE, in the middle of the Valerian persecution, when the administration had closed the Christian cemeteries, preventing Christians from visiting their graves. Even after the persecution, the Via Appia cult existed continuously — even after the *memoria* site had been given up and the Basilica of S. Sebastiano built on top of it around 325 CE. Among the literary and epigraphic evidence, three documents are the most important. First, the *Chronograph of the Year 354* mentions an annual celebration on June 29 ("III. Kal. Jul.") for the apostle Peter — not for Paul — at the Via Appia in connection with the year 258, marking the beginning of such a cult: *Petri in Catacumbas et Pauli Ostense, Tusco et Basso cons.,* which is the year 258.[37]

---

ently from Tertullian (*Anima* 55; *De resurrectione* 43), who limited an immediate heavenly existence to the martyrs, the *orantes* depictions show that also regular Christians were considered to be with God immediately after death.

35. For Peter's intercessor role at the Vatican site, especially in the Valerii mausoleum, see above.

36. See the archaeological evidence at the Via Ostiensis and at the Vatican. For early literary evidence of the Via Ostiensis Paul veneration, see again Gaius's testimony (above). For the Vatican, see also Eusebius, *De Theophania* 4.7: "even to this time," Peter's memory is "celebrated among the Romans . . . , worthy of an honourable sepulchre in the very front of their city"; "great multitudes of the Roman Empire" make pilgrimages to it "like to a great asylum and temple of God," which in view of the archaeological evidence can only refer to the Vatican cult.

37. That the chronograph of 354 only mentions a celebration for Peter and not for Paul at the Via Appia contradicts the graffiti evidence from the second half of the third and early fourth centuries, but also the Damasus inscription and other sources to be mentioned below. The chronograph of 354 seems to have made a mistake with regard to Paul. Or did its author have a tradition that at first only Peter was venerated here for a very short time, before Pauline

Second, an only slightly later inscription of Pope Damasus (366-384 CE) in the basilica of S. Sebastiano reminds the visitor that once Peter *and* Paul had "stayed here" *(Hic habitasse prius sanctos cognoscere debes/Nomina quisque Petri pariter Paulique requiris . . .).*[38] The epigraph thus implies that, at the time of Damasus, no remains of the two apostles were present at the S. Sebastiano cemetery and its basilica.

Third, the so-called *Martyrologium Hieronymianum* documents that an annual June 29th celebration still existed in the fifth century in the *Basilica Apostolorum* at the Via Appia for both Peter *and* Paul, while it also states that each apostle was venerated at his own location as well, that is, at the Vatican and the Via Ostiensis, respectively.

It is highly unlikely that the *memoria* site ever hosted any bones of the martyr apostles. During the Valerian persecution the Christians were forbidden to enter their cemeteries, and those who did were killed, like the Roman bishop Sixtus II in 258 (see below). Thus, that Christians illegally intruded into the Vatican necropolis, violated the peace of a grave, took some or all of its bones, transported them across town at night, and started illegal activities in a new cemetery site at the Via Appia seems highly unlikely — especially in light of the negative finding that no archaeological evidence for a resting place of bones could be discovered at the site of the *memoria* or in its vicinity. The very fact that the *memoria* site was *not* a Christian cemetery made it possible for Christians to start a cult here during the Valerian persecution. Thus the old hypothesis of a *translatio ad catacumbas* — either of the entire skeletons or

---

veneration — maybe still during the Valerian persecution — was added on? However, such a tradition would have not been echoed anywhere else in the extant sources. Ed. of the chronograph of 354: T. Mommsen, ed., *Auctores antiquissimi 9: Chronica minora saec. IV. V. VI. VII. (I),* Monumenta Germaniae Historica (Berlin: Weidmann, 1892), p. 71; cf. more recently M. R. Salzman, "Kalender II (Chronograph von 354)," *Reallexikon für Antike und Christentum* 19 (2001): 1177-91.

38. The complete text of the Damasus epigraph was copied by a seventh-century pilgrim and was preserved in an Einsiedeln manuscript of the eighth century. Critical edition by A. Ferrua, *Epigrammata Damasiana: Recensuit et Adnotauit,* SSAC 2 (Rome: Pontificio Istituto di Archeologia Cristiana, 1942), no. 20. For its discussion see, e.g., H. Chadwick, "Pope Damasus and the Peculiar Claim of Rome to St. Peter and St. Paul," in *Neotestamentica et Patristica,* FS O. Cullmann (Leiden: Brill, 1962), pp. 313-18; M. Lafferty, "Translating Faith from Greek to Latin: Romanitas and Christianitas in Late Fourth-Century Rome and Milan," *JECS* 11 (2003): 21-62, especially pp. 41-43; J. Curran, *Pagan City and Christian Capital: Rome in the Fourth Century,* Oxford Classical Monographs (Oxford: Clarendon, 2000), pp. 152-53; M. B. Rasmussen, "Traditio Legis — Bedeutung und Kontext," in *Late Antiquity — Art in Context,* ed. J. Fleischer et al., Acta Hyperborea 8 (Copenhagen: Museum Tusculanum Press, 2001), pp. 21-52, here pp. 33-34.

of single bones such as the skulls — is an unnecessary attempt to harmonize seemingly conflicting literary evidence.[39]

Nonetheless, the banquets at the *memoria* site clearly had a *funerary* character. One graffito, for example, reads, "Near Paul and Peter I made a *refrigerium*." But what, according to ancient standards, justified the "near" and funerary banquets? The most plausible explanation of the "near" and of the "habitasse" in the Damasus inscription is that the Christians in the Valerian persecution had kept some contact relics from the tombs at the Vatican and the Via Ostiensis. The recent excavations at Paul's alleged tomb at the Via Ostiensis show slits in the Constantinian lid of this tomb into which pieces of cloth or other objects could be inserted to touch the venerated bodily remains. Furthermore, the niche at the *memoria* site (above) is a perfect location to keep such contact relics, to which one could be "close" when celebrating the banquets and invoking the apostles. In a parallel epigraph from 406 CE in the North African province Mauretania Caesariensis, Christian parents talk about their child being buried "near [*apud*] the saint apostles Peter and Paul."[40] Thus, even in North Africa you could be "near" these martyrs because of such relics.

All of this means that already in the middle of the third century some Christians believed not only that the apostle martyrs are with God, where they can intercede in favor of the believers — just as Christ does because of *his* death — but that they also can be spiritually present with humans at the same time, with this spiritual presence being objectified, or condensed, in objects of matter. The *hic habitasse* of the Damasus epigraph thus gains concrete meaning. This theological concept, which paved the way for the cult of martyrs and saints after the extensive persecutions of the third and early fourth centuries, however, had its theological price. The uniqueness of Christ's martyrdom, of

39. In addition to the literary sources mentioned above, see, e.g., the following two that seemed to have been influenced by the "habitasse" of the Damasus inscription in the basilica. A pilgrim guide of 638-642 CE suggests that the apostolic bones were present at the *memoria* site for forty years but brought back to the Vatican — thus, at the end of the third century, a few years before the Diocletian persecution began in 303 CE (*Epitome de locis sanctorum* [638-642 CE]: "there are the graves of the Apostles Peter and Paul where they lay for forty years"). Furthermore, according to the *Liber Pontificalis* 22, Cornelius took the bodies from the Via Appia back to the Vatican and the Via Ostiensis ("de Catacumbas levavit noctu"). For a critical discussion of still other, even less likely, hypotheses, see Kirschbaum, *Gräber*, pp. 208-10.

40. *CIL* 8.9715; *CIL* 8, p. 2034; *ILCV* 2186; cf. Y. Duval, *Loca sanctorum Africae: Le culte des martyrs en Afrique du IVe au VIIe siècle*, Collection de l'École Française de Rome 58 (Paris and Rome: École Française, 1982), 1:392-94, no. 185, with photo fig. 254; W. H. Frend, "The 'Memoria Apostolorum' in Roman North Africa," *JRS* 30 (1940): 32-49.

its salvific power and of Christ's resulting role as heavenly intercessor, was jeopardized.

Why did a Christian group[41] choose this particular location at the Via Appia? (1) Until the middle of the third century, the location had been a burial place, which had been given up and more or less "buried" (see above). This mainly pagan cemetery, however, had already seen an occasional Christian presence. One Christian vestige, a graffito from about 200 CE, drawn into the fresh plaster, showed a Tau cross inserted into a fish *acrostichon*.[42] It is possible — nothing more — that descendents of the graffito author had something to do with those Christians who in 258 CE owned the place and had the modest *memoria* structure built. (2) More importantly, the Via Appia location was three miles away from the city in the countryside, where activities might have been less controllable. The Valerian administration had prohibited Christians from visiting their graves, for example, the Vatican necropolis and the burial place at the Via Ostiensis. Therefore, some kind of cultic alternative had to be found. A site in the countryside not used as a Christian cemetery seemed a reasonable choice. Once installed, this cult continued even after the Valerian persecution, as the plethora of graffiti shows. As contact relics warranted a materially condensed spiritual presence of the saints, there was no reason to give up the funerary banquets there. (3) On the contrary, as a pragmatic reason, for pilgrims the S. Sebastiano *memoria* was a very short walking distance to the Callisto Catacomb, in which — since the early third century — not only Christians of lower means had been interred with the support of the Roman bishops, but also the Roman bishops themselves had been laid to rest since 236, when bishop Anteros was buried there and a special crypt for the Roman bishops was established. (4) Access to this episcopal crypt was forbidden during the Valerian persecution, and those who violated this interdiction were killed, such as bishop Sixtus II,[43] who tried to visit the crypt and pay tribute to

---

41. Because pre-Constantinian Roman Christianity was fractioned, consisting of numerous different groups, one cannot automatically surmise that the *same* groups had their Peter cults at the Vatican *and* at the Via Appia, or that *all* Roman Christian groups endorsed the cult at the Via Appia. The different styles of the S. Sebastiano and Vatican graffiti, the latter not spelling out, e.g., the entire name of Peter (see above), seem to suggest different groups. See further Lampe, *From Paul to Valentinus*, pp. 357-408.

42. See n. 22 above.

43. Migne, *PL* 13.383-84 (Carmen X), falsely attributed to Bishop Stephen. As vivid homage to Sixtus II, the martyr bishop of the Valerian persecution, Bishop Damasus in the fourth century illustrated Sixtus's martyrdom in a poetic inscription at his tomb in the Callisto Catacomb.

his predecessors. He therefore was executed in the same year that the apostle *memoria* was established (258 CE) and laid to rest in this crypt. Thus, if Christians still wanted to venerate Peter cultically in the year 258, they had to avoid cemeteries, go to the less supervised countryside, take some contact relics with them, and, in addition, be in the neighborhood of Peter's successors as well. Guarducci, who also suggested that the proximity of the Callisto Catacomb played a role in choosing the S. Sebastiano location, overlooked an important detail concerning the perception of what a Roman bishop was for the Roman Christians at that time. Bishop Stephen, who had died only one year before in 257 CE, had related Matthew 16:18 to himself and openly propagated that he held "the succession from Peter, on whom the foundations of the Church were laid" (Cyprian, *Ep.* 74.17), implying that the church foundations were now resting on the Roman bishop. Thus, being in the vicinity of the Roman bishops' tombs already at that time meant to be close to representatives of Peter and his authority. Guarducci also overlooked an interesting coincidence: in the last third of the fourth century, sometime after the death of Roman bishop Liberius in 366 CE, a fresco in the Pretestato Catacomb was painted in which Peter and Paul are depicted together with Sixtus II. This is the *only* catacomb painting that shows Peter together with a Roman bishop.[44] This might be pure chance. But it parallels the coincidence of events in the year 258: those Christians who wanted to continue their veneration and invocation of Peter and Paul at the Via Appia also experienced the martyrdom of the current representative of Peter, Sixtus II, which made for a special association between the two martyr apostles and this Roman bishop.

Catacomb Fresco Iconography

An overview and a quantitative summary of images of Peter in the catacomb frescoes are displayed in the appendix to this essay, tables 1 and 2. Several results are striking when looking at these tables.

1. While Peter can be depicted without Paul, the apostle from Tarsus almost exclusively appears together with Peter, which shows a preference for Peter. A total of ten (or maybe eleven) frescoes depicting Paul are countered by a total of eighteen Peter frescoes.

---

44. See table 1 below, pp. 309-13. Peter and Sixtus II are shown on the same *sottarco* of an *arcosolium* — together with Paul. A separate fresco of the same *arcosolium* portrays Bishop Liberius (352-366 CE).

Not counted in these figures are seven fresco depictions of Peter as a martyr sheep or — one time — as a dove.[45] In these incidents Peter and Paul appear as an animal couple, usually (six times) flanking Christ, who is represented by either a sacrificial lamb (three times; one time with a nimbus), a Christogram, a cross, or a tree of life. The Roman *martyr pair* Peter and Paul has been a standard motif since *1 Clement* (5.4; 6.1-2) and Gaius (in Eusebius, *H.E.* 2.25.7). Apart from the catacomb frescoes, it reoccurs on glass objects[46] or on a medallion.[47]

2. The fresco showing Peter, Paul, and Sixtus II together (table 1) needs further interpretation: for mourning families, it apparently was consoling to know that the three prominent martyr saints, Peter, Paul, and Sixtus, who had conquered fear of death, surrounded their beloved deceased. Correspondingly, on other frescoes, Peter — either alone (two times) or together with Paul (two times) — is depicted together with an image of a buried person. Of the thirty-five[48] images of deceased persons in the Roman catacombs, 11.5 percent were accompanied by Peter, while only 5.7 percent[49] by Paul. We also saw the attempt to be close to Peter in death on the Vatican Hill, where several families tried to bury their beloved close to the apostle's grave.

3. Twice Peter's denial is shown at a tomb in different catacombs. What moved families to choose this motif? Had the deceased at one time in life, possibly during the Diocletian persecution,[50] denied Christ and hoped to be mercifully accepted by Christ as Peter had been, despite his failures? The Peter figure in catacomb frescoes was a subject of identification not only as someone who had to face the cruelty of death but also as someone who after repeated failures had received undeserved grace and forgiveness. One of the denial illustrations, a fourth-century, maybe even early-fourth-

---

45. This interpretation is supported by a parallel fresco in Commodilla (5), where Christ and the twelve apostles are represented as twelve doves flanking a dove with a nimbus.

46. E.g., on a glass fragment with Peter and Paul flanking a Constantinian Christogram with wreath (fourth century; photo: Guarducci, *Tomba*, p. 157, fig. 47) or on a glass plate with a martyr crown (Museo Sacro of the Vatican Library; photo: F. Mancinelli, *Katakomben und Basiliken: Die ersten Christen in Rom* [Florence: Scala, 1981], p. 5).

47. Third century, Domitilla Catacomb (Museo Sacro of the Vatican Library; photo: Guarducci, *Tomba*, p. 156, fig. 46).

48. See list in A. Nestori, *Repertorio Topografico delle Pitture delle Catacombe Romane*, 2nd ed. (Vatican City: Pontificio Istituto di Archeologia Cristiana, 1993), p. 193.

49. Only the aforementioned two times, together with Peter.

50. Cf. similarly F. Bisconti, "Pietro e Paolo: L'invenzione delle Imagini, la Rievocazione delle Storie, la Genesi delle Teofanie," in *Pietro e Paolo: La Storia, il Culto, la Memoria nei Primi Secoli,* ed. A. Donati (Milan: Electa, 2000), p. 48.

century,[51] fresco above a woman's tomb in the Cyriaca Catacomb (see table 1), was accompanied by an image of the manna miracle — as an illustration of God's grace. The other Petrine denial scene with a crowing cock on a column can be found in the Commodilla Catacomb cubiculum of an *officialis annonae* named Leo, dating from the second half of the fourth century, with its frescoes having been painted in the 370s/380s CE.[52] Both deceased could have experienced a "denial" on his or her own sometime in life; for the deceased woman in the Cyriaca Catacomb this may even have taken place in her youth during the Diocletian persecution, which did not end until the year 311 CE. Likewise, the reliefs of three early sarcophagi, one dating from the first quarter of the fourth century and two from the second, show the cock of denial between Peter and Christ, who, holding a scroll, commissions Peter.[53] At least for Epiphanius (*Pan.* 4.7.7-9), Peter was a symbol of Christ's forgiveness particularly for the repenting *lapsi* of the persecution in the early fourth century.

That only two roosters associated with Peter's denial occur in the frescoes, while more than fifty appear on the sarcophagi (tables 1 and 3 below), will be explained in connection with the sarcophagi reliefs. However, one reason can already be given now: Leo, the Roman official, acts like upper-class sarcophagi owners, using the rooster and the rock-miracle motifs just like them. Although his means were limited — in his *cubiculum* there was no room for an expensive sarcophagus — this did not prevent him from copying the upper-class iconographic preferences.

4. In 50 percent of the Peter frescoes, that is, nine times, Peter is shown together with Christ (and in 39 percent — seven times — with both Christ and Paul), while Paul, in the Roman catacombs, only appears together with Christ if Peter is present too (thus, seven times). In one fresco, Jesus' apparition before Peter (1 Cor. 15:5a) illustrates Peter's special role.

5. Peter's distinctive role is further expressed by the illustration of Matthew

---

51. A more precise date than the fourth century cannot be given. See Dresken-Wieland, *Bild*, p. 160. She even suspects the first half of the fourth century.

52. Dresken-Wieland, *Bild*, p. 158. H. Belting, *Bild und Kult: Eine Geschichte des Bildes vor dem Zeitalter der Kunst*, 6th ed. (Munich: Beck, 2004), pp. 104, 107: last quarter of the fourth century.

53. See G. Bovini and H. Brandenburg, *Repertorium der Christlich-Antiken Sarkophage: Rom und Ostia*, ed. F. W. Deichmann, vol. 1.1-2 (Wiesbaden: Deutsches Archäologisches Institut, 1967), nos. 674 and 43-44. In addition, these sarcophagi depict Peter's arrest and Peter, instead of Moses, performing the miracle of the rock. In no. 44, Peter — like Christ in the commissioning scene — holds a scroll when performing the rock miracle, giving life (water) with his teachings (scroll). For the sarcophagi scenes, see further below.

16:19 on a fresco in the Commodilla Catacomb. It displays a *traditio clavium* scene from the sixth century.[54] Christ Pantocrator, seated on the globe, hands the keys to Peter at his right side; Paul is only positioned at Christ's left.[55]

In Matthew 16:19 (and 23:13; 7:13-14), the keys — together with the image of "binding and loosing" on earth and in heaven — signify the authority to interpret the law in accordance with God's will:[56] whoever walks on the "path of righteousness" (Matt. 21:32) shown by Jesus and then Peter will enter the kingdom. Accordingly, two corresponding originally fourth-century (second half) mosaics in S. Constanza[57] not only present a *traditio clavis* but also a *traditio legis*. A bearded Pantocrator hands his keys to a young and shaved Peter, without Paul being present this time. The corresponding mosaic at the other side of the entrance depicts Christ handing over a scroll commissioning Peter to teach. The apostle tends the Lord's sheep with a shepherd's staff in his hand (John 21:15-19), portrayed as an old man (as in John 21:18). This time, Christ is not bearded and stands on a hill above the sheep, not as Pantocrator but as risen Christ (dressed in golden robes), in accordance with the scenario in John 21. Thus Peter and the Pantocrator are pictured in a chiastic way: while, in the *traditio clavis* scene, Peter is young and the Pantocrator a mature man, the *tradito legis* scene reverses the appearances — a young Christ commissions an old apostle. The scroll, after a poor restoration of the mosaics, now is inscribed

---

54. Testini, *Archeologia Cristiana*, p. 198. However, J. G. Deckers, G. Mietke, and A. Weiland, *Die Katakombe "Commodilla": Repertorium der Malereien* (Vatican City: Pontificio Istituto di Archeologia Cristiana; Münster: Aschendorff, 1994), p. 57, suggest the second half of the seventh century.

55. The flanking saints, Merita and Stephanus, are local martyrs of the third century, Felix and Adauctus Diocletian martyrs. Thus all six depicted persons were martyrs, hence, the palm trees at the left and right bottom.

56. In addition, the aspects of forgiveness and church discipline, respectively, are also implied: see 18:18 and its context (furthermore John 20:23). For the interpretation of Matthew, see, e.g., U. Luz, *Das Evangelium nach Matthäus: Mt 8–17*, EKK (Zürich: Benziger; Neukirchen-Vluyn: Neukirchener, 1990), vol. I/2, pp. 465-66.

57. *Traditio clavis* in the northern niche mosaic to the right of the entrance, *traditio legis* in the southern niche mosaic to the left of the entrance. The mosaics were poorly restored. Henck ("Constantius," pp. 283-84) ponders a fourth-century date under Constantius because of the similarity with the *traditio legis* apse mosaic of old St. Peter's. Similarly Noga-Banai ("Prototype," p. 177; see n. 72 below) suggests the third quarter of the fourth century. J. Rasch and A. Arbeiter posit the second half of the fourth century (*Das Mausoleum der Constantina in Rom* [Mainz: Philipp von Zabern, 2007]). With regard to the Constanza mausoleum itself, W. E. Kleinbauer argues for a Constantius date: "The Anastasis Rotunda and Christian Architectural Invention," *Journal of the Centre for Jewish Art* 23/24 (1988): 140-46; Rasch-Arbeiter, *Mausoleum*, p. 89, suggest the years 340-345 CE.

DOMINVS PACEM DAT because of the bucolic scenario, but originally probably read *DOMINVS LEGEM DAT.*[58]

In Matthew's Gospel,[59] Peter, as *typos,* represents all disciples, that is, the congregation (18:18), which Origen still clearly understood: "*We* become a Peter, and to *us* there might be said by the Word, '*You are Peter,*' etc. For a rock is *every* disciple of Christ."[60] The Roman artists of late antiquity, however, were interested in the individual person of Peter: he ruled the church in the name of Christ, and his regimen had been handed down to individual successors in Rome, who, since the third century, had underpinned their claims to primacy by means of Matthew 16:18-20. Bishop Stephen of Rome in the middle of the third century applied Matthew 16:17-19 to himself, but was nonetheless opposed by his African colleague Cyprian, who protested: Stephen "contends that he holds the succession from Peter, on whom the foundations of the Church were laid," which is an "open and manifest folly" (Cyprian, *Ep.* 74.17). Earlier third-century claims of a similar nature, possibly by some of Stephen's predecessors (although this is not specifically stated), were contested by Tertullian and Origen.[61] Not until the end of the fourth century did the entire West accept decrees of the Roman bishop, at that time Siricius's decrees (384-399 CE).[62] In the fifth century, finally Leo the Great suggested that St. Peter as primate of all bishops is to be honored in his successors.[63]

Sarcophagi Iconography

On the sarcophagi, Peter's commission to teach the church is far more prominent than in the frescoes.

---

58. Paul, for a change, is positioned at the right hand of Christ in this scene. The correct *Dominus legem dat* can be read in a catacomb in Naples from the early sixth century (Rasmussen, "Traditio Legis", p. 27; see also p. 25).

59. And still in Tertullian, *Pud.* 21.

60. The text continues: "and upon *every* such rock is built every word of the church, and the polity in accordance with it; for in *each* of the perfect, who have the combination of words and deeds and thoughts . . . , is the church built by God" (Origen, *Comm. Matt.* 12.10).

61. "If you suppose that upon that one Peter *only* the whole church is built by God, what would you say about . . . each one of the Apostles? Shall we otherwise dare to say, that against Peter in particular the gates of Hades shall not prevail, but that they shall prevail against the other Apostles and the perfect?" (*Comm. Matt.* 12.11, in the context of 12.10, see previous note). Tertullian, *Pud.* 21.

62. E.g., Rasmussen, "Traditio Legis," p. 34.

63. Leo the Great, *Sermones ad Romanam Plebem* 3-4.

1. An early depiction of Peter receiving the commission to teach the church as a new Moses is illustrated on a sarcophagus from the Vatican necropolis under St. Peter's from the first quarter of the fourth century.[64] It is one of the oldest extant sarcophagi depicting biblical scenes. It displays both Moses receiving the Torah tablets and, immediately beside this scene, Peter being commissioned by Christ, who holds an unrolled book scroll with a Christ monogram in his left hand and teaches Peter. In an interesting combination of motifs, in the same scene the rooster of denial stands between Christ and Peter, and Peter, albeit looking at Christ, performs the miracle of the rock, taking over this life-giving function of Moses as well. In another relief on the sarcophagus, in which Peter is arrested by soldiers and teaches them, the unrolled scroll (with Christ monogram) that Christ held in the commissioning scene is now in the hand of the teaching Peter himself.[65]

2. A beautiful teaching scene is also depicted in a mid-fourth-century relief of the sarcophagus of the senator Iunius Bassus, commissioned in 359 and found in St. Peter's in the sixteenth century.[66] In the centerpiece, that is, in the middle relief between four others, Christ, triumphantly seated between Peter and Paul, holds an unrolled scroll in his right hand, teaching them — and thereby through them. His left foot triumphantly rests on the head of a personified Caelus, showing Christ as Pantocrator (see, e.g., 1 Cor. 15:23-28). In later iconography, this detail develops into a globe as Christ's seat.[67] In a second row of reliefs underneath, Christ rides into Jerusalem with an imperial eagle flying above the scene. His entry echoes that of the *adventus* (parousia)

---

64. Bovini-Brandenburg, *Repertorium*, p. 674.

65. See also the commissioning scene on the early sarcophagus no. 40 in Bovini-Brandenburg, *Repertorium*, from the first third of the fourth century (S. Sebastiano): Christ with a book scroll in his left hand and with his right hand lifted up teaches Peter while looking at him. Peter holds his right hand to his chin, remorseful and pensive. The cock stands between them. On the same sarcophagus, Peter is arrested and, right beside this scene, performs the rock miracle for a drinking soldier. Furthermore, Moses is given the law on the same sarcophagus. For similar arrest, rock-miracle, and commissioning scenes (with book scroll in Jesus' hand and a cock), see Bovini-Brandenburg, *Repertorium*, no. 43 (second quarter fourth century); no 44 (second quarter fourth century): Christ here does not have a book, but Peter holds a book while performing the rock miracle; no. 45 (second third of the fourth century, from area at Paul's tomb): Christ is without a scroll, but Peter holds a scroll in the commissioning scene, his right hand again touches his chin, and a cock stands between them. During the rock miracle for a soldier, Peter again holds a scroll. Furthermore, Moses is given the law on this same sarcophagus.

66. Bovini-Brandenburg, *Repertorium*, no. 680.

67. Underneath, Peter as a lamb performs the rock miracle, and Moses (or Peter?) as a lamb receives the tablets of the law.

of an emperor. However, the other eight reliefs flanking these triumphal scenes create a contrast by showing the hardships and trials of life, three of them being arrests on the way to trial and martyrdom: Christ (upper row, second from right), Peter (upper row, second from left), and Paul (lower row, first from right). The same persons who compose the triumphant centerpiece are being arrested to face trial and martyrdom.[68] Christ's trial is further illustrated in a relief of a seated Pilate in the *praetorium*. The water has already been prepared for washing his hands; by sentencing Jesus, Pilate will fail his *own* trial of life (upper row, first from right). All three martyrdoms are thus only alluded to without displaying the executions of Peter, Paul, and Christ. The four New Testament scenes are typologically counterbalanced by four Old Testament scenes, showing again the hardships and tests of life: Daniel prevails in the lions' den (lower row, second from right); Job sits in his misery (lower row, first from left); immediately above, Abraham is asked to sacrifice Isaac;[69] and Adam and Eve are shown after the fall, being ashamed and turning away from each other. Thus, in both the New Testament and Old Testament cycles, the protagonists failed one out of four trials (Pilate as well as Adam and Eve), while the other protagonists stood their tests successfully. The picture program testifies that in all hardship and suffering there is hope, because Christ not only suffered for humanity but also is triumphantly enthroned in the center and teaches through Peter and Paul how his followers are to lead their lives (see the scroll of Christ's law, explaining God's will). The dialectic between despair and hope that characterizes the program is again reflected in the two Peter and the two Paul scenes, which move from capture and martyrdom to inauguration as teachers of the church. In a way, the reliefs of the newly baptized Iunius Bassus illustrate the pagan *per aspera ad astra* by means of biblical scenes. On the sarcophagus, they illustrate the deceased senator's move from the darkness of early death — the *prefectus urbi* Bassus was only forty-two when he died — to

68. It is unclear who is which apostle in the central *traditio legis* scene. If Peter, in the central relief, stands behind the unrolled scroll to Christ's left and Paul to Christ's right (as in the *traditio legis* mosaic above), then an interlocked setup is created: *Peter* (arrested) — *Christ* (triumphant) — *Peter* (receiving scroll) — *Christ* (arrested). There is a chance, however, that the order of Peter and Paul in the *traditio legis* scene was the reverse, creating a symmetric setup: *Peter* (arrested) — *Peter* (with scroll) — *Christ* (triumphant) — *Christ* (arrested).

69. The motif was already used in the years 300-325 CE, when a sarcophagus fragment under S. Sebastiano was carved, showing a bearded man who holds a knife in his raised right hand (a motif unknown to pagan sarcophagi); in the background a fluttering shoulder cloak and the foliage of a tree are visible. See Bovini-Brandenburg, *Repertorium*, no. 248; see also no. 674, prior to the Bassus sarcophagus.

the light of life eternal in Christ. The fascinating interplay of light and shadow in the deep three-dimensional reliefs illustrates this aspect in its own way.

As for the relation between Peter and Paul, Peter is only slightly more prominent: Not only was the sarcophagus originally placed close to Peter's grave in the basilica of St. Peter, but the relief of Peter's arrest is also positioned right beside the centerpiece scene, while Paul's capture is in the lower row at the right end.[70] However, both apostles are involved in the centerpiece: one of them — it is unclear who[71] — stands behind the unrolled scroll that the triumphant Christ holds, presumably being prepared to receive it from Christ. The other already holds a folded-up scroll in his left hand. Thus both are perceived as teachers of the church.[72]

3. Bovini and Brandenburg in their *Repertorium* do not count these two sarcophagi among the *traditio legis* illustrations, of which they enumerate 11(-13).[73] The eleven coffins, all from the fourth century, are younger than the two

70. That this is *Paul's* arrest is indicated by tall reeds in the background, congruent with the tradition that Paul was killed next to the Tiber. This tradition was also displayed on late-fourth-century coffins in the vicinity of Paul's tomb at the Via Ostiensis and in the poetry of Prudentius, *Peristephanon* 12. For the relief of Paul's arrest, see D. L. Eastman, *Paul the Martyr: The Cult of the Apostle in the Latin West* (Atlanta: Society of Biblical Literature, 2011). For a more detailed, and partly different, interpretation of the widely discussed picture program of the sarcophagus, see, e.g., E. S. Malbon, *The Iconography of the Sarcophagus of Junius Bassus: Neofitus Iit Ad Deum* (Princeton: Princeton University Press, 1990). She also deals with the fascinating blending of pagan and Christian motifs. Already F. Gerke published a comprehensive interpretation and pictorial documentation, including early drawings by Bosio (*Der Sarkophag des Iunius Bassus: Ein Meisterwerk der frühchristlichen Plastik,* Bilderhefte antiker Kunst 4 [Berlin: Mann, 1936]); more recent photos in D. Rezza, *Un Neofita Va in Paradiso: Il Sarcofago di Giunio Basso,* Archivum Sancti Petri: Bollettino d'Archivio 13 (Vatican City: Capitolo Vaticano, 2010).

71. See n. 68 above.

72. For the history of the *traditio legis* motif and its history of research, see esp. Rasmussen, "Traditio legis," pp. 21-52. Rasmussen also discusses the remote possibility that the Iunius Bassus artists copied the motif from Constantius's apse mosaic of old St. Peter's (pp. 38-45). Surprisingly, Rasmussen ignores Matt. 16:18-19 as another likely inspiration of the motif. Not only the juxtaposition of *traditio clavium* and *traditio legis* in S. Constanza calls for connecting these dots but also the Matthean text itself, where 16:19a is juxtaposed with, and thus specified by, 16:19b (see above). After Rasmussen, G. Noga-Banai argues for the apse mosaic of Old St. Peter's being the prototype of the set *traditio legis* scene, not necessarily of the Iunius Bassus scene ("Visual Prototype versus Biblical Text: Moses Receiving the Law in Rome," in *Sarcofagi Tardoantichi, Paleocristiani e Altomedievali,* ed. F. Bisconti and H. Brandenburg, Monumenti di Antichità Cristiana 2/18 [Vatican City: Pontificio Istituto di Archeologia Cristiana, 2004], pp. 173-83, here p. 178).

73. In chronological order *second third of the fourth century:* no. 26 (the oldest, but

discussed above; only one (no. 677; third quarter of the fourth century) might be still contemporaneous to the Bassus sarcophagus. Indeed, in a technical sense, the two older ones do not yet represent a *traditio legis* scene that actually shows Peter *receiving* a scroll from Christ, unlike Moses, who has been accepting tablets from God's hand in sarcophagi reliefs from the third century onward.[74] Nonetheless, the reliefs of the two older sarcophagi are evolutionary steps toward the more set *traditio legis* scene of the later sarcophagi and of the S. Costanza mosaics of the second half of the fourth century.[75]

4. The Petrine *traditio legis* motif is not only rooted in Matthew 16 and Moses iconography but also in standard imperial iconography.[76] In the latter,

doubted as *traditio legis* by the editors). *Third quarter of the fourth century:* no. 528 (from Domitilla Catacomb; doubted as *traditio legis* by the editors); 677 (from St. Peter's). *Last third of the fourth century:* no. 28 (from St. Peter's); no. 200 (from S. Sebastiano); no. 676 (from St. Peter's); no. 679 (from St. Peter's); no. 1008. *Last quarter of the fourth century:* nos. 116; 288 (from S. Sebastiano); 724 (from area close to Paul's tomb at Via Ostiensis; the scene is even depicted twice, one time with Peter carrying his own cross). *End of the fourth century:* no. 675 (from St. Peter's; the scene is depicted twice, one time with Peter carrying his own cross); no. 58. Five of these coffins are from St. Peter's, two from S. Sebastiano, and only one from the area of Paul's tomb at the Via Ostiensis. See further a gold glass (Vatican, Museo Sacro della Bibliotheca Apostolica, inv. no. 60771) and later the apse mosaics of SS. Cosmas and Damian (526-530 CE) and S. Prassede (early ninth century).

74. A century later, from about 350 to 450 CE, Moses can also receive a scroll like Peter — instead of tablets. It is likely that the handing over of a scroll to Moses was meant to symbolize God's mandate to go to Pharaoh, whereas the tablets were the Sinai commandments. In the fifth-century (first half) wooden door reliefs of S. Sabina in Rome, after Moses saw God's angel in flames from the burning bush and took off his shoes (Exod. 3:2-5; middle relief; the lower one shows Moses tending Jethro's flock: Exod. 3:1), God's hand reaches out of heaven handing him a scroll, i.e., the mandate to go to Pharaoh (Exod. 3:10; upper relief). Thus Exodus 3 is in the background, not Exod. 31:18. Furthermore, the Gorgonius sarcophagus of Ancona (first half of the fifth century) displays not only Christ giving a scroll to Peter, and Moses reaching for a scroll given by God's hand, but also a second Moses scene with him climbing a mountain and reaching for the wing of an Eros. This doubling of Moses scenes speaks in favor of two different interpretations: Sinai commandments *and* Pharaoh mandate. Like many authors in the past, Noga-Banai ("Prototype", pp. 173-83) does not make the distinction between the mandate to go to Pharaoh and the Sinai tablets, erroneously interpreting all these scenes as the Sinai law. For the Ancona sarcophagus, see J. Dresken-Weiland, *Repertorium der christlich-antiken Sarkophage, II: Italien mit einem Nachtrag Rom und Ostia, Dalmatien, Museen der Welt* (Mainz: Zabern, 1998), no. 149.

75. E. Stommel, *Beiträge zur Ikonographie der konstantinischen Sarkophagplastik*, Theophania 10 (Bonn: Hanstein, 1954), pp. 102-9, similarly argues for no. 674 (n. 64 above) being an early version of the *traditio legis*.

76. For analogies to imperial ritual and iconography, see, e.g., Rasmussen, "Traditio Legis," p. 36.

an enthroned emperor hands a scroll to one of his officials, thus mandating a task to him. In adaption of such imperial imagery, Peter is commissioned with a scroll to tend the Lord's sheep (John 21:15-19) and to teach them God's will (Matthew 16) — in the same way, God gave Moses a scroll, thereby commissioning him to go to Pharaoh (Exod. 3:10, see n. 74), and he gave him tablets to enable him to reveal God's will to the people at Sinai.

Two conclusions need to be drawn. First, the correspondence between the Peter and Moses motifs shows that Peter is the new Moses, bringing God's will to God's people. Whereas the pre-Matthean childhood stories had applied a Moses typology to Christ, the apostle now *shares* christological attributes: not only his martyrdom is set side by side with Christ's death, but also his interpreting God's will is juxtaposed with Christ's teaching, or better: the latter is *present* in the former. A similar Moses typology is seen when Moses' miracle of the rock appears as a Peter miracle (see below): Peter makes sure that the waters of life[77] and salvation can flow from the rock — which is Christ, according to 1 Corinthians 10.

Varying Moses-Christ/Peter typologies can be found in the literature from the early fourth century on, both in the West and the East, aiming in the same direction: as Moses brought water from the rock, Christ sent Peter, the rock, to spread Christ's teachings to the world.[78] Or, Peter producing water from the rock signifies Peter's bringing the life-giving gospel to the world from his mouth; Peter thus is the rock on which the church rests.[79] Or, Peter, replacing Moses (and Aaron), took over the true priesthood.[80] Or, as Moses doubted, so did Peter when denying his master.[81] Except for the last two examples, these typologies from the literary sources focus again on the teaching of Peter, as did the *traditio legis*.

A last aspect of the Moses-Christ/Peter typology on the sarcophagi is just a detail, but a significant one: the staff *(virga)* that Peter holds as a symbol of divine power in the rock miracle[82] and in several arrest[83] and denial[84] scenes.

---

77. Including eternal life, as often neighboring scenes such as the resurrection of Lazarus show (see Bovini-Brandenburg, *Repertorium,* e.g., nos. 6, 11, 15, 39, 42-44, 67, 85, 86, 24).

78. Aphrahat, *Demonstrations* 21.10 (early fourth century).

79. Maximus II Turinus, *Homily* 68 (*PL* 57.394); *Sermo* 66 (*PL* 57.666a) (late fourth century).

80. Macarius the Egyptian, *Homily* 26.23 (*PG* 34.689) (fourth century).

81. Augustine, *Sermo* 352.1.4 (*PL* 39.1554) (404 CE). For the literary tradition, see further, e.g., Dresken-Weiland, *Bild,* pp. 134-35, with older literature.

82. Bovini-Brandenburg, *Repertorium,* e.g., nos. 6, 11, 14, 17, 22, 42-43, 241, 369, 770, 772.

83. Bovini-Brandenburg, *Repertorium,* nos. 6-7, 11, 17, 22, 42-43, 220, 241, 369, 770, 772. In these arrest scenes, Peter teaches the soldiers in order to convert them (see below). He is given divine power for this task, symbolized by the staff.

84. Bovini-Brandenburg, *Repertorium,* nos. 43, 621, 770, 772.

As Moses used the staff to produce water from a rock, so Christ used it when performing miracles,[85] and now Peter holds it: after his denial, he is not only forgiven but also commissioned and given divine life-giving power.

Second, the adaption of imperial imagery shows that Peter's authority, and thus indirectly the authority of the Roman bishop, is seen in a triumphant light. For the Christians, Peter's — and thus the Roman bishop's — word weighs as heavily as the authoritative word of Roman magistrates or even the emperor. Together with the Peter-Moses typology, which started in the first half of the fourth century in Rome,[86] the imperial allusion helped to bolster the Roman bishops' supremacy claims (see below).

Significantly, in the catacomb frescoes it is predominantly Moses who performs the rock-water miracle, while on the sarcophagi reliefs this function shifts to a large extent to Peter.[87] There is a sociohistoric reason for this shift on the sculptured sarcophagi — which were far more costly and lavish than catacomb frescoes and only commissioned by upper-class people. Differently from the catacomb frescoes, the sarcophagi artists developed a Petrine picture program of their own that depicted Peter more than eight times more frequently than in the frescoes (see tables 2-3 below): (1) On the coffins, Peter performs the rock miracle more than fifty-five times for thirsty soldiers;[88] all of the rock miracles on the sarcophagi that can be

---

85. Bovini-Brandenburg, *Repertorium*, nos. 6-7, 11, 17, 42-43; cf. 369, 770, 772.

86. See especially *Repertorium* no. 674 (n. 64 above) and nos. 40 and 45 (n. 65 above). The silver casket from Nea Herakleia/Macedonia, fabricated in Rome, is later, dating from about 380 CE (Noga-Banai, "Prototype," pp. 174, 177), but it emphasizes the Moses-Peter typology neatly by giving both men similar appearances.

87. Cf. table 1, below (right column) with table 3, below. In the present study, the rock miracle is only categorized as Petrine iconography if soldiers drink from the water. Whether any images of the rock miracle depict Peter in the catacomb frescoes is debatable. In the following fresco examples, no sufficient clues are given to decide whether Moses or Peter is represented: frescoes in A. Nestori, *Repertorio,* pp. 55, 57, 61, 109, 116, 124, 128, as well as in A. Ferrua, *Catacombe Sconosciute: Una Pinacoteca del IV Secolo sotto la Via Latina* (Florence: Nardini, 1990), p. 65, fig. 63. In older literature, the beard was used as a distinctive trait of Peter, but Moses also sometimes wears a beard; an example in B. Christern-Briesenick, *Repertorium der Christlich-Antiken Sarkophage III* (Mainz: Zabern, 2003), p. 591.

88. Bovini-Brandenburg, *Repertorium*, nos. 4, 6, 11, 12, 14, 15, 17, 20, 22, 23, 33, 39-44, 52, 67, 73, 85, 86, 97, 100, 135, 153, 221, 241, 253, 255, 368, 369, 372, 421, 422, 425, 526, 541, 542, 621, 625, 636, 638, 651, 665, 673, 674, 770-72, 807, 934, 946, 990, 991; cf. also 624, 660; furthermore 45, 367, 838, 919, where the rock miracle is merged with the arrest by soldiers (see below). The above examples outnumber the reliefs in which it is doubtful whether Moses or Peter performs the miracle; in none of these do the soldiers drink: nos. 35, 95, 145, 332, 359, 417, 431, 442, 533, 543,

clearly attributed to Peter and not to Moses show soldiers drinking the water of life. (2) Furthermore, Peter's arrest by soldiers is absent in the catacomb frescoes, but is seen more than sixty-four times on the sarcophagi (table 3), for example, on Iunius Bassus's marble casket. In most of these reliefs Peter is seen teaching the arresting soldiers, often having a scroll in his hand.[89] Even more, in four cases,[90] the arrest by soldiers is directly merged with the motif of Peter performing his rock miracle for soldiers, illustrating the conversion of his two guards. (3) In addition, a rare scene portrays Peter as a learned man, reading aloud from a book scroll while his military guards listen.[91] The scene echoes the pagan motif of the reading philosopher, which was particularly popular in the third century.[92] The two last scenes are not only absent in catacomb frescoes (see table 1) but are also rarely seen outside of Rome.

The background of this set of three unbiblical scenes is a local hagiographic tradition that narrates Peter converting and then baptizing his two guards in his prison at the Capitol Hill by bringing water out of the rock. This is the common theme of the three sarcophagi scenes. The tradition seems not to have been

---

552, 677, 680, 689, 695, 748, 768, 783, 867, 932, 935, 951, 975, 987, 1007; doubtful rock miracles: 105, 371, 432, 692, 706, 726, 1018. Cf. table 3 below.

89. See already the old sarcophagus Bovini-Brandenburg, *Repertorium*, no. 674, discussed above. Peter is also clearly teaching them in, e.g., nos. 7, 11, 14, 17, 22, 39-40, 42, 44, 94, 220-21, 241, 369, 398, 434, 507, 621, 625, 636, 694, 771-72, 910, 915, 1007. Only when a scene of arrest or martyrdom of Paul and/or Christ corresponds to the Peter arrest in the picture program of a sarcophagus, Peter's arrest illustrates his martyrdom and he is not teaching (see the sarcophagi Bovini-Brandenburg, *Repertorium*, nos. 61, [frag. 201], 215, and the Iunius Bassus sarcophagus 680, all dating from the second third of the fourth century onward).

90. Bovini-Brandenburg, *Repertorium*, nos. 45, 367, 838, 919. Cf. Lange, *Ikonographisches Register für das Repertorium der Christlich-Antiken Sarkophage*, vol. 1, *Rome and Ostia*, Christliche Archäologie 2 (Dettelbach: Röll, 1996), p. 85, with n. 144.

91. Bovini-Brandenburg, *Repertorium*, no. 45 (second third of the fourth century, from area at Paul's tomb): Peter sits on a rock reading a book; he is approached by a soldier who touches the book scroll. Another soldier sits in a tree behind Peter listening and watching, one hand is holding on a branch, the other is stretched out toward Peter. In view of the second soldier, an interpretation as merely an arrest scene is unlikely, also because the moment of arrest is depicted somewhere else on the same sarcophagus. A similar scene is no. 262 (first third of the fourth century, from S. Sebastiano). Further reading scenes with Peter and soldiers nos. 42, 943, possibly 47, 576, 709, 981.

92. Cf., e.g., Dresken-Weiland, *Bild*, p. 143; F. Bisconti, "La Catechesi di Pietro: Una Scena Controversa," in *Esegesi e Catechesi nei Padri (Sec. II-IV)*, ed. S. Felici (Rome: LAS, 1993), pp. 171-79, here p. 178.

written down before the fifth century,[93] but the sarcophagi show that it is a century older. In view of this tradition, it is plausible that the water produced by Peter from the rock for soldiers not only symbolized the eternal life in Christ, but more specifically also the life-giving water of the baptism of his guards.[94]

One can plausibly conclude from these findings that the conversion and baptism of soldiers as representatives of Roman authority allude to the conversion of the upper-class Christians who commissioned these sarcophagi.[95] Ever since the "barracks emperors" of the third century in particular, who had heavily relied on the military, soldiers had also been given administrative functions. They were a perfect symbol of Roman authority, to which the sarcophagi-commissioning upper classes could easily relate.

Furthermore, Peter's denial, represented by a rooster, is shown about twenty-five times more frequently on sarcophagi than in catacomb frescoes (tables 1 and 3), often in the center of the front side.[96] Differently from the frescoes, Peter and the rooster are shown together with Christ either foretelling the denial (Luke 22:34) or commissioning Peter after forgiveness (Luke 22:32; John 21:15-19). That the denial itself is shown is less likely, because then Jesus would not stand beside Peter talking to him and using the gestures of a philosopher.[97]

---

93. Pseudo-Linus's *Passio Petri* 5 (fifth century) and the sixth-century *Passio of the Saints Processus and Martinianus* (*Acta Sanctorum, Iul. I*, ed. C. Ianninco et al. [1867], 28:270), which narrates that in prison Peter, by making a cross sign, let water spring from a rock in order to baptize his guards: "beatus Petrus in monte Tarpeio [i.e., the southern tip of the Capitol Hill] signum Crucis expressit in eadem custodia, atque eadem hora emanarunt aquae e monte: baptizatique beati Processus et Martinianus a beato Petro Apostolo."

94. Similarly Dresken-Weiland, *Bild*, pp. 135-36. She points out that, at least on a few late-fourth-century sarcophagi in France, the rock miracle corresponds to scenes of Jesus' baptism.

95. Thus also Dresken-Weiland, *Bild*, pp. 136, 162. However, that the rock-miracle/soldier scene also represented the fact that Christianity had overcome the pagan governmental authority in the fourth century, as Dresken-Weiland (*Bild*, p. 146) suggests, seems a little far-fetched. The interest of the deceased persons' families was less abstract and more personal: as the soldiers received water of life from Peter, they hoped for help from this apostle after death.

96. In, e.g., Bovini-Brandenburg, *Repertorium*, nos. 23, 52, 53 (here even as the only scene on the sarcophagus), 77, 177, 621, 665, 807, 989. In nos. 43, 621, 770 (cf. also 241, 772) the denial scene is directly juxtaposed to the arrest and rock-miracle scenes, showing equally strong interest in these subjects. In the last third of the fourth century, the rooster scene also occurs beside the *traditio legis* (nos. 676, 1008) and *clavium* (nos. 676, 755).

97. For a discussion of all details of the scene, see Dresken-Weiland, *Bild*, pp. 146-61. However, that the rooster in these reliefs also stands for Christ himself (pp. 151-53, 162, with third- and fourth-century sources) does not have to be assumed, especially since a human Christ figure is part of the scene. The scene rather conveys that Christ's forgiveness after denial and failure warrants eschatological life.

The image expresses hope that forgiveness, grace, and thus eternal life will be given to the deceased persons, despite all their failures.

Finally, Peter's gestures in many arrest and reading scenes echo similar gestures in images of philosophical discussion: Peter the philosopher talks with soldiers. In the same way, his own teacher, Christ, conversed with him like a philosopher when he commissioned him after his denial, both men acting as if they were involved in a philosophical discussion.[98]

Thus the upper-class Roman owners of the sarcophagi liked to associate themselves with Peter. Peter was learned like a philosopher and endowed with power and authority. Senatorial officials such as the *praefectus urbi* Iunius Bassus, who were interested in authority and power matters, showed an affinity for Peter. After all, the apostle was not only the *primus* among the disciples and the alleged first bishop of Roman Christianity (Irenaeus, *Adv. haer.* 3.3.3) but also Christ's representative — and, in turn, Peter with his authority was represented by the local Roman bishop. Vicarious representation of superior power, indeed, was one of the aspects of being a *praefectus* or a *legatus*. This ideological setup interested the sarcophagi owners and invited them to particularly venerate Peter,[99] to preferably bury their deceased close to Peter's tomb,[100] and hope for patronal support from him after death — just as Peter's military guards received the water of life brought by him from the rock. Finally, in view of the concept of vicarious representation, the numerous Peter scenes on the sarcophagi showed these Christian upper classes' affinity to the leadership of the Christian Roman church, which was endowed with Peter's authority. All of these aspects explain why Peter occurs *at least* eight times more often (see table 3) on upper-class sarcophagi than in catacomb frescoes (twenty-five times).[101]

---

98. The pagan image material of the third/early fourth century in Dresken-Weiland, *Bild*, pp. 150-51, with n. 292 and figs. 65-66.

99. And not Paul, the theologian of the cross, who had held that worldly power, wisdom, and crafty rhetoric are not compatible with the gospel (1 Cor. 1:18–2:5). Paul is seldom featured on the sarcophagi. The predominance of Petrine images in catacomb frescoes is repeated on the sarcophagi. Pauline images (his martyrdom; fourth century) can be found on only eight sarcophagi reliefs (incl. Bovini-Brandenburg, *Repertorium,* no. 724: Peter and Paul as martyr lambs flank Christ). In addition, there might be three possible occurrences, making for a total of eleven, as opposed to more than two hundred Peter reliefs. Not included are scenes in which Paul seems present among several other apostles, e.g., Bovini-Brandenburg, *Repertorium,* no. 26. There the individual Paul is not of interest but the apostolic group.

100. Old St. Peter's was a distinguished place for upper-class burials, not only for Iunius Bassus. It was naturally here that Peter's image occurred particularly often on the sarcophagi (for this, see Dresken-Weiland, *Bild,* p. 145).

101. For a similar interpretation, see Dresken-Weiland, *Bild,* p. 162.

Two Damasus Inscriptions and Their Background

1. The association of the Peter tradition with political power dynamics can also be observed in the S. Sebastiano inscription (n. 38 above) by Damasus (366-384 CE). It is only slightly later than the Iunius Bassus sarcophagus (359 CE). Two observations are important in this respect.

First, the epigraph clothes the old idea of Peter and Paul being accepted into heaven immediately after their martyrdom in political images, picturing the two apostle martyrs as ascending to heaven by alluding to the emperor's apotheosis as a star or stellar constellation *(per astra secuti)*.[102] Damasus's push for the cult of local martyrs, above all Peter's and Paul's, whom he glorified like emperors, was part of the attempt to underpin a superiority of the Roman bishop. It was during his episcopacy that the set *traditio legis* motif was established (see above, especially n. 73), placing Peter and Paul at the sides of the ruling Christ.

Second, Damasus's epigraph shows how much the Roman Christians by now had naturalized both apostles as genuine "citizens" of the city of Rome *(cives)* because of their martyrdom there. Although they were immigrants from the East *(discipulos Oriens misit)*, their blood offering in Rome had made them true Romans, Damasus claims. Another Damasus epigraph, the *Elogium Saturnini* (46),[103] espouses the same concept: Although Saturninus was of Carthage, "he changed his citizenship with his blood, as well as his name and family. His birth among the saints [i.e., his death as martyr] made him a [genuine] Roman citizen" with all implied political rights.

2. Damasus's Romanization and thus usurpation of Peter's and Paul's authority, moving it from the East to Rome, needs to be seen in a larger church political context.[104] It fits with the contemporaneous attempts of the West to influence Eastern affairs, for example, in Antioch, where the church also claimed Peter as their first leader. In Antioch, Rome backed Paulinus against Meletius in their power struggle. However, the opposition to Meletius was not very successful; in 381, Meletius even presided over the Council of Constantinople. Nonetheless, when Meletius died, Damasus again backed Paulinus and now opposed Flavian. The West also opposed the appointment of Nectarius in Constantinople in 381. Moreover, the West convened a general

102. See also Lafferty, "Translating," p. 42. Dan. 12:3 was not the only inspiration for this motif.

103. Text in U. Reutter, *Damasus, Bischof von Rom (366-384): Leben und Werk* (Tübingen: Mohr Siebeck 2009), pp. 91-92.

104. See also, e.g., Chadwick, "Pope Damasus," p. 314.

council in Rome in 382 presided over by Damasus, but the Eastern bishops were not interested in Western meddling; they only sent three emissaries. In these contexts, the Damasus usurpation of Petrine and Pauline authority speaks volumes. Jerome bravely supported his friend Damasus in his claims and, in a letter, called him "successor of the fisherman [*successor piscatoris*] to the disciple of the cross. Following no leader but Christ, I unite myself in fellowship with none but your Beatitude, that is, with Peter's chair. On this rock, I know, the church is built. Whoever eats the paschal lamb outside this house is profane. Who is not found in Noah's ark shall perish when the flood prevails."[105] The only rock within the floods of water: this is what has become of a little Galilean fisherman.

Conclusion

1. Since the end of the first century, the memories of Peter and Paul as local martyrs were closely associated with one another (see already *1 Clement*, Ignatius, and Gaius above). The association continued to be expressed throughout the centuries of late antiquity in various media, with the martyr pair even occurring on medals and glass objects. From the middle of the third century onward, their martyr deaths were liturgically celebrated on the same day (June 29). Nonetheless, despite this close association, Peter is significantly more prominent in the catacomb paintings and sarcophagi reliefs.

2. Peter played several roles in the documents of early Christian archaeology and art. First, as Roman martyr, he overcame death and was accepted into heavenly glory, where he could be invoked as intercessor before God — just as Christ after his own sacrifice. To a certain extent, this concept jeopardized the uniqueness of Christ's salvific death — although this may be an all too Protestant perception. In the ancient perspective, the purpose of the juxtaposition of Christ's, Peter's, and Paul's martyrdoms was to break down the universal importance of Christ's death to the local level, to make it tangible there. Since Peter and Paul died as martyrs in Rome, it was here — and nowhere else, as Damasus pointed out in his S. Sebastiano inscription — that the martyrdom of Christ was locally made accessible by its representation in the martyrdoms of the two apostle martyrs, who frequently were depicted as sacrificial lambs right beside the Christ lamb (see tables 1 and 3). Also the Wall g graffito *Ad*

105. Jerome, *Letter* 15.2, to Damasus (376/377 CE).

Petrum Christos[106] says it all, as well as the PE key beside the Christogram. Peter in his local martyr tomb is the key to the universal. He in his martyrdom, materially tangible in a tomb, is the mediator between Christ and believers such as Leonia, whose L was merged with a PE and immediately preceded by a Christogram. Without a doubt, popular pagan religiosity exerted its influence here. The divine is only perceivable on the local level, in hero cults and local deities.[107]

Another reason for the concept of representation of Christ's death in Peter's and Paul's martyrdoms might have been New Testament tradition. If Mark wrote in Rome — there are excellent reasons for this[108] — a Roman first-century document at least prepared the later close association of the apostle Peter's martyrdom with that of Christ: in Mark 8:34, after his confession, Peter, together with the "people," is encouraged to carry his own cross in the footsteps of Christ. Moreover, in Romans 6, the Romans had read that Christians *die with Christ* in the sacramental ritual of baptism, in which the Jerusalem cross and the individual baptism became simultaneous.[109] Paul's participatory Christology, in which he as apostle identified with the crucified Christ, perceiving himself as crucified with Christ[110] and thus ultimately also "mirroring" Christ's *doxa* (2 Cor. 3:18), certainly helped to pave the way for the later representation concept that guided the Peter-Paul ideology in Rome.

The special veneration of the martyr apostle Peter, documented in archaeological evidence since the second century and jointly with Paul since the middle of the third century, paved the way for a similar cultic veneration of other martyrs in Rome after the severe persecutions of the third and early fourth centuries.

---

106. If the A P letters are to be read like this (see above). *Christos* is represented in a Christogram.

107. For the latter, cf., e.g., W. Wischmeyer, "Märtyrer II: Alte Kirche," in *Die Religion in Geschichte und Gegenwart*, 4th ed. (Tübingen: Mohr-Siebeck, 2002), 5:862-65.

108. See, e.g., M. Hengel, "Entstehungszeit und Situation des Markusevangeliums," in *Markus-Philologie: Historische, literargeschichtliche und stilistische Untersuchungen zum zweiten Evangelium*, ed. H. Cancik, WUNT 33 (Tübingen: Mohr Siebeck, 1984), pp. 1-45.

109. The same idea also guided the later liturgical readings of the martyr narratives: in the liturgical context, the listener was drawn into the story so that it became present and the time difference disappeared.

110. For the application of this concept to various aspects of Paul's apostolic existence, see P. Lampe, *New Testament Theology in a Secular World: A Constructivist Work in Philosophical Epistemology and Christian Apologetics* (London: T&T Clark, 2012), pp. 117-20, and see, e.g., Rom. 8:17b; 6:5, 8; Gal. 2:19b; 6:17; Phil. 3:10; 2:5-8; furthermore 2 Cor. 4:7-12, 16-17; 11:23b-33; 1 Cor. 4:9-13.

Second, the story of Peter's denial, ending in John 21, served as an illustration of God's grace and forgiveness even after death, making Peter an identification object for many.

Third, in reference to Matthew 16:18-20 and John 21:15-17, Peter was considered to be the teacher of the church, as the representative of Christ authoritatively explaining what God wants Christians to do, thereby also having the power to forgive or to discipline. Already in the third century, at the latest in the middle of it, Roman bishops claimed the same authority for themselves, in their own way using Peter as identification object. Thus, in Rome from now on, depicting Peter in art could also mean indirectly hinting at the authority of the Roman bishop.

3. The latter was one of the reasons why in the art commissioned by upper-class Christians, that is, in sarcophagi reliefs, Peter occurs significantly more often than in catacomb frescoes (ratio 1:8), documenting a special Peter veneration in the Christian upper classes of Rome. It pleased the Christians of worldly status and power to associate themselves with the authority of Peter and the Roman bishop, while less aristocratic Christians, commissioning less expensive catacomb paintings, shied away from this kind of association or were not interested in it (see also p. 290 above).

4. All of those, however, who depicted Peter at their tombs, aristocrats or commoners, were united in the hope of having Peter as an intercessor at their side when facing God after their death — a mediator who, as a pardoned sinner himself, could put in a good word for them and bring them the water of eternal life, as he had done for the soldiers who had arrested him.

5. In his S. Sebastiano inscription of the fourth century, Damasus claims that Peter's and Paul's martyrdoms in town made these two Eastern immigrants true Romans *(cives)*. By naturalizing them, he usurps them, attempting to monopolize all of their authority in the West in order to boost his attempts to uphold influence in the political power struggles of the East.

6. The importance of Peter does not lie in the historical Peter's individual theology, about which we know nothing for sure.[111] Nevertheless, Peter was given the role of teacher of the church. What then was the content of his teachings for the church? In the eyes of many Roman Christians, at the latest from the third century onward, the content was defined by the local Roman bishop's teaching. Peter as recipient of Christ's *traditio legis et clavium* guar-

---

111. In view of Gal. 2:12-13, he might have propagated a reconciliatory, integrative theology, in Antioch anticipating Paul's own later advice to the "strong" in 1 Corinthians 8–10; Romans 14–15.

anteed that the bishop of Rome, as his representative, was given the mandate to lead the church and teach the truth, especially in ethical matters. The fact that the apostle, contrary to Paul, had not left a written legacy must have been convenient for his "successors" on the Roman episcopal cathedra.

7. Peter's and Paul's local martyr tombs as local representations of Christ's universally salvific passion, as well as Peter's representation of Christ, the authoritative teacher, giving direction to the church (*traditio legis,* Moses-Peter typology), show how much the ancient category of representation influenced these Christian concepts. One might call it a vulgar Platonism, according to which the higher being reflects itself on material lower levels of the being and becomes tangible there. But one can also look at the concepts of Roman administration and society, where the vertical system of representation is ubiquitous, with prefects, legates, and procurators. Iunius Bassus, as *praefectus urbi,* was the vicar of the emperor, for example. Even on lower levels, entrepreneurs were represented by freedmen as procurators of their affairs in other cities. Paul calls himself an ambassador of Christ. Thus the martyrdom of Peter did not have a salvific power in its own right; it rather reflected the salvific power of Christ's death in a locally tangible way. Similarly, the Roman bishop did not possess an authority of his own but an authority reflected through Peter from Christ (as Christ himself reflects God's *doxa,* 2 Corinthians 3). In these two ways, Peter became a key to Christ and to Christ's work of salvation — which is quite a reinterpretation of Matthew 16:19–18:18, where Peter was portrayed as representative of the congregation.

Table 1: Images of the Apostle Peter in Catacomb Iconography (third to seventh centuries)

The table begins on p. 310.

Abbreviations used in the final column of table 1

B	F. Bisconti, *Le Pitture delle Catacombe Romane: Restauri e Interpretazioni* (Todi: Tau Editrice, 2011)
D	J. G. Deckers, *Commodilla*
DS	J. G. Deckers, H. R. Seeliger, and G. Mietke, eds., *Die Katakombe "Santi Marcellino e Pietro": Repertorium der Malereien* (Vatican City: Pontifio Istituto di Archeologia Cristiana; Münster: Aschendorff, 1987)
EW	C. Edwards and G. Woolf, eds., *Rome as Cosmopolis* (Cambridge: Cambridge University Press, 2003)
RP	A. Nestori, *Repertorio*
WMM	J. Wilpert, *Die römischen Mosaiken und Malereien der kirchlichen Bauten vom IV. bis XIII. Jahrhundert*, vol. 4 (Freiburg: Herder, 1916).
WP	J. Wilpert, *Die Malereien der Katakomben Roms,* Tafelband (Freiburg: Herder, 1903)

Catacomb	Location	With deceased	With Paul
Anonymous Via Ardeatina (Balbina?)	1 (*arcosolium:* lunette)	x (veiled woman, *orante*)	x
Commodilla	3 (small basilica: decorated loculus in left wall)		x (and other martyr saints: Merita, Adauctus, Felix, Stephanus)
	5 (*cubiculum: arcosolium* in right wall: lunette)		
	5 (*cubiculum: arcosolium* in back wall: *sottarco* right side)		
Domitilla	18 (*cubiculum: arcosolium* in right wall: lunette)	x (woman, *orante*)	x
	19 (*cubiculum:* niche in back wall: *sottarco* center)		x
	38 (*arcosolium:* lunette)	x (veiled *orante*)	
	41 (loculus)	x (person, probably the deceased)	
	[46] (*arcosolium:* lunette)		
	50 (*arcosolium:* lunette)		
Giordano ed Epimaco	1 (*cubiculum:* vault)		x
Pietro e Marcellino	3 (*cubiculum:* vault; late 4th to early 6th cent.)		x
Pretestato	5 (*arcosolium: sottarco*)		x
	[5] (*arcosolium:* front)		
	6 (*arcosolium:* lunette)		x
	19 (*arcosolium:* lunette)		x
Via Latina (Via D. Compagni)	9 (*sala:* left wall: 3rd section: lunette)		x
Ciriaca	4 (*arcosolium: sottarco*)		

With Christ	With martyr bishop Sixtus II	Peter's denial	Peter as sheep (= martyr)	Description or photo
				RP 118; WP 249,1
x seated on globe, handing over keys				RP 140-42; WM 148f
		x		RP 143; EW 95; D 104 (ca. 380 CE or later)
x (Jesus' apparition before a man, probably Peter)				RP 142
				RP 123; WP 179,1; 154,1
x				RP 123 (*sottarco* right side: miracle of the rock)
				RP 126; WP 154,2
				RP 126; WP 153,2
				RP 127; WP 127,1 (bearded man: Peter?)
x				RP 128; WP 182,1; 248 (same *arcosolium,* front: miracle of the rock. With Moses?)
x				RP 71 (on the same vault *a traditio legis.* With Moses?)
x x (the 2nd time as lamb with 4 paradisiacal rivers and 4 other saints)				RP 50; EW 97; WP 252-254; DS 201
x	x			RP 91; WP 181.1
				RP 91 (bearded man: Peter?)
x				RP 92 (*sottarco:* maybe the miracle of the rock)
				RP 95
x				RP 80
		x		RP 45; WP 242.1; B 247: end 4th cent.

Theriomorphic			
Catacomb	**Location**	**With deceased**	**With Paul**
Pretestato	5 (*arcosolium:* lunette)		x as sheep
	5 (*arcosolium:* lunette)		[x] as dove
Callisto	18 (crypt of S. Caecilia: *lucernario*)		x as sheep
	[31] (cubiculum: front) identification as Peter and Paul very uncertain		x as sheep
Panfilo	1 (*arcosolium:* lunette)		x as sheep
Commodilla	5 (*cubiculum: arcosolium* in back wall: *sottarco* left side)		x as sheep
Priscilla	40 (loculus)		x as sheep

Theriomorphic				
With Christ	*With martyr bishop Sixtus II*	*Peter's denial*	*Peter as sheep (= martyr)*	*Description or photo*
x as sheep			x	RP 91
x represented by a Christogram			[x] not as sheep, but as dove	RP 91 (end 4th cent.)
x represented by a cross			x	RP 105
			x	RP 107
x as sheep with nimbus			x	RP 6
x as sheep			x	RP 142
[x] represented by a tree of life			x	RP 28

Table 2: Summary of Table 1[a]

Total of Paul images in catacombs	Total of Peter images in catacombs	Peter and the deceased		Peter and Paul
10 (or 11[b])	18	4 (22%)		10 (56%)
			Peter, Paul and the deceased	
			2 (11%)	
Theriomorphic				
7 as martyr sheep (or dove)	7 as martyr sheep (or dove)			7
Totals				
17 (or 18)	25	4	2	17

a. Frescoes in which Peter occurs as only one among the twelve apostles flanking Christ are discounted (e.g., Commodilla 5, where the Twelve are represented by doves and Christ by a dove with a nimbus). In these cases, "the Twelve" is a motif on its own without particular interest in Peter. Percentage numbers relate to 18 as a total number of Peter images.

b. See Nestori, *Repertorio,* p. 208. Ten of them together with Peter (see table 1). The identification of a man with a pointed beard with Paul on the eleventh image in Domitilla 12 (*arcosolium: lunette;* Nestori, *Repertorio,* p. 119) is as uncertain as the identity of a second (today headless) person in the same fresco — who could have been Peter again.

		Peter and Christ			Peter's denial
		9 (50%)			2 (11%)
Peter, Paul, and Christ			Peter and risen Christ	*Traditio clavium*	
7 (39%)			1 (6%)	1 (6%)	
	Peter, Paul, Christ and Sixtus II				
	1 (6%)				
Theriomorphic					
6		6			
Totals					
13	1	15	1	1	2

Table 3: More than Two Hundred Petrine Scenes on Roman Sarcophagi (Rome and Ostia)[a]

R = Bovini-Brandenburg, *Repertorium*

Numbers without R = frequency. If two numbers are given the first one reflects definite occurrences, the second one the total of definite and possible occurrences.

Traditio legis	*Traditio clavium*	Christ saves Peter from the waters	Miraculous(?) fish catch	Healing of a blind person
13 / 15 (1st quarter to end of 4th cent.); *included in these figures are R 674 and 680 (as precursors of the motif; see above), and*	**6** (last third of 4th cent.)	**2** (1st quarter to 2nd third of 4th cent.)	**1** (3rd quarter of 4th cent.)	**0 / 1** (R 12; 1st third of 4th cent.)
8 with Peter carrying a cross (last third to end of 4th cent.)				

a. See the lists in U. Lange, *Register*, pp. 9-12, 40, 65, 82-88, 90-93, 102-106, 124 (some of the totals on p. 124 are corrected here). In addition to the figures here, Peter is globally included in numerous scenes in which, by way of example, *several* apostles acclaim Christ or carry wreaths to Christ *(aurium coronarium)*.

Peter reading, with soldiers	Denial motif: rooster (Matt. 26:34)	Miracle of the rock, with soldiers drinking	Arrest	Martyrdom (cross)	Lamb symbolism: several apostles as lambs, parallel to depictions of Christ with apostle figures
4 / 8 (from the 320s to 2nd half of 4th cent.); in addition cf. R 26: standing among other apostles, Peter is not reading but points to an open scroll in left hand while teaching	**47 /63** (1st quarter of 4th cent. [or 3rd quarter of 3rd cent.] to end of 4th cent.); including	**55 / 57**[b] (beginning of 4th cent. to last 3rd of 4th cent.); **plus** see R 680 (Peter as lamb; 359 CE) and the combinations of rock miracle and arrest on R 45, 367, 838, 919	**64 / 75** (1st quarter to end of 4th cent.), including	**3 / 4** (2nd third to end of 4th cent.) **plus** see *traditio legis* (left) with Peter carrying cross, and lamb symbolism (right)	**6** (last third to end of 4th cent.); also included is R 724: *only* Peter and Paul as martyr lambs flank Christ (4th quarter of 4th cent.)[c]
	Combination of both scenes		**Combination of rock miracle and arrest**, illustrating the conversion of soldiers		
	1 (R 674; 1st third of 4th cent.)		**4** (1st quarter to 2nd third of 4th cent.)		

b. Thus, not included are reliefs in which it is unclear whether Moses or Peter is depicted, because no drinking soldiers are visible. There are 25/32 such undeterminable reliefs.

c. Not included is Bovini-Brandenburg, *Repertorium*, p. 777 (cf. above).

Concluding Reflection

CHAPTER 19

Scripture's Pope Meets von Balthasar's Peter

Markus Bockmuehl

Simon Peter's New Testament profile had an enormous — some might say disproportionate — effect on subsequent construals and controversies in Christian ecclesiology.[1] But what bearing, if any, does the New Testament Peter really have for the idea of an ongoing "Petrine" role in the church, whether or not this is linked in any way with the role of the pope? Nowadays, this question features only rarely in biblical scholarship.[2] The Roman Catholic Church, by contrast, has long held that there is indeed a vital connection between the historic apostle and an ongoing ecclesial office, even if this idea may remain less familiar or plausible to Christians in other churches.

Much ink was, of course, spilled on this issue by apologists and polemicists of previous generations, in both pro- and anti-Catholic mode. It was, for instance, an item of explicit and largely critical concern to Oscar Cullmann in his well-known book about Simon Peter half a century ago; and the debate gained particular interest among ecumenical study groups in the immediate aftermath of the Second Vatican Council.[3] Within the Catholic

---

1. I am grateful for comments received on previous versions of this material from Mark Elliott, Jane Heath, Cyril O'Regan, Benedict Viviano, and the participants in the 2013 Edinburgh conference on Peter. The remaining shortcomings of the argument are of course my own.

2. My own published work also only touches on this in passing: e.g., Markus Bockmuehl, *Simon Peter in Scripture and Memory: The New Testament Apostle in the Early Church* (Grand Rapids: Baker Academic, 2012), pp. 85-86, 181-83.

3. Oscar Cullmann, *Peter: Disciple, Apostle, Martyr. A Historical and Theological Essay,* trans. Floyd V. Filson (London: SCM, 1953); and see, e.g., Raymond E. Brown, Karl P. Donfried,

Church, the "Petrine office" continues to feature in papal encyclicals and in the Catechism.[4]

For the last forty years, by contrast, there has been less explicit debate about the scriptural grounding of this notion — perhaps because, in the spirit of ecumenical cooperation, biblical scholars have tended to agree that the New Testament actually says little of direct historical or exegetical relevance to the subject.

In that case, such an abeyance of debate may have been entirely suitable. Two generations and three popes later, however, it does not seem inappropriate for a symposium on Simon Peter to ask where we now stand on that question of an "office" of Peter — exegetically, historically, or, indeed, ecclesiologically.

My own expertise lies rather more in biblical scholarship than in Catholic doctrine, in the history of ecumenical relations, or for that matter in the work of Hans Urs von Balthasar. Nevertheless, this highly influential twentieth-century Catholic theologian's work on the subject seems a useful point of reference for a renewed interaction of historical and exegetical concerns. In what follows, therefore, I briefly introduce von Balthasar and his relevance to this debate before going on to bring his conception of a Petrine office in the church into constructive critical dialogue with the profile and memory of the New Testament Peter. My conclusion will also articulate several suggestions for future ecumenical engagement about the church's Petrine inheritance.

Hans Urs von Balthasar

The Swiss scholar Hans Urs von Balthasar was one of the most influential Roman Catholic theologians of the twentieth century. Born in Lucerne in 1905, he initially gained a Ph.D. on the role of eschatology in German idealism[5] (1928) before entering the Jesuit novitiate in 1929 and being ordained a priest in 1936. Initial philosophical studies at Munich were followed in the mid-1930s by an

---

and John Reumann, eds., *Peter in the New Testament: A Collaborative Assessment by Protestant and Roman Catholic Scholars* (London: Chapman, 1974).

4. See *Catechism of the Catholic Church*, e.g., §§85, 194, 857, 877, 880-92.

5. His thesis was eventually published in three volumes under the somewhat grandiose title, *Apocalypse of the German Soul*: Hans Urs von Balthasar, *Apokalypse der Deutschen Seele: Studien zu einer Lehre von letzten Haltungen*, 3 vols. (Salzburg: Anton Pustet, 1937); cf. further his book, *Prometheus: Studien zur Geschichte des deutschen Idealismus* [Heidelberg: Kerle, 1947]).

intensive three-year apprenticeship in the church fathers under the guidance of Henri de Lubac in Lyon, a period on the importance of which he reflected extensively in later life.[6] It was this patristic engagement with Scripture that he experienced as a genuine liberation from the confines of traditional scholastic approaches to Thomas Aquinas. After spending most of the Second World War in fruitful pastoral and literary activities at Basel, where he first began to work with his mystic muse and confidante Adrienne von Speyr (1902-1967), he left the Jesuit order in 1950 under something of a cloud.

At this point he began a prolific but somewhat marginalized decade of theological writing and teaching outside the framework of any university post. This was a mark, perhaps, of the suspicion with which he was regarded in some quarters, and which in turn may have led to his omission from the list of contemporaries invited to attend the Second Vatican Council.

Works during this period include books on individual patristic figures such as Origen, Gregory, and Maximus as well as on contemporaries such as Karl Barth, Reinhold Schneider, and Martin Buber. He produced a *Theology of History*[7] along with several studies and a commentary on Thomas Aquinas. After a period of illness he then embarked in 1961 on the twenty-five-year project combining his interests in the drama of redemption and eschatology that would become the monumental seven-thousand-page trilogy for which he is best known. Completed only in 1987, this work consisted of seven volumes of "theological aesthetics" titled *The Glory of the Lord,* followed by five volumes of "theological dramatic theory" called *Theo-Drama,* and finally three volumes of *Theo-Logic.*[8] Beginning in the mid-1960s, the influence of his books and his rising star in the global Catholic Church and beyond resulted in numerous international lectures and conferences as well as academic and public honors, culminating a month before his death in 1988 in his nomination as a cardinal by Pope John Paul II, whose favorite theologian he was said to be. At his fu-

---

6. E.g., Hans Urs von Balthasar, *My Work: In Retrospect* (San Francisco: Communio Books, 1993).

7. Hans Urs von Balthasar, *Theologie der Geschichte: Ein Grundriss,* 2nd ed. (Einsiedeln: Johannes, 1950); ET: *A Theology of History* (London: Sheed & Ward, 1963).

8. Hans Urs von Balthasar, *Herrlichkeit: Eine theologische Ästhetik,* 3 vols. (Einsiedeln: Johannes-Verlag, 1961); ET *The Glory of the Lord: A Theological Aesthetics,* trans. Erasmo Leiva-Merikakis, 7 vols. (San Francisco: Ignatius, 1983); *Theodramatik,* 4 vols. (Einsiedeln: Johannes-Verlag, 1973); ET *Theo-Drama: Theological Dramatic Theory,* trans. Graham Harrison, 5 vols. (San Francisco: Ignatius, 1988); *Theologik,* 3 vols. (Einsiedeln: Johannes-Verlag, 1985-1987); ET *Theo-Logic: Theological Logical Theory,* trans. Adrian J. Walker, 3 vols. (San Francisco: Ignatius, 2000).

neral, the future Pope Benedict XVI endorsed a widely cited opinion that von Balthasar was "perhaps the most learned man of his age."[9]

Von Balthasar's vast oeuvre has continued to be the subject of several hundred books and conferences to the present day. Despite understandable superlatives there have also been criticisms in recent years — not only of his acknowledged lack of precision or conciseness in expression, but more pertinently of a certain flamboyance and perceived overreaching in theological style. Whereas von Balthasar's writings for laypeople could be admirably direct and accessible, the bulk of his more scholarly work has struck many readers as combining an astonishing range of reference and learning with a notable opaqueness, convolution, and "indirection" of argument.[10] On these and other fronts, a number of early enthusiasms are being rethought and his heritage is now more contested.[11] But all in all, there remains little doubt about von Balthasar's stature as one of the giants of Catholic theology in the later twentieth century.

Von Balthasar's Peter

For perfectly understandable reasons of both method and substance, von Balthasar is not widely cited by biblical scholars as an expert on Simon Peter. And, to be sure, this apostle is not indeed the subject in which he was most interested. But for the present, more limited engagement I wish to draw on one particular volume that does, I believe, hold catalytic value for our question. The English version is titled *The Office of Peter and the Structure of the Church*, and was published in two editions (1986, 2007; German original 1974 and 1989), the second of which incorporated a further essay on the same topic included in a Festschrift for then Cardinal Joseph Ratzinger.[12] In this book, von

9. Joseph Ratzinger, "Homily at the Funeral Liturgy of Hans Urs von Balthasar," in *Hans Urs Von Balthasar: His Life and Work*, ed. David L. Schindler (San Francisco: Ignatius, 1991), quoting Henri de Lubac, "A Witness of the Church: Hans Urs von Balthasar," in the same volume, p. 272 (German original, "der gebildetste Mann seiner Zeit").

10. A term used by Karen Kilby, *Balthasar: A (Very) Critical Introduction* (Grand Rapids: Eerdmans, 2012), p. 36. Cf. Vincent Holzer, *Hans Urs von Balthasar, 1905-1988*, Initiations aux Théologiens (Paris: Cerf, 2012), cover blurb: "Il y a certes une logique de la totalité qui traverse l'écriture balthasarienne, mais elle se déploie toujours sous le profil irréductible des fragments."

11. Kilby, *Balthasar*, is particularly critical of overconfidence in von Balthasar's authorial voice.

12. Hans Urs von Balthasar, *The Office of Peter and the Structure of the Church* (San Francisco: Ignatius, 1986; 2nd ed., 2007); German: *Der antirömische Affekt* (Freiburg: Herder,

Balthasar offers a sympathetic yet critical engagement with prevalent Roman Catholic notions of the Petrine office in light of the New Testament — as well as with Christian opposition to such an office. Although I have been unable to find a single review of the book by a New Testament scholar, I believe that it is in fact a useful point of reference for the current topic of dialogue.

Given its unfamiliarity to Protestants and to biblical scholars, we will begin with a summary of von Balthasar's case. The first thing to note is that the English title in both the 1986 and 2007 editions rightly identifies the ecclesial ministry of Peter as one of von Balthasar's central concerns in this book. This differs dramatically from the 1974 German original, however, which was titled *Der antirömische Affekt*, "the anti-Roman temper."[13] It may appear at first sight that these two titles are incompatible to the point of contradiction — a problem that is not helped by the absence of a translator's preface to help explain the oddly unexpected change of title. In fact, however, the titles represent two sides of the same coin, capturing a concern that von Balthasar delineates as a crisis of confidence in the life of the church after Vatican II. This concern is also evident in his unfulfilled intention in 1987 to revise the book substantially and release it under a new title that would foreground the problem of how to integrate the papacy within the Christian church as a whole.[14] He commented on the book once again in a short autobiographical reflection published as *My Work: In Retrospect*.[15]

From the opening lines of *The Office of Peter*, von Balthasar confronts

---

1974; 2nd ed. Einsiedeln: Johannes-Verlag, 1989). Note the Festschrift article included in the second edition: Hans Urs von Balthasar, "The Anti-Roman Attitude: The Catholic Church Self-Destructing," in his book, *Office of Peter*, pp. xiii-xxv (original publication: "Der antirömische Affekt als Selbstzerstörung der katholischen Kirche," in *Weisheit Gottes — Weisheit der Welt: Festschrift für Joseph Kardinal Ratzinger zum 60 Geburtstag*, ed. Walter Baier, Stephan Otto Horn, and Vinzenz Pfnur (Sankt Ottilien: EOS, 1987), pp. 1173-79.

My discussion here will cite this work primarily according to the better-known first English edition, but the second (differently paginated) English edition will also be referenced in case of significant alterations.

13. See n. 12 above.

14. *Wie läßt sich das Papsttum in der Gesamtkirche integrieren* (the subtitle of the 1989 German second edition; cf. *Office of Peter* [2nd ed. 2007], p. xi).

15. He wrote that in *Office of Peter*, "it was not at all a question of a pure defence of the isolated principle of the papacy, as if this were an individual element that could be added in its own right to the rest or from which one could abstract. It was instead a question of demonstrating in general terms the organic unity of the revelation of God in Jesus Christ, of investigating the different aspects and stratifications of this unity, and only after that of integrating the Petrine factor of unity with the other wider factors": Hans Urs von Balthasar, *My Work: In Retrospect* (San Francisco: Communio Books, 1993), p. 104.

the existence of a widespread hostility to the Roman papacy, specifically in the Catholic Church (though of course pertaining by extension in Protestantism too, beginning with Luther's notorious instruction to his followers, "Preserve this one thing when I am dead: hatred of the Roman Pontiff").[16] Von Balthasar sets out to demonstrate that the problem lies in a distortion of the ecclesial balance between the several defining apostolic missions of the church, a distortion in which the papacy itself has at times colluded. In this, he contends, there has too often been an Ultramontane confusion of the pope with the church, and of either or both of them with the power of secular jurisdiction.[17] By contrast, he sees the mission of the church symbolically focused in the balance between the four apostolic missions of James and Paul, Peter and John.[18]

Within this typology, Peter's pastoral office is accompanied by the constancy of love associated with John, by James's reverence for tradition and divine law, and by Paul's freedom in the Holy Spirit. Each of these apostolic "charisms" only holds validity as a function of the three others. Von Balthasar goes on to map these four apostolic graces onto the traditional fourfold sense of Scripture, so that the Jamesian themes of tradition and law relate to the historical sense (including the historical Jesus), the Petrine pastoral office represents the tropological or moral sense (including church discipline), the Johannine permanence of love connects with the anagogical sense (including the vision of eternity as already present), and Paul's freedom in the Holy Spirit promotes the allegorical sense (including the Christ of faith).

Von Balthasar concedes that from a secular perspective this diagrammatic arrangement might appear to be reducible to the four poles of positivism versus rationalism and church organization versus gnosticism and experience. He strongly resists such a caricature, but also acknowledges its popularity and abiding influence (pp. 313-14).

---

16. Von Balthasar, *Office of Peter*, p. 16 and n. 4. He credits this quote to Yves Congar and references only a secondary source; but it resonates with the ailing Luther's reported parting shot to his followers on leaving Schmalkalden in 1537, "May the Lord fill you with his blessing and hatred of the Pope" *(Impleat vos Dominus benedictione sua et odio papae)*. See, e.g., Martin Brecht, *Martin Luther* (Philadelphia: Fortress, 1985), 3:186. Luther articulated his hardening views on the matter shortly before his death in a tract titled "Against the Papacy in Rome, Founded by the Devil" (*Wider das Papsttum zu Rom, vom Teufel gestiftet*: WA 54:228-63).

17. See esp. von Balthasar, *Office of Peter*, p. 74 and passim), citing Kraus. Elsewhere, he characterizes such confusion of the person with the office as "Donatist" (von Balthasar, "The Anti-Roman Attitude," p. xiii).

18. Von Balthasar, *Office of Peter*, pp. 308-30 and passim.

Interestingly, von Balthasar insists that the Catholic Church's imbalances among the four apostolic poles require a retuning and correction, in keeping with the historic Protestant principle of *ecclesia semper reformanda,* "the church is continually in need of Reformation" (p. 314). In relation to the Petrine ministry, this means that its task cannot be carried out in isolation, but only in continual learning and dynamic interplay with the other apostolic missions: The "office" of Peter is never "above" the church nor on the other hand reducible to the church. Indeed, there is a sense in which, despite its juridical nature, that office requires a deliberate self-critique and abrogation of the will to power as a precondition for the very possibility of legitimate governance.[19]

The New Testament figure of Peter is, for von Balthasar, characterized by three basic features. First, he is chosen for office, and accepts his calling irreversibly, well before he is empowered by the Spirit to be a responsible leader — and while he is still in need of hard words of correction from the Lord. Second, his task of holding the keys to the kingdom and pasturing the Good Shepherd's lambs is, in its scope, an "utterly excessive" assignment. Third, Peter's catholic and universal outlook, drawing on the vision at Joppa (Acts 10), allows him to be the ecumenical bridge between James and the Twelve, on the one hand, and Paul's missional universalism on the other.[20]

Corresponding to this, writes von Balthasar, the "Petrine" ministry of the pope requires three chief qualities: truthfulness and authenticity in love, the capacity for unity and openness to learn, and the "eschatological centre of gravity" that serves to guard intact the deposit of faith.[21]

Additionally, von Balthasar places great emphasis on the Marian profile of the church alongside his conception of the fourfold apostolic framework: "Mary . . . belongs to the innermost circle of that human 'constellation' around Jesus which is of theological significance" (p. 197). In his discussion of the office of Peter it is the balance with the three other apostolic figures that predominates, although von Balthasar does also note that Mary's role as "mother and teacher" *(mater et magistra)* sometimes places her quite close to Peter in medieval developments, especially those that entail an emphasis on the singular personal authority of the pope.[22] And both of them exercise a liberating ministry at the core of the church, freeing people from spiritual

---

19. I am indebted to Cyril O'Regan on this point.

20. Von Balthasar, *Office of Peter,* pp. 151-57.

21. Von Balthasar, *Office of Peter,* pp. 316-31.

22. Von Balthasar, *Office of Peter,* pp. 166-67.

shackles (p. 210). Nevertheless, he regards the relationship between Mary and the church as uniquely "perichoretic" (adopting a term more commonly used of the triune divine persons).[23]

Unlike Mary, whose self-giving ministry stands invariably at the center of Christ's love,[24] Peter's ministry is both central and yet in some sense "excentric," granted to a former sinner and yet one who exercises love in a *juridical* role of lawgiving, even though this authority must never be reduced to an "abstract" exercise of "power."[25] In this sense there is in von Balthasar a strong defense of the magisterium, although, as Cyril O'Regan notes, "The [Petrine] magisterial office is still [also] an expression of the Marian and Johannine dimensions of the Church."[26] In the end, the Petrine and the other apostolic principles are together coextensive with the church in a way that is always subject to the self-offering of Christ:

> It is only because Christ unceasingly offers himself to, and within, the Church in the Eucharist, that she is called the "fullness of him who fills all in all" (Eph 1:23); naturally, therefore, the Marian motherliness as well as the Petrine pastoral care must be patterned after this christological model of self-sacrifice.[27]

Evaluation

This very rapid survey has only sketched what is a far more complex and at times rather diffuse argument in von Balthasar. Here, I have neither time nor competence to trace his typologizing application of the Petrine office throughout the history of Catholic theology.

As I hinted in my introduction, von Balthasar's concerns about inner-Catholic resistance to the office of Peter do not feature prominently in his oeuvre of over one thousand publications. Indeed, he himself once wryly suggested that the reason this particular book had sold poorly was that "no one

---

23. Von Balthasar, *Office of Peter,* p. 200; but note that he sees the profiles of Peter, John, and Paul similarly to be in perichoresis with each other (p. 144).

24. Kilby, *Balthasar,* p. 118 and passim, however, is highly critical of the unreconstructed traditionalism in his characterization of Mary.

25. Von Balthasar, *Office of Peter,* pp. 209-10.

26. Cyril O'Regan, "Balthasar: Between Tübingen and Postmodernity," *Modern Theology* 14 (1998): 325-53, here p. 332.

27. Von Balthasar, *Office of Peter,* pp. 204-6.

stricken with the illness would have bought it."[28] Nevertheless, his repeated return to the subject matter in the Ratzinger Festschrift, in his autobiographical reflections, and in the intended revision of the work shows that it evidently remained dear to his heart.

A number of observations may be made by way of contextual assessment. Some of these concern von Balthasar's indebtedness to key German thinkers representing both the idealism of the nineteenth century and the political philosophy of the twentieth. In his lectures on the philosophy of revelation, for example, Friedrich Schelling (1775-1854) described the history of the world as God coming to himself. In Schelling's scheme, there are three great historical eras of Christianity. Of these, Petrine Catholicism and Pauline Protestantism already belong to an obsolete past, whereas in their place will now arise the Johannine Christianity of the future.[29] Von Balthasar explicitly repudiates Schelling's or any other scheme that attempts to play off a church abstractly associated with one apostle against another.[30]

More interesting, and for our purposes more telling perhaps, is the influence of a towering twentieth-century thinker whom the book never cites but who is evidently significant at least as a foil for von Balthasar (as indeed he has been reappropriated for a number of postmodern political theologies). The Catholic political philosopher Carl Schmitt (1888-1985) controversially argued during the Weimar period for totalitarian definitions of sovereign political power as equivalent to secularized theological claims. He went on to become a strong supporter (and beneficiary) of the Nazi regime, especially in the mid-1930s. His 1923 treatise *Roman Catholicism and Political Form* opens with the statement,

> There is an anti-Roman temper [*Es gibt einen antirömischen Affekt*] that has nourished the struggle against popery, Jesuitism and clericalism with a host

---

28. Von Balthasar, "The Anti-Roman Attitude," p. xiii.

29. The apostolic quartet of Peter, James, John, and Paul is also pivotal in Clement of Alexandria (*Strom.* 1.1.11.3), although Schelling's structure may at least formally echo the Father-Son-Spirit supersession scheme of Joachim of Fiore. In keeping with his teacher de Lubac, von Balthasar recognized a "deformative lineage of Böhme and Joachim in Schelling," Berdyaev, and others, as Jennifer Martin interestingly puts it: "Hans Urs von Balthasar and the Press of Speculative Russian Religious Philosophy" (Ph.D. diss., University of Notre Dame, 2012), p. 158. Cf., similarly, Aidan Nichols, *Say It Is Pentecost: A Guide through Balthasar's Logic* (Edinburgh: T&T Clark, 2000), pp. 98-99, in relation to gnosticizing supersession schemas in Swedenborg, Hegel, and Marx.

30. Von Balthasar, *Office of Peter*, pp. 146-48.

of religious and political forces, and that has impelled European history for centuries. Not only fanatical sectarians but entire generations of pious Protestants and Greek-Orthodox Christians have seen in Rome the Antichrist or the Babylonian whore of the apocalypse.[31]

In place of this "anti-Roman temper," unlike von Balthasar, Schmitt articulates a Catholic rationalism of visible institutions, in isolation from any corresponding charism. In other words, he tends to that identification of the church with its governing institutions that von Balthasar criticizes as characteristic of Ultramontane error (see above).[32] It is significant to note here the contrast between Schmitt's wholly futile resistance to the theology of Vatican II and von Balthasar's meteoric ascent in the council's wake. That contrast notably illustrates an important inner-Catholic aspect of von Balthasar's portrayal of Peter, which positions itself not only over against Schmitt's Hobbesian presuppositions and totalitarian sympathies on the right, but also against a perceived tendency on the intellectual left to decry any and every exercise of authority as authoritarian.[33]

Von Balthasar's Peter Meets Scripture's Pope

Several useful lines of engagement suggest themselves from a perspective of New Testament interpretation. Von Balthasar presents an attractive appeal to the scriptural Peter in support of a quite nuanced and sophisticated account of

---

31. Carl Schmitt, *Römischer Katholizismus und politische Form* (Hellerau: Hegner, 1923), p. 5; ET *Roman Catholicism and Political Form,* trans. G. L. Ulmen (Westport, Conn.: Greenwood, 1996).

32. In a highly critical study, Christoph Schmidt ("Review Essay of Jacob Taubes' *The Political Theology of Paul,*" *Hebraic Political Studies* 2 [2007]: 232-41) suggests that von Balthasar's fierce resistance to Carl Schmitt was in this respect unduly influential on Jacob Taubes's *The Political Theology of Paul,* ed. Aleida Assmann, Cultural Memory in the Present (Stanford: Stanford University Press, 2004). Taubes had been exposed to both Barth and von Balthasar during his war years in Basel and Zürich. Cf., similarly, Michael Maidan, review of Jacob Taubes, *Occidental Eschatology* (Stanford: Stanford University Press, 2009) and *From Cult to Culture: Fragments towards a Critique of Historical Reason* (Stanford: Stanford University Press, 2010), *Philosophy in Review* 30 (2010): 449-56, here p. 449. In a significantly related observation on his notion of authority, Cyril O'Regan notes that von Balthasar's resistance to monolithic institutions subverts Vincent of Lerins's famous definition of catholic tradition as that which is the same everywhere and at all times (O'Regan, "Balthasar," pp. 329-30).

33. I owe this point to Cyril O'Regan.

the papal office within the wider context of the church's mission. For present purposes we may characterize von Balthasar's presentation of Peter as deployed to oppose two or perhaps three perceived distortions of ecclesiology. Specifically, these are

1. exaggerated or Ultramontane views of the pope's authority,
2. anti-Roman attitudes within Catholicism, and to a lesser extent
3. Protestantism, construed as a kind of radically inverted papism of the individual.[34]

It will be most expedient here to foreground what is probably the most obvious point of critical engagement with our Petrine subject. This is the question of whether in fact, despite its nuance and sophistication, von Balthasar perpetuates a classic Roman Catholic category error in continuing to tether the papal office to the New Testament figure of Peter. After all — so goes the most common objection — the New Testament Peter's profile is nothing like that of a pope or even, arguably, a bishop. What is more, Protestant exegetes usually claim to see nothing in the biblical evidence to suggest that the role and authority entrusted to this apostle are in any way transferable to anyone after his death, let alone to a unilinear succession of bishops of Rome.

This is a robust and effective Protestant criticism, and one that finds support among Eastern Orthodox churches too. Certainly careful attention to the flow of the scriptural text must be allowed to pose questions to institutional assumptions of entitlement.

Oscar Cullmann is characteristic of this emphatic Protestant resistance to the notion that the New Testament Peter's role might have any meaningfully formative aftermath in the history of the church. On this question of continuity, old confessional divides remained firmly entrenched in Cullmann's day, as in some circles they continue into our own. His skepticism in this matter incurred Roman Catholic reviewers' wrath (even while appreciating his sympathetic account of Peter's role as a bridge builder) and Protestants' praise (even while voicing misgivings about his catholic-sounding portrait of Peter in Matthew 16). One of the latter expressed his approval as follows:

34. On this point von Balthasar, *Office of Peter,* p. 172 n. 69, quoting J. A. Möhler: "Protestantism is papism carried to the extreme, that is, complete egoism in principle. In papism each gives himself unconditionally to one person: in Protestantism, each one is in a position to oppose all others (in so far as he makes of himself the principle of interpretation of revelation)." Also cited in John McDade, "Von Balthasar and the Office of Peter in the Church," *The Way* 44 (2005): 97-114, here p. 98; cf. further discussion in O'Regan, "Balthasar," p. 335 and passim.

The fact that, from the beginning of the second century onwards, Rome assumed a leading and increasingly important role in the Church is not disputed, what is denied is that that has anything to do with the Apostolic Age, or that the primacy promised to Peter in Matt. 16.17, a primacy which was actually exercised by him for a short time in Jerusalem, can possibly be transferred to the Bishops of Rome.[35]

Von Balthasar was, of course, aware of the difficulty. He explicitly acknowledged Oscar Cullmann's challenge on the basis of Matthew 16 that "he who proceeds without prejudice, on the basis of exegesis . . . cannot seriously conclude that Jesus here had successors of Peter in mind," and, indeed, that "in the entire New Testament, the apostolic function is always unique, christologically possible only at the beginning of the building of the edifice."[36]

Nevertheless, von Balthasar retorted in somewhat traditional fashion that the merely literalist substitution of *sola Scriptura* for the living voice of the church is a rather artificial failure to recognize the fuller sense of the Lord's words to Peter, "When you have turned back, strengthen your brothers" (Luke 22:32).[37]

He conceded that Jesus did not indeed straightforwardly establish a Petrine "office." But von Balthasar insisted, "The transfer of Christ's pastoral ministry to Peter cannot be expurgated from the Gospel." And yet, the ministerial authority entailed in that transfer to Peter consists precisely in Christ's "privilege and ability to give his life for his sheep"; and the twin conditions for this authority include both the demand for Peter's "greater love" and the prophecy of his martyrdom on a cross.[38]

I suspect this type of antiliteralist retort carries rather greater force than conventional Protestant exegesis might like to acknowledge. The more one attends to Peter both in New Testament texts and in the memory of the early church, the more one discovers each to be already a function of the other: the second-century remembered Peter is clearly shaped by a scriptural persona, which in turn is already indebted to a corporate ecclesial memory. As a result, both inherited caricatures (e.g., of a vacillating bumbler who misunderstood both Jesus and Paul) and imagined historical certainties (e.g., of Peter's sole magisterial authority as the first in an unbroken line of popes on his chair at

35. William Neill, Review of Oscar Cullmann, *Petrus: Jünger, Apostel, Märtyrer* (Zurich: Zwingli-Verlag, 1952), *SJT* 7 (1954): 207-10, here 210.

36. Von Balthasar, *Office of Peter*, p. 75, quoting Cullmann, *Petrus*, pp. 238-40.

37. Von Balthasar, *Office of Peter*, p. 76.

38. Von Balthasar, "Anti-Roman Attitude," pp. xiv-xvii.

Rome) may give way to a picture of the man that is both fresher, more unstable, and yet more engaging than either surface readings or inherited caricatures suggest.

To read the Gospels with an eye to their inescapably public liturgical function and effect requires a sensitivity to the possibility that their hearers may discover something universally exemplary and typological in features like the faithful listening of Mary of Bethany or like the eschatological expectancy of Zechariah's song. The same, perhaps, is true for the task of penitent shepherding assigned to Peter — even if that alone does not of course give us a papal line of succession.

The problem with von Balthasar's approach is not that it allows a *sensus plenior* or a fuller meaning to the narrative of what Christ entrusts to Peter. That is surely discussable and open to scrutiny. But my query arises more from the ahistorical and highly allegorized way in which von Balthasar achieves his appropriation, not only for Peter but also for Mary.

This in turn makes particular exegetical claims seem at times arbitrary and in any case insufficiently self-critical, let alone falsifiable. Von Balthasar's scriptural characters too often appear reduced to ciphers or principles in the service of contemporary ecclesial agendas. Just as Mary is "the all-inclusive, protective and directive form of all ecclesial life" (p. 208)[39] so that "the entire church is Marian" (p. 205), so also "Peter" alone "as shepherd who has to pasture the whole flock . . . has a right to claim authority (in doctrine and leadership) and to demand unity" (p. 158). Peter receives "infallibility" for his governing office as "a partial share in the total flawlessness of the feminine, Marian church" (167). "Peter" is now evidently the pope, and patently *not* Scripture's Peter.

The problem may be that this sort of allegorical abstraction lends itself, beyond appropriate moral and pastoral exhortation, to the perpetuation of an institutional status quo. Is there not a danger that, contrary to von Balthasar's best intentions for a plural and collegial ecclesiology, and despite his explicit call for mutuality and communion, such use of Peter and Mary as institutional ciphers in fact might paradoxically aid and abet an ecclesial Realpolitik in ways that are either subtly or overtly totalizing in their ecclesial application to both characters?[40]

It is at the same time important to acknowledge that von Balthasar's por-

---

39. I am indebted for these and several of the following quotes to the discussion in McDade, "Von Balthasar," pp. 100-104.

40. I am not wholly reassured on this point by the explanation of McDade that for von Balthasar "obedience has the same dignity as commanding": "Von Balthasar," pp. 112-13, citing Laberthonnière via von Balthasar, *Office of Peter*, pp. 264, 315.

trayal of Peter achieves several aims rather well. He recognizes that misplaced conceptions of authority skew Christian appraisals of the role of governance in general, of apostolicity in particular, and of Peter most especially. He accepts that the early Christian organizational chart must not be misconstrued as a pyramid, let alone one with Peter at the top. Its continuing popularity notwithstanding, that misconception strikes him as a wholly lamentable relic of Roman imperial ideas of power.[41] This form of top-down governance did not pertain in Jerusalem, where even some Protestant scholars still assume Peter to have been in authority until James staged a palace coup in order to become "the first pope" (as Martin Hengel memorably put it[42]). There was also no such pyramid in Antioch or even in Rome itself. Despite periodic assertions of episcopal primacy by Victor in the second century and Stephen in the third, throughout antiquity the dominant line of the Roman church's apologetic, whether in literary sources like 1 *Clement* or Irenaeus, in iconic inscriptions like those of the founder in the Church of Santa Sabina or of Pope Damasus at San Sebastiano, was based on the claim of Rome's *dual* apostolic foundation by Peter and Paul, representing the Jewish and the gentile missions. Von Balthasar rightly focuses on the church's *collegial* and *pluriform* apostolic foundation, symbolized by Peter alongside Paul, John, and James as well as Mary. A welcome effect of this way of proceeding is to ground the papacy not in itself but ecclesiologically and in scriptural principles of apostolic leadership, thereby quite explicitly "displacing" the office of Peter from its position misguidedly imagined atop an authoritarian pyramid.[43]

These well-framed arguments poignantly interrogate and diminish a certain kind of traditionalist Roman Catholic rhetoric that tethered a Petrine "office" all too narrowly and (as other churches would argue) arbitrarily to a unilinear succession of Roman pontiffs. As we saw, von Balthasar achieves this in part by insisting on a nuanced, collegial, and complementarian reading of the New Testament Peter's profile in relation to several *other* prominent apostolic figures. Despite the stereotyped repetition of authoritarian claims in some popular Roman Catholic teaching, an exclusively *unilinear* Petrine office cannot in fact be plausibly grounded either in Scripture's Peter or for that matter in patristic attestations of second-century Roman episcopal succession *(diadochē)*.

All these are among the undeniable strengths of von Balthasar's approach.

41. Von Balthasar, *Office of Peter*, p. 21.

42. Martin Hengel, "Jakobus der Herrenbruder — der erste 'Papst'?" in *Glaube und Eschatologie: Festschrift für Werner Georg Kümmel zum 80. Geburtstag*, ed. Erich Grässer and Otto Merk (Tübingen: Mohr Siebeck, 1985), pp. 71-104.

43. Cf. McDade, "Von Balthasar," p. 104.

And yet the question remains whether, even while decentering and relativizing the authority of the papacy, von Balthasar's allegorical approach does not in the end replace the early church's complex profile of Simon Peter a little too neatly with a cipher of Peter that straightforwardly equates to the bishops of Rome. Examples of such comfortable slippage from Peter to Pope include unabashedly contemporizing statements such as the following:

> Peter too must be continually learning: he must not think that he can carry out his office in isolation (which could easily tempt him to overvalue it). He too must take his bearings by the all-encompassing totality of the Church, which expresses itself concretely in the dynamic interplay of her major missions and in the laws inherent in her structure. . . . Revelation is entrusted to the whole Church, and all, under the leadership of Peter, are to preserve it, interpret it and produce a living exposition of it. And since the office of Peter is borne by fallible human beings, it needs everyone's watchful but loving co-operation so that the exercise of this office may be characterized by the degree of "in-fallibility" that belongs to it. More precisely, this means that a pope can exercise his office fruitfully for all only if he is recognised and loved in a truly ecclesial way, even in the context of instruction or dispute.[44]

However unobjectionable this appears as a statement of the Petrine office, it remains the case that its New Testament contours are here absorbed and subsumed, apparently without remainder, beneath the institutional reality of a soi-disant Petrine papacy.

A side-effect of this allegorical abstraction will be to flatten and impoverish the rich and diverse scriptural profile of Peter. Five aspects of that biblical profile may here suffice to illustrate in brief what is arguably a much broader pattern, which I have tried to expound more extensively elsewhere:[45]

1. The New Testament Peter is not James: he is a pioneering missionary rather than a sedentary ruler or caliph.
2. Peter bridges not only between apostolic individuals (so von Balthasar) but also, and just as importantly, between early Christianity's very diverse geographic centers and their churches. No other apostolic figure connects Jerusalem credibly with both Antioch and Rome, for example. The broadest ecumenicity seems an inalienable aspect of Peter's ministry.

44. Von Balthasar, *Office of Peter,* p. 315.
45. Bockmuehl, *Simon Peter,* passim.

3. The first letter of Peter is widely acknowledged as bringing together an almost unparalleled range of early Christian traditions.[46] This document illustrates that the New Testament Peter's "catholicity" will be Pauline as much as Petrine, a point that is almost wholly submerged in von Balthasar's account.

4. The scriptural Peter relates to secular power neither competitively nor complementarily but subversively, relativizing its claims and suffering costly consequences as a result (his repeated imprisonment, exile, and eventual martyrdom). This point is again documented across a wide range of sources, and presumably has cognate implications for the continuing exercise of a Petrine "office."

5. More broadly, it matters for the understanding of Peter in the New Testament and in the first three Christian centuries that with very few exceptions he serves no one group or cause as patently parti pris, "our man" (whether to endorse or to oppose an alternative). Peter in the New Testament is *both* a visionary *and* the guardian of the Jesus tradition. In second-century polemic (whether "gnostic" or "catholic") that balance is admittedly on occasion distorted into a bipolar alternative, but even those exceptions prove and confirm the rule that *both* aspects are vital for understanding his biblical and early Christian profile.

The Question of Continuity: Peter's Ministry and the Pope's

Having offered a critical acknowledgment of von Balthasar's laudable concern to relate the "Petrine office" to the Peter of the New Testament, we must now turn the question on its head: might biblical scholarship in its turn recognize something of a Petrine ministry emerging in its own text, connecting von Balthasar's Peter to a New Testament pope, as it were?

What surfaces in Scripture is Peter the uneducated fisherman, Peter the

---

46. Scholars have long recognized 1 Peter as an "epistle of the tradition" (C. Spicq) "at the crossroads" of New Testament theologies (A. Vanhoye), manifesting catholicity more than distinctiveness. It is conversant with a wide range of early Christian ideas without patently representing one particular "school"; in addition to extensive links with the Jesus tradition as well as with quasi-Pauline theological tropes, 1 Peter belongs with Romans and Hebrews as one of the NT books most replete with echoes of the Old Testament. For documentation see, e.g., Lauri Thurén, *Argument and Theology in 1 Peter: The Origins of Christian Paraenesis,* JSNTSup 114 (Sheffield: JSOT Press), p. 14 n. 7; and John H. Elliott, *1 Peter: A New Translation with Introduction and Commentary,* AB 37B (New York: Doubleday), p. 30 (citing numerous others).

irascible disciple, Peter the miracle worker, Peter the eyewitness and the pillar, the bishop and the martyr, the apocalyptic visionary and yet the repository and guarantor of the tradition about the Lord. The variety of images, evidence, and texts can be disorientating, whether we begin with Paul's polemical early testimony in Galatians or work backward from much later hagiographies of Roman or pseudo-Clementine perspective. Although one may feel an occasional sense of intellectual whiplash about this diversity, there are nevertheless areas of striking continuity between the New Testament memories of Peter from different historical and geographical locations.

Peter emerges into the Gospel narrative as an undistinguished rustic whose house in Capernaum served as a base for Jesus' ministry. His profile is that of the leading disciple in the privileged group of three, present with James and John at key moments in Jesus' ministry such as the transfiguration. The first half of Acts continues that picture of Peter, while portraying him as something of a missionary pioneer, a powerful miracle worker, and one who played a role in every major event in Jerusalem Christianity until around 49 CE. Paul's heated comments in Galatians 2 grudgingly concede Peter's prominence as well, even if Peter was in the wrong at Antioch, as Paul thought. Paul himself soon afterward in 1 Corinthians sounds markedly more irenic about this paradigmatic apostle, pioneer witness of the resurrection and fellow "steward of the mysteries of God" (1 Cor. 3:21–4:1; 9:5; 15:5-8). For all their contrasts in theology, language, and evidently authorship, the two Petrine letters agree in portraying an apostle who is at least implicitly presented as an eyewitness of Jesus (of his passion and transfiguration, respectively: 1 Pet. 5:1; 2 Pet. 1:16-18), and as in some sense a senior shepherd of Christ's flock, as is already adumbrated in the Fourth Gospel (1 Pet. 2:25; 5:1-4; John 21:15-17).

Second-century sources are variously supportive or occasionally critical of Peter and the profile he fills in the larger church. Appreciative texts stress Peter's importance in the ministry of Jesus and his position of authority and eminence. To be sure, a handful of others read in certain esoteric Egyptian Christian circles implicitly accept his importance for the orthodox position while seeking to subvert his authority relative to other figures such as Thomas or Mary Magdalene (as in the *Gospel of Thomas* or the *Gospel of Mary*). Yet most of the more widely read Eastern texts, too, take for granted Peter's ministry from Jerusalem to Rome. The Petrine *Acts* and the pseudo-Clementine literature, for example, are among popular pro-Petrine texts that colorfully portray his leadership, his rhetorical power, his miracles, and his resistance against heresy, ultimately in Rome.

All this, to be sure, still leaves us wrestling with von Balthasar's question about a Petrine "office." On this point, I suggest that Cullmann and his Protestant reviewers were both profoundly right and profoundly misguided. On the one hand, and despite his undoubted prominence, the remembered Peter of the Gospels and the Epistles is *not* exceptional in his role as a fellow shepherd and fellow servant of the flock of Christ (see 1 Pet. 5:1-4). The apostle's very fallibility and fragility place him on the same road of discipleship as all other believers — and in particular all those who exercise the pastoral task. Simon Peter is first and foremost neither an authority nor an institution, neither powerful nor infallible, but a flawed disciple and shepherd of Christ's flock.

On the other hand, and by the same token, the scope of the task assigned to Peter (whether in Matthew 16 or John 21) does seem coextensive with the life on earth not merely of the apostle personally but also of Christ's flock globally. And thus, as long as the church endures, there must be a question of the proper continuation or succession of this Petrine ministry.

In his cantankerous dispute with Pope Stephen, Cyprian (d. 258) may be judged right to conclude that *all* those shepherds who confess the faith of Peter constitute the "rock" on which, according to Matthew 16, the church is founded.[47] This is the appropriate challenge to any maximal papal arrogation of Peter's ministry — and one to which, one might argue, von Balthasar's project could rightly be sympathetic.

Nevertheless, it is also the case that the remembered Peter's profile before long encompassed the sense that his ministry on Christ's behalf was indeed entrusted to a continuing succession of ecclesial shepherds in various places of his activity (including Antioch) but also, and perhaps most prominently, in Rome. This in turn continues to make it feasible and permissible to ask about successors to Peter, however much later institutional trappings of authority and opulence ill-become the early church's memory of a Galilean fisherman whose way of discipleship neither sought nor obtained any power or wealth. (The early years of Pope Francis have in this respect hinted at a welcome change of the Roman mood music.)

Pope John Paul II was famously, and perhaps justly, grieved that the institutionally visible form of that Petrine ministry had itself become such a frequent instrument not of unity but of division.[48] Whereas that divisive effect has been sadly exemplified in certain phases of ecumenical relations with other ecclesial communions, the converse of this paradox is that the ministry of

---

47. Cyprian, *Ep.* 26.1; 73.7; cf. *Ep.* 74.17 of Firmilian to Cyprian.
48. Classically stated in his 1995 encyclical *Ut unum sint.*

several recent occupants of the Petrine chair has repeatedly foregrounded a desire in some appropriate way to serve *all* the servants of Christ.

Consensus about these matters, and about their bearing on Jesus' prayer for his followers' unity (John 17:21-22), remains an eschatological hope. Yet regardless of the right ad hoc and particular answers, the principle of a continuation of the Petrine ministry *as such* seems clear in the early profile of the man, beginning perhaps with classic "Petrine primacy" texts such as Matthew 16:17-19; Luke 22:31-32; and John 21:15-17. All three texts imply a post-Easter continuation of Peter's assignment, and hence perhaps of a role that seems intrinsically permanent in nature and not as such tied to the historic identity of the one apostle.[49] The labor of pasturing the flock and guarding them from attack was clearly a requirement that would continue; and so it seems patently untrue to take for granted, as many Protestant exegetes still do, that Peter's pastoral task self-evidently "expired with his death."[50]

Peter's profile in the vast majority of early Christian texts embodies the archetype of an apostolic ministry that serves the entire church, and a task of pastoral service that necessarily endures as long as the church endures. It is in this sense, above all, that Peter is remembered as the rock on which the church is built, as feeder of Christ's flock, as caretaker of the kingdom's keys, as binder and looser. In the end, the diverse and unharmonizable sources of Peter's memory nevertheless attest an important consensual insight on this point: The enduring magnitude of the mission is greater than the volatile fragility of the man to whom it was first entrusted. In this sense, indeed perhaps in this sense first and foremost, we see Peter remembered as the one to whom Christ's pastoral task is entrusted (as his place-taker or "vicar," in the old-fashioned Roman Catholic language). The fragility and yet indispensability of this ministry of unity, its strength in weakness, and its witness to this apostle's peculiar grace of a "second-chance" discipleship might indeed serve the continuing heritage of Peter's memory among all the Christian churches.

If one is willing in principle to grant such an implied Petrine ministry, then one useful abiding question for debate is its ecclesial locus. Does its identity now subsist in an office, in an office holder, or only derivatively there but

---

49. Cf. Rudolf Pesch, "Was an Petrus sichtbar war, ist in den Primat eingegangen," in *Il primato del successore di Pietro: Atti del Simposio Teologico — Roma, Dicembre 1996*, ed. Joseph Ratzinger (Vatican City: Libreria Editrice Vaticana, 1998), pp. 37-39 (22-111); Ettore Malnati, *Simone detto Pietro, nella singolarità del suo ministero*, Pro Manuscripto (Lugano: EUPress FTL, 2008), p. 82.

50. Thus Jürgen Becker, *Simon Petrus im Urchristentum*, Biblisch-Theologische Studien (Neukirchen-Vluyn: Neukirchener, 2009), p. 139.

first and foremost in the body of the faithful at large? It seems important to note the recurrent resistance of patristic reflection to any premature foreclosure of this question as though exclusively focused on the bishop of Rome.

Attentiveness to this ecclesial locus of Petrine ministry may shed further light on Pope John Paul II's aforementioned sadness that the office of Peter's visible successor in Rome should of all things be the cause of division in the church. Peter's charism of feeding and tending the Good Shepherd's flock should perhaps be understood to devolve to all who pastor the faithful. That said, von Balthasar's study of Peter certainly reminds us that the question of authority in the church does not fade away whenever it becomes politically incorrect or culturally inconvenient to ask it.

It seems appropriate to come away from this exercise with a genuine appreciation for von Balthasar's desire to assess the function of Peter first and foremost within the variegated *plurality* of apostolic leadership. At the same time it would seem that, in reading Scripture's Peter and his ongoing task and office in the church, abstract ecclesial allegorizing may be no more exegetically useful or faithful than a more specifically *personal* typology — documenting and expounding leaders past and present who exemplify this apostle's discipleship, his faith, and his pastoral call. Perhaps the authority in Peter's office of shepherding and guarding the mission of Christ's flock subsists first and foremost in the faith, the love, and the hope of all believers, from which individual leaders derive their contingent task. An office of Peter so construed might grant more tangible meaning and authority to that other scripturally grounded title of the pope: "the servant of the servants of Christ."

Index of Modern Authors

Adams, Sean A., 64n.9, 131n.5, 146n.2,
    155n.33
Adan-Bayewitz, David, 27, 27n.22, 28n.23
Allison, Dale C., 1n.1, 40n.46
Andresen, Georg, 82
Arav, Rami, 25n.19, 28, 28n.25, 28n.26
Arbeiter, Achim, 293n.57
Ascough, Richard, 123, 123n.5-6, 124,
    124n.7-10
Assmann, Jan, 50n.10, 53, 53n.18
Aubert, Jean-Jacques, 78n.7
Aune, David E., 54n.19

Bagnall, Roger, 188n.19
Balthasar, Hans Urs von, 322, 322n.5, 323,
    323n.6-8, 324, 324n.12, 325, 325n.13-15,
    326, 326n.16-18, 327, 327n.20-22, 328,
    328n.23, 328n.25, 328n.27, 329, 329n.28-
    30, 330, 331, 331n.34, 332, 332n.36-38,
    333, 333n.40, 334, 334n.41, 335, 335n.44,
    336-38, 338n.48, 340
Barclay, John M. G., 45n.62
Barclay, William, 77n.6
Bardenhewer, Otto, 172n.13
Bar-Ilan, Meir, 132n.11
Barnes, Timothy D., 44n.60, 45n.65,
    53n.16, 76n.1, 80n.14, 81n.16, 83n.24-25,
    88n.41, 89n.44, 91n.49

Barnier, Amanda J., 51n.11
Barrett, C. Kingsley, 70, 70n.42, 71n.47,
    85, 85n.29, 112n.9, 113n.10, 116n.22,
    117n.23, 119n.31, 132, 132n.10, 133,
    133n.13
Barry, Catherine, 204, 204n.26
Barth, Karl, 3n.4, 323, 330n.32
Bauckham, Richard J., 37n.34, 45, 45n.64,
    47n.3, 48n.6, 51n.12, 56n.27, 57n.31,
    59n.37, 77n.6, 86, 86n.33, 95n.67,
    109n.1, 110, 110n.4-5, 117, 117n.27,
    120n.34, 136n.26, 147n.4, 155n.34,
    201n.17, 249n.61, 255n.69
Bauer, Johannes B., 172n.12
Bauer, Walter, 85, 86n.31, 264, 264n.3-4,
    267, 267n.14, 271, 271n.24
Baumeister, Theofried, 196n.1
Beasley-Murray, George R., 86, 86n.32,
    243n.46
Becker, Jürgen, 14n.61, 127n.15, 127n.17,
    339n.50
Bedrossian, Matthias, 265n.9
Belting, Hans, 292n.52
Bennema, Cornelis, 109n.1, 119n.33
Berding, Kenneth, 172, 172n.14, 174,
    174n.21, 175, 175n.24-25, 176, 176n.28-
    33, 177, 177n.38-39, 178, 178n.43,
    178n.46-47, 179, 179n.49

Berger, Klaus, 196n.1

Best, Ernest, 52n.14, 58n.34, 59n.38, 99n.4, 104, 104n.16

Bethge, Hans-Gebhard, 152n.24, 205n.30, 206n.33, 208n.42-43

Beyschlag, Karlmann, 171n.11

Bickell, Gustav, 224n.10, 225n.11

Bigg, Charles, 154n.32

Binsfeld, Andrea, 285n.32

Birmelé, André, 3n.4, 6n.20, 7n.23

Bisconti, Fabrizio, 291n.50, 301n.92

Black, C. Clifton, 48n.6

Blaine, Bradford, 109n.1, 113n.11, 116n.21, 118n.30

Bock, Darrell L., 74n.69, 74n.71, 133n.13

Bockmuehl, Markus, 10-11, 11n.46-47, 12, 12n.48-54, 13, 13n.55, 14, 14n.56-61, 15, 31n.4, 33n.14, 34, 34n.15, 34n.19-20, 35, 35n.23-25, 37n.32, 38n.36, 58n.31, 59n.37, 76, 76n.3, 77, 77n.5, 86, 86n.33-34, 88, 95n.68, 99, 99n.2, 123n.4, 130, 130n.1, 136n.24, 156, 157n.41, 161, 161n.3, 164n.8-9, 169, 169n.2, 170n.8, 175n.26, 222n.4, 260n.78, 261n.79, 321n.2, 335n.45

Bond, Helen K., 78n.9, 80n.13, 166

Boobyer, G. H., 155n.36

Boomershine, Thomas E., 57n.31, 59, 59n.37

Borrell, Augusti, 58n.34

Bovini, Giuseppe, 292n.53, 295n.64-66, 296n.69, 297, 299n.77, 299n.82-83, 300n.84-86, 300n.88, 301n.89-91, 302n.96, 303n.99

Bovon, François, 151n.21

Bowersock, Glen W., 89n.44

Brakke, David, 199, 199n.11, 200, 200n.13

Brandenburg, Hugo, 292n.53, 295n.64-66, 296n.69, 297, 299n.77, 299n.82-83, 300n.84-86, 300n.88, 301n.89-91, 302n.96, 303n.99

Brankaer, J., 206n.33, 208n.42-43

Branscomb, B. H., 50n.9

Brecht, Martin, 326n.16

Bremmer, Jan N., 95n.67, 238, 238n.40

Brock, A. Graham, 216n.59

Brown, Raymond E., 85n.28, 100, 104-5, 105n.18, 109n.2, 222n.1, 321n.3

Brox, Norbert, 154n.30, 211n.48

Bruce, F. F., 63n.5, 69n.39, 71, 71n.51, 230n.21

Bubar, Wallace W., 104n.17

Buchanan, E. S., 90n.46

Bullard, Roger A., 211n.47, 258n.74

Bultmann, Rudolf K., 2n.4, 50n.9, 85, 85n.30, 106, 106n.23, 111n.7, 113n.10, 243n.48, 254n.68

Burkitt, F. C., 247n.58

Burridge, Richard A., 54n.19, 58n.33

Bussières, Marie-Pierre, 148n.10

Cadbury, Henry J., 63, 63n.7

Cambe, Michel, 183n.7-8, 184, 184n.11, 191n.25

Caragounis, Chrys C., 40n.45, 41n.48, 42n.53

Carr, David M., 143n.41

Chadwick, Henry, 287n.38, 304n.104

Champlin, Edward J., 81n.17, 82, 82n.23, 92, 92n.56, 93, 93n.61-63, 94n.64

Christern-Briesenick, B., 300n.87

Clark, Andrew C., 127n.15

Clivaz, Claire, 213n.52

Collins, Adela Yarbro, 4n.10, 257n.73

Collins, Raymond F., 109n.2, 156n.40

Congar, Yves, 326n.16

Conway, Colleen M., 118n.29

Corbo, Virgilio C., 25n.19

Cranfield, Charles E. B., 50n.9

Cribiore, Raffaella, 131n.4

Crook, John A., 38n.39

Cullmann, Oscar, 2, 2n.4, 3, 3n.5-7, 4, 4n.8-10, 5, 5n.11-14, 6, 6n.15-20, 7, 7n.21-24, 8, 8n.31, 10, 12-15, 31n.4, 35n.23, 38n.35, 85, 85n.30, 99, 99n.1, 99n.3, 222n.2, 263, 263n.1, 264, 287n.38, 321, 321n.3, 331-32, 332n.35-36, 338

Culpepper, R. Alan, 109n.1-2, 110n.5, 117n.24, 118n.30, 119n.31

Curran, John, 287n.38

Curtis, Robert I., 24n.15

Dahl, Nils A., 154n.31
Damgaard, Finn, 127n.16
Dassmann, Ernst, 76, 76n.2, 274n.6, 279n.17-18
Davidson, James N., 21n.7
Davies, W. D., 40n.46
Davila, James R., 156n.39
de Boer, Esther A., 216n.59, 233n.29, 234, 234n.31
de Boer, Martinus C., 163n.7, 179n.50
Deckers, J. G., 293n.54
DeConick, April D., 232n.25
Dehandschutter, Boudewijn, 170n.7, 175n.26, 177, 177n.40, 178n.44
Deissmann, Adolf, 38n.37
Dewey, Joanna, 47n.2
de Zwaan, Johannes, 70, 70n.40
Dibelius, Martin, 50n.9, 62n.3-4, 63, 63n.5, 63n.7, 71, 71n.48
Dicken, Frank, 62n.1
Dietrich, Wolfgang, 123n.4
Dobschütz, Ernst von, 183n.7
Dodd, Charles H., 63n.5, 67n.28, 68n.33, 69n.38, 70, 70n.41
Doering, Lutz, 130n.3, 149n.13
Donfried, Karl P., 100, 104-5, 223, 223n.5, 223n.6
Dresken-Weiland, Jutta, 285n.33-34, 298n.74, 299n.81, 301n.92, 302n.94-95, 302n.97, 303n.98, 303n.100-101
Droge, Arthur J., 110n.3, 116n.22, 117n.24
Dudley, Merle Bland, 65n.15
Dunderberg, Ismo, 197n.3, 201n.17, 205n.31
Dunn, James D. G., 2n.2, 15n.62, 65n.18, 101n.12
Dupont, Jacques, 63n.5
Duval, Yvette, 288n.40

Eastman, David L., 297n.70
Eck, Werner, 78n.8
Ehrenberg, Victor, 30n.2
Ehrman, Bart D., 1n.1, 88n.43, 91n.52, 147n.3, 162n.4, 165n.10
Elliott, J. K., 1n.1, 88n.42, 90n.47, 137n.28,

224n.8, 244, 244n.50-51, 253n.67, 255n.69
Elliott, John H., 134, 134n.18, 135n.19, 153n.27, 154, 155n.35, 157, 250n.62, 336n.46
Elliott, Mark, 321n.1
Epp, Eldon Jay, 125n.12, 127n.15
Eshel, Hanan, 191n.26

Farrer, Austin, 47n.5
Ferguson, Everett, 90n.45
Ferreiro, Alberto, 218n.65
Ferrua, Antonio, 287n.38, 300n.87
Festugière, André-Jean, 79n.11, 190n.21
Filson, Floyd V., 3, 3n.7
Fitzmyer, Joseph A., 30n.3, 34n.16, 41n.52, 74n.68
Fleddermann, Harry T., 237n.38
Foakes-Jackson, Frederick John, 86, 86n.33
Fornara, Charles W., 65n.16
Forster, E. M., 167, 167n.12
Frend, W. H. C., 242n.45, 288n.40
Frey, Jörg, 237n.39
Freyne, Sean, 22n.10
Foster, Paul, 137n.27, 150n.18, 225n.11, 228n.17-18, 229n.20, 245n.55, 258n.75
Fulda, Hermann, 78n.9, 86n.31

Gardner, Jane F., 38n.38
Garnsey, Peter, 78n.7
Gasque, Ward, 63n.5, 69n.39, 70, 70n.43, 71, 71n.51
Gathercole, Simon, 202n.20
Gaventa, Beverly Roberts, 118n.28
Geiger, Joseph, 78n.8
Gempf, Conrad H., 64, 64n.11, 64n.14, 65n.15
Gerke, Friedrich, 297n.70
Giet, Stanislas, 170n.8
Gill, Christopher, 58n.33
Glasson, Thomas F., 55, 56n.25
Gnilka, Christian, 86n.35
Goulder, Michael D., 68n.34
Grant, Mark, 21n.9
Grappe, Christian, 2n.3, 132n.10

Green, Peter, 40n.47
Gregory, Andrew F., 169, 169n.4-5,
    235n.34-35, 236, 236n.37
Gruenwald, Ithamar, 152n.23
Grünstäudl, Wolfgang, 183n.9
Guarducci, Margherita, 14n.58, 274n.6,
    276n.8, 277n.9, 277n.11, 278, 278n.13-
    14, 279n.16-18, 282, 282n.24, 285n.31,
    290, 291n.46-47

Hachlili, Rachel, 32n.13, 39n.40
Haenchen, Ernst, 62n.4, 85, 85n.31,
    132n.10
Hägg, Thomas, 54, 54n.20, 55-56, 55n.22-
    24, 60, 60n.40
Hagner, Donald A., 174n.21
Hahnemann, Geoffrey Mark, 90n.45
Hakola, Raimo, 58n.32
Halbwachs, Maurice, 50n.10
Hanson, Kenneth C., 21n.5, 24, 24n.16
Harnack, Adolf von, 148n.8, 151, 151n.19,
    266, 266n.12, 268n.15, 270, 271n.23
Harrington, Daniel J., 34n.16
Harris-McCoy, Daniel E., 79n.10, 80n.12
Harris, Celia B., 52n.13
Harris, William V., 131n.4, 135n.22
Harrison, P. N., 175, 175n.27
Hartenstein, Judith, 203n.25, 204,
    204n.27, 208n.40
Hartog, Paul, 172n.15, 175n.24, 177n.42,
    178n.45-46
Havelaar, Henriette, 211n.47, 212n.49,
    212n.51
Heath, Jane, 321n.1
Heil, John Paul, 106, 106n.22
Helyer, Larry R., 75n.73
Henck, Nick, 274n.4, 293n.57
Henderson, Timothy P., 229n.19
Hengel, Martin, 8, 8n.26-32, 9, 9n.33-39,
    10, 10n.40-44, 11, 11n.45, 15, 48n.6,
    49n.8, 80, 80n.14, 100n.4, 100n.9,
    110n.3, 133n.15, 166n.11, 198n.6, 222n.3,
    306n.108, 334, 334n.42
Hercher, Rudolf, 79n.11
Herron, Thomas, 171n.10
Heubner, Heinz, 82, 82n.21

Hezser, Catherine, 133n.11
Hill, Charles E., 175, 198n.6
Holmes, Michael W., 173n.18, 174n.21,
    175, 176n.31, 178n.45-46, 179n.50
Holzer, Vincent, 324n.10
Hooker, Morna, 40n.44, 60n.39
Hornschuh, Manfred, 147n.6
Horrell, David, 146n.2, 153n.28, 154
Horsley, Greg H. R., 24n.17, 31n.6, 35n.26,
    71, 71n.50
Hovhannessian, Vahan, 148n.7
Hultgren, Arland, 128, 128n.21, 129n.22
Hurtado, Larry W., 70n.45, 71n.54, 72,
    72n.56, 72n.58-59, 73, 73n.61, 73n.64-
    65, 146n.2, 226n.14, 281n.21

Ilan, Tal, 31n.5, 32, 32n.8, 32n.11, 34n.16-
    17, 34n.22, 36, 36n.30, 37, 37n.31, 37n.33,
    40n.43, 41n.49-50, 43
Incignieri, Brian J., 49n.8
Irmscher, Johannes, 139n.32, 140n.34

James, Montague Rhodes, 147, 147n.4,
    148, 223n.8, 244, 244n.53, 255n.70
Janßen, M., 214n.54
Jensen, Morten H., 19n.2
Jobes, Karen H., 135n.19
Johnson, Luke Timothy, 63n.6, 71,
    71n.49, 126n.14
Johnson, Scott Fitzgerald, 266n.11
Jones, A. H. M., 30n.2
Jones, F. Stanley, 141n.36, 181n.2
Joshel, Sandra R., 38n.38
Junod, Eric, 266, 266n.13

Kaler, Michael, 148n.10, 152n.24, 208n.41
Käsemann, Ernst, 157n.42
Keener, Craig S., 63n.8, 64n.11-12, 65,
    65n.17, 65n.20, 66n.21, 66n.23-24,
    66n.26, 67n.28, 69n.39, 70n.45, 71n.53,
    73, 73n.62-63, 74n.67, 74n.69, 112n.9
Keith, Chris, 50n.10, 53, 53n.18, 133n.16,
    143, 143n.42, 143n.43, 144n.46, 181
Kelber, Werner, 53, 53n.18, 57, 57n.29-30
Kelly, John N. D., 264, 264n.5, 269n.16,
    269n.18

Kemp, Richard I., 52n.13
Khomych, Taras, 173, 173n.19
Kilby, Karen, 324n.10-11, 328n.24
King, Karen L., 197, 197n.3, 203, 203n.22, 233n.27
Kingsbury, Jack D., 100, 100n.9
Kirk, Alan, 50n.10
Kirschbaum, E., 274n.6, 275n.7, 279n.17, 279n.18, 285n.30, 288n.39
Klauck, Hans-Josef, 150n.17
Kleinbauer, W. Eugene, 293n.57
Klijn, A. F. J., 246n.57, 247n.59
Knoch, Otto, 169n.6, 177n.40
Knox, Wilfred L., 72n.60
Kodell, Jerome, 123n.6
Koester, Helmut, 70n.44
Koschorke, Klaus, 208n.41
Krafft, Eva, 114n.15, 116n.20, 117n.24
Kraus, Thomas J., 94n.66, 95n.67, 132n.8, 133, 133n.12, 133n.14, 135n.22, 182n.4, 225n.11-13, 326n.17
Krautheimer, Richard, 274n.4
Kruger, Michael J., 227n.15
Kuhn, Heinz-Wolfgang, 20n.3, 28, 28n.24, 78n.7, 82n.20

Lafferty, Maura, 287n.38, 304n.102
Lake, Kirsopp, 91n.52
Lampe, Peter, 4n.8, 40n.46, 77, 81n.18, 88, 143n.39, 146n.2, 205n.29, 274n.3, 277n.10, 278n.15, 280n.20, 282n.22, 283n.25, 284n.28-29, 289n.41, 306n.110
Landolt, Jean-François, 128n.19
Lane, William L., 61n.41
Lapham, Fred, 130n.3, 137n.28, 139n.32, 223n.7
Lawson, John A., 175n.27
Leibniz, Gottfried Wilhelm, 146n.1
Leipziger, Ursula, 285n.30
Levick, Barbara, 30n.1
Lewis, N. Denzey, 203n.21
Liddell, H. G., 84n.26
Lietzmann, Hans, 90n.46
Lieu, Judith M., 149n.15
Lightfoot, Joseph Barber, Bp., 88n.43, 89n.44, 92, 92n.54-55

Lincoln, Andrew T., 112n.9, 114n.18, 117n.25, 243n.47
Lindars, Barnabas, 34, 34n.21
Lindemann, Andreas, 171n.9, 171n.11, 173, 173n.18, 174n.21, 179, 179n.50
Lipsius, Richard Adelbert, 88n.42, 90n.47
Logan, Alastair H. B., 83n.25, 200n.12
Lohmann, Hans, 174, 174n.20
Löhr, Helmut, 170n.7
Löhr, W. A., 218n.63
Lona, Horacio E., 86n.35, 169n.4
Lüderitz, Gert, 44n.58
Lührmann, Dieter, 49n.7, 225n.11
Luomanen, Petri, 214n.55
Luther, Martin, 1, 326, 326n.16
Luttikhuizen, Gerard P., 199n.10
Luz, Ulrich, 293n.56

MacMullen, Ramsay, 44n.61
Maidan, Michael, 330n.32
Maier, Paul L., 78n.8
Malbon, Elizabeth Struthers, 57n.31, 297n.70
Malnati, Ettore, 339n.49
Mancinelli, Fabrizio, 291n.46
Marcus, Joel, 47, 47n.2, 47n.4-5, 48, 48n.7, 49, 49n.8, 53n.16, 56, 56n.26, 59n.37, 104n.17
Marguerat, Daniel, 179n.50
Marichal, Robert, 285n.31
Marjanen, Antti, 209n.44
Markley, John R., 101n.11, 101n.13, 106n.21, 107n.26, 255n.71
Markschies, Christoph, 197n.3, 205n.28
Marshall, I. Howard, 67n.31, 70n.46, 72n.55
Martin, Jennifer, 329n.29
Martini, Carlo M., 127n.15
Mason, Hugh J., 90n.48
Mason, Steve, 23n.14
Massaux, Édouard, 174n.21
Mathews, Mark. D., 156n.38
Maynard, Arthur H., 110n.3
McDade, John, 331n.34, 333n.39-40, 334n.43

McHugh, John F., 34n.18
McIver, Robert Kerry, 51n.12
Meade, David C., 144n.45
Meeks, Wayne, 114n.16-17
Menoud, Philippe-Henri, 128n.20
Merenlahti, Petri, 58n.32
Merz, Annette, 47n.5
Metzger, Bruce M., 105n.20, 178n.46, 267
Meyer, Marvin W., 215n.57, 258-59,
    259n.76-77
Michaels, J. Ramsey, 116n.22, 117n.26
Michie, Donald, 57n.31
Mietke, Gabriele, 293n.54
Millar, Fergus, 91n.50
Minear, Paul S., 117, 117n.27
Möhler, J. A., 331n.34
Molinari, A. Lorenzo, 211n.46
Moloney, Francis J., 116n.22
Mommsen, Theodor, 77-79
Moulds, Michelle L., 52n.13
Moule, C. F. D., 73n.60

Nagel, Titus, 198n.6, 200, 200n.14, 201,
    201n.15
Nau, Arlo J., 100n.10, 102n.15
Nave, Guy D., Jr., 126n.13
Neill, William, 332n.35
Nestori, Aldo, 291n.48, 300n.87
Neyrey, Jerome H., 155n.37
Nichols, Aidan, 329n.29
Nicklas, Tobias, 77, 94n.65-66, 95n.68,
    137n.27, 146n.2, 181, 203n.23
Niederwimmer, Kurt, 47n.5, 49n.7
Nielsen, Charles M., 176, 176n.34
Nineham, Dennis E., 50n.9
Noga-Banai, G., 293n.57, 297n.72,
    298n.74, 300n.86
Nolland, John, 34n.22, 38n.36
Norelli, Enrico, 92n.57, 93n.59, 93n.60,
    95n.67, 193, 193n.30
Novenson, Matthew V., 44n.60
Nun, Mendel, 20n.4, 23n.12

Oakes, Peter, 177n.41
Oakman, Douglas E., 24n.16
O'Connor, Daniel W., 4n.8, 14n.58

Odelain, Olivier, 31n.4, 32n.9
Ogg, George, 90n.46
O'Neill, John Cochrane, 71n.50
O'Regan, Cyril, 321n.1, 327n.19, 328,
    328n.26, 330n.32, 330n.33+C43, 331n.34

Padilla, Osvaldo, 74n.72, 131n.5
Pagels, Elaine, 203, 203n.22, 206n.34
Panchaud, Louis, 148n.10
Parvis, Sara, 271n.26
Paterson, Helen M., 52n.13
Pearson, Birger A., 218n.63-64
Peel, Malcolm L., 206n.35
Penner, Todd C., 149n.16
Perkins, Pheme, 2n.3, 7n.21, 7n.25, 100,
    100n.9, 109n.2
Pervo, Richard, 132, 132n.6
Pesch, Rudolf, 2n.3, 49n.7, 339n.49
Peterson, David, 132, 132n.9
Petit, Françoise, 265
Pichler, Josef, 69n.36
Plisch, Uwe-Karsten, 205n.30
Polhill, John B., 167n.12
Popkes, Enno E., 214n.53
Porten, Bezalel, 41n.51
Praeder, Susan Marie, 127n.15
Pratscher, Wilhelm, 196, 196n.1, 197,
    197n.2, 199n.6, 199n.9, 203, 207n.39,
    208n.41, 210n.45, 215n.58, 217n.61, 218,
    218n.62, 219n.66
Prete, Benedetto, 125n.11
Price, S. R. F., 79n.10
Prieur, Jean-Marc, 239, 239n.41

Quast, Kevin, 109n.1

Rasch, Jürgen, 293n.57
Rasmussen, Mikael Bøgh, 287n.38,
    294n.58, 294n.62, 297n.72, 298n.76
Ratzinger, Joseph, 324, 324n.9
Read-Heimerdinger, Jenny, 133,
    133n.12-13
Redman, Judith C. S., 51n.12, 52n.13
Rehm, Albert, 282n.23
Rehm, Bernhard, 139n.32, 182n.3
Reich, Ronny, 26n.20

Rensberger, David K., 174n.23
Resseguie, James L., 201n.17
Reumann, John, 100, 104-5
Reutter, Ursula, 304n.103
Rezza, Dario, 297n.70
Rhoads, David, 57n.31
Richards, E. Randolph, 135n.19
Ridderbos, Herman N., 66n.25, 68n.35,
   73n.66
Riesner, Rainer, 86n.35
Rist, John M., 76n.4
Rius-Camps, Josep, 133, 133n.12-13
Robbins, Vernon K., 54n.19
Robert, Jeanne, 78n.7
Robert, Louis, 78n.7
Robertson, A. T., 69-70, 70n.40
Robinson, Gesine Schenke, 183n.8,
   200n.12
Robinson, John A. T., 73n.60
Robinson, Joseph Armitage, 255n.70
Rokeah, David, 44, 44n.58
Römer, Franz, 82, 82n.21

Saldarini, Anthony, 143, 143n.42
Salzman, Michele R., 287n.36
Schelling, Friedrich, 329, 329n.29
Schenke, Hans-Martin, 200, 200n.12-13,
   220n.68
Schmidt, Carl, 244, 244n.52
Schmidt, Christoph, 330n.32
Schmidt, Karl Ludwig, 50n.9
Schmitt, Carl, 329-30, 330n.31-32
Schneemelcher, Wilhelm, 151, 151n.20
Schneider, Gerhard, 122n.2
Schoedel, William, 173, 173n.17
Schreiber, Johannes, 57, 57n.29
Schröter, Jens, 214n.53
Schultheiss, Tanja, 199n.7
Schürer, Emil, 43n.57
Schwartz, Barry, 50n.10, 54n.18
Schweizer, Eduard, 66n.25
Schwener, Anna Maria, 5n.26
Scott, Robert, 84n.26
Séguineau, Raymond, 31n.4, 32n.9
Sevenster, Jan Nicolaas, 148n.7
Shepherd, Massey Hamilton, 175, 175n.27

Simon, Marcel, 192n.28
Skiba, Paulette, 206n.35
Skinner, Christopher W., 110n.3
Smalley, Stephen S., 73n.60
Smallwood, E. Mary, 32n.10
Smith, Abraham, 58n.33
Smith, Morton, 170n.8
Smith, Terence V., 104, 104n.17, 106,
   106n.24
Snodgrass, Klyne R., 67n.30
Snyder, Graydon F., 4n.8, 14n.58, 278n.11,
   279n.18
Snyder, H. Gregory, 143, 143n.40, 144n.44
Soards, Marion L., 62n.2, 63n.7, 66,
   66n.25, 67n.27, 71n.52
Spicq, Ceslas, 153n.28, 336n.46
Stead, G. C., 90n.47
Steffy, J. Richard, 25n.19
Stern, Menahem, 45n.63
Still, Todd, 46n.1
Stock, Augustine, 59n.36
Stock, Brian, 187n.18
Stommel, Eduard, 298n.75
Stoops, Robert F., 240n.42-43, 241n.44
Strecker, Georg, 99, 100, 100n.5, 139n.32,
   140n.33, 237n.39
Streeter, B. H., 172, 172n.13
Stuckwisch, D. Richard, 176, 176n.35,
   177n.36-38, 178
Sturdevant, Jason S., 110n.6
Sutton, John, 51n.11
Syreeni, Kari, 58n.32, 58n.35, 100, 100n.9

Talbert, Charles H., 54n.19
Tannehill, Robert C., 57n.31, 128n.18
Tardieu, Michel, 219n.67
Taubes, Jacob, 330n.32
Taylor, Vincent, 46n.1, 50n.9, 60, 60n.39
Tcherikover, Victor A., 37n.34
Testini, Pasquale, 274n.3, 293n.54
Theissen, Gerd, 47n.5
Theobald, Michael, 179n.48
Thümmel, Hans Georg, 83n.25
Thurén, Lauri, 336n.46
Tite, Philip, 148n.7
Tolmie, D. Francois, 109n.1

Tuckett, Christopher M., 46, 46n.2, 53n.16, 216n.59, 216n.60, 232n.26, 233, 233n.28, 233n.30, 234, 234n.32, 234n.33
Turner, C. H., 57n.31
Turner, Jon D., 202n.19
Tyson, Joseph B., 57, 57n.29

Valantasis, Richard, 231, 231n.24
van den Broek, Roeloef, 197-98, 198n.4
Vanhoye, Albert, Cardinal, 336n.46
van Minnen, Peter, 94n.66, 188n.19
van Voorst, Robert E., 181n.2
Verheyden, Joseph, 227, 227n.16
Vielhauer, Philip, 237n.39
Viviano, Benedict, 321n.1

Wachsman, Shelley, 25n.19, 26
Walbank, Frank W., 65n.19
Weeden, Theodore J., 57, 57n.29
Weiland, Albrecht, 293n.54
Werker, Ella, 26n.21
Werner, Andreas, 211n.47
Wessel, Ineke, 52n.13
Wiarda, Timothy, 58n.31, 59n.38, 100, 100n.9, 105, 105n.19, 119n.32
Wiedemann, Thomas, 38n.38

Wiegand, Theodor, 282n.23
Wilcox, Max, 69n.38
Wilkins, John, 21n.8
Wilkins, Michael J., 100, 100n.9-10, 102, 102n.14-15, 106-7, 107n.25
Williams, Jacqueline A., 206, 206n.36
Williams, Margaret H., 1n.1, 32n.11, 36n.29, 45n.63
Williams, Michael A., 197, 197n.3, 199, 199n.10
Wischmeyer, Wolfgang, 306n.107
Wisse, Frederik, 199n.10
Witherington, Ben, 66n.24
Wordsworth, Christopher, 92, 92n.53
Wright, William, 246n.57

Yardeni, Ada, 41n.51

Zahn, Theodor, 148n.8
Zangenberg, Jürgen, 25n.18, 25n.19
Zehnle, Richard F., 66n.25, 69, 69n.37, 72, 72n.57
Zelyck, Lorne R., 198n.6, 202n.20
Zwierlein, Otto, 86, 86n.36, 87, 87n.37-39, 88

Index of Scripture and Other Ancient Writings

OLD TESTAMENT

Genesis

2:23	91
4:3-8	89
17	39n.42
17:4-5	111
27:41-42	89
29:33	32n.7
32:28-29	111
37:12-36	89
41	79

Exodus

2:11-15	89
3	298n.74
3:10	299
31:18	298n.74

Numbers

12:1-15	89
16:12-15	89
16:23-33	89

Deuteronomy

21:23	80
33:2-4 LXX	192n.27
33:24 LXX	94n.66

Joshua

22:12 LXX	91n.52

1 Samuel

7:7 LXX	91n.52
18:10-11	89
19:9–24:22	89

1 Kings

11:14 LXX	91n.52

Psalms

22:18	78

Proverbs

12:22 LXX	94n.66
14:35 LXX	94n.66

Isaiah

42	72
49	72
66:1-2	192

Jeremiah

29	149
31:31-32	190
36	149

Daniel

	105-6
8:26	152
8:27	105
10–12	105
12:4	152
12:8	105
12:9	152

Amos

5:25-27	192

Zechariah

4	102
13:7 (LXX)	225

Malachi

1:52	91n.52

APOCRYPHA

Baruch	149
Epistle of Jeremiah	149

2 Maccabees

8:22	36

NEW TESTAMENT

Matthew 5, 13, 19, 35, 38,
38n.6, 42, 47-48,
60, 74, 74n.70, 78-
79, 99-100, 103-4,
121, 155, 213, 215,
223, 225, 236-37,
255n.71, 294
4:8 228
4:13 19n.1
4:18 35-36, 38n.36, 167
7:13-14 293
8:5 19n.1
8:14 236
8:15 236
8:21-22 236
9:13 126
10:2 228, 236
10:3 39
10:4 39
10:16 163
10:24 236
11:21 19n.1
11:23 19n.1
12:18 72
12:28 163
13:11 103
13:16-17 103-4
13:45-46 252
14:28-31 48
15:1-21 102
15:6 103
15:8-9 103
15:11 102
15:15 101-3, 108
15:15-16 104-5
15:16 102-3
16 298-99, 331-32,
338
16:13-17 215, 230
16:17 33-34, 332
16:17-18 4-5
16:17-19 7, 48, 294, 339
16:18 4-6, 40, 153, 167,
212, 290

16:18-19 6n.19, 11,
297n.72
16:18-20 278, 294, 307
16:19 6, 167, 292-93,
297n.72, 308
16:22-23 5, 106-8
16:23 101, 107, 107n.27
17:1-8 155
17:4 104
17:24 19n.1
17:24-27 48
17:27 144
18:15 236
18:18 293n.56, 294, 308
18:19 282
18:20 237
18:21 101, 249
18:21-22 236
19:23 237
19:27 101, 121n.1, 237
20:2 236
21:32 293
23 213
23:13 293
26:30-31 225
26:31 126
26:33 122
26:33-34 225
26:34 317
26:37-75 153
26:39 94
26:40 121
26:42 94
26:44 94
26:52 247
26:56 126
26:72 122
26:75 122
27:35 78, 80n.12
27:57-61 80n.13
28 208
28:20 213

Mark 9, 13, 19-20, 22-23,
39-40, 40n.44,
41-42, 46-61, 70,

74, 74n.70, 100,
101n.12, 104-6, 121,
126, 126n.14, 129,
165-66, 207n.37,
223-25, 306
1:1-15 48
1:14-15 67n.28
1:16 19, 23n.11, 167
1:16-18 56
1:16-20 52
1:19-20 19
1:20 26
1:21 19n.1
1:21-28 48
1:29 61n.41, 236
1:35-37 61n.41
1:35-38 126
1:40-45 50n.9
2:1 19n.1
2:3-5 50n.9
2:13 23n.11
2:15-17 48
2:17 126
3:1-6 48
3:5 50n.9
3:16 38, 41, 228
3:16-19 236
3:17 4, 4n.10, 39, 41
3:18 39
4:1-2 23n.11
4:36 23n.11
5:1-2 23n.11
5:6 23n.11
5:45 23n.11
5:53 23n.11
6:30-44 48
6:45 19n.1
7:17 102
7:18 102
7:31 .11
8:1-9 48
8:10 23n.11
8:22 19n.1
8:27-29 230
8:27-30 215
8:31-33 126

8:32-33	106	4:23	19n.1	22:34	124, 167, 302
8:33	101, 107n.27	4:31	19n.1	22:42	94
8:34	306	4:38	236	22:45	122
9:5	106	5:7	20	22:59	124
9:5-6	104-5	5:8	126	22:60	124
9:5-7	126	5:11	121	22:61	124
9:6	101, 104, 104n.17,	5:32	126	22:61-62	127n.14
	105-6	6:8	144	22:62	123
9:7	106	6:14	38, 41, 228	23:22	124-25
9:33	19n.1	6:14-16	236	23:23	124
10:17-31	20	6:15	39	23:43	285
10:28	101, 121n.1	7:36-50	67n.28	23:48	123
10:38	116n.22	9:10	19n.1	23:49	129
14:26-27	225	9:18-20	215, 230	23:50-56	80n.13
14:27	123, 126, 225	9:21-22	121	24:12	75, 129
14:28	59	9:33	101, 104-6, 121	24:13-49	182
14:29	122	9:45	125	24:34	182n.5, 129
14:29-30	225	10:3	163	24:39	164
14:36	94, 116n.22	10:13	19n.1	24:43	75
14:37	121	10:15	19n.1	24:44-49	67
14:37-41	126	10:23-24	103-4	24:46	67
14:39	94	10:25-37	67n.28	24:47	67, 126, 129
14:43-52	48	12:4-5	163	24:48	67
14:50	123, 126	12:16-21	67n.28		
14:53	59	13:6-9	67n.28	**John**	9, 13, 35, 42, 77, 80,
14:54	59, 126	15:3-7	67n.28		109-20, 121, 198-99,
14:55-65	59	15:8-10	67n.28		199n.7, 200-202,
14:66-72	59, 126	15:11-32	67n.28		206-7, 215, 220,
14:71	122	16:1-13	67n.28		228-29, 237, 243
14:72	115n.19, 117n.25,	16:19-31	67n.28	1	208
	126, 129	17:3-4	236-37	1:35-42	33
15:42-47	80n.13	18:1-8	67n.28	1:40-42	111-12
16:7	59, 126, 129	18:9-14	67n.28	1:41	111
16:8	52	18:13	123	1:41-42	111-12
		18:28	101	1:42	4, 33, 34n.18, 38,
Luke	20, 39, 41-42, 48,	18:34	125		41-42, 111, 118,
	60, 70, 74, 74n.70,	19:11-27	67n.28		163n.7
	76n.4, 99-101, 103-	19:48	125	1:44	19, 19n.1
	6, 121-26, 128-29,	21:12-15	132	1:47	111
	132, 182, 215, 264-	22:14-30	125	1:48	144
	65, 267, 269	22:28	126	1:49	111
1:59-61	32n.12	22:31	126	2:12	19n.1
2:1	77n.4	22:31-32	11, 339	4:22	207
2:2	76n.4	22:32	122-23, 125n.11,	4:33	199n.8, 207
2:43	72		302, 332	4:46	19n.1
3:23	236	22:33	122	6:17	19n.1

6:24	19n.1	18:26-27	117	2:4	127
6:59	19n.1	18:36	116	2:5	125
6:68-69	112	19:31-37	80	2:14	68
6:69	112	19:38-42	80n.14	2:14-40	66
10:10	115	20:2	119n.31	2:21	67
10:11	114n.14, 116, 276	20:8-9	118	2:22	72
10:15	116	20:19-20	254n.68	2:23	67, 124
10:17-18	112-13	20:19-29	118	2:24	67, 178, 178n.46
10:28	115	20:20	254n.68	2:29	66n.22, 123, 127
12:12-13	116	20:23	293n.56	2:32	67
12:21	19, 19n.1	20:26-29	229	2:36	67, 72, 124
13	112-15, 201	20:27	254, 254n.68	2:37	125
13:1-18	112-13	21	14, 29, 117-19, 276, 293, 307, 338	2:38	67
13:4-5	112			2:40	67
13:6	112	21:1	229	2:41	124, 127
13:7	113	21:1-14	84	2:47	124-25
13:8	113, 113n.12	21:1-23	228	3:1-4:37	259
13:9	113	21:2	228	3:1-10	167
13:10	113	21:2-3	26	3:1-11	127
13:12	113	21:7	84	3:6	72
13:15	113-14, 114n.13	21:7b-8	118	3:12	68
13:31-38	113	21:9	118	3:12-26	66
13:33	114	21:15	118-19	3:13	72, 124
13:34	114, 114n.13	21:15-17	33, 115, 167, 307, 337, 339	3:13-14	124
13:36	114, 115			3:15	67
13:37	114, 117	21:15-18	11	3:17	123, 125
13:38	115	21:15-19	164, 293, 299, 302	3:19	67, 125
14:2	285	21:16	153	3:20	70
15:13	114, 114n.14	21:17	117, 119	3:21	70
15:14	230n.21	21:18	83-87, 119	3:26	67, 72
17:12	115	21:18-19	77, 112, 114n.18, 273	4:1-22	131
17:21-22	339			4:2	68
18	114-17	21:19	119	4:3	127
18:1-11	115			4:4	124, 127
18:3	115	Acts	9-10, 43-44, 51, 62-75, 90, 123-29, 131-34, 136, 141, 144-45, 150, 154, 170n.8, 178n.46, 181n.2, 182, 192, 208, 208n.41, 221, 247, 259, 269, 337	4:8	127
18:5	115, 117			4:8-13	182n.2
18:8	115-17			4:9	68
18:9	115, 117			4:10	67, 72
18:10	116			4:11	67
18:11	116, 247			4:12	67
18:15	116	1:3-8	182	4:13	131-34, 141, 144
18:17	117	1:16	66n.22	4:21	125
18:18	118	1:22	68	4:24-30	72
18:18-27	116-17	2	210	4:25	72
18:19-24	117			4:33	68
18:25	117			5:1-10	144

5:1-11	127	10:40	67	16:9-10	127
5:12-16	127	10:41	67	16:16-18	127
5:13	125	10:42	67	16:19-24	127
5:14	124	10:43	67	16:25-40	127
5:15	127, 167	10:44-46	127	17:11	193
5:16	127	10:45	167	17:18	68
5:18	127	11:2	123n.3	17:22-31	69, 127
5:19-25	127	11:2-3	127	17:32	68
5:26-33	127	11:16	72	18:5	68-69
5:29	67-68	12:3-5	127	18:9	127
5:30	67	12:6-19	127	18:23	123
5:31	67	12:12	49n.7, 154n.29	18:28	68
5:32	67	12:25	49n.7, 154n.29	19:8	68
5:42	68	13	68-69	19:11-12	127
6-7	68, 192	13:4	127	20:7-12	127
6:13	192	13:5	49n.7	20:18-35	69
7:2	66n.22	13:6-12	127	20:22	127
7:37-53	192	13:9	127	20:25	68
7:38	192	13:13	49n.7	20:30-31	90
7:53	192	13:15	66n.22	20:37	72
8-10	127	13:16-41	66, 68n.32, 69	20:39	72
8	68	13:27	68	21:33	127
8:5	68	13:28-29	68	22:1	66n.22
8:9-24	218	13:30	68	22:15	69
8:12	68	13:31	68	22:17-21	69
9	68	13:42-43	127	23:1	66n.22
9:1-2	129	13:46	127	23:1-10	127
9:20	68	14:3	127	23:6	68-69
9:22	68	14:15-17	69	24:10-20	69
9:23-29	129	14:21	123	24:21	68
9:28	127	15-18	154n.29	25:8-11	69
9:32	167	15	150, 253	26:4-23	69
9:32-43	127	15:1-6	127	26:16	69
9:40	167	15:7	66n.22, 154	26:19-20	122
10	70, 327	15:7-11	127, 129, 150	26:22-23	69
10:3	127	15:13-21	150	26:23	68
10:14	126n.14	15:22	154	26:26	127
10:17	127	15:27	154	27:10	144
10:19	127	15:32	154	28:3-6	127
10:34-43	66	15:37	49n.7, 154	28:17	66n.22
10:34-48	127	15:37-39	154n.29	28:23	68
10:36	70-71	15:39	49n.7, 154	28:31	68, 127
10:36-41	61n.41	15:40	154		
10:37	72	15:41	123	**Romans**	1, 13, 206,
10:38	70, 72	16:5	123		336n.46
10:39	67	16:6-7	127	6	306

7:12	206
8:17	306n.110
14:10	175
14:12	175
15:20	6n.17
15:28	90
6:5	306n.110
6:8	306n.110
14–15	307n.111

1 Corinthians 1, 163, 168-69, 169n.4, 206, 337

1:12	42n.55, 163, 163n.7, 168-69
1:17	134n.17
1:18–2:5	303n.99
2:11	107n.27
3:10	6n.17
3:21–4:1	337
3:22	42n.55, 163n.7, 168-69
4:9-13	306n.110
5:7-8	206
5:9	148n.11, 155
6:2	174n.21, 175
6:9-10	175
7:1	149n.11
8–10	307n.111
9:5	42n.55, 163n.7, 167-68, 337
10	299
11:23-25	67n.28, 75n.73
15	206
15:1-11	8, 67n.28
15:3-5	210
15:3-8	1
15:5	1n.1, 42n.55, 75n.73, 163n.7, 168, 206, 219, 292
15:5-8	337
15:23-28	295
15:50	219

2 Corinthians 1, 206

3	308
3:9	306
3:18	306
4:10	306n.110
4:7-12	306n.110
4:16-17	306n.110
6:7	175
7:8	149n.11
10:9	149n.11
11:22-28	171
11:23-33	306n.110

Galatians 1, 13, 129, 168, 170, 269-70, 337

1:7-8	67n.28
1:18	9, 42, 42n.55, 43, 163n.7
2	337
2:7-8	67n.28, 163n.7, 167
2:7-9	170
2:9	6n.17, 42n.55, 163n.7
2:11	42n.55, 163n.7, 269
2:11-21	8, 10
2:12-13	307n.111
2:14	42n.55, 163n.7
2:19	306n.110
3:19	192n.27
6:7	175,
6:17	306n.110

Ephesians 73, 148, 154, 206

1:23	328
2:5	175
2:8-9	175
2:15	206
2:20	6n.17
3:14	206

Philippians 148, 174, 206

2:5-8	306n.110
2:6-11	73, 148n.9
2:16	148n.9

3:10	306n.110
3:12	148n.9
4:5	148n.9

Colossians 148, 154, 206

4:10	10, 49n.7, 154n.29
4:16	149, 149n.12

1 Thessalonians

1:1	154n.29

2 Thessalonians 148

1:1	154n.29

1 Timothy 148

6:7	175
6:10	175

2 Timothy 148, 156-57

4:6-8	156
4:10	175
4:11	10, 49n.7, 154n.29

Titus 148

Philemon

24	10, 49n.7, 154n.29

Hebrews 73, 135n.21, 149, 206, 336n.46

2.2	192n.27
7:25	285

James 149, 151, 153, 205n.32

1:1	150n.16
2:1	151, 151n.19
4:11	151, 151n.19

1 Peter 9, 13, 130-31, 134-36, 139, 141, 144-45, 149-51, 153-57, 161, 172, 175-79, 206-7, 249-50, 336n.46

1:1	45, 153-54, 166, 266	1:14	273	5:35-37	107
1:8	175	1:16-18	337	5:40	107
1:11	153n.26	1:17-18	155	6:32-33	107
1:12	175	2:4-5	249	7:15	107
1:13	175	2:4-10	137	7:19	107
1:15	44n.60	3:1	135n.20, 137, 155, 157, 166	7:[67]-[77]	107
1:21	175			8:47a	107
2:4-8	153	3:15	223	8:47b-54	107
2:9	153n.26	3:15-16	10n.44, 148	10	105
2:11	175	3:16	137	10:30	105
2:12	176			10:31	105
2:17	176	**1 John**	149, 176-78	10:35	105
2:21	153n.26, 176			10:38-39a	105
2:22	176	**2 John**	149	10:38-40	107
2:24	176			10:55-58	107
2:25	337	**3 John**	149	13:53-56	107
3:6	153n.26			14:1-6	107
3:8	176	**Jude**	149	14:37-48	107
3:9	175			14:9	107
3:19-20	249-50	**Revelation**	135n.21, 149		
3:19-22	250n.62	17	103	**Jubilees**	
4:7	175	17:7	103	1.27-29	192n.27
4:8	153n.26, 207	21:14	6n.17		
4:16	153, 176	21:19	6n.17	**Testament of**	
5:1	75n.73, 167, 337	22:10	152	**Abraham**	102-3
5:1-2	154	22:13	278	8.8	103
5:1-4	164, 167, 337-38				
5:1-5	153, 153n.26				
5:5	153, 153n.26, 176-78	**OTHER ANCIENT JEWISH WORKS**		**NEW TESTAMENT APOCRYPHA AND CHURCH FATHERS**	
5:12	10n.44, 144-45, 136, 136n.23	**4Q389 (Apocryphon**			
5:12-13	45, 154	**of Jeremiah)**	149	**Act of Peter**	
5:13	10n.44, 47, 47n.5, 49n.7, 153, 165	**4 Baruch/**		**(BG 8502.4)**	147n.5, 150, 220, 250-51
		Paraleipomena Jeremiou			
2 Peter	13, 135-38, 149-51, 153, 155, 155n.34, 156-57, 206-7, 207n.37, 223, 223n.6, 249-50	6-7	149	**Acts of Andrew**	238-40
		4/5 Ezra	105-7	20	86n.34, 239
		2.33	192n.27	**Acts of Carpus, Papylus,**	
		2.44-48	192n.27	**and Agathonice**	81n.16
1:1	137, 166	4:2	107		
1:1-2	155	4:10-11	107	**Acts of John**	213, 219, 238-39, 245-46, 257
1:12-15	156-57	4:21	107	87	245
1:12-16	137	4:34	107	88	245
		5:33	107		

90	245	15.36	250	**39756/Rainer**	
91	246			**Fragment)**	94-95
97.7-10	257	*Acts of Thomas*	238-39, 246-48	**(Ethiopic)**	138, 255,
Acts of Paul	238-39, 244, 246	1	247		255n.69, 256,
		86	247		256n.72
Acts of Peter (Codex Vercellenis 158)	138, 238-43, 250, 261-62, 266, 337	*Actus Petri cum Simone* (BHL 6656)	90n.47	**(NHC VII 3)**	150, 196, 211-14, 221, 255, 257-58
		Allogenes			
5	240	**(NHC XI 3)**	208-9	70.14-84.14	211
12-18	240				
20	138	*Apocalypse of Adam*		70.14-20	257
23-32	240	**(NHC V 5)**	200	71.15-72.3	212
31[2]	241				
32[3]	241	*Apocalypse of James,*		72.2-3	213
35[6]	242	*First*	147n.5, 208, 214-15	72.4-81.3	211
37[8]	243	**(CT)**		72.4-73.10	212
		2	205		
Acts of Peter and		12.8-17	206	72.5-6	213
Andrew	150	22.26-23.2	206	73.10-81.3	213
		42.21-24	206		
Acts of Peter		**(NHC V 3)**	205	73.16	212
and Paul	150, 262	25.24-26.1	206		
		29.18-25	206	77-78	257
Acts of Peter and the		36.1-5	206	79.22-30	258
Twelve Apostles		41	231	80.23-81.3	258
(NHC VI 1)	147n.5, 150, 196, 198n.6, 220, 251-53	*Apocalypse of*		81.3-82.17	211
		James, Second		81.4-24	258
1.1-2.10	251	**(NHC V 4)**	147n.5, 205n.32	81.8	213
2.2-4	252			81.16	213
2.10-5.18	251	*Apocalypse of Paul*			
2.35	252	**(NHC V 2)**	147n.5, 148	81.21	213
5.19-8.11	251			82.9.28	213
8.11-12.19	251	*Apocalypse of*			
9.11-12	251	*Peter*	94-95, 144n.45, 147n.5, 150,	82.18-26	213
10.14-30	252		155n.34, 220-2	82.18	213
		(Greek/Akhmîm		82.31-33	213
Acts of Philip	247-51	**Fragment)**	137-38, 255,		
2	248		255n.69, 256n.72	83.3	213
3.1	248			84.8-9	213
3.3	248	**(Greek/P. Vindob.G.**			
8.1	249			84.10	213
8.12	249				

Apocryphon of James

(NHC I 2) 147, 205n.32

Apocryphon of John

(NHC II 1; III 1; IV 1;

BG 8502.2) 147n.5,

199n.6, 200-203,

208, 220-21

Ascension of

Isaiah 92-94

Birth of Mary. See

Protevangelium of James

Book of Thomas the

Contender

(NHC II 7) 147n.5

3 Corinthians 148

Correspondence of

Paul and Seneca 148

Didache 173n.19

9.2-3 72

10.2 72

Epistle of Barnabas 149

9.7-9 282n.22

Epistle of James

(NHC I 2) 196, 217, 221

Epistle of Paul to the

Alexandrians 148

Epistle of Paul to

the Laodiceans 148-49

Epistle of Peter

to James 151, 153, 156-57

Epistle of Peter

to Philip 147, 151-53,

157, 196, 208-12,

220-21, 258-61

(CT)

1.1-4 209

2 209

5-6 209

(NHC VIII 2)

132-33 152

133 152-53

132.10-133.8 209

133.8-11 209

133.12-16 209

133.22 209

134.4-5 209

134.20-24 259

138.13-17 209

138.18-20 259

139.1 209

139.11-12 259

139.19 209

Epistle of Titus 149

Epistula

Apostolorum 147, 149-50,

253-54, 254n.68

1 253

2 253

5 254

11 254

Epistula

Clementis 139, 151

2.1-4.4 139

2.3 139

20.1 139

Epistula Petri 139

1.1-2 151

1.2 139

2.1 139

3.1 139

Eugnostos 204n.25

(NHC III 3) 203

(NHC V 1) 203

Gospel of the

Ebionites 235

Gospel of the

Hebrews 206, 237

Gospel of the

Nazoreans 236, 236n.36,

237

Gospel of Judas

(CT) 202-3, 208-11, 221

Gospel of Mary

(BG 8502.1) 147n.5, 196,

208, 216-17, 220,

231n.23, 232-35,

259-61, 337

7.10-12 232

7.13 232

10.1-6 233

17-18 216

17.13-15 233

17.13-22 259-60

17.16-22 182n.6, 234

17,19-20 216

18.5 216

18.7-21 217

(P.Oxy. 3525) 216

(P.Ryl. 463)   216-17,
                234n.32

Gospel of Peter
(**P.Cair. 10759**)   144n.45,
                150, 219, 224,
                224n.10, 225,
                227-29
7.26a   137, 227-28
7.26-27   228
14.59   228-29
14.60   137, 228-29

Gospel of Philip
(**NHC II 3**)   147n.5, 205-6
111b   207

Gospel of Thomas
(**NHC II 2**)   147n.5, 196,
                214-16, 223, 229-32,
                234, 261, 337
1   214
12   214
13   182n.6, 215,
                229-30
114   182n.6, 215, 231,
                234, B50261
(P. Oxy. 1, 654, 655)   214

Gospel of Truth
(**NHC I 3**)   205-6,
                207n.37

*Kerygmata
Petrou*   150-51, 196, 219

*Infancy Gospel
of Thomas*   224n.9

*Interpretation of
Knowledge*
(**NHC XI 1**)   205

1 Jeu   200n.24

Kerygma Petrou   128-39,

                150, 181-89, 207,
                207n.38
Frg. 1   183, 183n.7,10,
                185n.16, 190n.22
Frg. 2   183n.7, 184-85,
                185n.14, 185n.16,
                186
Frg. 3   183n.7, 184,
                185n.14, 185n.16,
                186
Frg. 4   183n.7, 184,
                185n.14, 185n.16,
                186, 191, 191n.25
Frg. 5   183n.7, 185n.14,
                185n.16, 186, 190,
                190n.22, 192
Frg. 6   183n.7, 184,
                184n.13, 185n.14,
                185n.16, 186
Frg. 7   183n.7, 184,
                184n.13, 185n.14,
                185n.16, 186
Frg. 8   183n.7, 184,
                184n.13, 185n.14,
                186
Frg. 9   183n.7, 185,
                185n.14, 185n.16,
                187-88
Frg. 10   183n.7, 185

*Letter to Reghinos /
Treatise on Resurrection*
(**NHC I 4**)   205-6

*Martyrdom of
Peter*   86, 88, 240-42, 262

*Martyrdom of
Polycarp*   177n.38

Melchisedek
(**NHC IX 1**)   200

Pistis Sophia   196,
                200n.24, 217, 221
1-3   217

4   217

*Prayer of the Apostle
Paul* (**NHC I 1**)   147n.5,
                148, 205

*Protevangelium of
James*   147n.5, 224n.9

*Pseudo-Clementine
Homilies*   139-42

*Pseudo-Clementine
Recognitions*   139-42

*Shepherd of
Hermas*   103, 173n.19
25.3   103

Sophia of Jesus Christ
(**NHC III 4; BG 8502.3;
P.Oxy.1081**)   203-4, 208

Tripartite Tractate
(**NHC I 5**)   205

Valentinian Exposition
(**NHC XI 2**)   205

Zostrianos
(**NHC VIII 1**)   200, 208,
                210